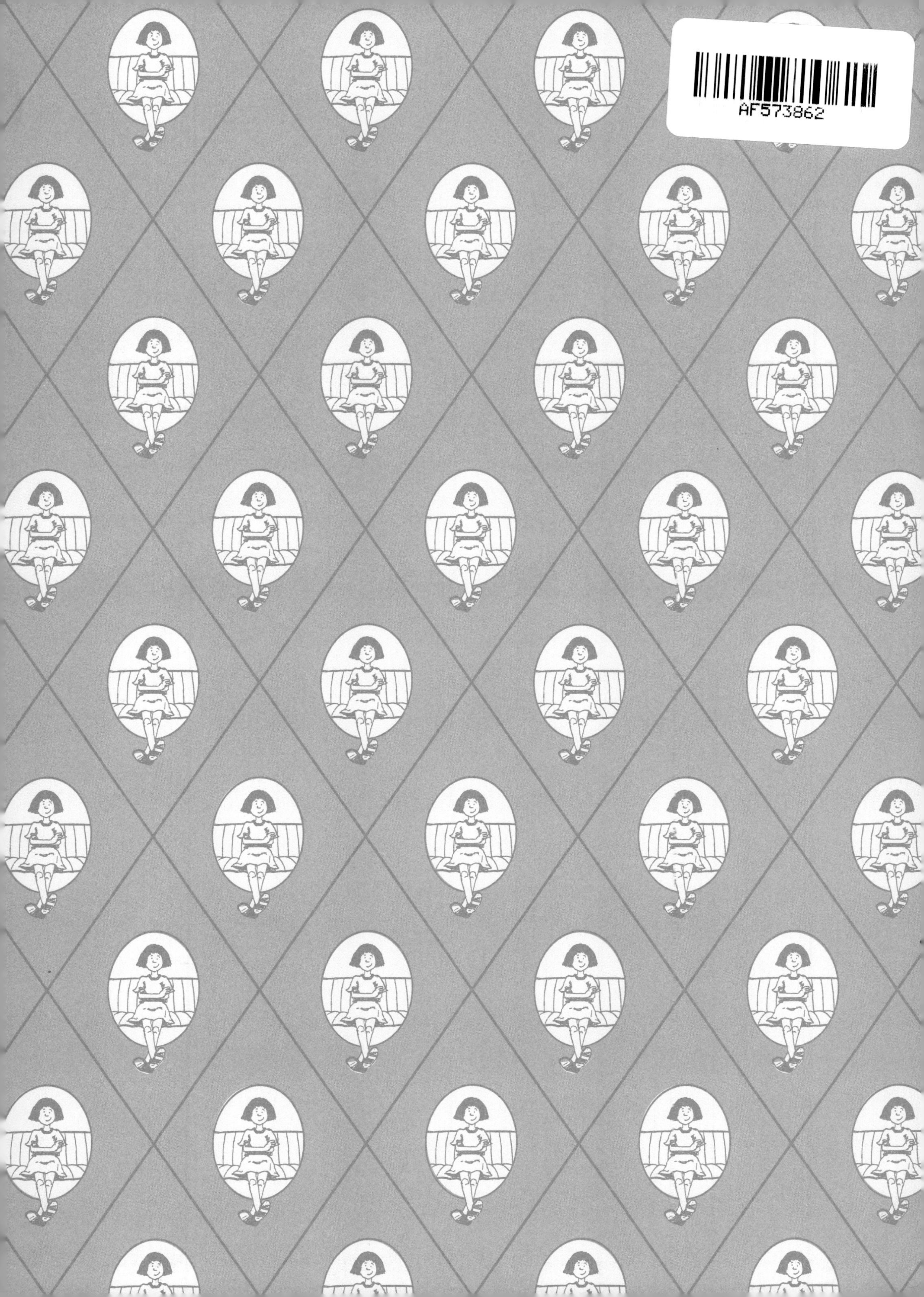
AF573862

THE ART OF
Ramona Quimby

Sixty-Five Years of Illustrations from
Beverly Cleary's Beloved Books

THE ART OF Ramona Quimby

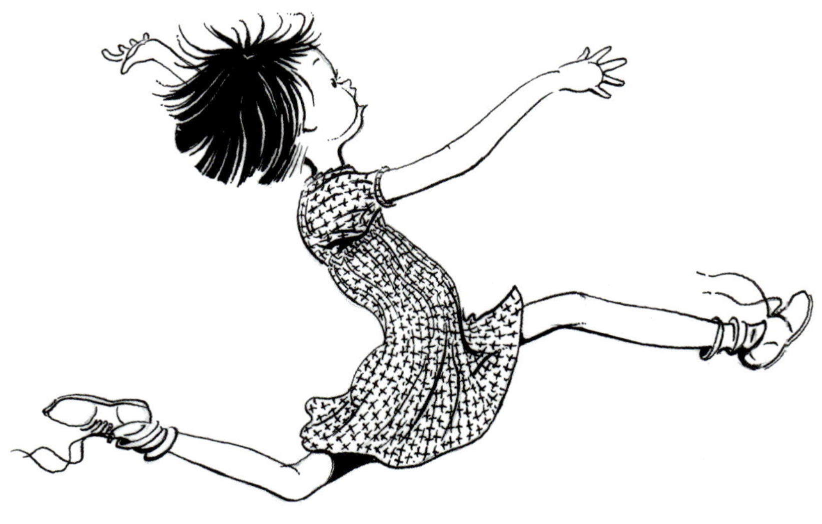

by ANNA KATZ
Essays by ANNIE BARROWS and JACQUELINE ROGERS

CHRONICLE BOOKS
SAN FRANCISCO

Library of Congress Cataloging-in-Publication Data

Names: Katz, Anna, 1984- author. | Barrows, Annie, author of foreword. | Rogers, Jacqueline, 1958- author of afterword.
Title: The art of Ramona Quimby : sixty-five years of illustrations from Beverly Cleary's beloved books / by Anna Katz ; essays by Annie Barrows and Jacqueline Rogers.
Identifiers: LCCN 2020000358 | ISBN 9781452176956 (hardback)
Subjects: LCSH: Cleary, Beverly—Illustrations. | Darling, Louis. | Tiegreen, Alan. | Scribner, Joanne. | Dockray, Tracy. | Rogers, Jacqueline, 1958- | Illustration of books—20th century. | Illustrators—20th century.
Classification: LCC NC975.5.C54 K38 2020 | DDC 741.6/40922—dc23
LC record available at https://lccn.loc.gov/2020000358

Manufactured in China.

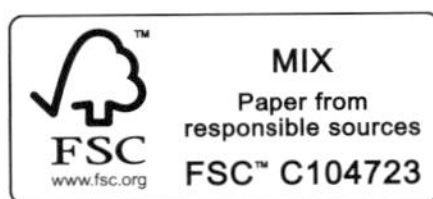

Design by Allison Weiner.
Photography by Kyle Chan.

10 9 8 7 6 5 4 3 2

Chronicle Books LLC
680 Second Street
San Francisco, California 94107
www.chroniclebooks.com

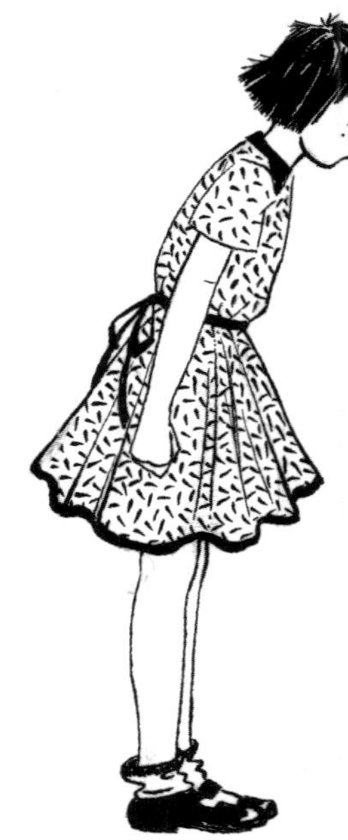

Contents

FOREWORD

Annie Barrows

Bad Author/ Good Witch: What I Learned from *Ramona the Pest*

When I made the extremely practical decision to abandon my career in publishing to become a writer, I didn't know I wanted to write children's books. I thought I wanted to write for adults. Accordingly, my first published work was an illustrated book about fortune-telling; my second was about opera; my third, about urban legends; my fourth, I'm not exactly sure, because right about that time, I stopped being interested in adults.

I had had some babies, you see, during this period, and suddenly, I was spending all my time with children; I read only children's books; I talked only to children; I thought only about children. I had nothing to say to grown-ups, and most of the time, I didn't understand what they were saying to me. Why did they want to talk about real estate when they could talk about pterodactyls? Why were they obsessed with traffic when they could be obsessed with buried treasure? Adult conversation had become incredibly dull, and adult books, duller.

It was in this spirit that I decided I would become a children's book writer.

And in this spirit, I was totally, completely WRONG.

WRONG, WRONG, WRONG.

The problem, the wrongness, was rooted, as it usually is, in arrogance. *I* decided that *I* should become a children's book writer because *I* was bored by adult books and *I* loved children's books. *I* was going to write children's books because it would gratify *me*. This is not an attitude that leads to great children's books.

However, I didn't know that, and I set about my new goal industriously. My first attempt was a picture book manuscript entitled *Audrey and the Fire Engine*, a story about Audrey, who is scared of the sound of sirens. She's so scared of sirens that she starts dreading the noise even when she's not hearing it. But—whew!—Audrey has a wise mother who helps her surmount her fear through several ingenious stratagems. Oh, lucky, lucky Audrey, to have such a wise mother! The end.

I thought it was pretty good. I sent it around to some writer friends and one of them connected me to a genuine children's book author who kindly agreed to give me her opinion on the manuscript. What this kind and brilliant children's book author said was: No. This is a book about how great Audrey's mom is, not about Audrey. This is not a kids' book because it's not really about kids. This is a book that will make grown-ups feel good about themselves.

I didn't get it. It was a story about a kid, so of course it was a kids' book! I kept reading my manuscript, trying to figure out which sentences I could change to make it better. Should I add more about Audrey? Should I put the mom in fewer scenes? I didn't know how to fix the problem because I didn't understand what the problem was.

Luckily for me, my oldest daughter was at this juncture beginning to move beyond picture book into books with chapters. Also luckily for me, she considered my central duty as a mother to be reading to her. So together, we embarked upon chapter books. Like every red-blooded American family, we began in the Magic Tree House and then ascended the slopes of literature until we reached Beverly Cleary and *Ramona the Pest* and, above all, Chapter Six, "The Baddest Witch in the World."

I very well remember my daughter's response to this segment of the book: complete identification with the emotional roller coaster of Ramona's Halloween, which starts with Ramona's passionate desire to be the "baddest" witch in the world; proceeds to her fear of her scary witch mask, happily overcome by her pride in her costume when Halloween finally arrives; moves on to a scene of liminal mayhem in the schoolyard as all the children, released from responsibility and consequences by their disguises, indulge in forbidden behavior; and then culminates in one of the most extraordinary moments of kid-understanding in children's literature. In this scene, after tearing around the playground in her witch costume, Ramona realizes with a shock that she is, actually, unidentifiable behind her mask; her teacher, Miss Binney, truly does not know that she is speaking to Ramona. And at this, Ramona experiences a profound and profoundly human terror—is she anyone if no one knows who she is? This is followed by an even more shocking thought: What if her own mother can't identify her? Here, we are privy to, even participating in, one of childhood's primary fears—the mother denying her child (this is what separation anxiety is all about). Ramona wonders, "What if her mother forgot her? What if everyone in the whole world forgot her?" She removes her hard-won mask.

Right there, as I read "The Baddest Witch in the World," I understood what the kind children's author had been telling me. I understood what a children's book is supposed to be. It's writing from *inside* the kid's world, inside the kid's perspective, almost from inside the kid's eyeballs. Beverly Cleary doesn't *tell* us what Ramona's experiencing; she doesn't separate herself far enough from Ramona to tell us. She doesn't say "Ramona's mother would never forget her, but Ramona was worried that she might." She doesn't even insert herself into proceedings to say "Ramona thought for a moment that her mother would forget her." Nope, Beverly Cleary gives the story to Ramona herself to experience, and she does it by withdrawing herself from the equation.

There are certainly other ways to write a good children's book; it is possible for a narrator to be part of the tale in a non-oppressive, non-colonizing, non-grown-uppy way. But to me, the best children's books, like the Ramona books, are the result of serious unselfishness, even humility. The author sets up the furniture, props the door open, and then covers herself with an author-cozy and disappears, leaving the entertainment to be directed, acted, and understood by the kid-characters. The wise and kindly adult who interprets the meaning of the action or, worse, teaches the befuddled youngster an improving lesson—that person is banished in great kids' literature. The main characters, the kids, learn things on their own.

But how do you do it? How do you enter the kid-world so thoroughly? I think there are three major routes. The first is a willingness on the part of the author to be erased (which most grown-ups don't have; they want more attention, not less); the second is a deep and serious sympathy with kids; and the third is a pretty good memory. I'm guessing Beverly Cleary has all three.

I'm certain she also has the fourth thing, the special extra that's not required but is lovely: generosity of spirit. Because "The Baddest Witch in the World" doesn't end with Ramona so fearful of loss of identity that she can't partake of the Halloween parade she's been anticipating for years. It ends with Ramona's brilliant solution to the problem: She runs into her classroom, grabs a piece of paper, and writes "RAMONA Q." Then, with nametag affixed and selfhood firmly reestablished, she pulls her mask back over her face and races out to enjoy being the baddest witch in the world in all her disruptive glory. What a great ending! How satisfactory! Are children helpless? NO! Are children resourceful? YES! Are children going to be forgotten as a punishment for donning the guises of wickedness? NO WAY! Children are going to have a great time on Halloween and overcome any problems that might arise! Plus, they are going to eat candy! What could be better?

The lesson in "The Baddest Witch in the World" for Ramona is that there *is* no lesson—or maybe it's that she has the power to make herself known. But the lesson for me was profound. The lesson was this: It's not about you. Of course, Beverly Cleary's understanding of her own position and her mastery of what's called "kidbrain" in industry circles didn't stop with the baddest witch; it's apparent in all of the books about Ramona. It's in her glorious red galoshes and her impatience with Howie's dullness and her dawnzer-lee-light humiliation and her response to Miss Binney's substitute. She knows

Ramona from the inside out, and she loves and respects her.

Hmm, I thought, holding *Ramona the Pest* on my lap while my daughter went off to the kitchen to make a potion, *maybe I should forget about Audrey and her wise mom. Maybe I should try writing about something I know inside out. Like what?* I thought, watching my daughter get out the food coloring (a good potion requires a lot of food coloring). All I know are seven-year-olds. Seven-year-old girls. Seven-year-old girls who want to be witches. Or paleontologists. I know a few of those. Let's say there are two. Yeah, let's say there are two seven-year-old girls who are very different. Let's say their moms want them to be friends. Let's say they don't like each other. . . .

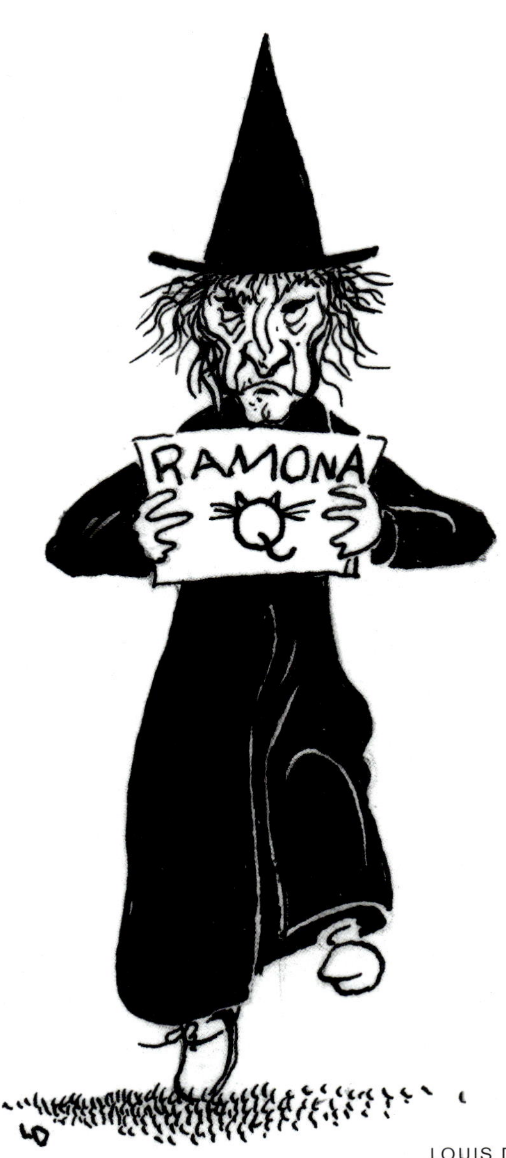

LOUIS DARLING

The Many Paths to Ramona Quimby

Based on purely anecdotal research, one might conclude that Ramona Quimby readers remember the illustrations with which they grew up as *the* illustrations. Baby boomers wax nostalgic about Louis Darling's ink illustrations, with their elegant simplicity and retro styling. His illustrations are especially cherished because you can only find them in the first two books of the series, due to Darling's early death in 1970, at the age of fifty-three.

For children born in the 1970s through the 1990s, the late Gen Xers and vintage Millennials, Ramona and Beezus had pageboy haircuts, dots for eyes, and funny little mushroom noses. They wore decidedly seventies-style outfits, rendered in slashy and crosshatched ink lines. This was the work of Alan Tiegreen, who took over the series from the late Darling for the publication of the third book of the series in 1975. Tiegreen created cover art for the first seven books but only illustrated the interiors of the last six.

Around this same time, Joanne Scribner painted covers for the first seven books, stunning artwork that has been credited with raising the bar for children's book covers across the board. If you belong to this generation of Ramona fans, you might remember her realistic rendering of Ramona dancing before a wall of mirrors in *Ramona Forever*, or a big-eyed, turtleneck-wearing Ramona on the cover of *Ramona Quimby, Age 8*.

The younger folk of Generation Z grew up with the shaded, more inclusive, cartoonish renderings of Tracy Dockray, who took over the job in 2006. And those being raised on the 2013 edition of the Ramona Quimby series will likely claim the illustrations by Jacqueline Rogers as the ultimate expression of the Quimbys and their world.

Many Beverly Cleary fans don't realize that the Ramona Quimby series has benefited from the efforts of more than one illustrator. Or they may have been shocked when they picked up a Ramona Quimby book to read to their own kids only to find illustrations different than those from their childhoods. When a person discovers that "their" illustrations are in fact just one set among many, a certain kind of tribalism can emerge. It's the same kind of tribalism that has old-timers—anyone over, say, twenty-five—complaining that they just don't make music, movies, politicians, panty hose, or polar ice caps like they used to.

But the range of illustrations points to the fact that the Ramona stories themselves transcend generational divides. They have had such staying power because Cleary's writing, like all good writing, makes the universal specific and the specific universal. She mostly left out details that would freeze the story within a particular time period, but you can spot evidence of zeitgeist if you are looking for it. For example, second-wave feminism was rippling across the United States during the 1960s and 1970s and just so happened to coincide with Mrs. Quimby's choosing to work outside the home in *Ramona the Brave*, published in 1975. In *Ramona and Her Father*, published in 1977, Mr. Quimby loses his job and the family must "pinch and scrimp" to make ends meet, just like so many families did during and following the recession of the mid-1970s. It's not just big national affairs, however, that hint at the broader context; in *Ramona and Her Mother*, Beezus is desperate for a haircut that looks like "that girl who ice skates on TV. You know, the one with the hair that sort of floats when she twirls around and then falls in place when she stops." She might be referring to Dorothy Hamill who, along with her famous wedge hairstyle, won gold at the 1976 Winter Olympics.

Then again, it could all be a coincidence. Cleary never names that figure skater, or any other politician or celebrity who might tie the books down to a particular era. Girls will always have floaty-haired ice skaters to idolize. There will continue to be new social movements and recessions, mothers going to work and fathers losing their jobs, and children worrying, feeling unloved, or, if they are very, very lucky, being cared for by parents like Mr. and Mrs. Quimby.

It is the changing of the art that allows each new generation of children to see themselves and their lives represented on the pages of Cleary's books. The changes range from the more explicit and obvious, like style of clothing—Darling's lace-trimmed hats and day gloves, Tiegreen's pageboys and paisley, Dockray's and Rogers's jeans and T-shirts—to the style of the art itself—Darling's comic book pen-and-ink drawings, Tiegreen's messy sketches, Scribner's Rockwellian realism, Dockray's cartoons, and Rogers's clean ink drawings. My hope is that this book will show how every illustrated version of the Ramona Quimby series is beautiful and illuminating in its own way, and that the ongoing pairing of art with story has allowed the series to endure through decades of significant change in the United States and around the world.

First published in 1955, the Ramona Quimby series has maintained its relevance and relatability for sixty-five years and counting, because Ramona and Beezus ride childhood's roller coaster of feelings with such humor and honesty. Their experiences are true in a way that transcends era, as are those of the adults who inhabit the Ramonaverse. Just as Ramona becomes aware of her parents and the other grown-ups as their own separate entities, with their own thoughts and feelings, we readers, as we age, can see our adult selves in the story, too. We might relate to Mr. and Mrs. Quimby's marital bickering, their graying hair, their worry over bills, their struggles with addiction. The way they love their kids.

Twenty years have passed since the final Ramona Quimby book was published, and young readers may notice the absence of smart phones, streaming television, or other technologies ubiquitous in contemporary life. (In an interview in 2006, the ninety-five-year-old Beverly Cleary admitted that she did not know how to use the internet.) Even if the books begin to appear dated, the themes not just of childhood but also of life endure: everyday elation and insecurity, pride in artwork and hard-won callouses, the desire to be liked and seen, the hope that the people we love are happy. The joy of stomping in mud puddles and eating whipped cream.

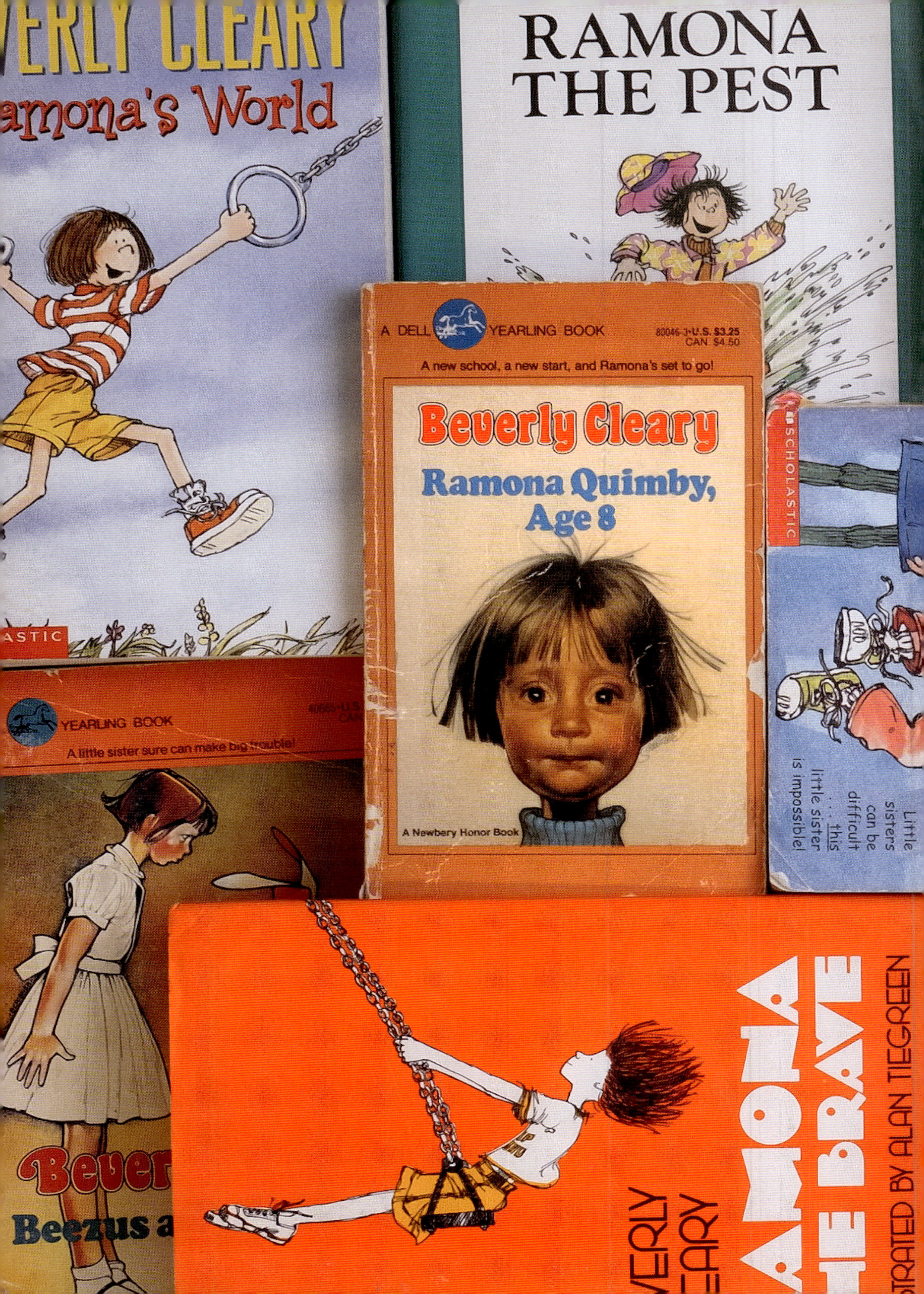

RAMONA
THE PEST
A DELL YEARLING BOOK
80046-3•U.S. $3.25
CAN. $4.50
A new school, a new start, and Ramona's set to go!
Beverly Cleary
Ramona Quimby,
Age 8
A Newbery Honor Book
SCHOLASTIC
Little sisters can be difficult . . . this little sister is impossible!
YEARLING BOOK
A little sister sure can make big trouble!

Before We Begin

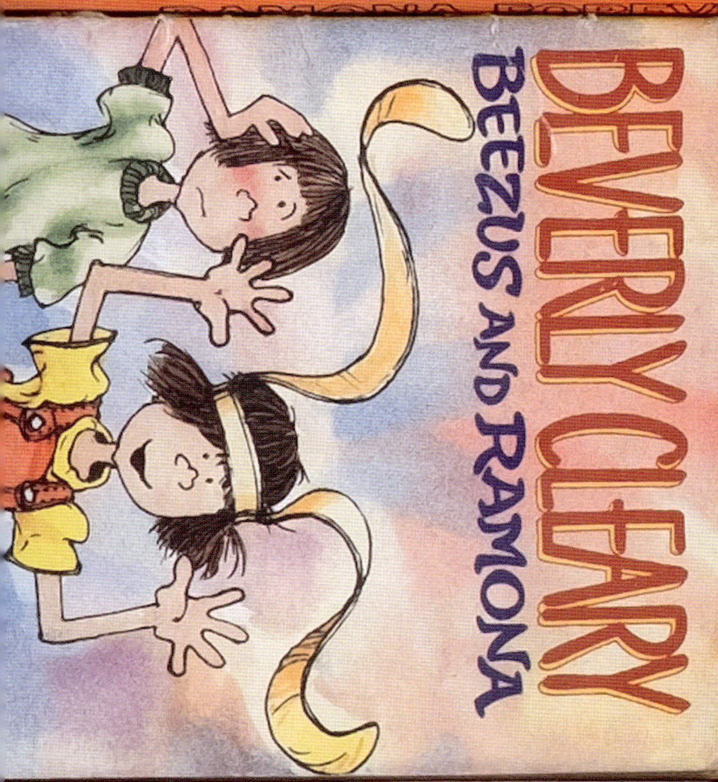

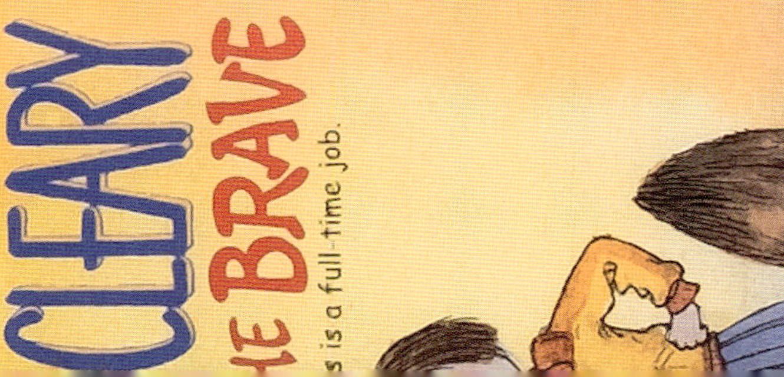

The Creators

The Author: Beverly Cleary

Beverly Cleary née Bunn was born on April 12, 1916, and spent her first years in Yamhill County, Oregon. One of her earliest memories is of the town's bells ringing to mark the end of World War I.

At the time of this writing, Cleary is 103 years old. She came of age in Portland, Oregon, during the Great Depression and attended Chaffey Junior College near Ontario, California. After narrowly passing the harrowing English Comprehensive, she earned her undergraduate degree in 1938 from the University of California, Berkeley. There she met Clarence Cleary, the man who later would become her husband.

At the University of Washington's School of Librarianship the following year, Cleary learned the now lost art of cataloguing and finally got a pair of eyeglasses, despite her mother's disapproval. (Her theory is that her mother was worried that she wouldn't be able to attract a husband while wearing bifocals.) Postgraduate work took her to Yakima, Washington, where she learned how to tell a story during Saturday story hours in the library and in local parks and schools. In Yakima, she also met the little boys from St. Joseph's School, who wanted to know where the books about kids like them were, inspiring her writing more than a decade later.

Against her parents' wishes—Clarence's family was Catholic, while the Bunns were Presbyterian—Beverly Bunn and Clarence Cleary married. After she finished her graduate degree, the two moved to near Sacramento, then to San Francisco, and on to Oakland. There Cleary got a Christmas job at the Sather Gate Book Shop in Berkeley, seasonal work she'd take on for many years. During World War II, she served her country at Camp Knight and Oakland Regional Hospital as Post Librarian.

It wasn't until January 2, 1949, when she was nearly thirty-three years old, that Cleary finally sat down at a desk in the back bedroom of their new home in the Berkeley Hills with a pile of paper, a few freshly sharpened pencils, and a noisy cat named Kitty and began to write.

When reading Cleary's two memoirs, *A Girl from Yamhill* and *My Own Two Feet*, it's difficult not to see Ramona and Beezus within Cleary's own character. Some of the connections are overt, like Cleary's taking one bite out of every apple because "the first bite of an apple tastes best," just as Ramona did in *Beezus and Ramona*. Others are perhaps less specific to Cleary as an individual. How many children start as a rambunctious, creative, volatile Ramona and, after a few years of experience and conditioning, become more like the conscientious and careful Beezus?

Along with the Ramona Quimby series, readers have celebrated Cleary's other works of fiction: the Henry Huggins series, the Ralph Mouse series, and thirteen other novels, including the Newbery Medal–winning *Dear Mr. Henshaw*. For her contribution to children's literature, she has won the American Library Association's 1975 Laura Ingalls Wilder Award, the Catholic Library Association's 1980 Regina Medal, and the University of Southern Mississippi's 1982 Silver Medallion. She was named a "Living Legend" by the Library of Congress in 2000.

The Illustrators

Over the past sixty-five years, the following five illustrators have contributed their talent and skill to the Ramona Quimby series. There have been other, perhaps less widely known, editions with the work of other illustrators or photographers, which are not covered in this book, including those whose covers use photographs of the 1988–1989 Canadian television series, those in languages other than English, and those published by Avon Camelot.

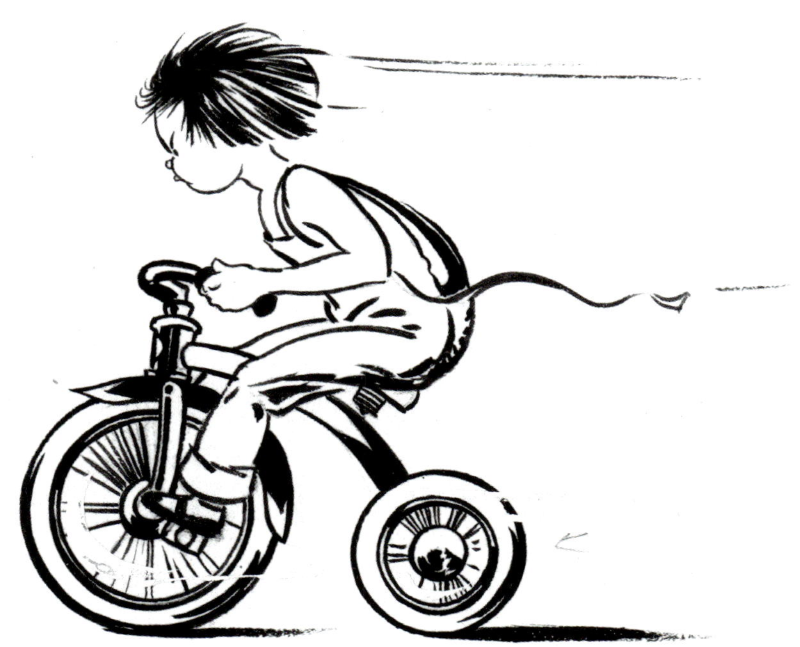

Louis Darling

Born two weeks after Beverly Cleary, on April 26, 1916, Louis Darling was an illustrator, writer, and pioneering environmentalist. He grew up in Stamford, Connecticut, and he developed an interest in natural history and the great outdoors at an early age. His was a childhood of hunting, fishing, and camping, along with a burgeoning passion for illustration. After two years at the Grand Central Art School in New York, two years studying under private tutelage, a stint in advertising, and four years as an Air Force photographer during World War II, Darling began his book illustration career in earnest.

During his short life, Darling illustrated sixty books, including the fourteen that he wrote. He primarily used pen and ink. Early in the environmentalist movement, he and his wife, Lois Darling née MacIntyre, collaboratively illustrated Rachel Carson's best seller *The Silent Spring*, as well as other books, including *Before and After Dinosaurs*, *Turtles*, *The Science of Life*, *Bird*, and *A Place in the Sun: Ecology in the Living World*. In 1956, as the president of Connecticut Conservationists, Inc., Darling appeared in court to defend Sherwood Island State Park from the state's plan to dredge the Long Island Sound.

Darling illustrated many of Beverly Cleary's books, including the first two of the Ramona Quimby series, until his death in 1970. *Runaway Ralph*, published that same year, is the last book he illustrated for Cleary—the author dedicated it to him.

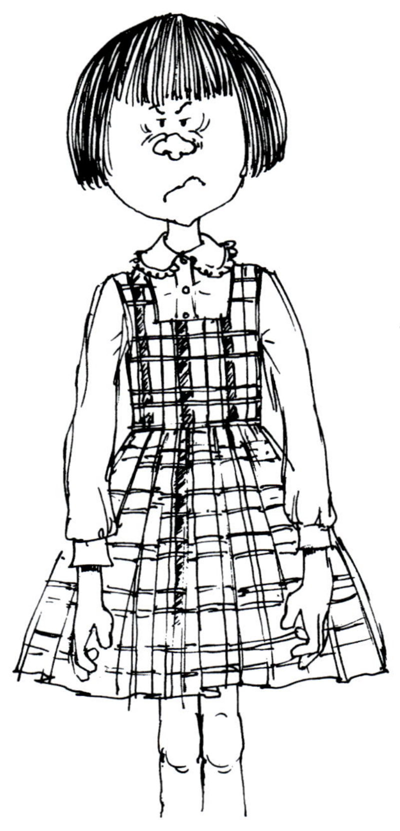

Alan Tiegreen

Alan Tiegreen was born in Boise, Idaho, in 1935. He and his family moved around the country throughout his childhood, following his father's employment with the government. An artist and musician, Tiegreen chose to focus on art and illustration in college, earning a Bachelor of Arts degree from the University of Southern Mississippi in 1957 and a Bachelor of Professional Arts degree from the ArtCenter College of Design in Los Angeles in 1961. Starting in 1965, he taught painting, drawing, and illustration at Georgia State University in Atlanta.

It wasn't until he and his wife, Helen Hurt Tiegreen, became parents that he grew interested in illustrating children's books. He illustrated the Pee Wee Scout series by Judy Delton, *Silver Woven in My Hair* by Shirley Rousseau Murphy, *Blueberries for Steven* by Beth Rice Lutrell, and many books by Joanna Cole and Stephanie Calmenson, including *Bug in a Rug: Reading Fun for Just-Beginners, Six Sick Sheep: 101 Tongue Twisters, Crazy Eights and Other Card Games, Why Did the Chicken Cross the Road, The Eentsy, Weentsy Spider: Fingerplays and Action Rhymes, Miss Mary Mack and Other Children's Street Rhymes, Anna Banana: 10 Jump Rope Rhymes*, and *Asking About Sex and Growing Up: A Question-and-Answer Book for Boys and Girls*, among others. Alongside Cleary, Tiegreen won many honors and awards for the work he did on the Ramona Quimby series: the 1977 Golden Archer and 1978 Mark Twain for *Ramona the Brave*, the 1978 Boston Globe Horn Book fiction honor and Newbery Medal for *Ramona and Her Father*, the 1981 American Book Award for *Ramona and Her Mother*, and the 1984 New York Times Notable Book of the Year for *Ramona Forever*.

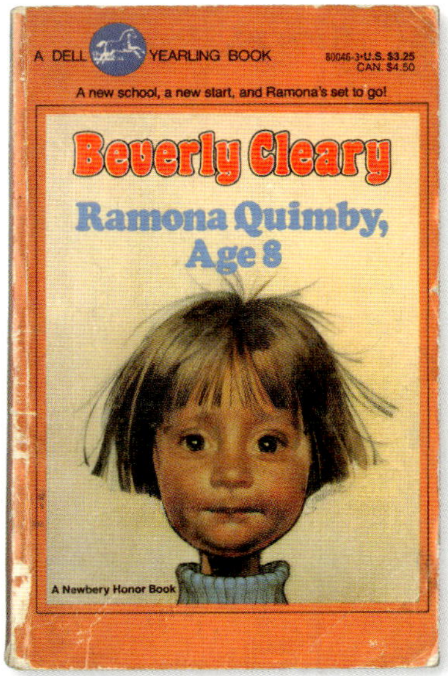

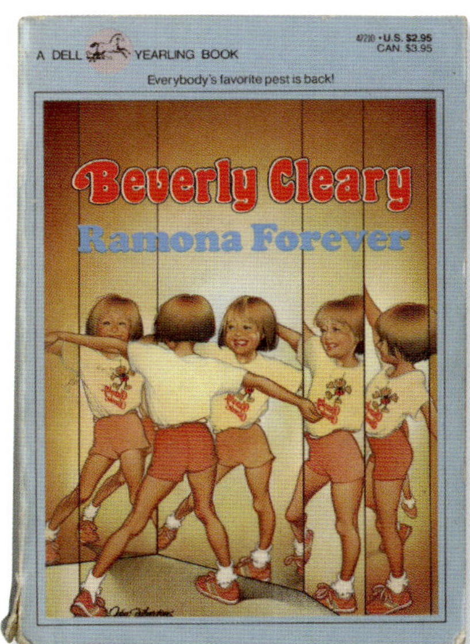

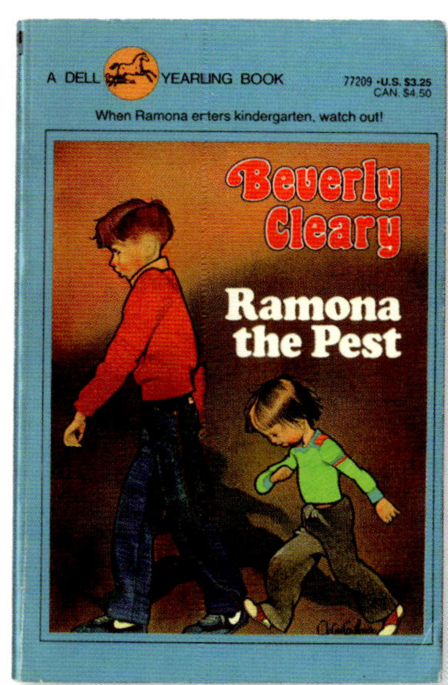

Joanne Scribner

Joanne Scribner studied art for advertising at Spokane Falls Community College in Washington State and started out as a fashion illustrator for Bloomingdale's in New York City. One day, a fellow illustrator told her that Dell Publishing was looking for illustrators to create covers. Scribner showed up without an appointment, and when the receptionist told her that she could fit her in in three months, Scribner told her that she would just wait. That day, she met the editor with whom she would work for years to come.

For a while, Scribner lived in New York and illustrated covers for adult and children's books. After returning to her hometown of Spokane, she was introduced to the work of Beverly Cleary. Her first cover for the author was for *Emily's Runaway Imagination*, released in 1980.

For her cover art, Scribner painted in layers. She used pencil, ink, acrylic, and, as she said in a telephone interview, "the kitchen sink if [she] could flatten and glue it in there." Then she would apply resin after each layer of paint, wait a few days for it to dry, and sand it down so that it would be smooth and the layers wouldn't show.

Many of the books for which Scribner created cover art do not explicitly credit her in the front matter or back matter. But if you look closely, you can find variations of her name on some of the book covers: to the left of the doll's head in *Ramona and Her Father*, near Ramona's feet in *Ramona the Pest* and *Ramona Forever*, on the bathroom sink in *Ramona and Her Mother*, under the bow on Beezus's dress in *Beezus and Ramona*.

For the Ramona series, Scribner used her daughter, Jami, as the model. Jami was six years old when Scribner was hired to paint the cover for *Ramona the Brave*, in which Ramona happens to be around the same age. This resulted in beautiful, realistic renderings of Ramona, as well as an awkward parent-teacher conference for Scribner. Jami, the teacher told the illustrator, had signed a drawing "Ramona" with a kitty cat Q in Ramona's signature style. "Who's Ramona?" the teacher had asked. "Why, Ramona Quimby, of course!" Jami had replied.

To get the pattern on the blanket right on the *Ramona the Brave* cover, Scribner cut apart a quilt and glued it in. For all her covers, she worked tirelessly to draw the people realistically, with the theory that the face, rather than background details, would be powerful enough to draw a potential reader's eye.

She was correct—to this day, Scribner's covers for the Ramona books are widely celebrated. Over the course of her career, she illustrated more than one hundred books, including the Kids of Polk Street School series by Patricia Reilly Giff and the Danger Guys series by Tony Abbott.

Tracy Dockray

Tracy Dockray hails from West Texas. She moved to New York, earning a Master of Fine Arts degree at Pratt Institute in 1985. Before beginning her career illustrating books, she made puppets and painted murals for children's rooms and playgrounds.

Dockray first experienced the Ramona books as most people do, while reading them as a child. The books contained Louis Darling's pen-and-ink drawings, which she adored despite the cars and clothes being dated; that was part of their charm. So when she was asked to illustrate the stories in the early 2000s, she was curious as to why anyone would want to change Darling's original Ramona, who looks remarkably like Beverly Cleary did as a child. She then discovered that Alan Tiegreen had already created a second version of Ramona, so reinterpreting this winsome child and her family *had* been done before.

Dockray's illustrations were a bit different. She proposed using flat gray shading because there are so many shades of people, and she wanted to make the stories more inclusive. She created sketches with pencil and inked them, then used a computer to add the shading afterward.

The deadline to complete the illustrations for the Ramona series was incredibly tight, so Dockray lived and breathed Ramona and her family for two years. To start off, she reread all the books, avoiding the drawings so she wouldn't be influenced by them. At the time, her daughter, Audrey, was the same age as Ramona in the first books. She was jealous of this 2-D girl who got so much of Dockray's undivided attention, but she wasn't too proud to mention to people that drawing Ramona was her mother's full-time job.

Along with the Ramona series, Dockray also drew pictures for Cleary's Henry Huggins series and the Ralph Mouse series. For the latter, Cleary suggested that she use a real mouse as a model for Ralph. Rumor has it that Louis Darling had used a dead one propped on a toy motorcycle as his model, but Dockray found that method a little too ghoulish. Soon after, Dockray discovered a tiny baby mouse crouched on the sidewalk in New York City. She scooped him into a paper cup, brought him home, and nursed him with a dropper. He stayed in his new mouse house by her drawing table and became the muse for her Ralph.

Dockray has also illustrated numerous picture books, including the Fix-It Friends series by Nicole C. Kear. She is a literacy advocate for Literacy Inc. and Learning Leaders, and a part-time librarian at a local school.

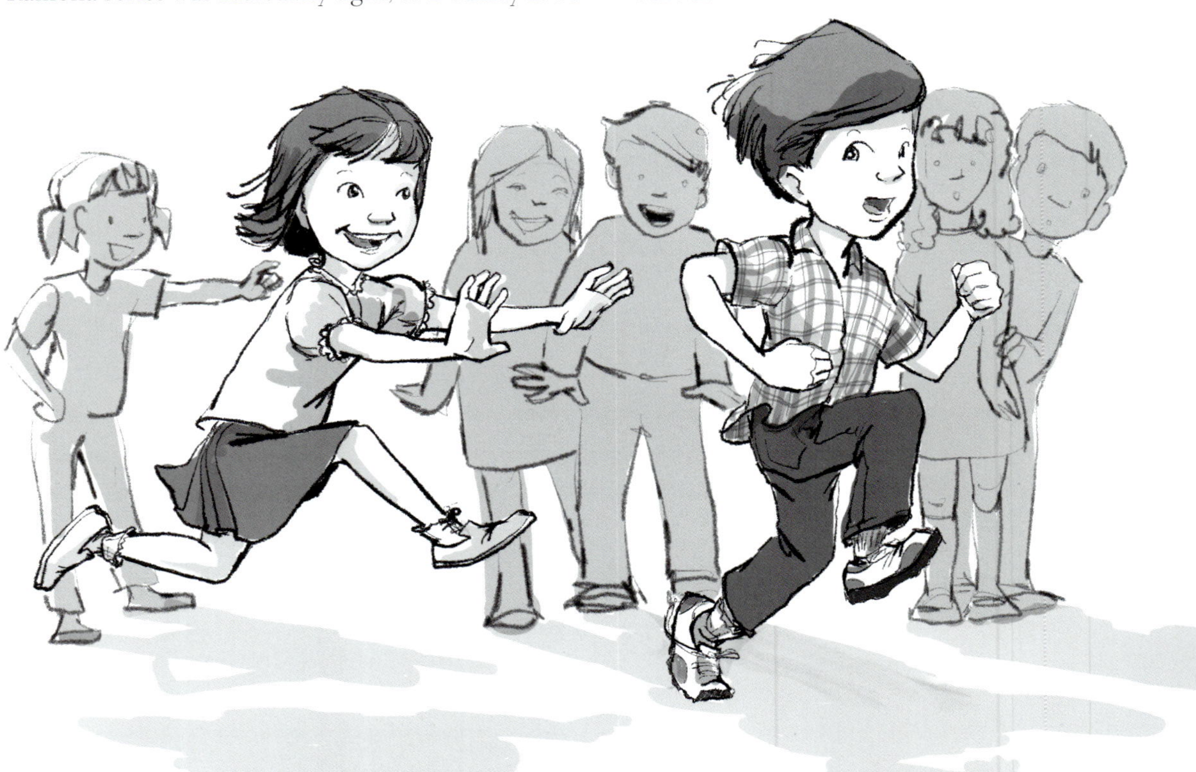

Jacqueline Rogers

Born in Westport, Connecticut, in 1958, Rogers was the youngest of six children in a family of artists. Her mother was a portrait and landscape painter; her father was a businessman who did leathersmithing, photography, knot tying, and jewelry making as hobbies. There were always art supplies lying around the house, and the entire family encouraged Rogers, signing her up for sculpture lessons, taking her along to their painting and drawing classes, passing down art books, and giving her the time and space to draw and do calligraphy in her room.

By the time she was in high school, it was clear to her that she was going to have a career in art. She went to the Rhode Island School of Design to study painting. She loved the school but was unhappy in the painting department, so she eventually switched to studying illustration halfway through her sophomore year. Two of her favorite teachers were the award-winning children's book illustrators David Macaulay and Chris Van Allsburg. Even so, she didn't decide to work on children's books until well after she graduated college, first trying other types of illustration, including magazine, newspaper, advertising, store windows, and even scrimshaw. Ultimately, she sought work in children's books because it was the most fun and provided lots of opportunity for creativity.

Rogers has illustrated over a hundred children's books, including *Our Great Big Backyard* by Laura Bush and Jenna Bush Hager and the Little Ree series by Ree Drummond. She illustrated Beverly Cleary's backlist, including the Ramona Quimby series, in 2013 and 2014. She continues to experiment in different media, painting (mostly in oil), making tiles, throwing pots, and working in reverse scratchboard with ink, acrylic, and watercolor. In 2019, HarperCollins published *Goblin Moon*, a picture book that Rogers both wrote and illustrated herself.

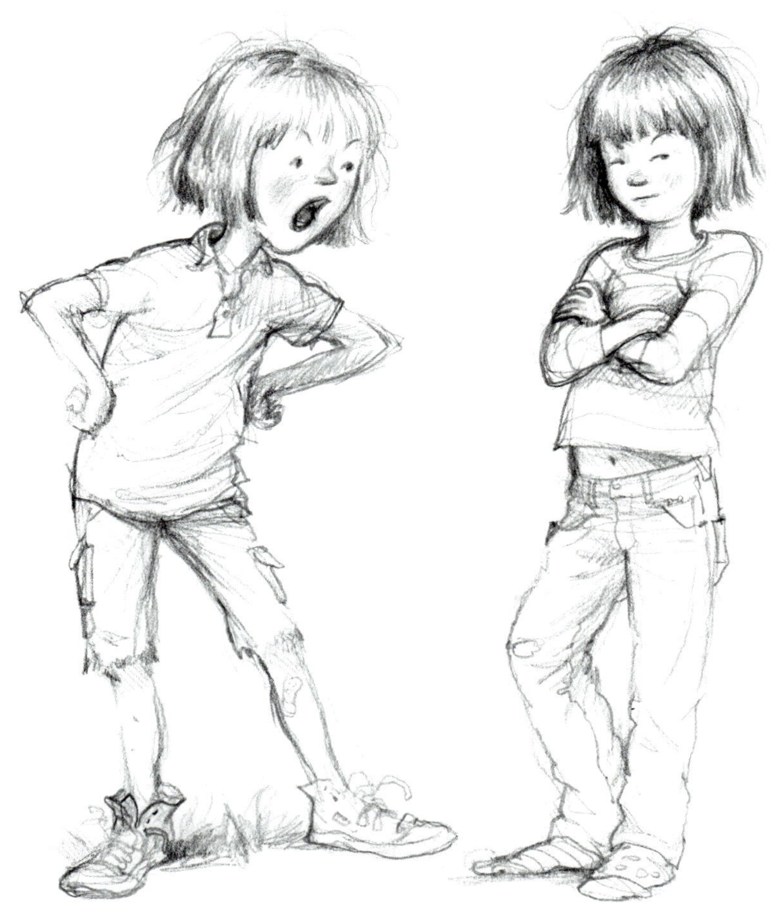

Cast of Characters

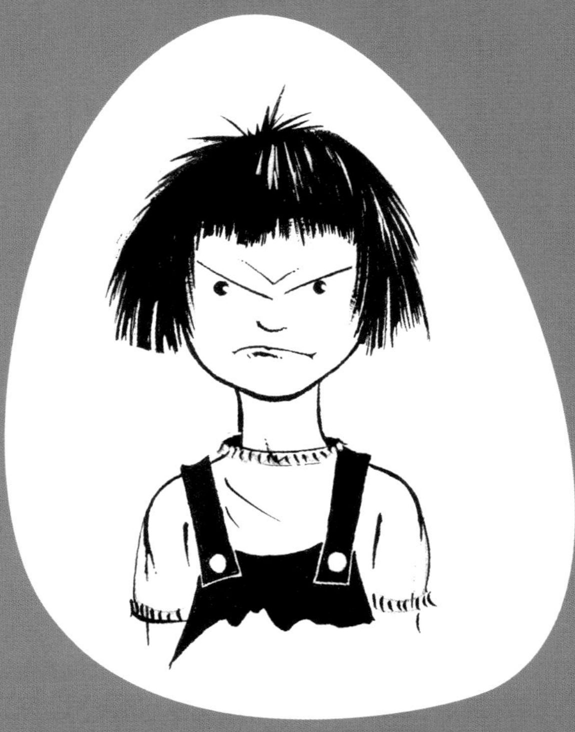

Ramona

Ramona scowled. "I am too a Merry Sunshine!" she shouted angrily.

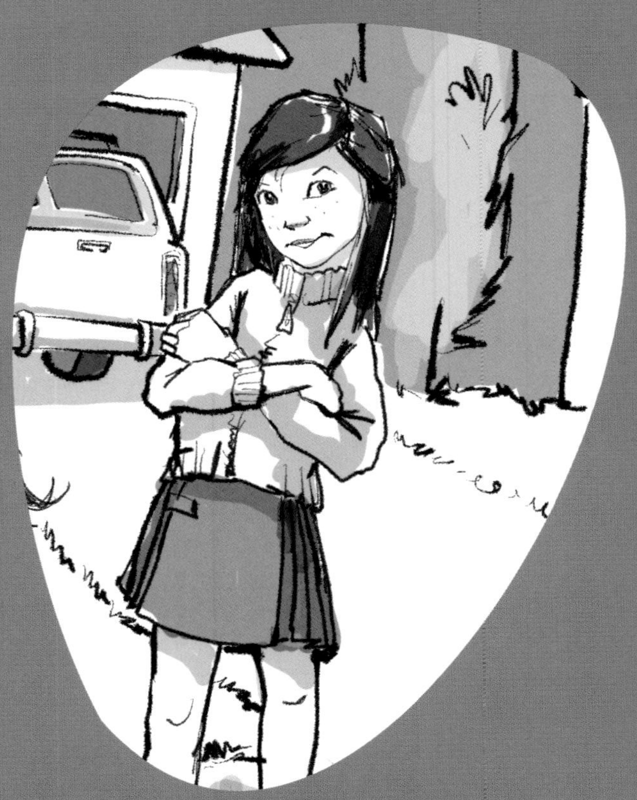

Beezus

Nobody, reflected Beezus, ever says anything about my imagination. Nobody at all. And she wished, more than anything, that she had imagination.

ABOVE: LOUIS DARLING (LEFT) AND ALAN TIEGREEN (RIGHT). OPPOSITE: JACQUELINE ROGERS (LEFT) AND ALAN TIEGREEN (RIGHT).

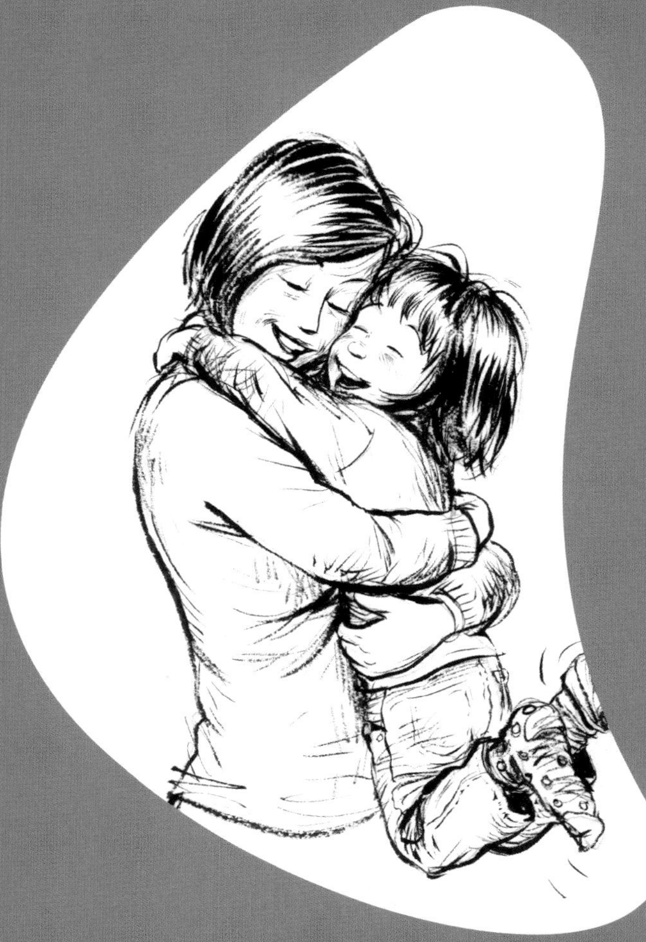

Mrs. Quimby

"Love isn't like a cup of sugar that gets used up," said Mrs. Quimby. "There is enough to go around."

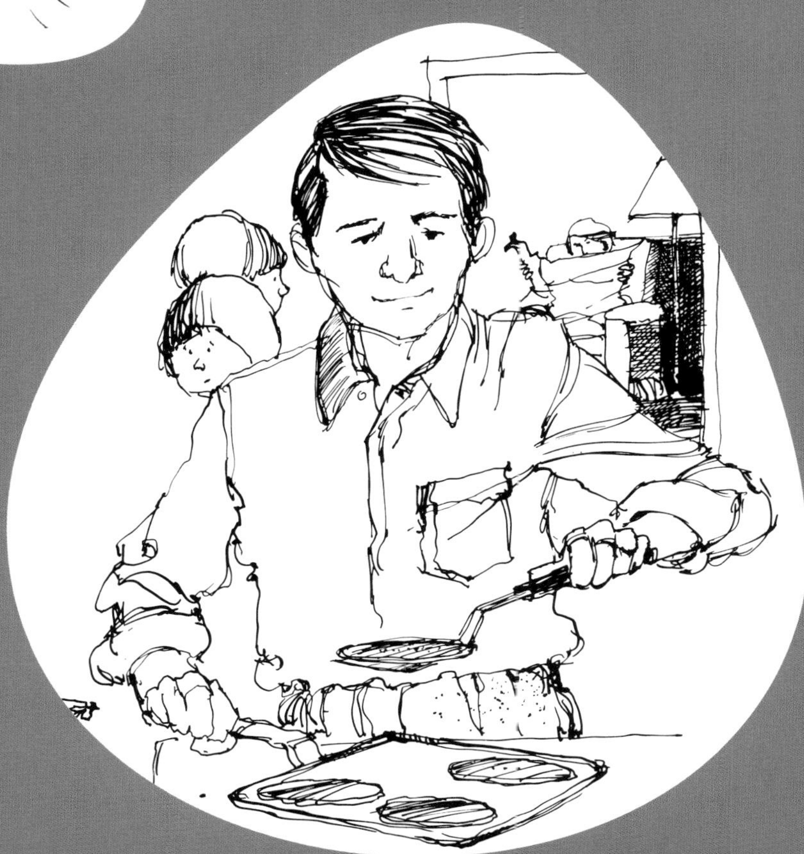

Mr. Quimby

"Buck up, Ramona," said Mr. Quimby. "Show us your spunk."

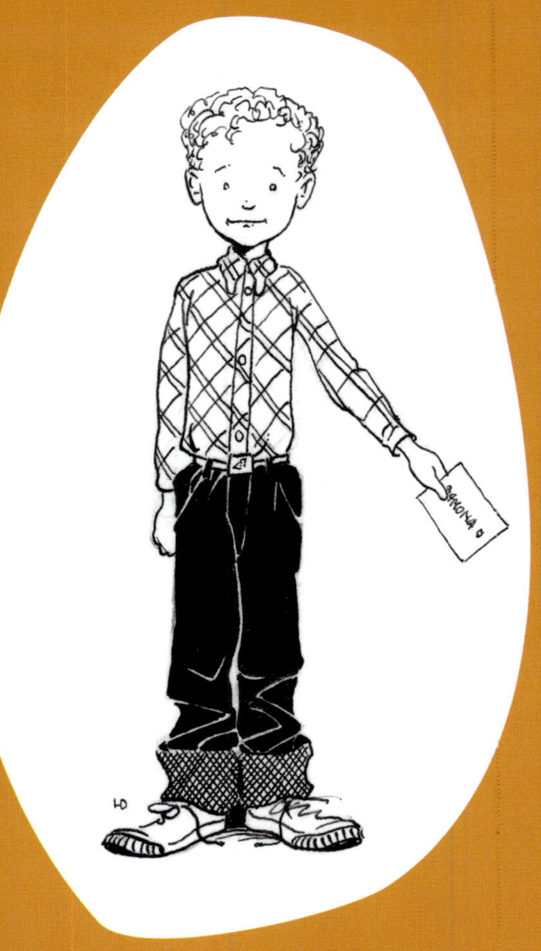

Howie

"I'm tired of sharing," said Howie. "Share, share, share. That's all grown-ups ever talk about."

Susan

"Miss Binney, Ramona scribbled all over her house," said Susan, who by now had revealed herself as the kind of girl who always wanted to play house so she could be the mother and boss everybody.

ABOVE: JACQUELINE ROGERS (LEFT) AND LOUIS DARLING (RIGHT). OPPOSITE: ALAN TIEGREEN (LEFT) AND LOUIS DARLING (RIGHT).

Willa Jean

"You have to be the dog," said Willa Jean.

"Why?" Ramona kept an eye on Mrs. Kemp as she wondered how far she dared go in resisting Willa Jean's orders.

"Because I'm a beautiful rich lady and I say so," Willa Jean informed her.

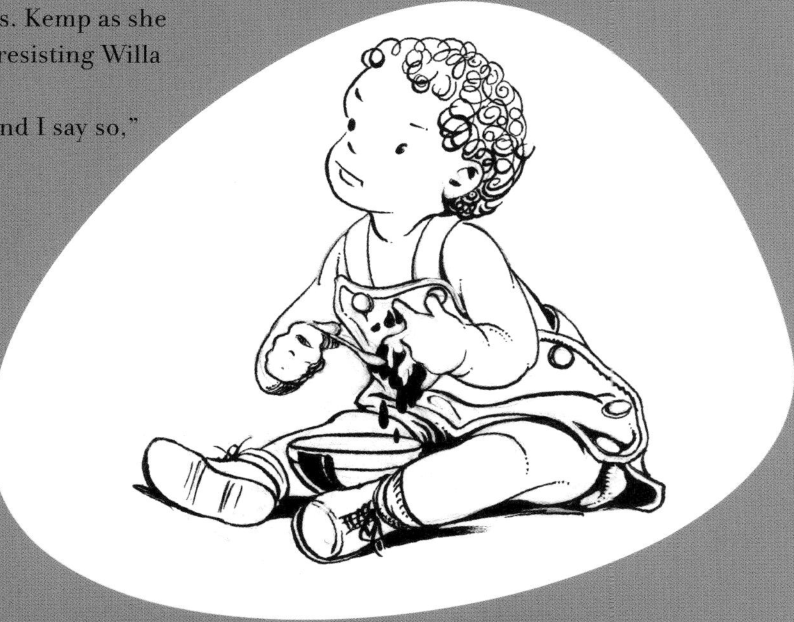

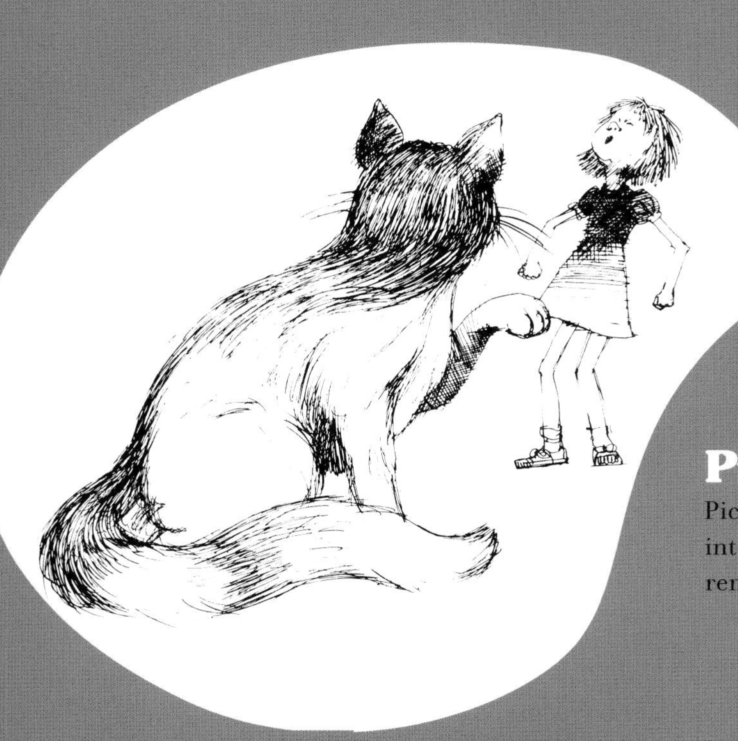

Picky-picky

Picky-picky, purring like a rusty motor, walked into the dining room and rubbed against legs to remind the family that he should eat too.

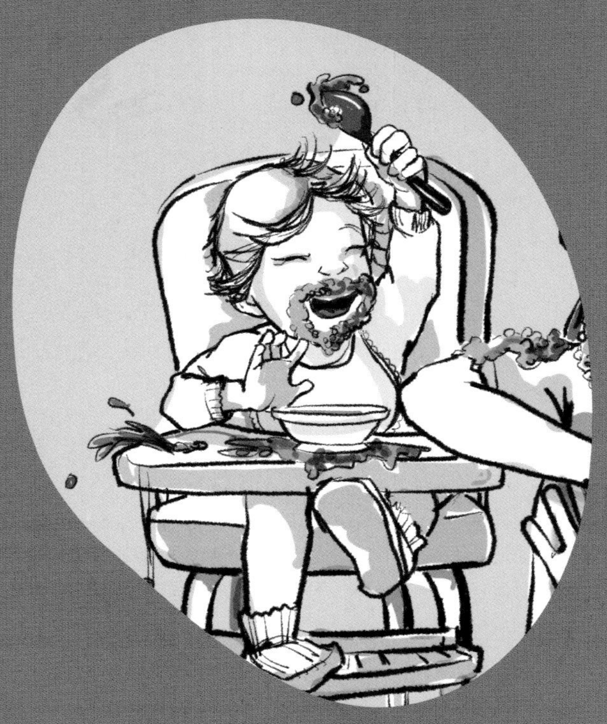

Roberta

With her mouth full of peas, Roberta looked both surprised and disappointed, as if her sister had betrayed her. Then she blew hard, spraying mushy, squishy, smelly green peas all over Ramona.

Yard Ape

She half rose from her seat to look across the aisle toward Yard Ape and read in his neat uphill cursive, "My name is Daniel. Call me Yard Ape. I am nine years old. I am not married. I am a kid and proud of it."

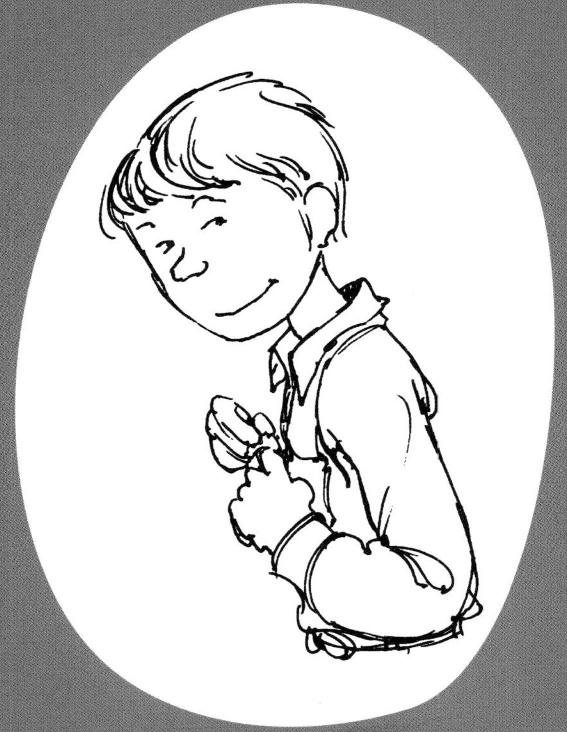

ABOVE: TRACY DOCKRAY (LEFT) AND ALAN TIEGREEN (RIGHT). OPPOSITE, CLOCKWISE FROM LEFT: LOUIS DARLING, JACQUELINE ROGERS, AND ALAN TIEGREEN.

Mrs. Kemp

"Now Howie," said Mrs. Kemp, busy with her endless knitting, "play nicely with your sister. She's little, you know."

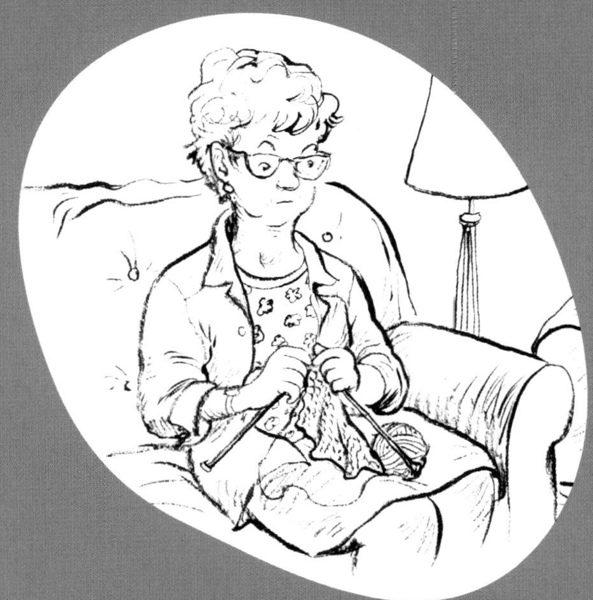

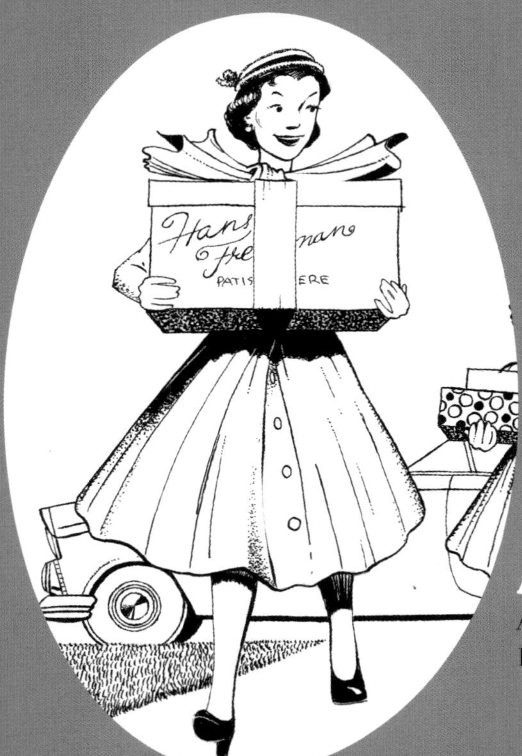

Aunt Bea

And the way Aunt Beatrice laughed made Beezus laugh too.

Daisy Kidd

Now Daisy spoke up. "I think that's silly. I'm going to eat my cake. I've eaten birthday cake all my life and I'm still alive." Ramona was glad she had Daisy for a best friend.

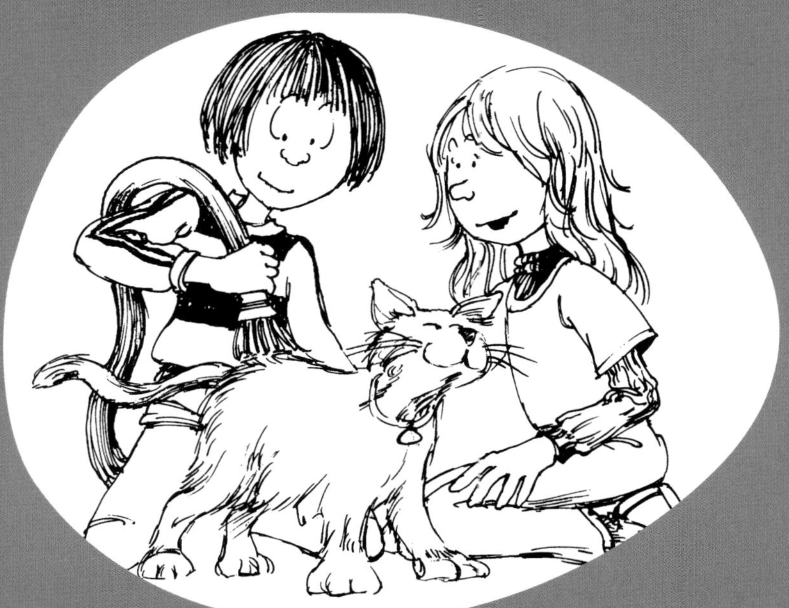

A Note About Henry Huggins

BEFORE RAMONA AND BEEZUS, there was Henry Huggins. This charming third-grader with hair like a scrubbing brush and a best friend named Ribsy was Beverly Cleary's very first brainchild. He was inspired by a group of grubby little nonreaders, schoolboys who visited the library in the rural town of Yakima, Washington, in 1939. "Where are the books about kids like us?" they asked the newly minted librarian.

Cleary wrote the first of the three-book Henry Huggins series in 1949; it was published by Morrow Junior Books in 1950. Beezus, whose real name is Beatrice, and her lively little sister, Ramona, first pop into existence in the book's second chapter, "Gallons of Guppies." They agree to adopt one of Henry's fast-breeding guppies, even though they already have a cat, three white rats, a turtle, and one fish. (By the time they got their own series, they were down to the one cat, Picky-picky.)

That was consistent with the characteristic courteousness of the Beezus we would come to know and love. Ramona doesn't show her true colors until the book's final chapter, when she says, "Mewow, mewow," a creative variation of a cat's meow (or "miaow" per the 1950 spelling).

"What does she mean, 'Mewow'?" asked Henry.

"Oh, don't pay any attention to her," answered Beezus. "That's the way she says miaow. She's pretending she's a cat."

"Mewow," said Ramona and patted the curlers in her hair. "I'm a cat with curly hair."

And so began our enduring enthusiasm for everything Ramona.

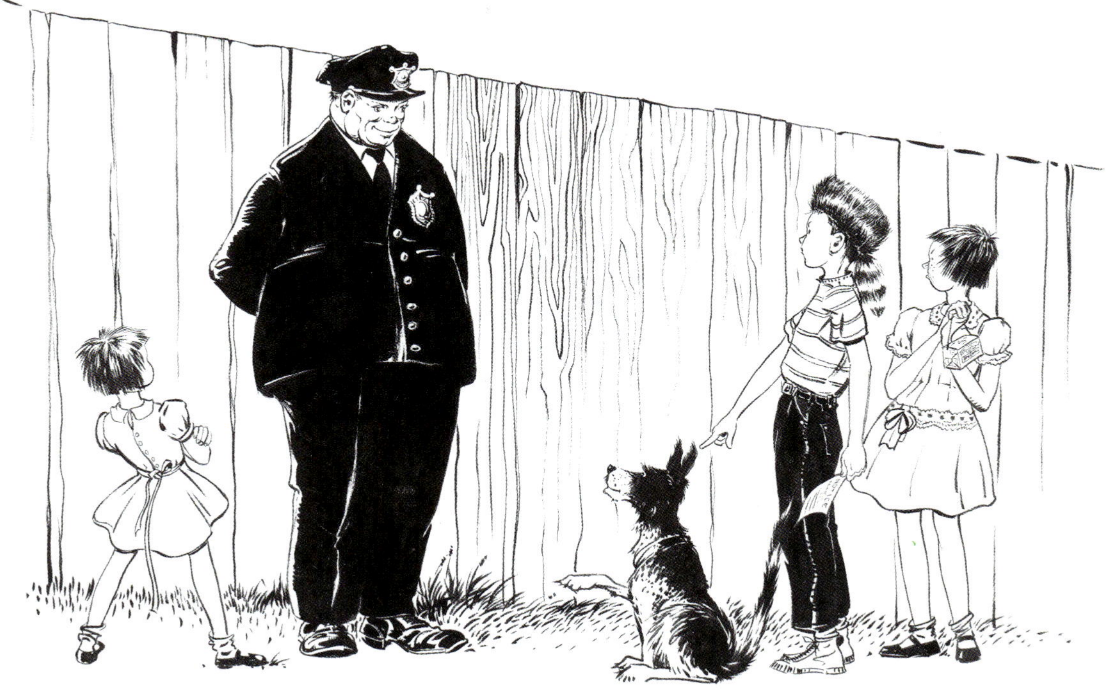

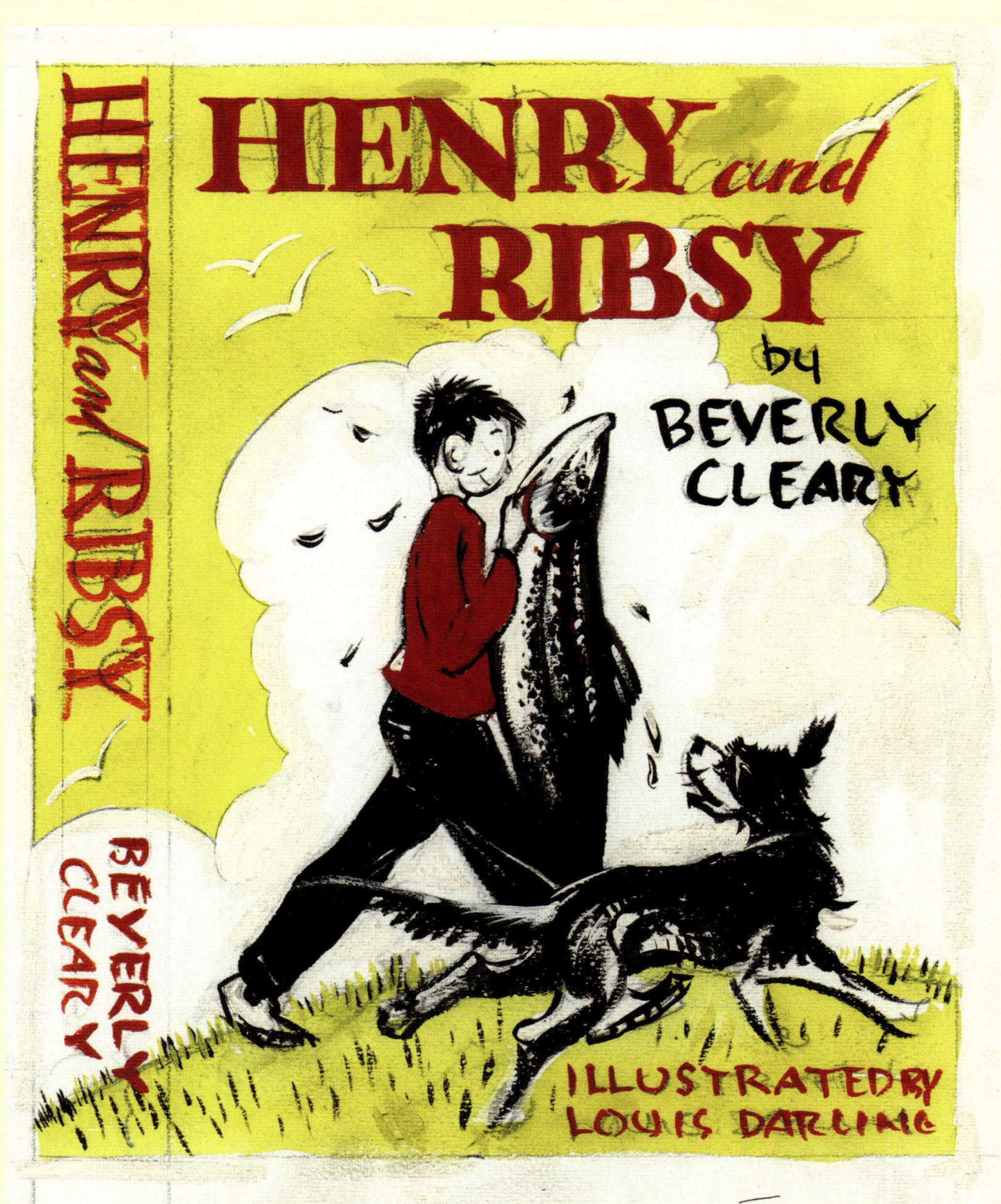

LOUIS DARLING (ABOVE AND OPPOSITE).

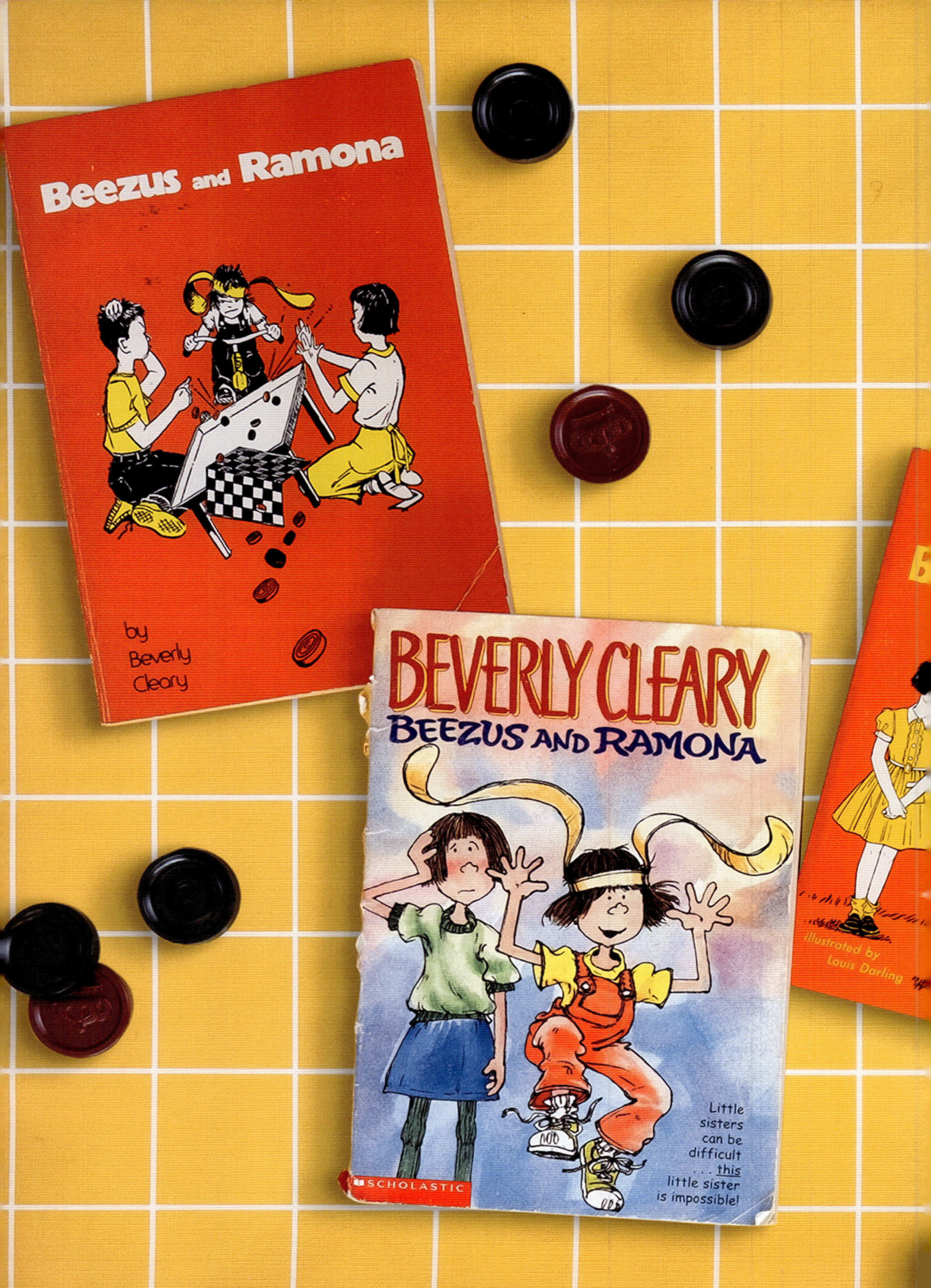
Beezus and Ramona
by
Beverly
Cleary
BEVERLY CLEARY
BEEZUS AND RAMONA
Little
sisters
can be
difficult
. . . this
little sister
is impossible!
SCHOLASTIC
illustrated by
Louis Darling

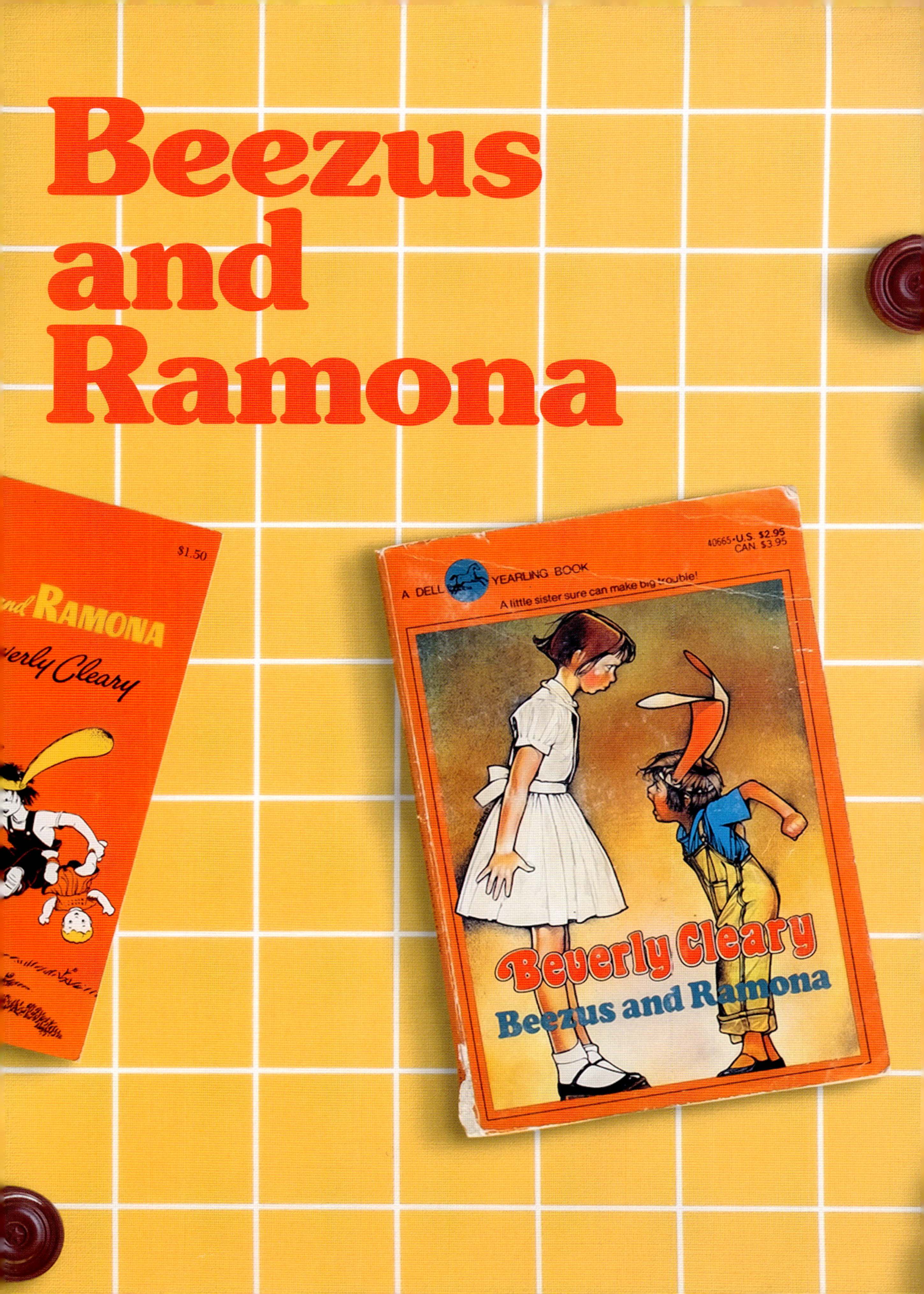
Beezus and Ramona
$1.50
RAMONA
40665 U.S. $2.95
CAN. $3.95
A DELL YEARLING BOOK
A little sister sure can make big trouble!
Beverly Cleary
Beezus and Ramona

Chapter One

Beezus and Ramona

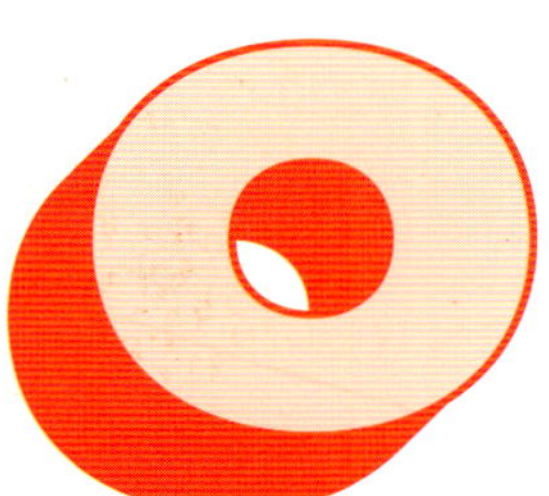

On her head Ramona wore a circle of cardboard with two long paper ears attached. The insides of the ears were colored with pink crayon, Ramona's work at nursery school. "I'm the Easter bunny," announced Ramona.

"Mother," wailed Beezus. "You aren't going to let her wear those awful ears to the library!"

From the get-go, Ramona is a force unto herself, and the bane of Beezus's existence. Even a mature nine-year-old girl can get tired of always having to be the nice, responsible one, while her babyish four-year-old sister gets to do whatever she wants and everyone thinks she's oh-so-adorable. Showing off her scabs, scribbling in library books, sneaking into the big kids' art class—Ramona is just impossible!

Published in 1955, *Beezus and Ramona* is the first of the Ramona Quimby series, and the first book starring the two sisters and their parents. It marks a transition from Beezus as a minor character in Henry Huggins's story to Beezus as the protagonist. It isn't until the second book of the series that Ramona becomes the leading actor in this saga, with Beezus as her sometime antagonist, sometime ally, always sister.

OPPOSITE: JACQUELINE ROGERS (LEFT) AND LOUIS DARLING (RIGHT).

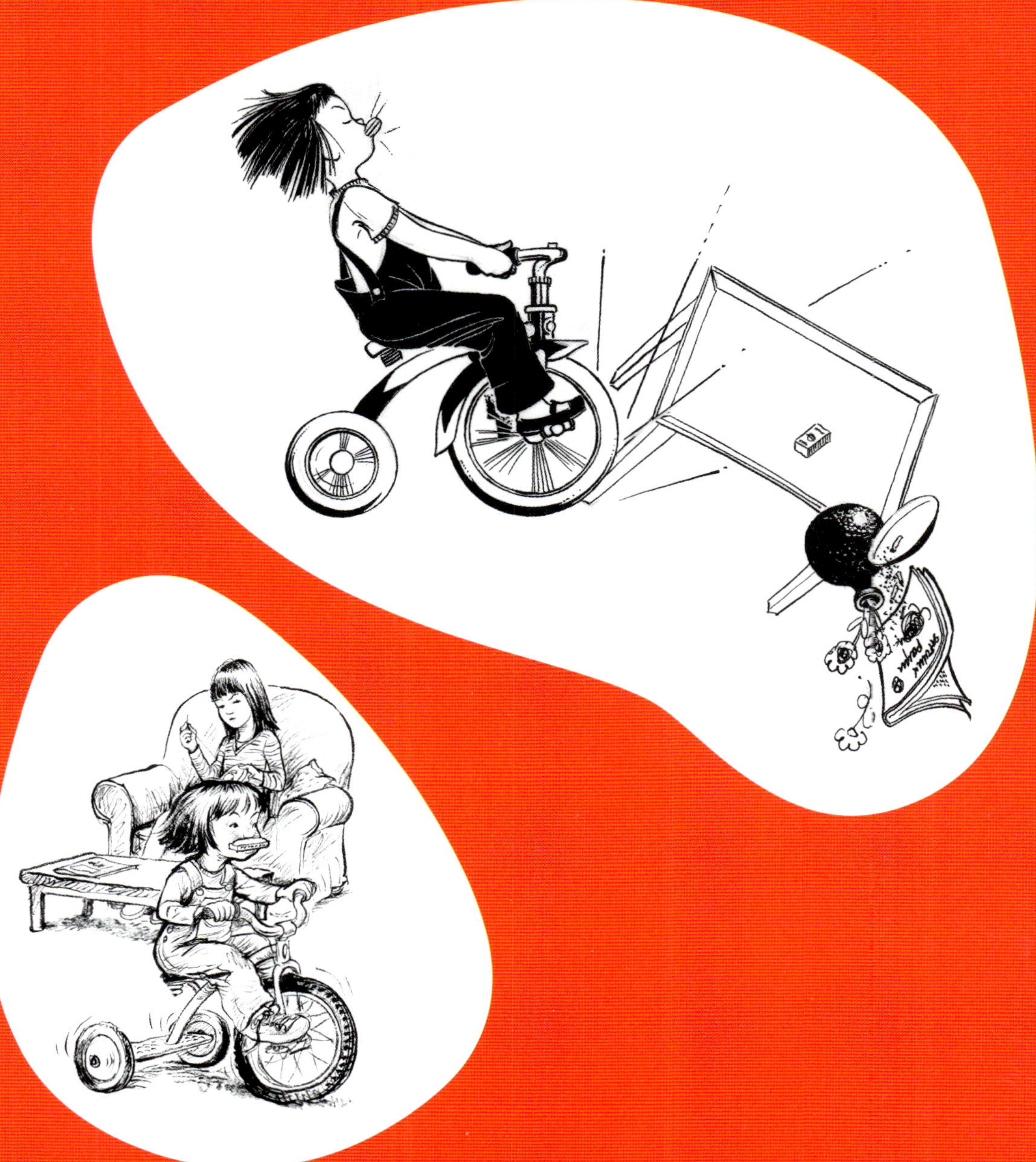

Ramona, blowing in and out of her harmonica, rides her tricycle around the living room with her eyes closed while Beezus attempts to embroider a potholder for their aunt's Christmas present. And so we meet Ramona and Beezus and see the dynamic between the sisters that will carry on throughout the books. Darling forgoes a more realistic rendering of subject meeting object and emphasizes the chaos of the moment when the younger girl inevitably crashes into the coffee table. Rogers draws the period after the crash, with a determined Ramona back on her tricycle and an annoyed-looking Beezus sewing in the background. Ramona is essentially extorting her older sister: If Beezus agrees to read aloud her favorite book, *The Littlest Steam Shovel*, then she will stop.

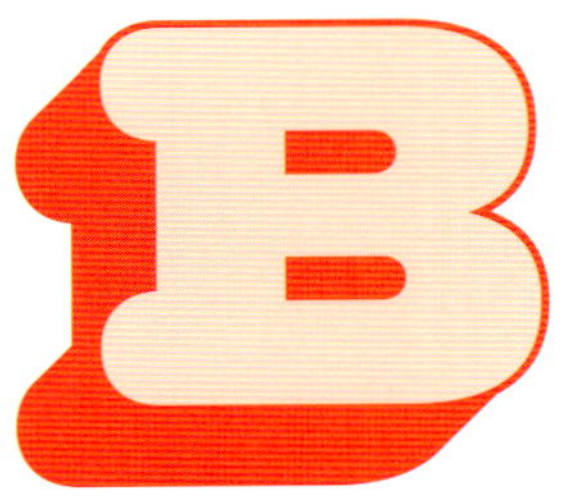

But the girls had no sooner left the house when they saw Mrs. Wisser, a lady who lived in the next block, coming toward them with a friend. It was too late to turn back. Mrs. Wisser had seen them and was waving.

"Why, hello there, Beatrice," Mrs. Wisser said, when they met. "I see you have a dear little bunny with you today."

"Uh . . . yes." Beezus didn't know what else to say.

Ramona obligingly hopped up and down to make her ears flop.

Mrs. Wisser said to her friend, as if Beezus and Ramona couldn't hear, "Isn't she adorable?"

Both children knew whom Mrs. Wisser was talking about. If she had been talking about Beezus, she would have said something quite different. Such a nice girl, probably. A sweet child. Adorable, never.

Tired of reading the same book over and over again, Beezus offers to take Ramona to the library to check out a new one. On the way, they run into a neighbor and her friend. Judging from her internal reaction to the woman's comment, Beezus, at nine years old, is already resigned to her role as the responsible older sister, and maybe also a little bit jealous.

The characters' clothes set these illustrations in the time and place of their creation. In Darling's 1955 drawings, Mrs. Wisser and friend wear full-skirted circle dresses with robust collars, day gloves, little purses, hats, and modest heels; Beezus wears a dress and bobby socks. Dockray's 2006 illustration features all characters in more casual attire, with the women in pants and shorts with sneakers, and Beezus in a skirt and jacket. In Tiegreen's cover art showing the same moment (see page 28), the girls have the seventies-style haircut that the illustrator replicates throughout the series (and Beezus's cheeks are flushed pink with embarrassment). In the latest illustration of this scene, created by Rogers for the 2013 re-edition, the women appear to be wearing the sneakers and jogging suits that make up modern workout gear. Perhaps they are out doing their daily exercise, something women would not have done in public during Darling's era. But in all three versions, Ramona sports dungarees and, of course, bunny ears.

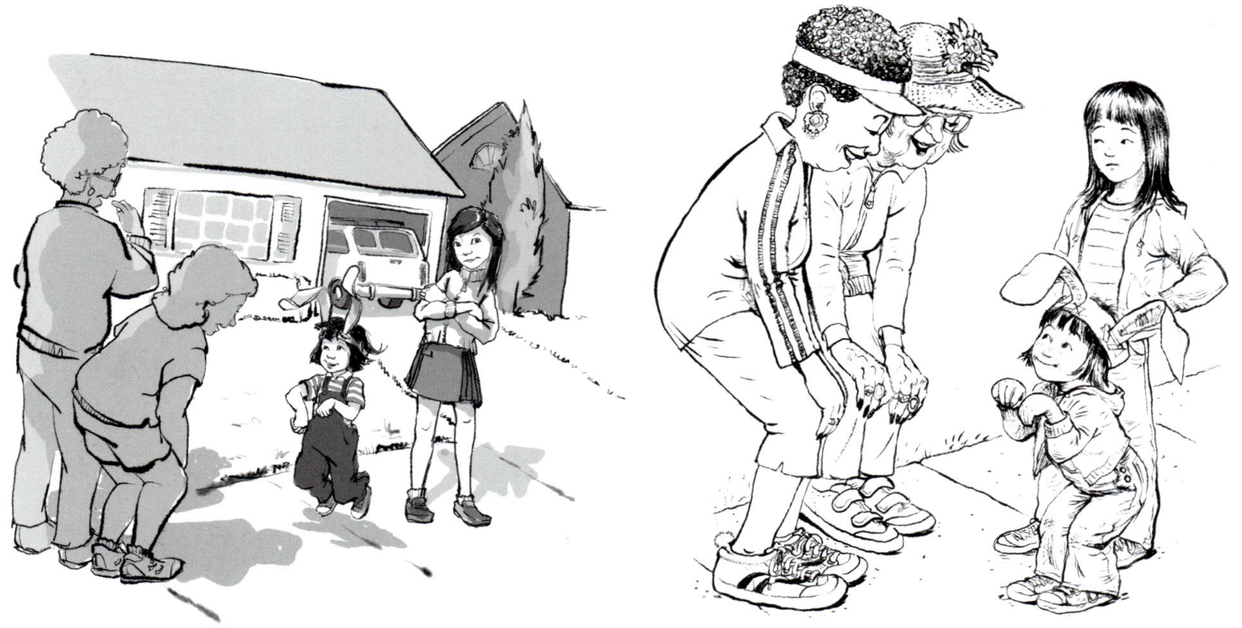

ABOVE: TRACY DOCKRAY (LEFT) AND JACQUELINE ROGERS (RIGHT). OPPOSITE: LOUIS DARLING.

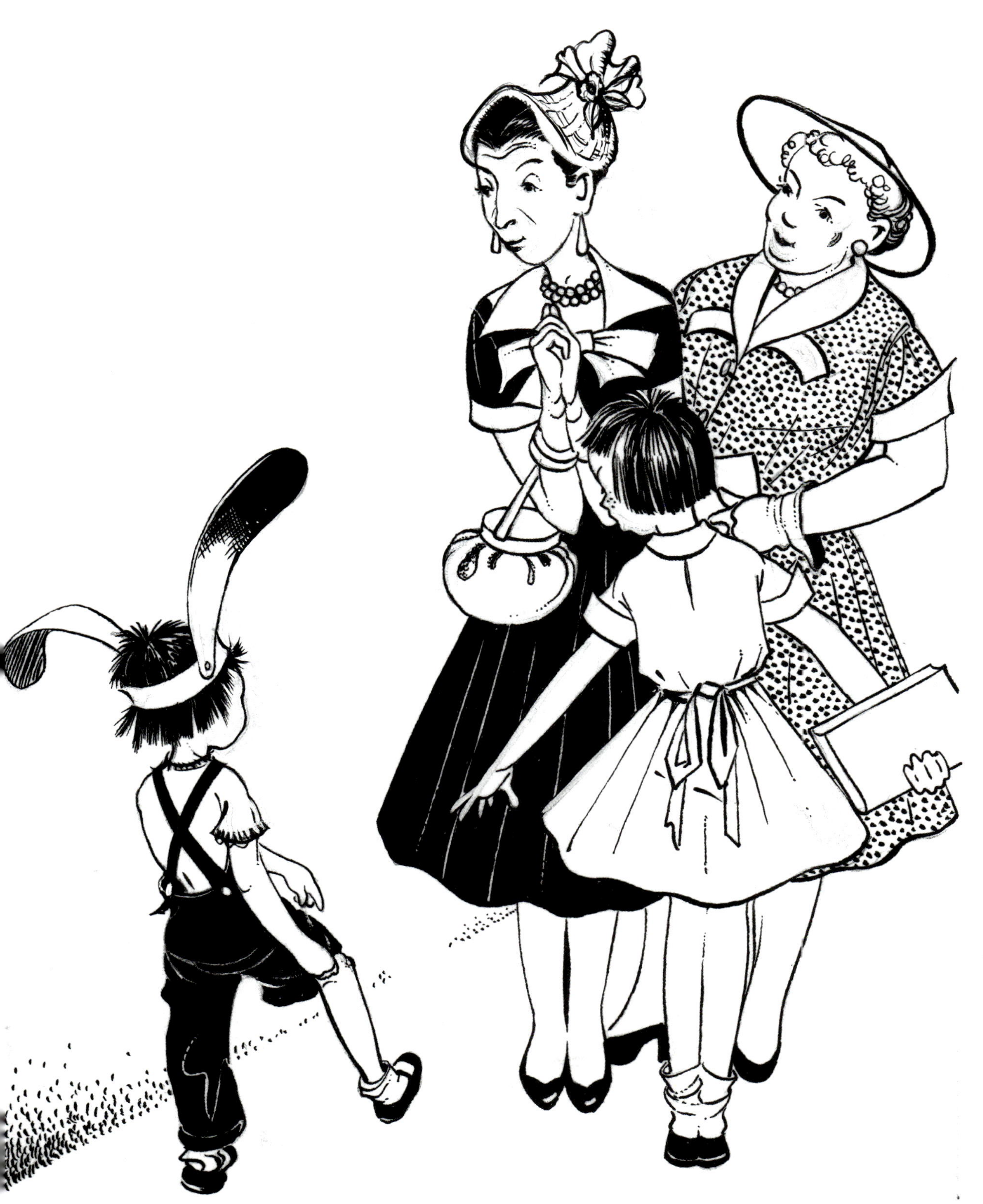

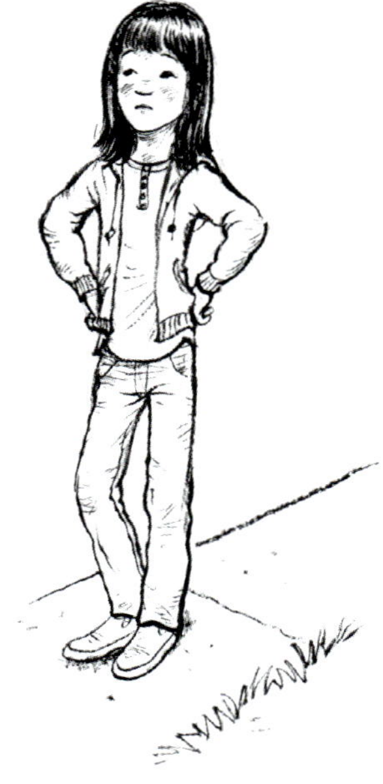

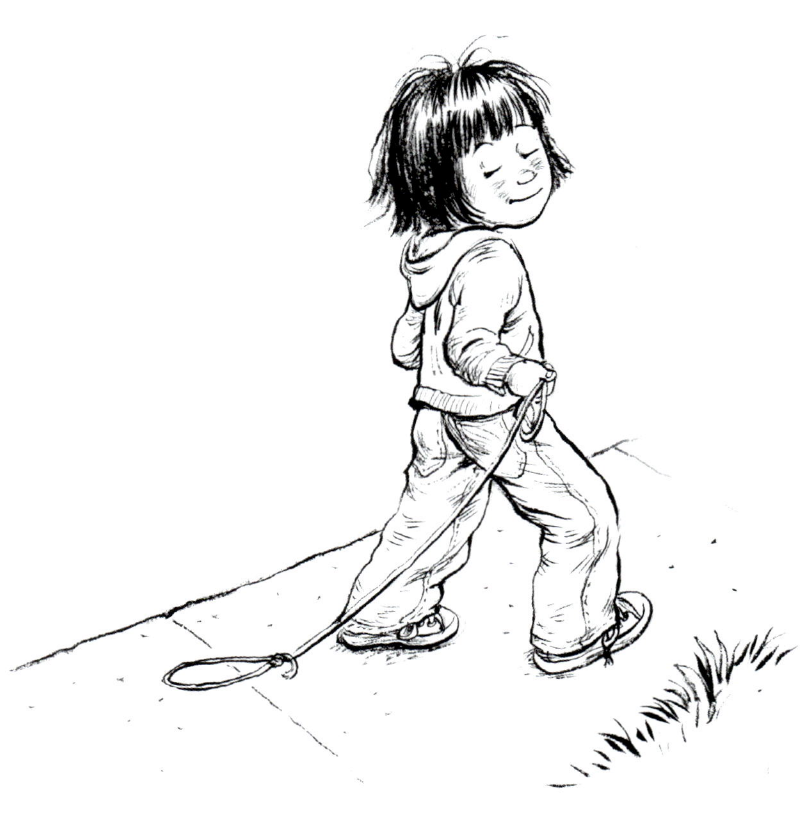

"That's my name," said Ramona proudly.
"That's just scribbling," Beezus told her.

Ramona has seen her sister write "Beatrice" and therefore assumes that all names must be made up of dots and lines; she doesn't understand that her name doesn't have the letters *t* and *i*. This is how she signs her name when attempting to get her first library card. Ultimately, the librarian lets her check out a book on Beezus's card.

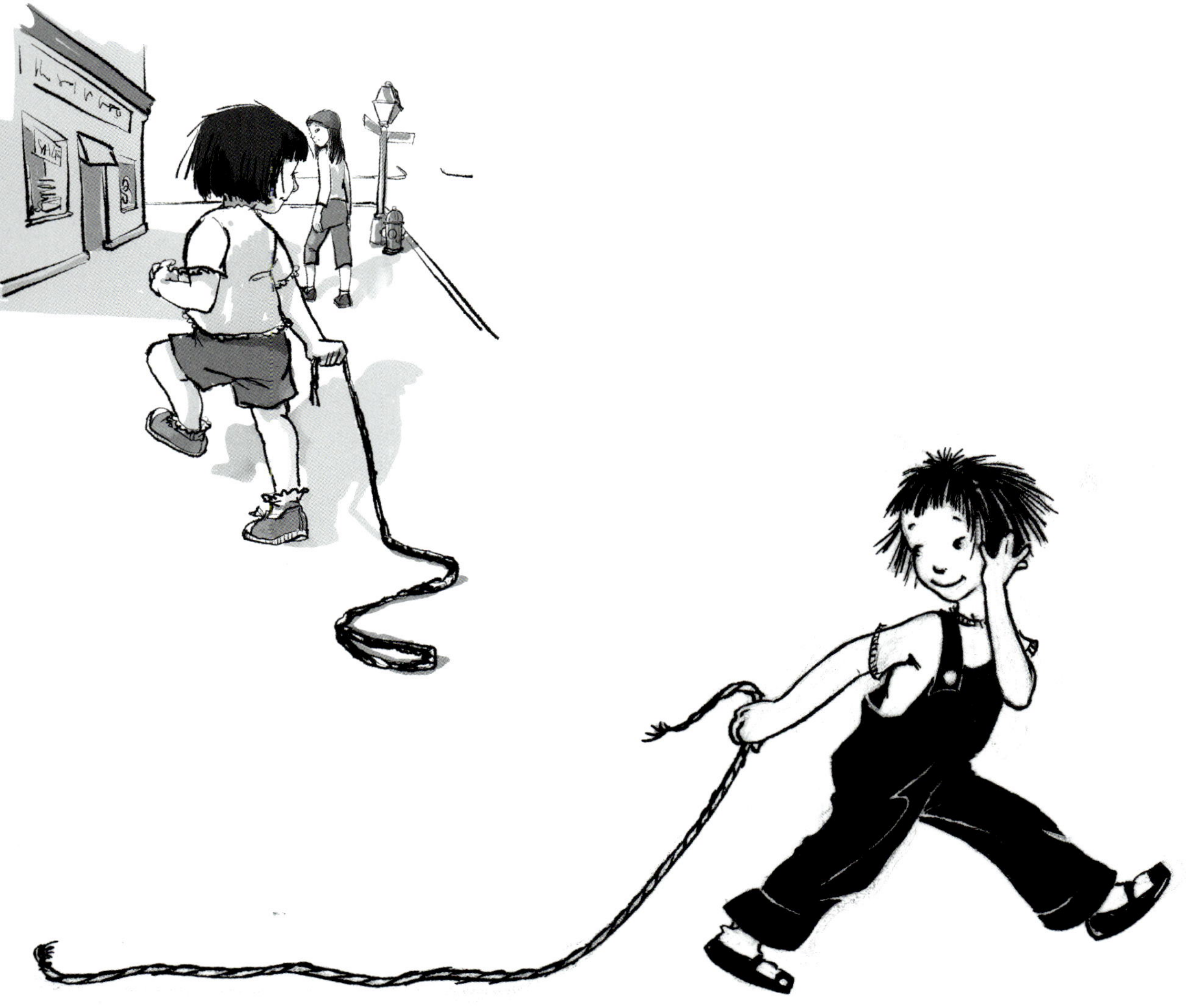

Ramona leads her imaginary lizard, Ralph.

One day, the assignment in Beezus's art class is to paint an imaginary animal. Miss Robbins, the art teacher, encourages freedom of expression and enjoyment, but while Ramona is famous—or, at times, infamous—for her wild imagination, Beezus tends toward neatness and drawing within the lines. Will Beezus be able to tap into the creative energy that Ramona so easily channels?

Coincidentally, Ramona had brought her own imaginary animal, a lizard named Ralph, along on their outing. The illustrators show Ramona and Ralph on his lead from different angles. Darling includes only those two characters in the scene, shown in simple profile. Rogers separated the two sisters, drawing Beezus with hands on hips and presumably counting the seconds until the lollygagging Ramona catches up with her. In Dockray's version, the leash occupies the foreground to the right, drawing the eye up to Ramona in jaunty mid-step; in the background, Beezus impatiently looks over her shoulder from up the street.

JACQUELINE ROGERS (OPPOSITE), TRACY DOCKRAY (LEFT), AND LOUIS DARLING (RIGHT).

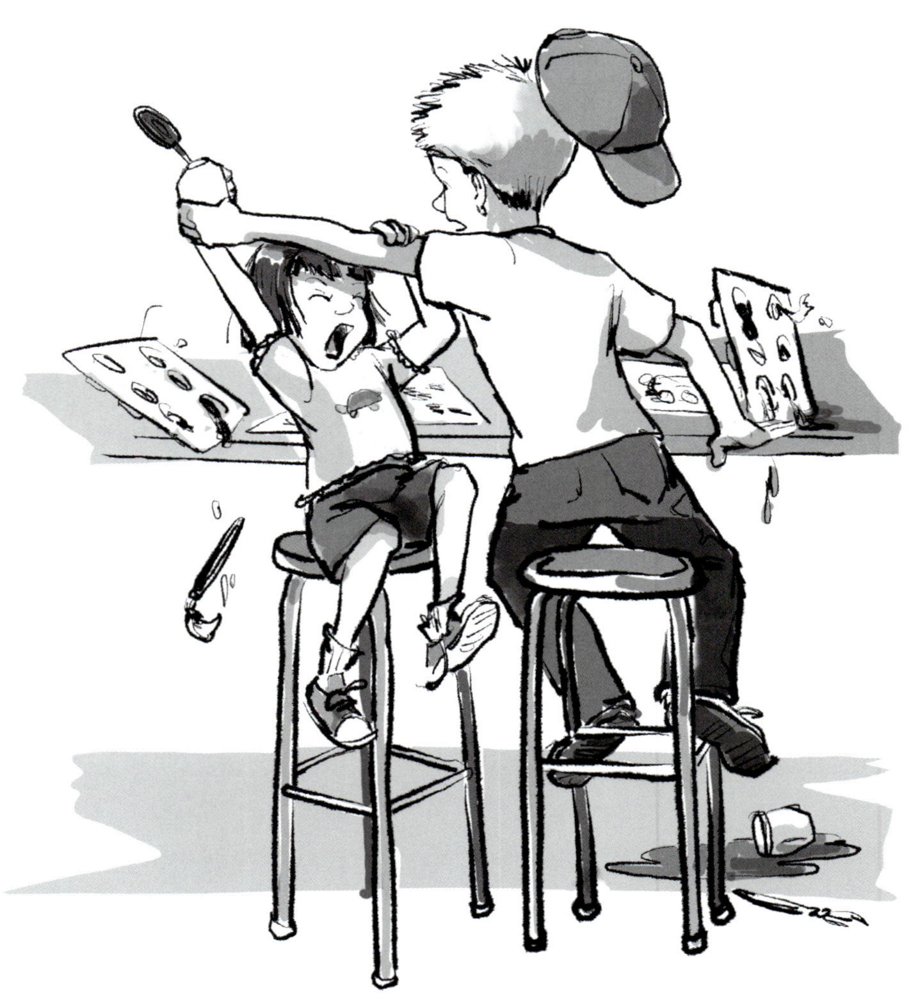

Ramona embarrasses Beezus by stealing classmate Wayne's sucker.

After her real friend Howie throws sand on her imaginary friend Ralph outside in the park, Ramona walks into the art classroom determined to join Beezus in her pursuit of art. And though the class is the one place she's not supposed to tag along, the art teacher lets her stay, and even share her sister's paints! Of course, soon Ramona discovers the purple lollipop that classmate Wayne had put beside his muffin tin of paints to save for later.

After the tussle shown in this illustration, Beezus will first defend her little sister, then make the ultimate threat: leave, or get tickled.

TRACY DOCKRAY

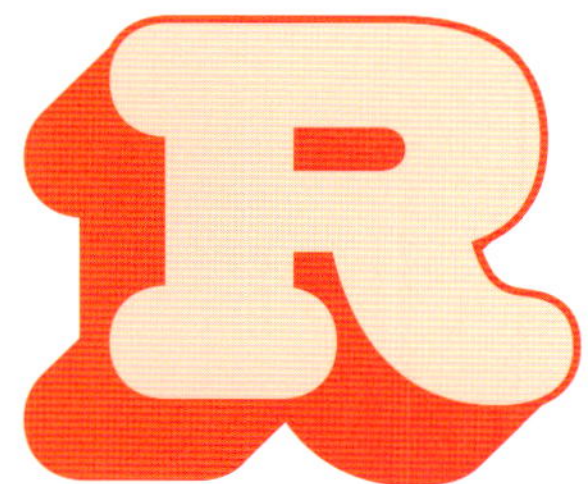

Ramona was not the only one in the family with imagination. So there!

Beezus seized her brush and painted in another sky with bold, free strokes. Then she dipped her brush into green paint and started to outline a lizard on her paper. Let's see, what did a lizard look like? She could not remember. It didn't matter much, anyway—not for an imaginary animal. She had started the lizard with such brave, bold strokes that it took up most of the paper and looked more like a dragon.

Beezus promptly decided the animal was a dragon. Dragons breathed fire, but she did not have any orange paint, and she was so late in starting this picture that she didn't want to take time to mix any. She dipped her brush into pink paint instead and made flames come out of the dragon's mouth. Only they didn't look like flames. They looked more like the spun-sugar candy Beezus had once eaten at the circus. And a dragon breathing clouds of pink candy was more fun than an ordinary flame-breathing dragon.

Forgetting everyone around her, Beezus made the pink clouds bigger and fluffier. Dragons had pointed things down their backs, so Beezus made a row of spines down the back. They did not look quite right—more like slanting sticks than spines. Lollipop sticks, of course!

At that Beezus laughed to herself. Naturally a dragon that breathed pink spun sugar would have lollipops down its back. Eagerly she dipped her brush into red paint and put a strawberry lollipop on one of the sticks. She painted a different flavor on each stick, finishing with a grape-flavored lollipop like the one Wayne and Ramona had shared.

Then she held her drawing board at arm's length. She was pleased with her dragon. It was funny and colorful and really imaginary. [. . .]

"Those who have finished, wash your hands clean," said Miss Robbins. "And I mean clean." Then she came across the room to Beezus. "Why, Beezus!" she exclaimed. "This is a picture to be proud of!"

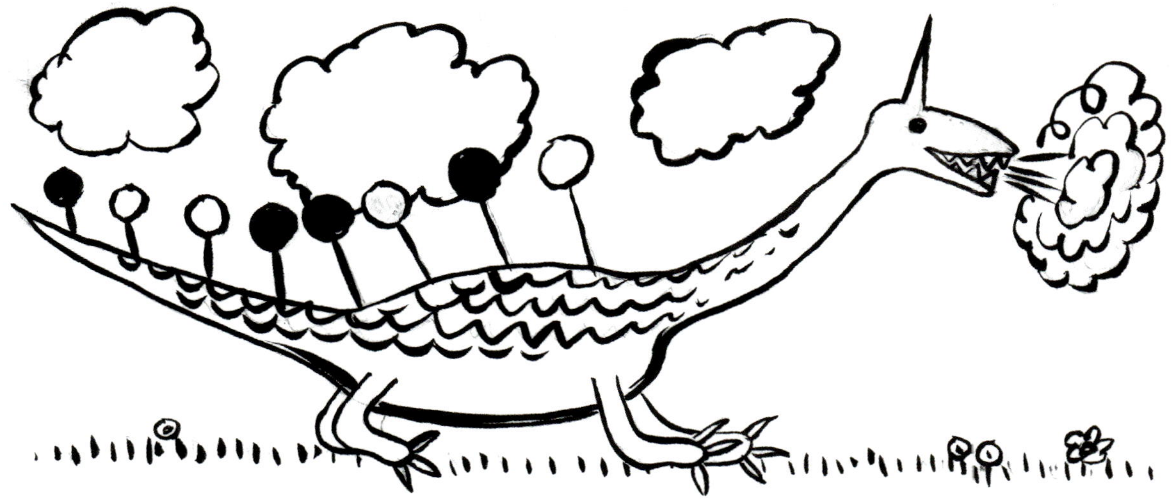

LOUIS DARLING

Henry and Beezus play checkers.

Henry Huggins and Ribsy venture off the pages of the Henry Huggins series to make this cameo in *Beezus and Ramona*. Here, he and Beezus play checkers, a game that Ramona is too little to play (and, besides, checkers allows for only two players). In Dockray's illustration, the younger sister still seems to be optimistic about the possibility of convincing her sister to include her, and perhaps even switch to a more young-kid-friendly game of tiddlywinks. In Rogers's version, Ramona, tired of being ignored, appears to be ramping up toward a tantrum.

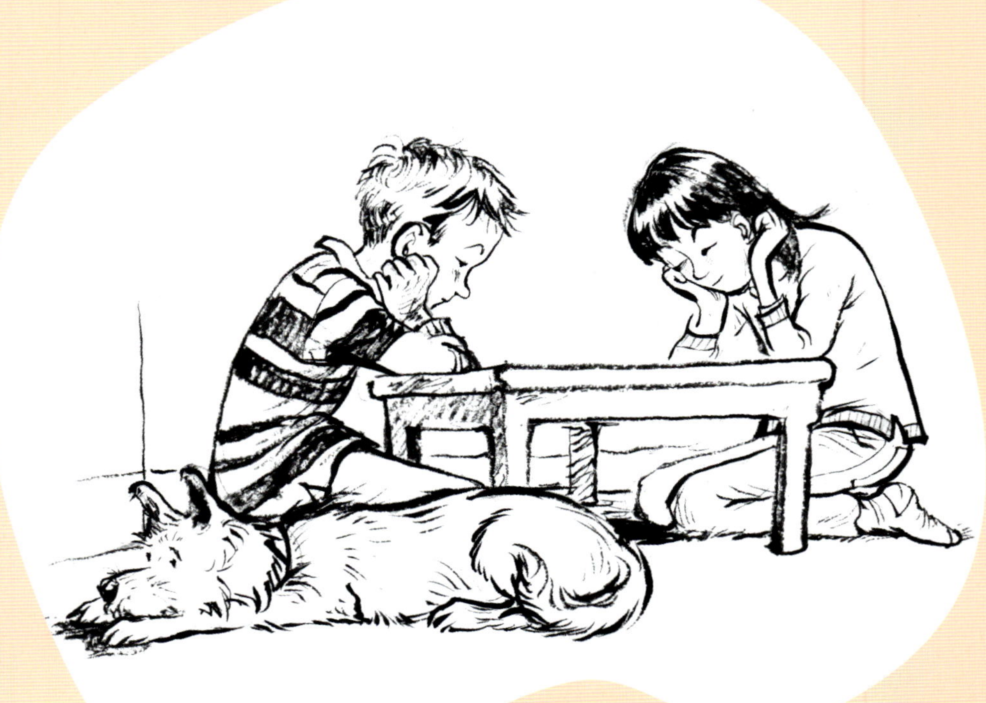

ABOVE: JACQUELINE ROGERS. OPPOSITE: TRACY DOCKRAY (TOP) AND JACQUELINE ROGERS (BOTTOM).

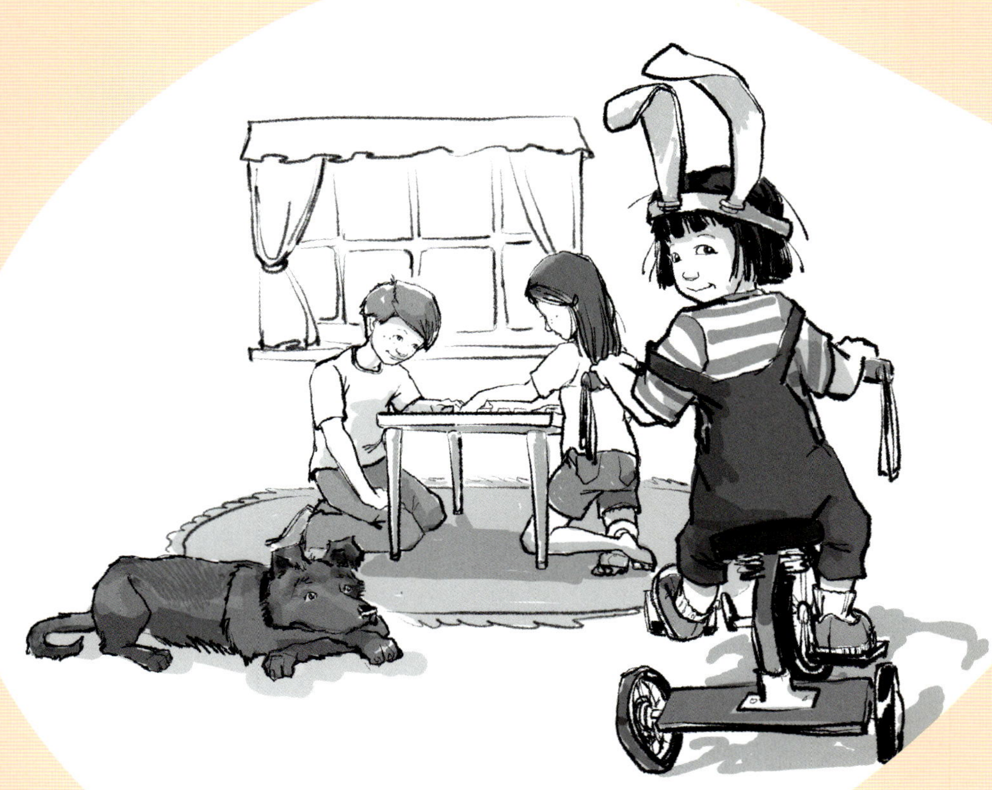

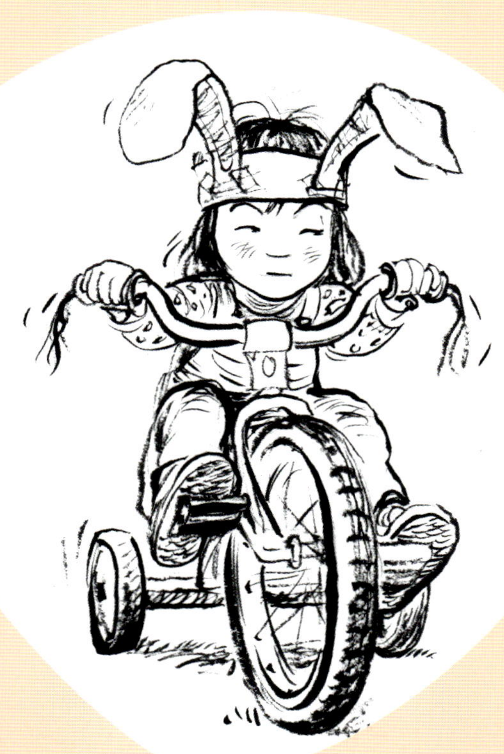

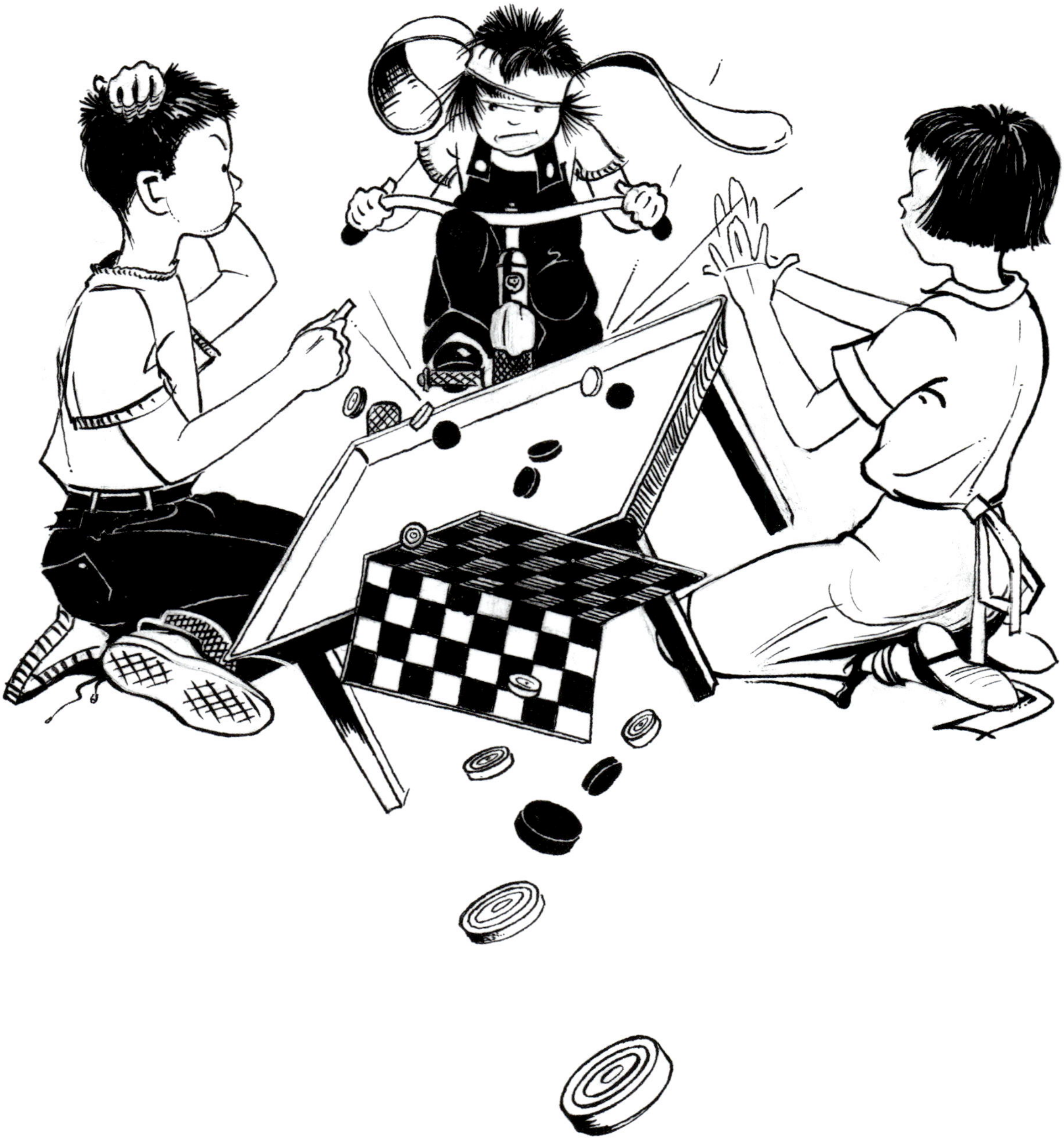

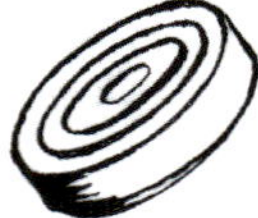

Ramona won't be ignored.

If Beezus refuses to listen, well, Ramona will have to make her listen. Wearing her signature rabbit ears and scowl, Ramona rides her tricycle into the coffee table, sending checkers flying into the foreground. (Later, as an older and wiser second-grader, she will conveniently forget all about this when Howie's little sister, Willa Jean, disrupts Ramona's own game of checkers.) For the cover of the book (page 28), Darling added red to the background and half the checkers, and yellow to Beezus's skirt, Henry's shirt and shoes, and Ramona's ears and trike.

ABOVE: LOUIS DARLING. OPPOSITE: TRACY DOCKRAY.

I'll bet she has a tantrum, thought Beezus, as she picked up the checkers.

Ramona kicks and screams while Mrs. Quimby counts to ten, a wary Ribsy watching from a safe vantage. Motion lines indicate the flailing of hands and feet and the ongoing disturbance of the checkers.

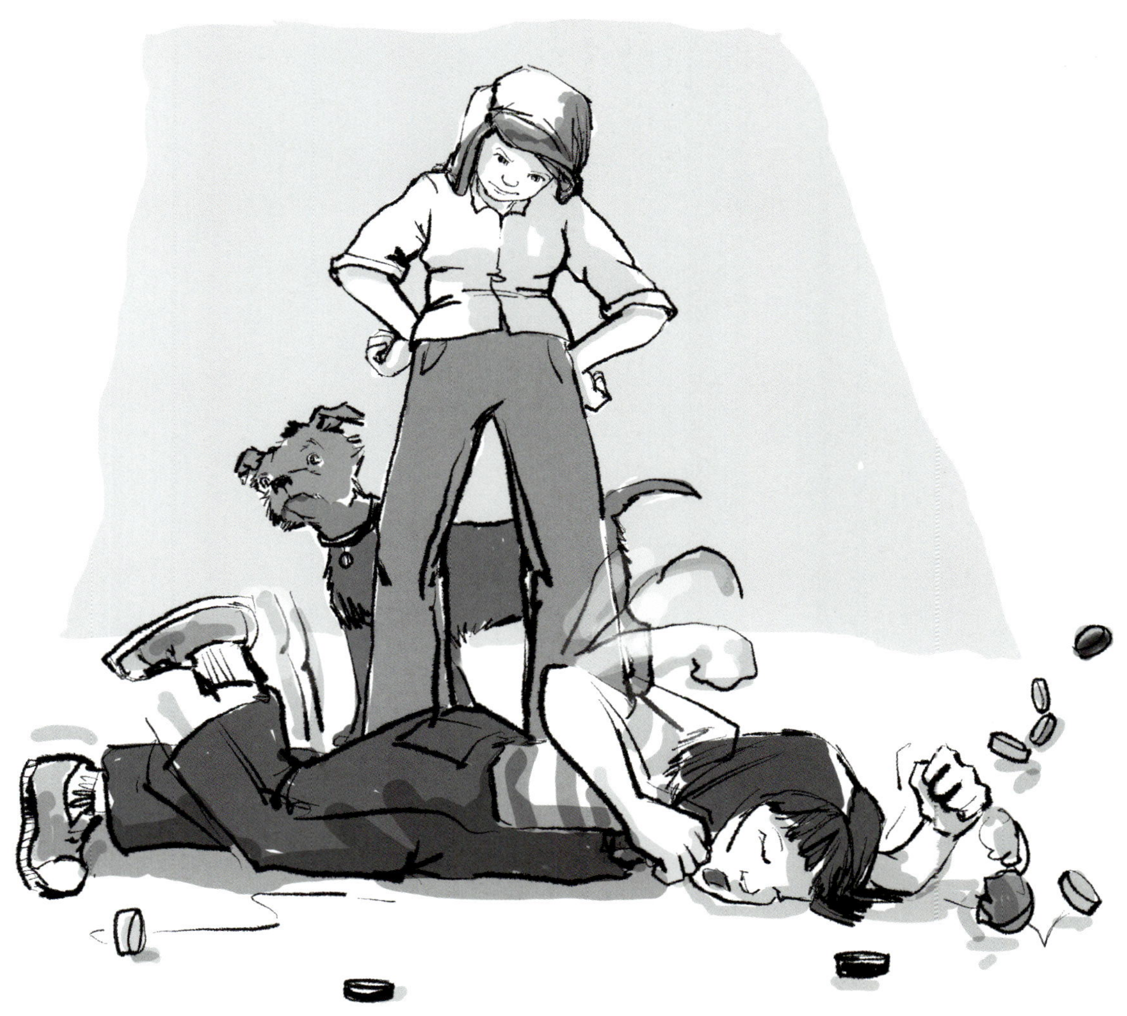

“Open the door and let him out,” said Mother.

“I can’t,” shouted Ramona angrily, above Ribsy’s furious barks. “The bad old dog went and locked the door.”

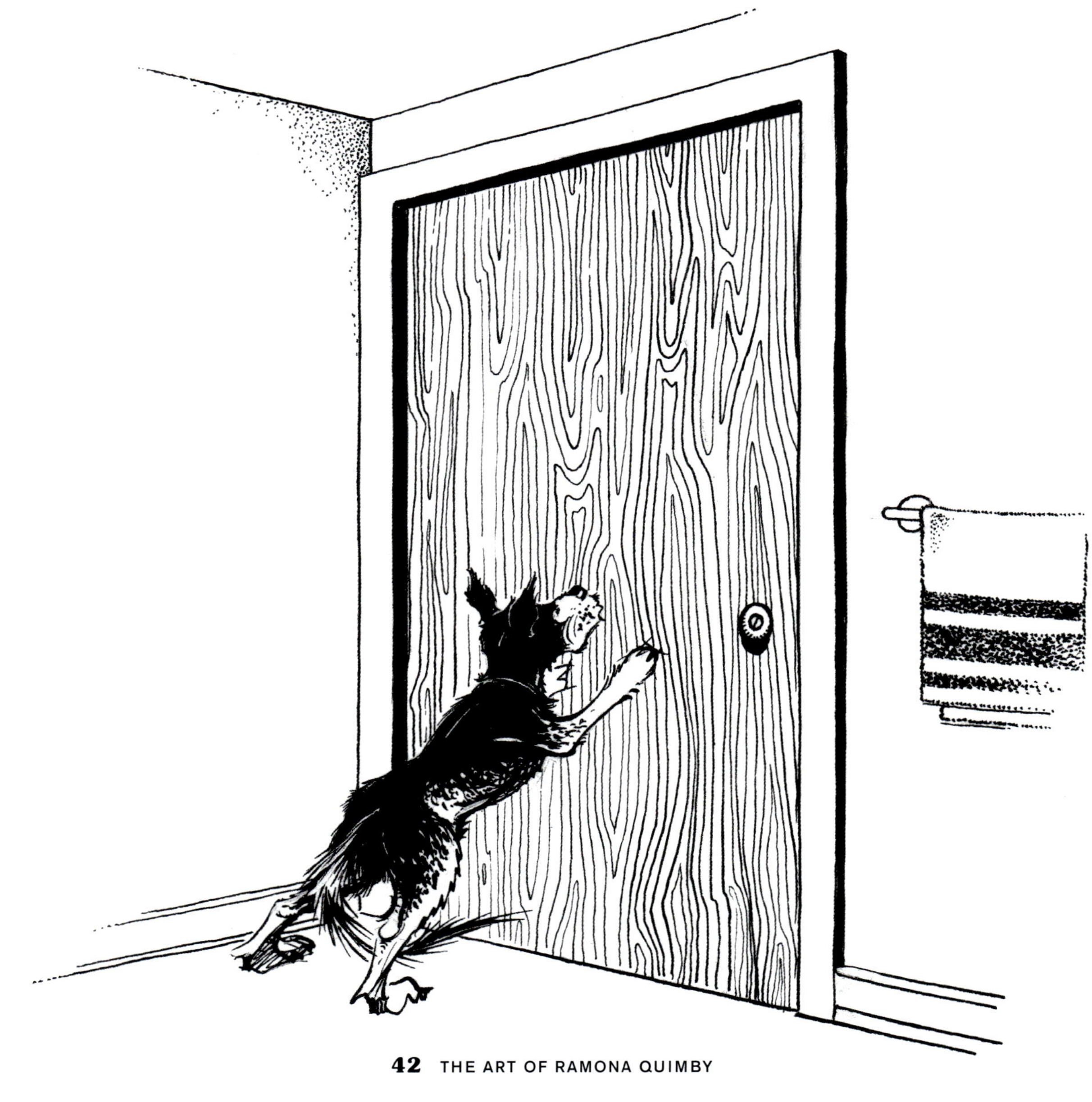

After going to her room, Ramona emerges somewhat calmer, only to accidentally lock poor Ribsy in the bathroom for stealing her cookie. (In fact, Ribsy was the one who locked himself in by pressing the little button in the center of the knob while pawing at the door.) Darling chose to show the situation from both the dog's and the little girl's perspective, signifying the door's bathroom side by the towel rack to the right. Ramona and Ribsy seem equally agitated.

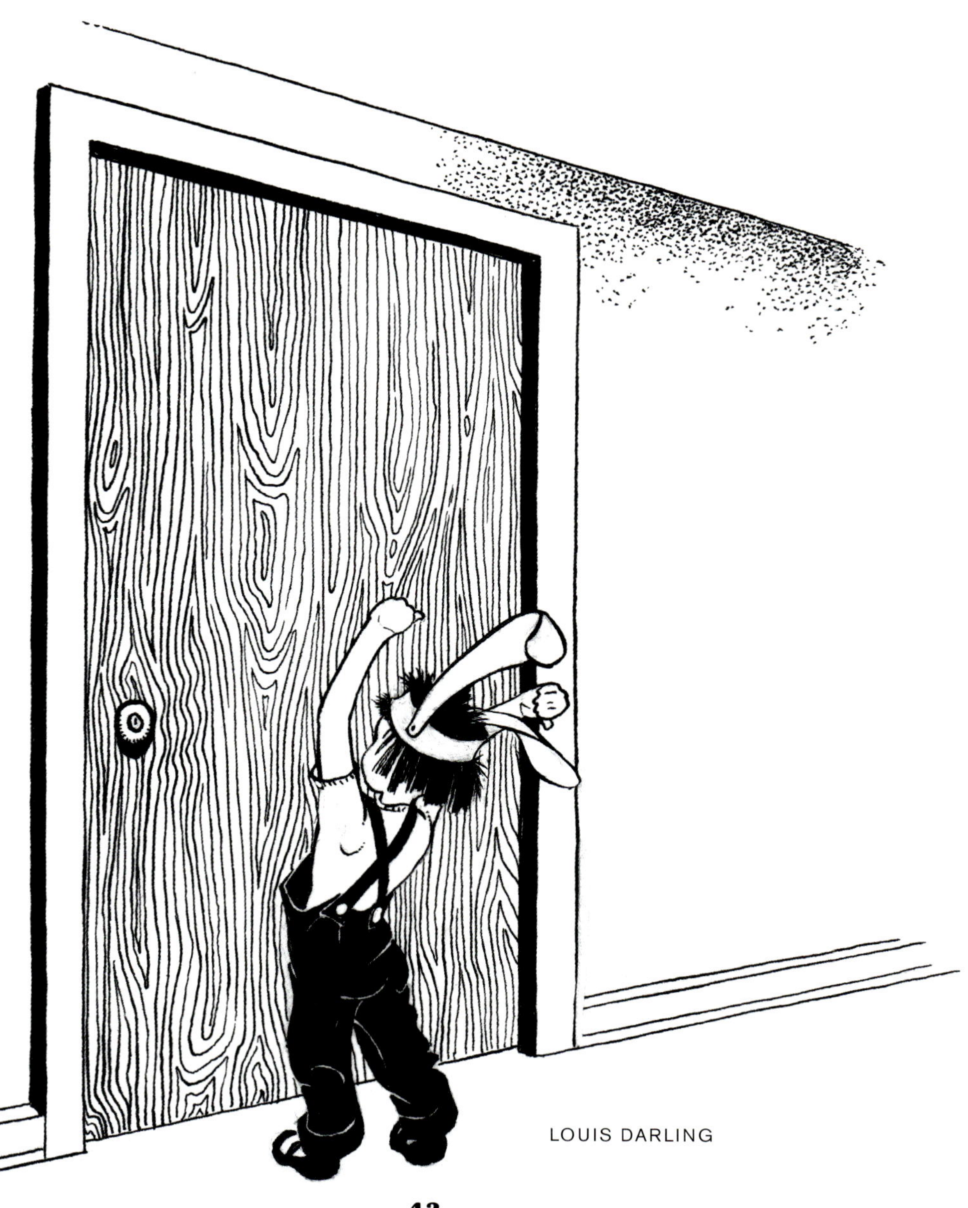

LOUIS DARLING

With a joyous bark Ribsy bounded out and jumped up on Henry. "Good old Ribsy," said Henry. "Did you think we were going to leave you in there?" Ribsy wriggled and wagged his tail happily because he was free at last.

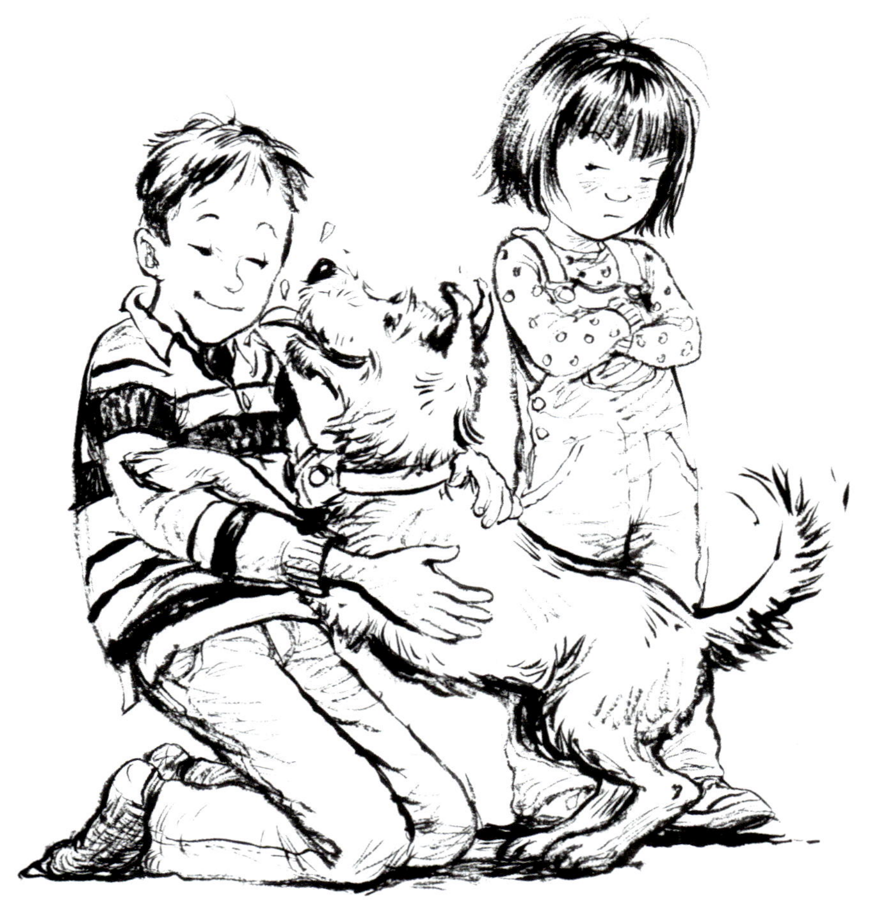

JACQUELINE ROGERS (ABOVE) AND LOUIS DARLING (OPPOSITE).

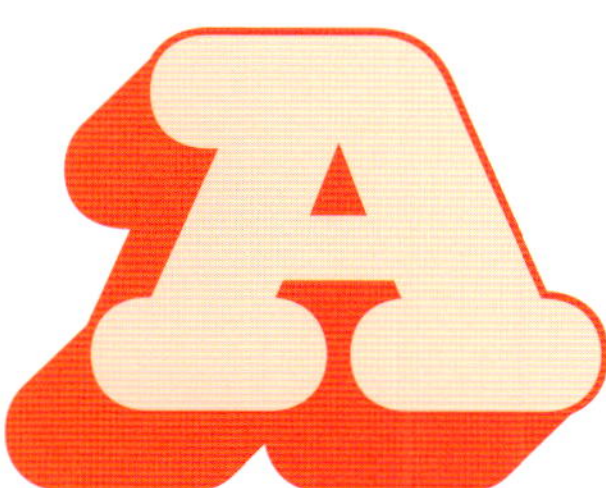

At that moment Beezus heard a noise. She thought it came from the basement, but she was not certain. Tiptoeing to the cold-air intake in the hall, she bent over and listened. Sure enough, a noise so faint she could scarcely hear it came up through the furnace pipe. So the house wasn't empty after all! Just wait until she got hold of Ramona!

Beezus snapped on the basement light and ran down the steps. "Ramona, come out," she ordered. "I know you're here."

The only answer was a chomping sound from the corner of the basement. Beezus ran around the furnace and there, in the dimly lit corner, sat Ramona, eating an apple.

Beezus was so relieved to see Ramona safe, and at the same time so angry with her for hiding, that she couldn't say anything. She just stood there filled with the exasperated mixed-up feeling that Ramona so often gave her.

"Hello," said Ramona through a bite of apple.

"Ramona Geraldine Quimby!" exclaimed Beezus, when she had found her voice.

"What do you think you're doing?"

"Playing hide-and-seek," answered Ramona.

"Well, I'm not!" snapped Beezus. "It takes two to play hide-and-seek."

"You found me," Ramona pointed out.

"Oh. . . ." Once again Beezus couldn't find any words. To think she had worried so, when all the time Ramona was sitting in the basement listening to her call. And eating an apple, too!

As she stood in front of Ramona, Beezus's eyes began to grow accustomed to the dim light and she realized what Ramona was doing. She stared, horrified at what she saw. As if hiding were not enough! What would Mother say when she came home and found what Ramona had been up to this time?

Ramona was sitting on the floor beside a box of apples. Lying around her on the cement floor were a number of apples—each with one bite out of it. While Beezus stared, Ramona reached into the box, selected an apple, took one big bite out of the reddest part, and tossed the rest of the apple onto the floor. While she noisily chewed that bite, she reached into the apple box again.

"Ramona!" cried Beezus, horrified. "You can't do that."

"I can, too," said Ramona through her mouthful.

"Stop it," ordered Beezus. "Stop it this instant! You can't eat one bite and then throw the rest away."

"But the first bite tastes best," explained Ramona reasonably, as she reached into the box again.

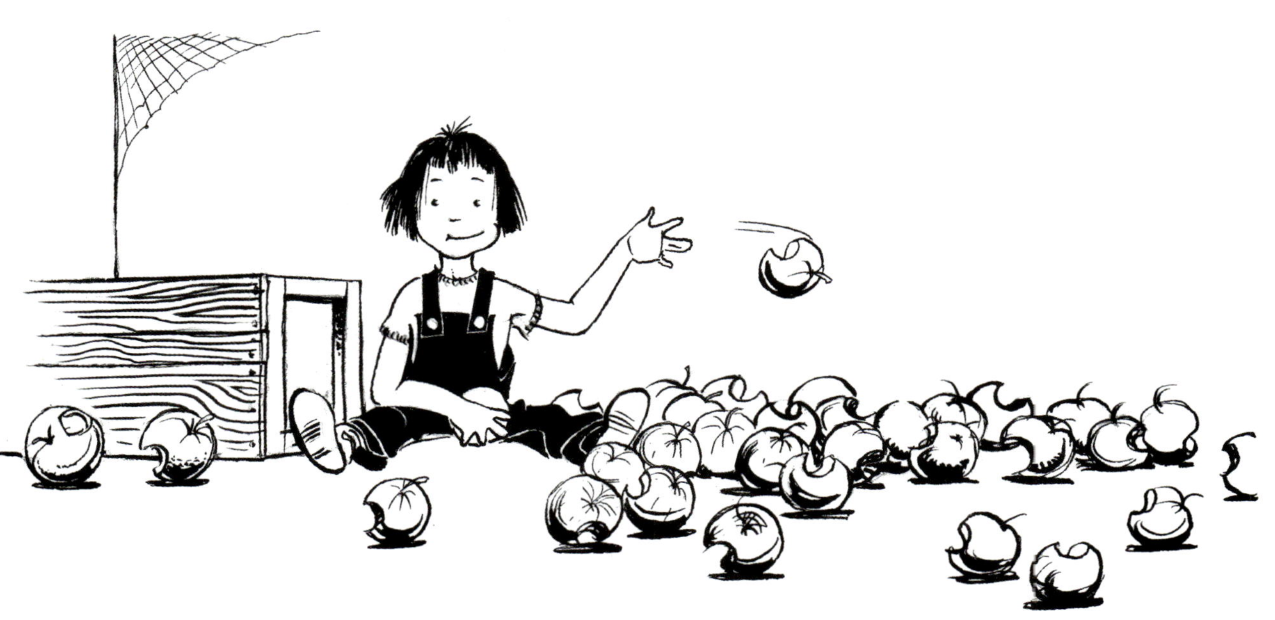

Over the phone, Beezus's aunt and namesake has convinced her to not give Ramona the attention she is clearly trying to get through bad behavior. So instead of scolding or punishing her sister, Beezus makes a plan with her mother: Just as when life hands you lemons you make lemonade, they will pretend like nothing happened and make applesauce out of all those singly bitten apples.

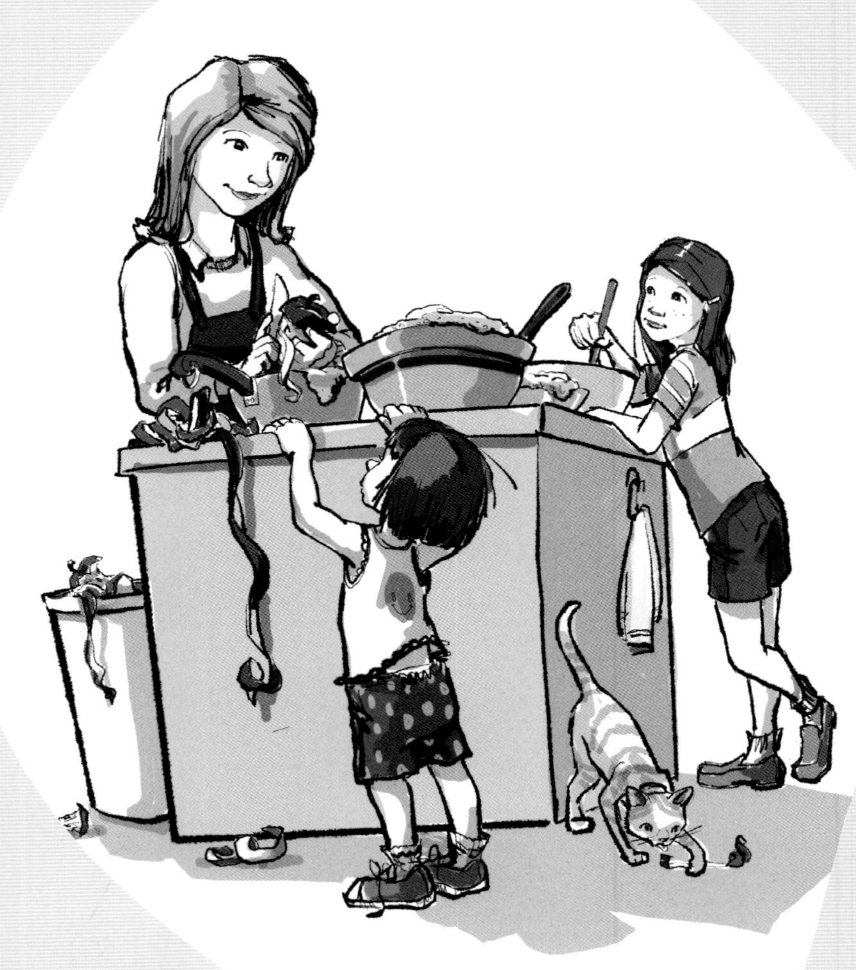

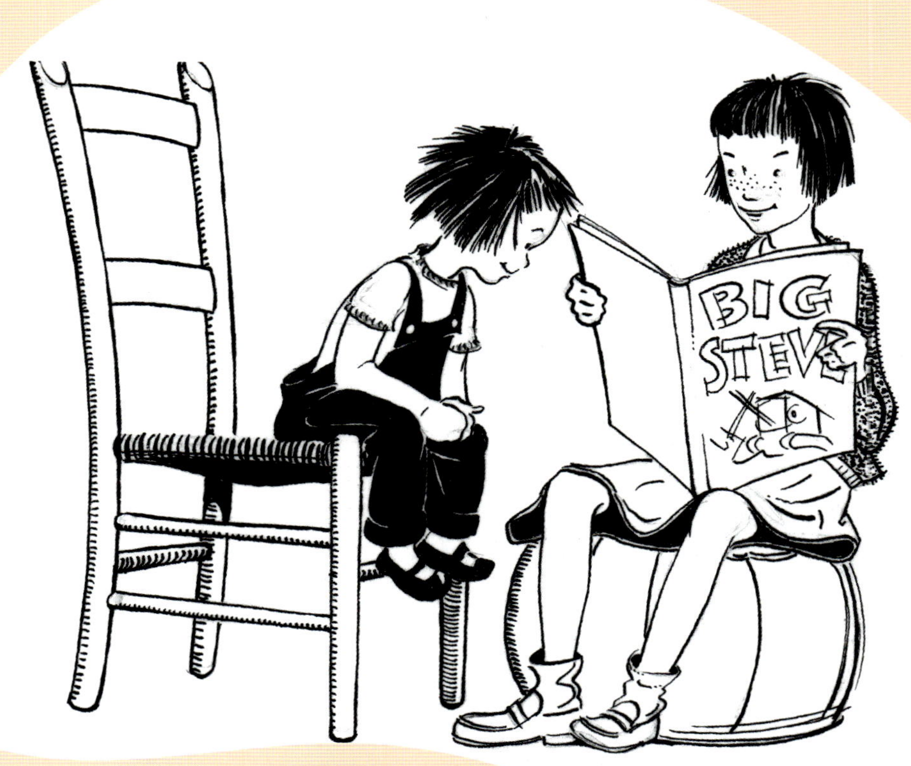

Instead of saying no and potentially giving Ramona an excuse to make a fuss, Beezus sticks to the game plan by giving in to her sister's request that she read *Big Steve and the Steam Shovel* yet again. Here, we come full circle. This raises the question: Isn't Ramona getting her way after all?

TRACY DOCKRAY (OPPOSITE) AND LOUIS DARLING (ABOVE).

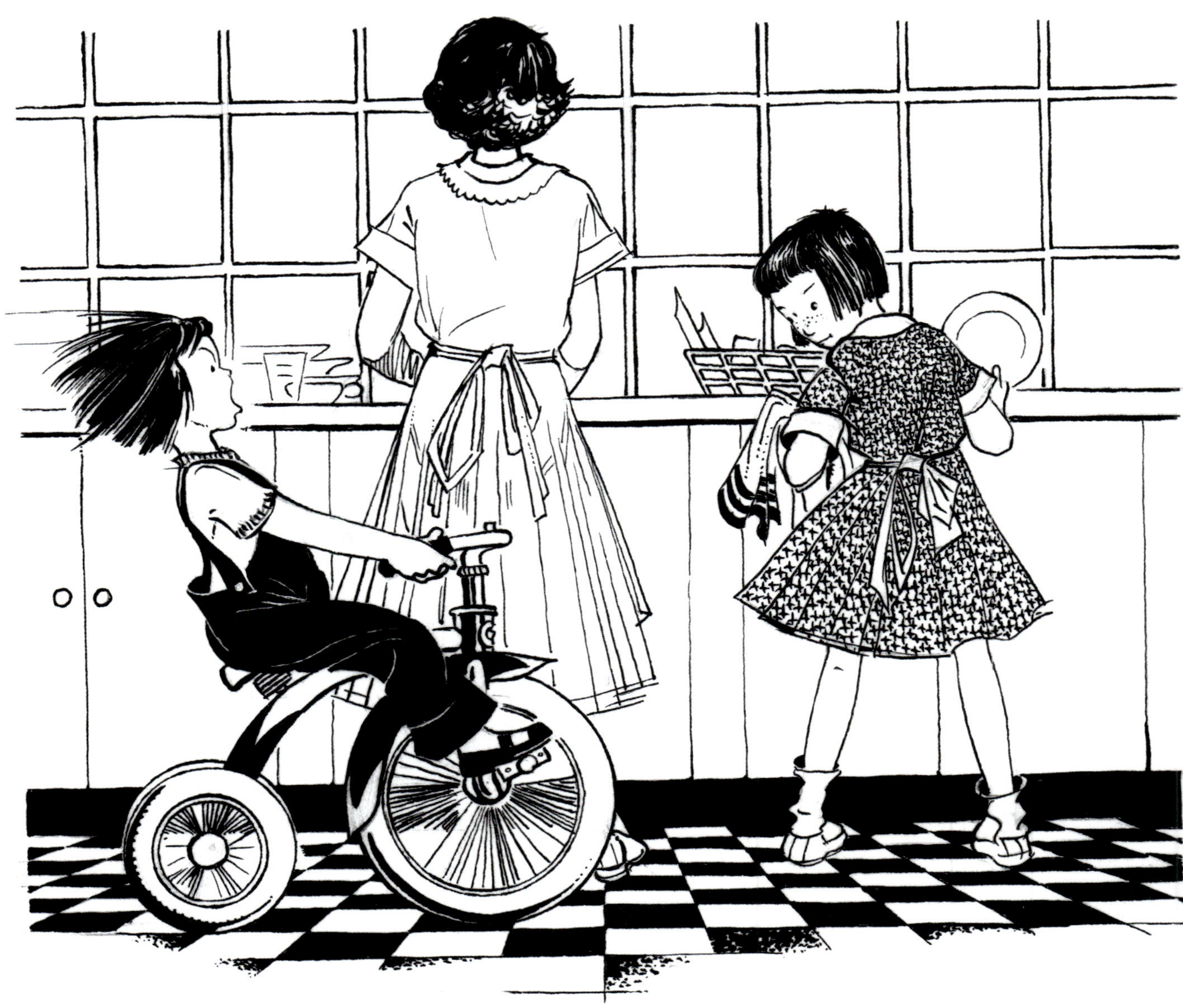

The par-tee.

Beezus and her mother, in dresses and aprons, wipe the breakfast dishes while Ramona rides her tricycle, singing, "I'm going to have a par-tee, I'm going to have a par-tee." This reminds Mrs. Quimby to ask what Beezus would like to do for her birthday next week, not realizing that Ramona means what she says. (Note the fabulous retro black-and-white checkered floor.) It seems that Ramona has invited friends over without asking, because she's learned that when she asks permission, she often doesn't get what she wants.

LOUIS DARLING (ABOVE) AND JACQUELINE ROGERS (OPPOSITE).

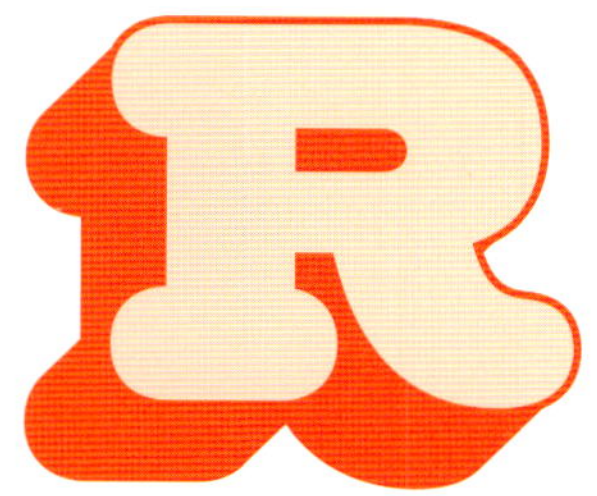

amona offered Susan her panda bear, but Susan did not want it. Ramona hit Susan with the panda. "You take my bear," she ordered. "This is my party and you're supposed to do what I say."

"I don't want your old bear," answered Susan.

Here, for the first time, we meet Susan, one of Ramona's unexpected guests. She (and her curls) will come to play a large role in the series, primarily as a prissy antagonist who ruins everyone's fun. (It isn't until the last book that Ramona gets insight into Susan's character and develops some sympathy for the girl.)

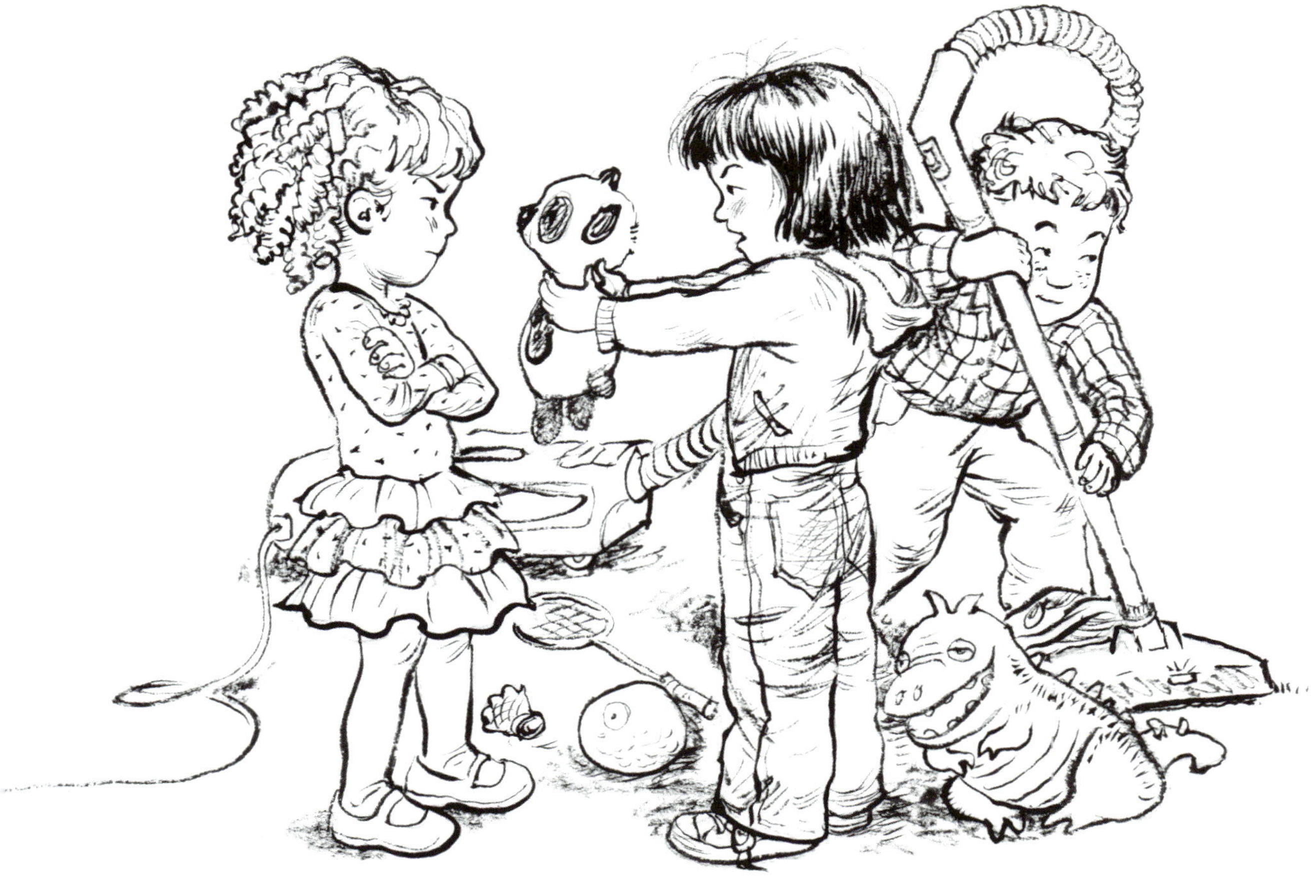

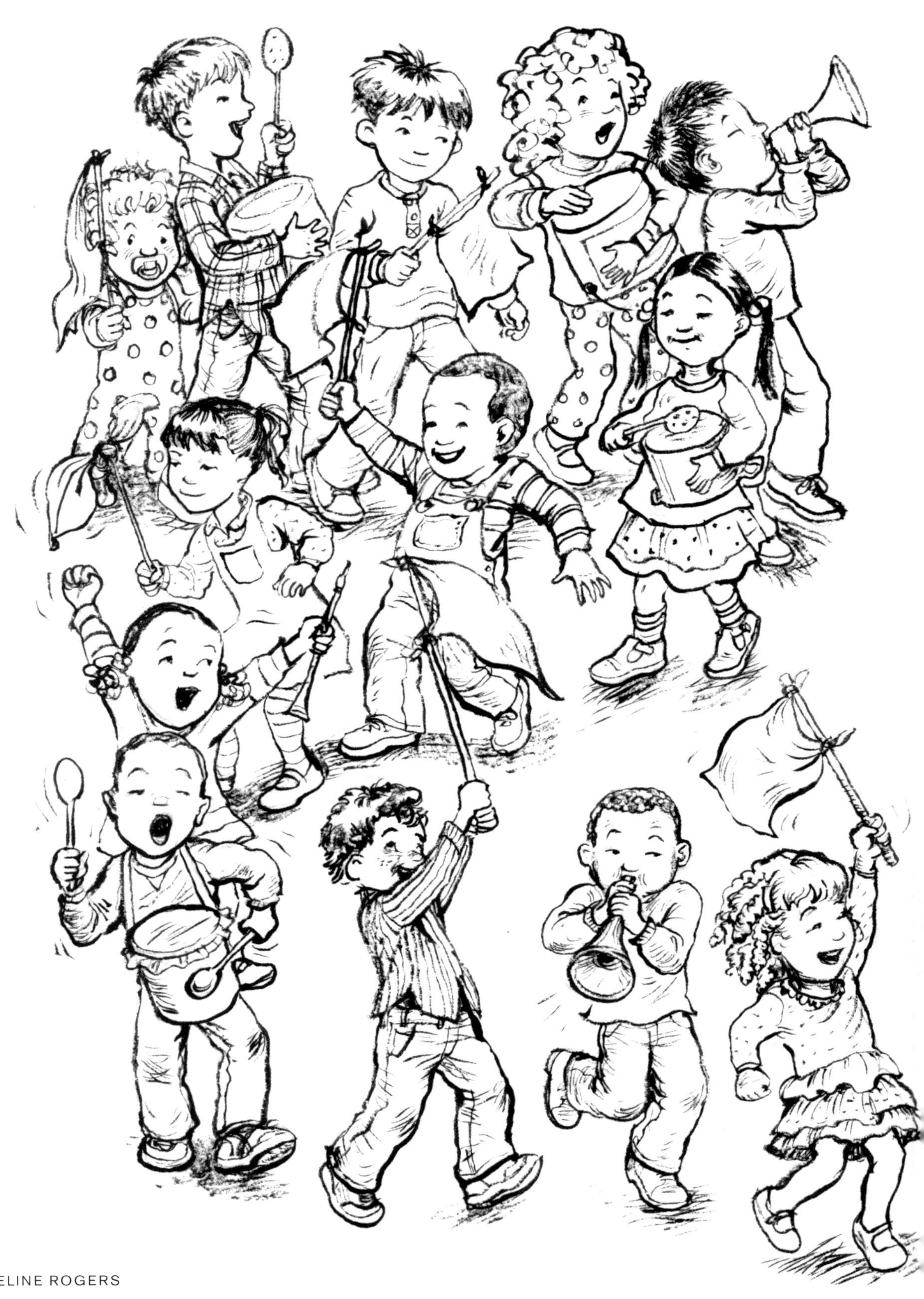

JACQUELINE ROGERS

Beezus helps along the party parade.

Tasked with managing the impromptu party, Beezus comes up with the idea of having a parade. Note Howie, banging a drum, in the lead, with Ramona sulking behind him. She feels that, since this is *her* party, she should be the boss and therefore in that spot. Susan marches behind. Beezus, as ever, is the patient and helpful Quimby daughter.

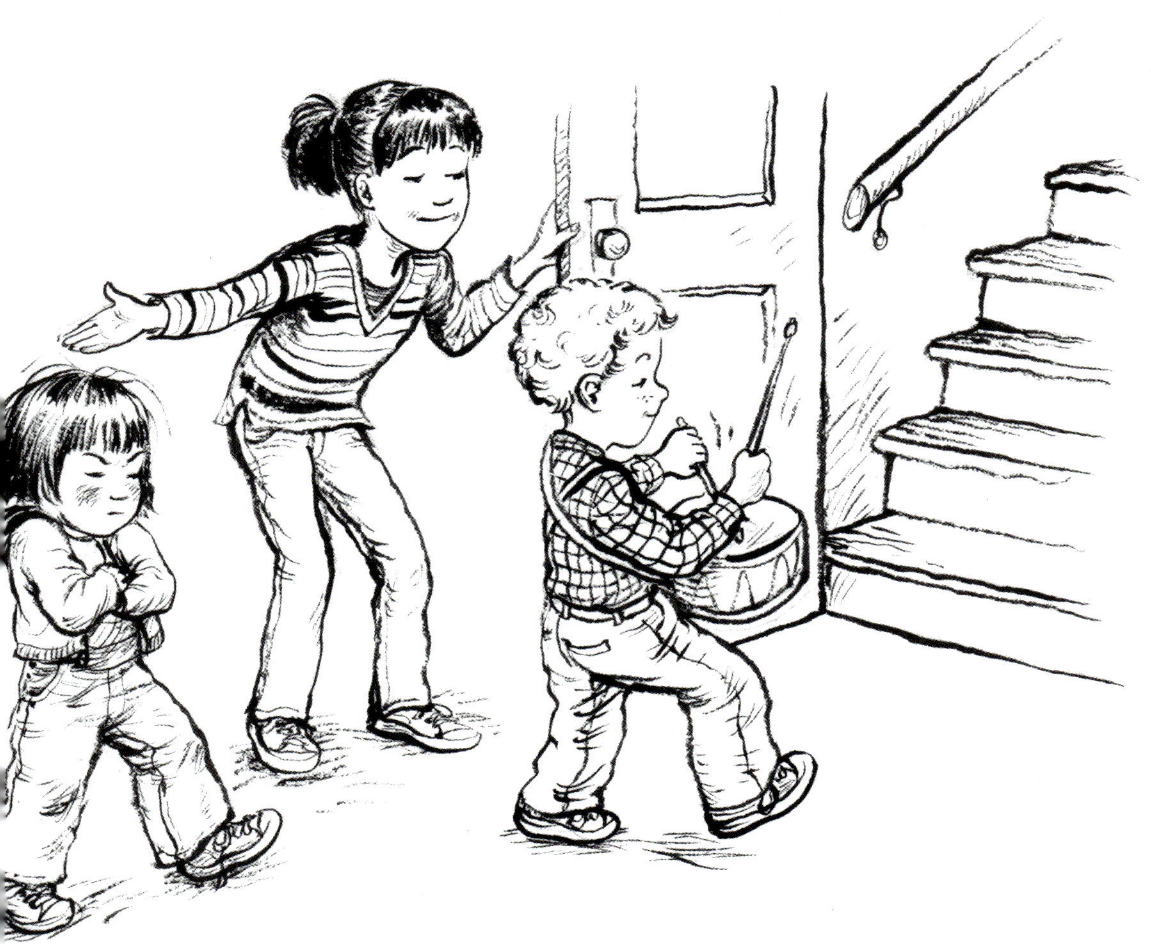

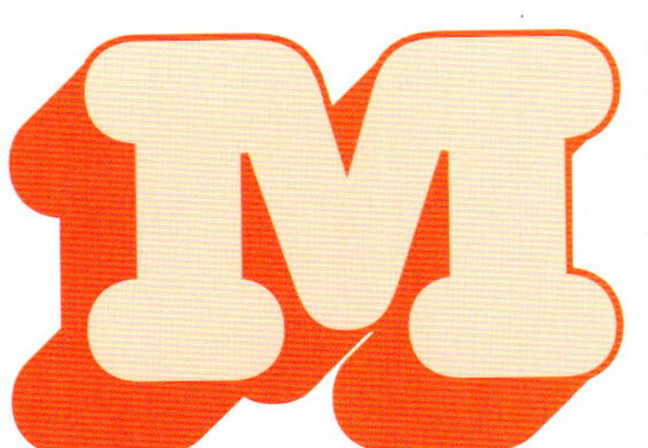

Mother came into the living room from the bedroom. "Beezus, do you smell something rubbery?" she asked anxiously.

"Yes, and it smells awful," said Beezus. Ramona held her nose.

Mother sniffed again. "It smells as if something is scorching, too."

Beezus went into the kitchen, where she found the smell so strong that it made her cough. "It's worse in here, Mother," she called, as she looked to see if anything was burning on the stove. Then Beezus remembered the oven. "Mother," she said in a worried voice, "you don't suppose something has happened to my birthday cake again?"

"Of course not," said Mother, coming into the kitchen and opening the window. "What could happen to it?"

Just to be sure, Beezus cautiously opened the oven door. "Mother!" she cried, horrified at what she saw. "Look!" Ramona's rubber doll, Bendix, leaned over the edge of the cake pan, her head and arms buried in the batter. Her dress was scorched to a golden tan. "Oh, Mother!" repeated Beezus. Her birthday cake, her beautiful, fragrant birthday cake, was ruined.

"Is the witch done yet?" Ramona asked.

"Ramona—" began Mother and stopped. She couldn't think of anything to say. Silently she turned off the oven and, with a pot holder, pulled out the doll and the remains of the cake.

"Ramona Geraldine Quimby!" said Beezus angrily. "You're just awful, that's what you are! Just plain awful. Spoiling your own sister's birthday cake!"

"You told me to pretend I was Gretel," protested Ramona. "And Gretel pushed the witch into the oven."

Beezus looked at the cake and burst into tears. Ramona promptly began to cry too. This made Beezus even angrier. "You stop crying," she ordered Ramona furiously. "It was my birthday cake and I'm the one that's supposed to be crying."

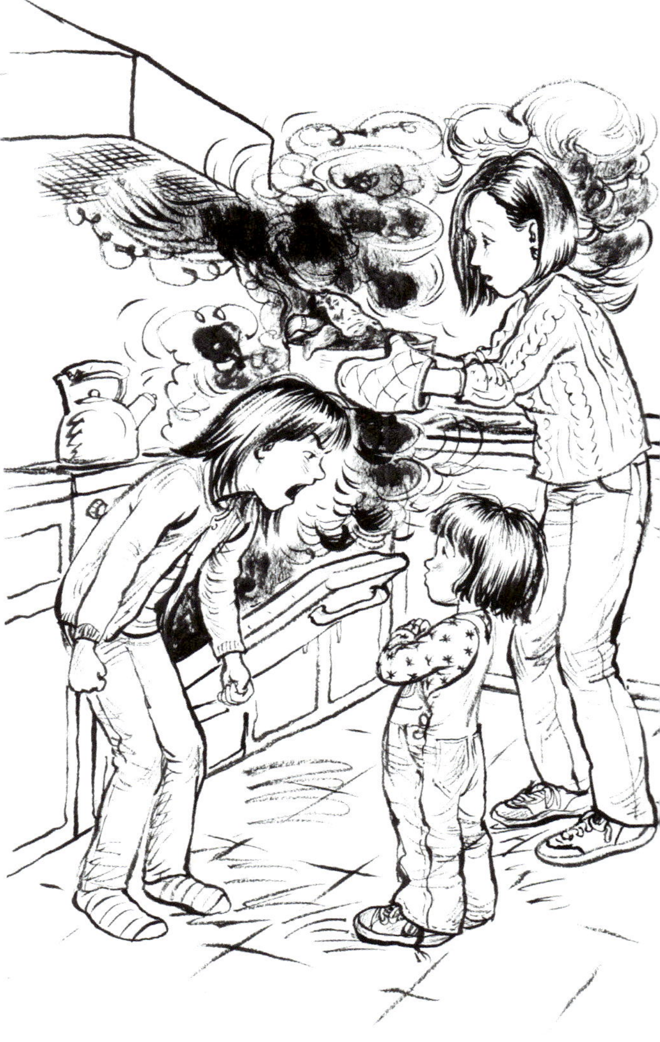

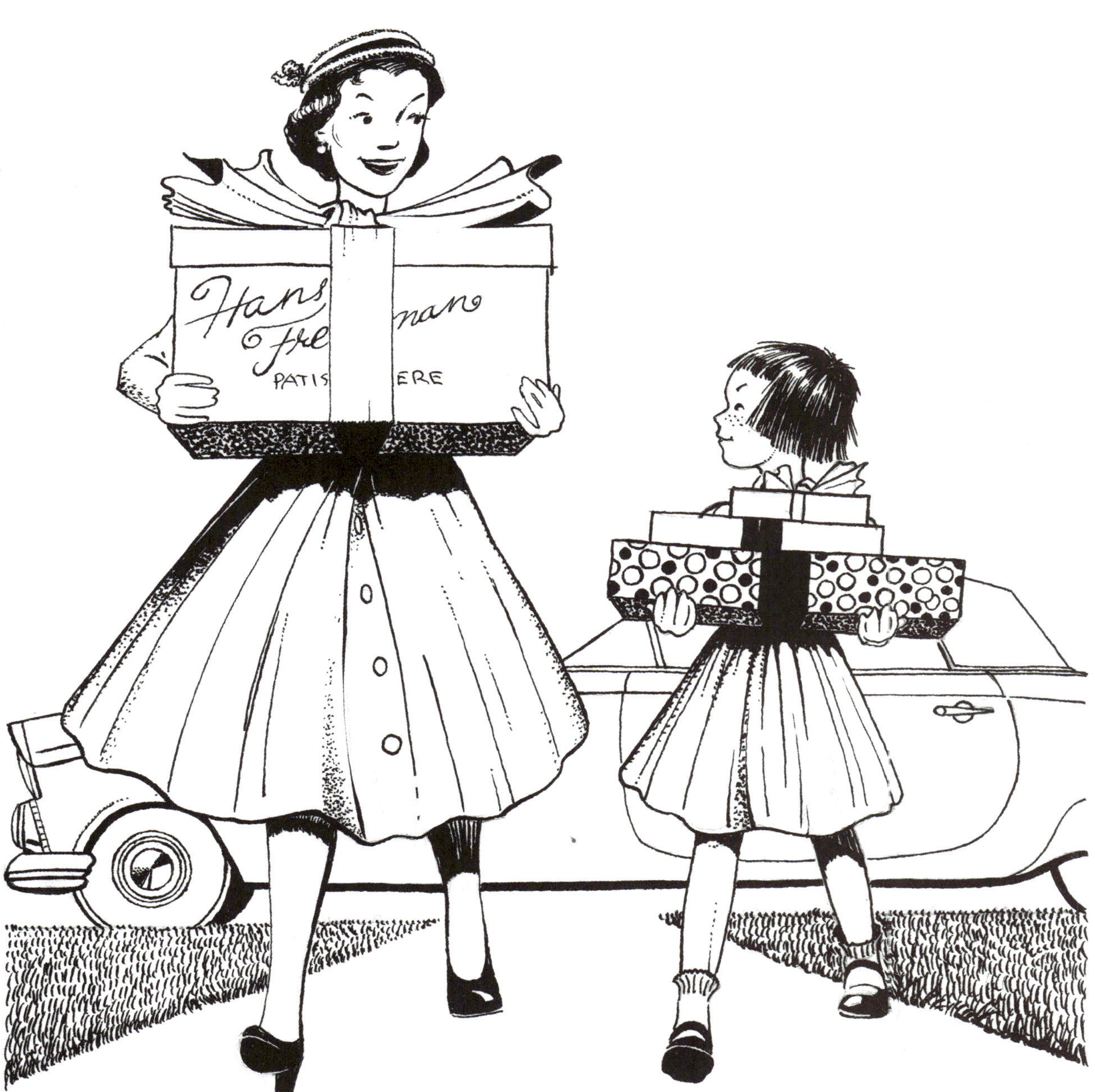

Aunt Bea comes to the rescue.

With gifts and a beautiful store-bought cake—pink with a wreath of white roses made out of icing—Beezus and Ramona's aunt saves the day. Here she arrives dressed to the nines, in 1950s style, her yellow convertible parked at the curb.

JACQUELINE ROGERS (OPPOSITE) AND LOUIS DARLING (ABOVE).

"Make a wish," said Father.

Beezus paused a minute. Then she closed her eyes and thought, I wish all my birthdays would turn out to be as wonderful as this one finally did. She opened her eyes and blew as hard as she could.

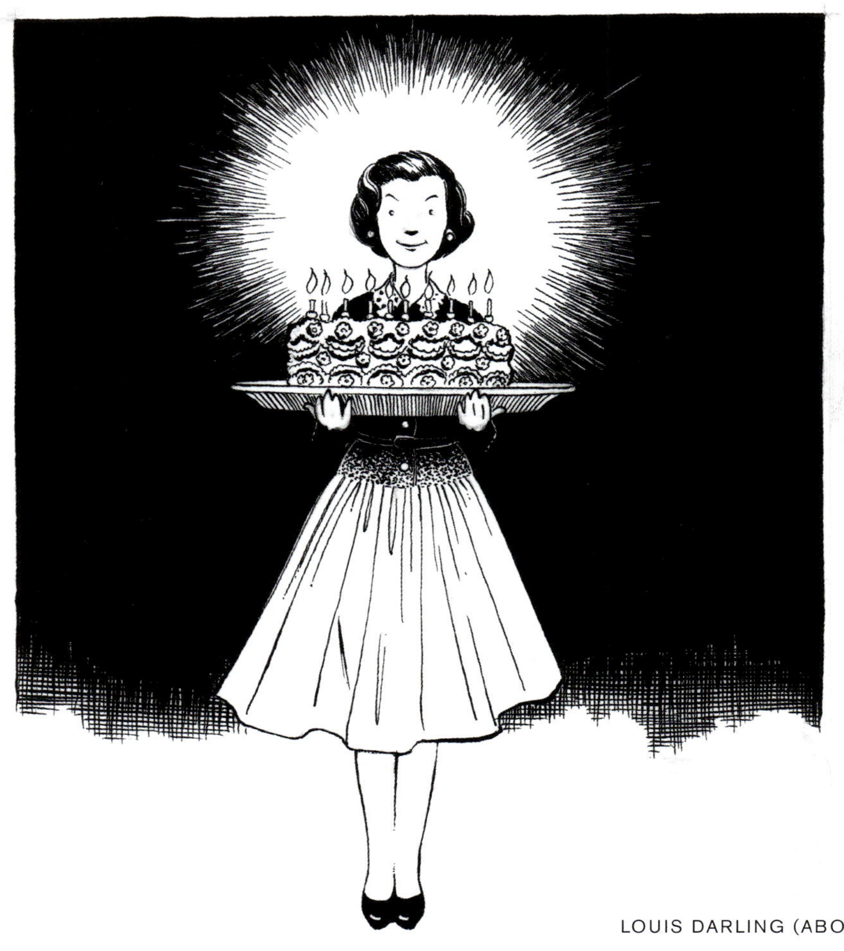

LOUIS DARLING (ABOVE AND OPPOSITE).

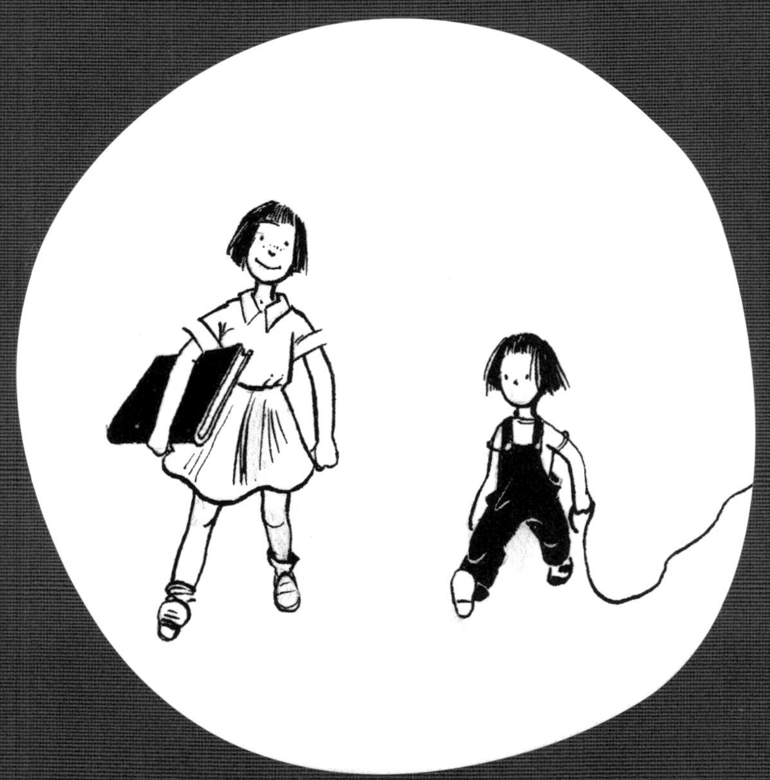

Beezus and Ramona.

Over dinner, at which Ramona is sent to her room for being naughty yet again, Mrs. Quimby and Aunt Bea recount their childhood together. Beezus is surprised to learn that her mother was, like her, the responsible older sister, and Bea was the big troublemaker who always spoiled everything. It's normal, they tell Beezus, to not love your sister all the time. Relieved of that guilt, and with the newfound understanding that what's terrible today might be funny in the future, Beezus and Ramona make up. Darling's Beezus and Ramona stand apart, the younger girl leading her imaginary lizard. Her face is just three dots, while the elder sister has a single line for a smile.

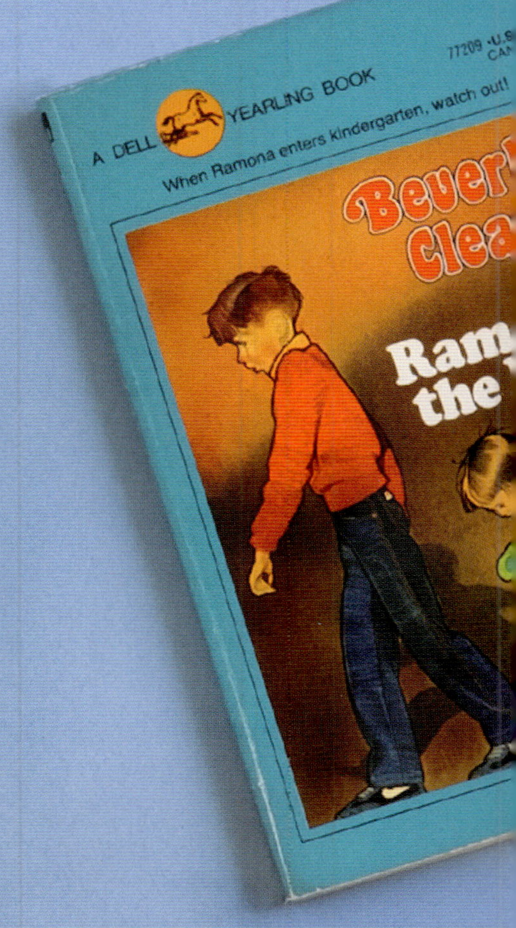
A DELL YEARLING BOOK
When Ramona enters kindergarten, watch out!

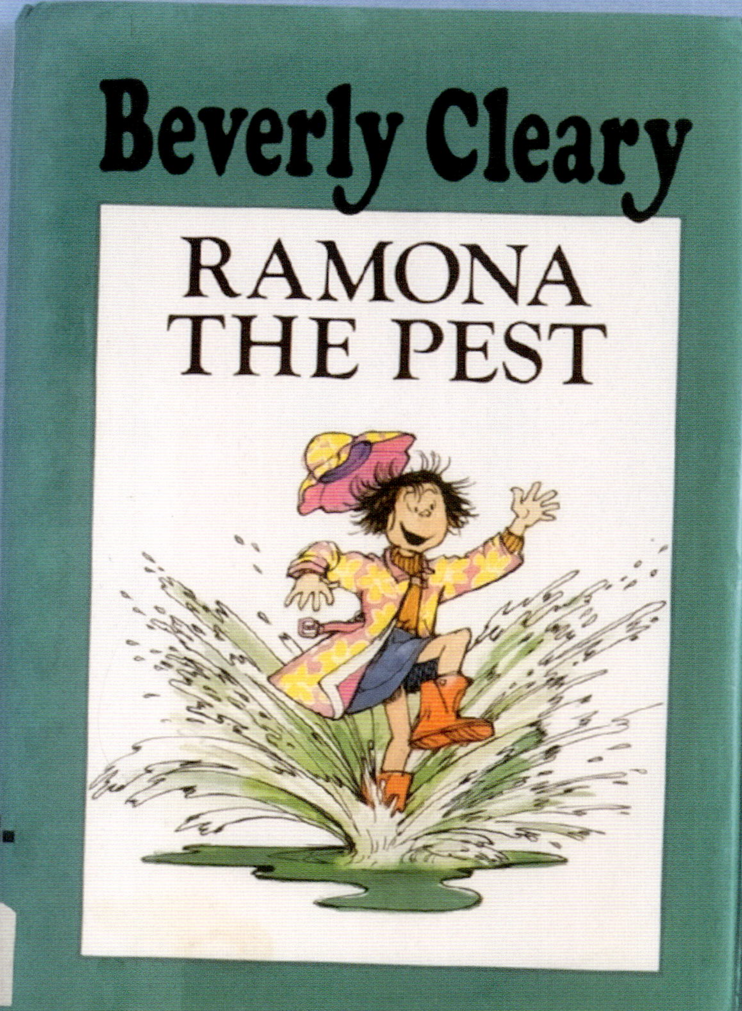
Beverly Cleary
RAMONA
THE PEST

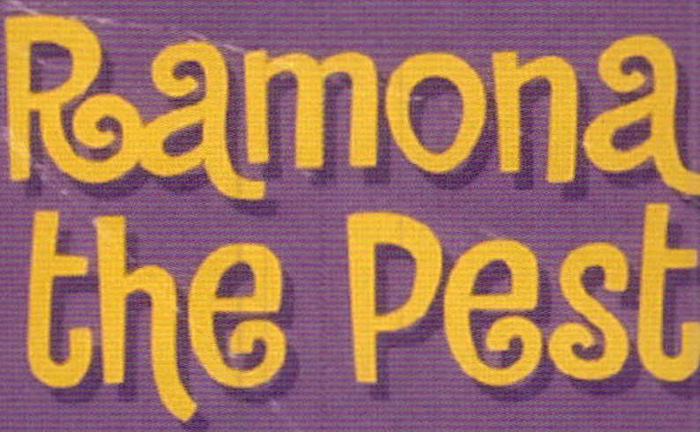
Ramona
the Pest

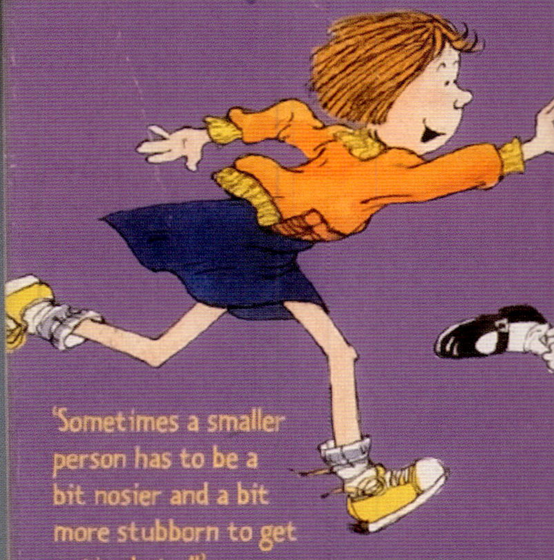
'Sometimes a smaller
person has to be a
bit nosier and a bit
more stubborn to get
noticed at all'

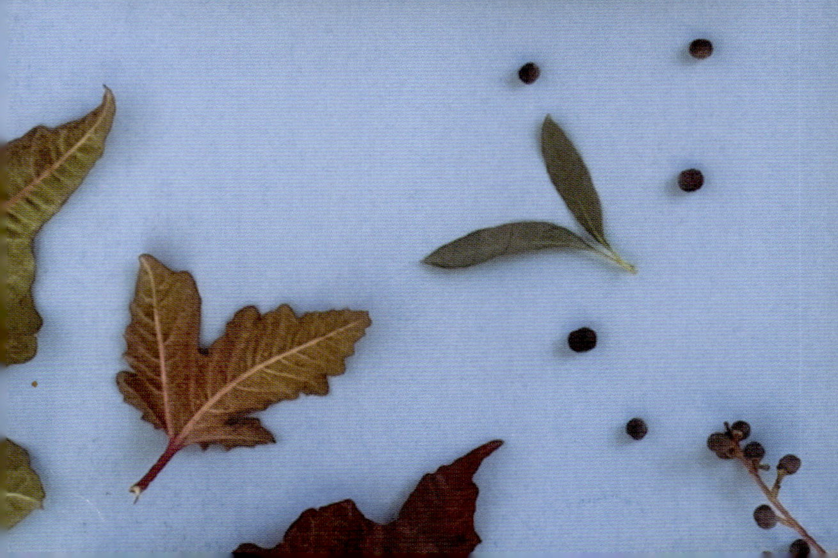

Ramona the Pest

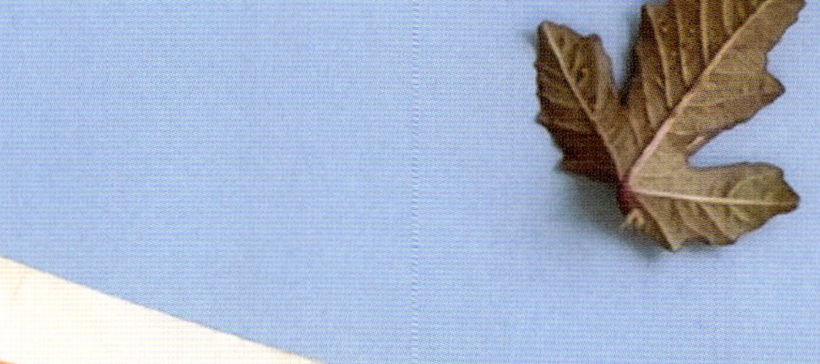

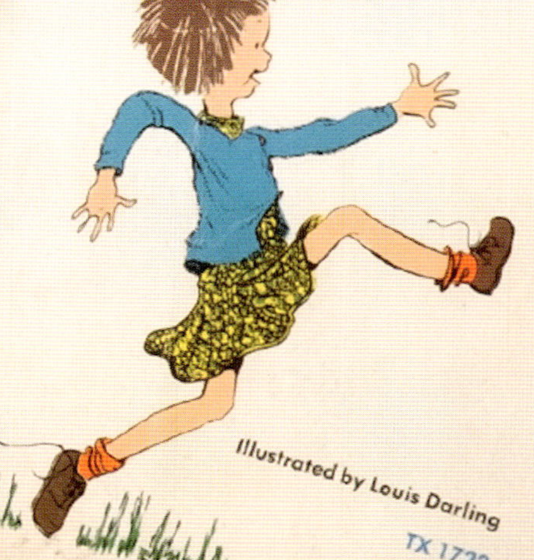

Ramona the Pest

Chapter Two

"I am not a pest," Ramona Quimby told her big sister Beezus.

"Then stop acting like a pest," said Beezus, whose real name was Beatrice. She was standing by the front window waiting for her friend Mary Jane to walk to school with her.

"I'm not acting like a pest. I'm singing and skipping," said Ramona, who had only recently learned to skip with both feet. Ramona did not think she was a pest. No matter what others said, she never thought she was a pest. The people who called her a pest were always bigger and so they could be unfair.

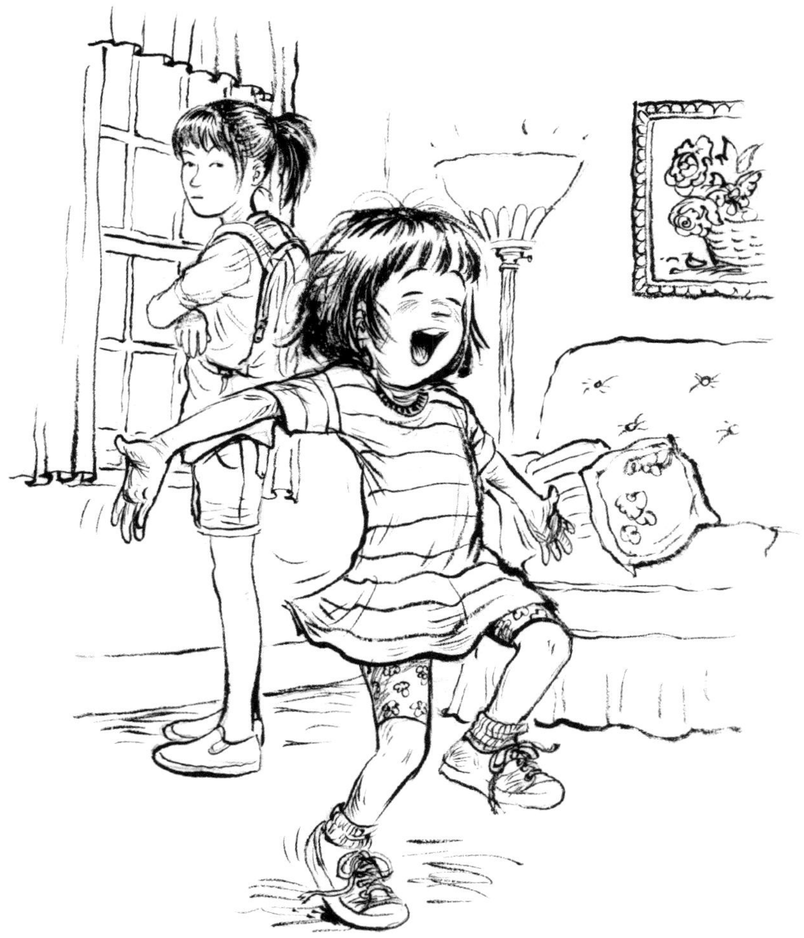

Ramona cannot wait to grow up. She's five years old and more than ready to start kindergarten—she's been waiting for practically forever! Of course, some big adjustments and even bigger feelings lie ahead.

Ramona the Pest was published in 1968, thirteen years after the first of the series. In an interview with the author on her website, Beverly Cleary explains that the primary reason for that lengthy gap between books was her own lack of experience with kindergarten; she didn't start her formal education until the first grade, at Fernwood Grammar School in Portland, Oregon. It wasn't until Cleary's own children—twins—started kindergarten and began to discuss their daily trials and tribulations over the dinner table that she felt confident enough to send Ramona into this earliest phase of elementary school.

As she does with everything, Ramona brings her unique flair to this new experience. Cleary was adamant that she did not write stories to teach lessons—she wrote stories to entertain children. Even so, while Ramona is learning kindergarten fundamentals like how to write her name, she also manages to encounter a life lesson or two through the drama of sharing and the consequences of pulling a classmate's curls. And, most challenging of all, she'll be forced to recognize how stubbornness can be self-defeating, like refusing to take off brand-new red boots once they're stuck in the mud. Will Ramona overcome her hurt feelings over the unfairness of it all, or will she become a kindergarten dropout?

JACQUELINE ROGERS

Ramona's heart was filled with love for her teacher. Miss Binney was not like most grown-ups. Miss Binney understood.

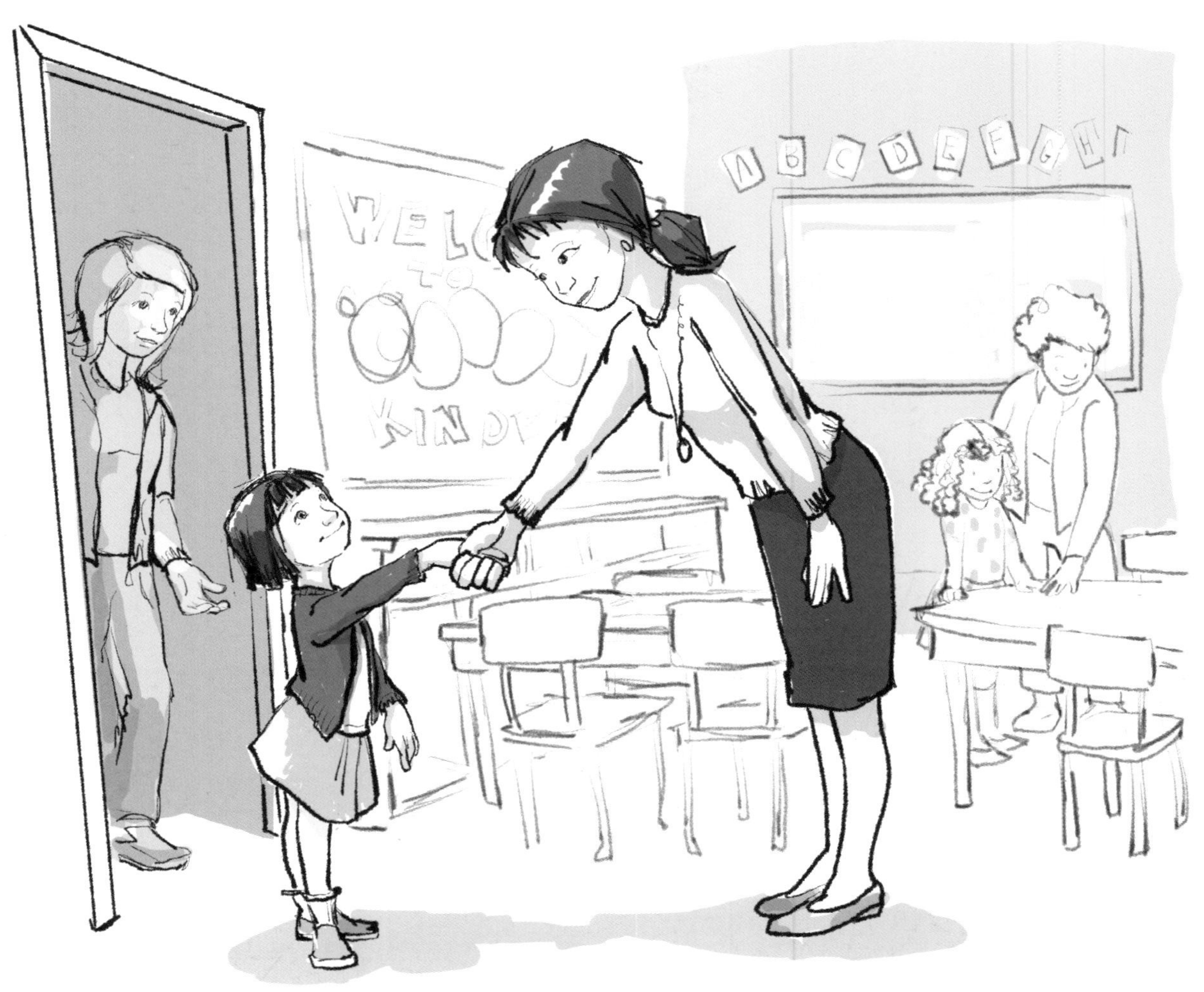

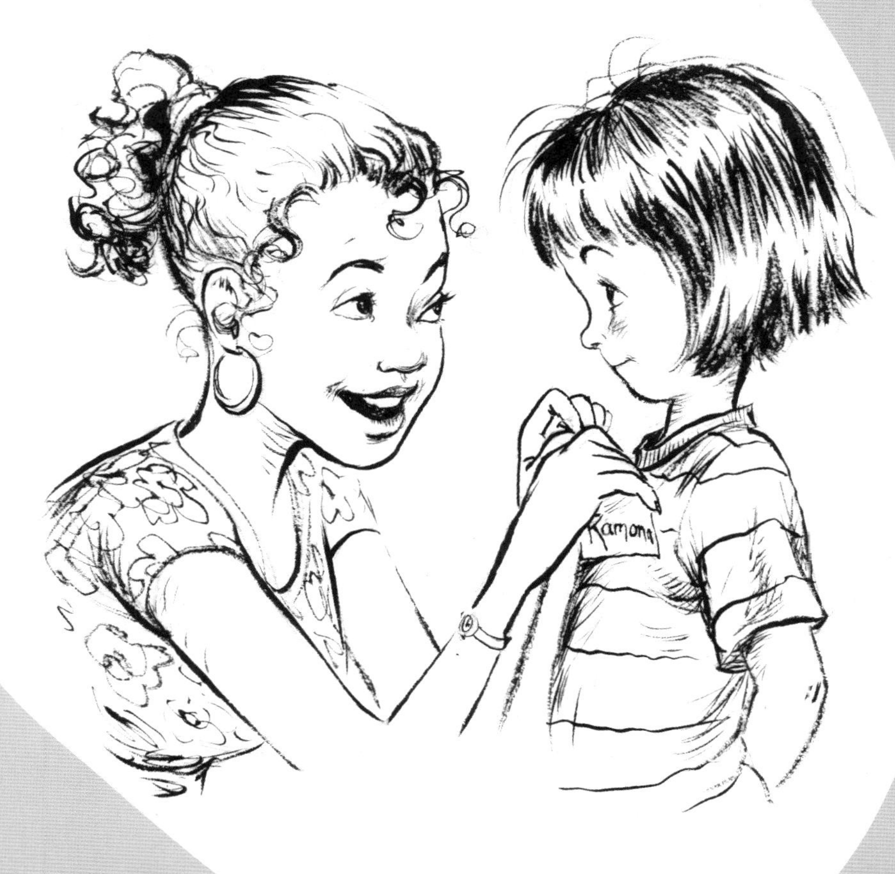

OPPOSITE: TRACY DOCKRAY.
ABOVE: JACQUELINE ROGERS.

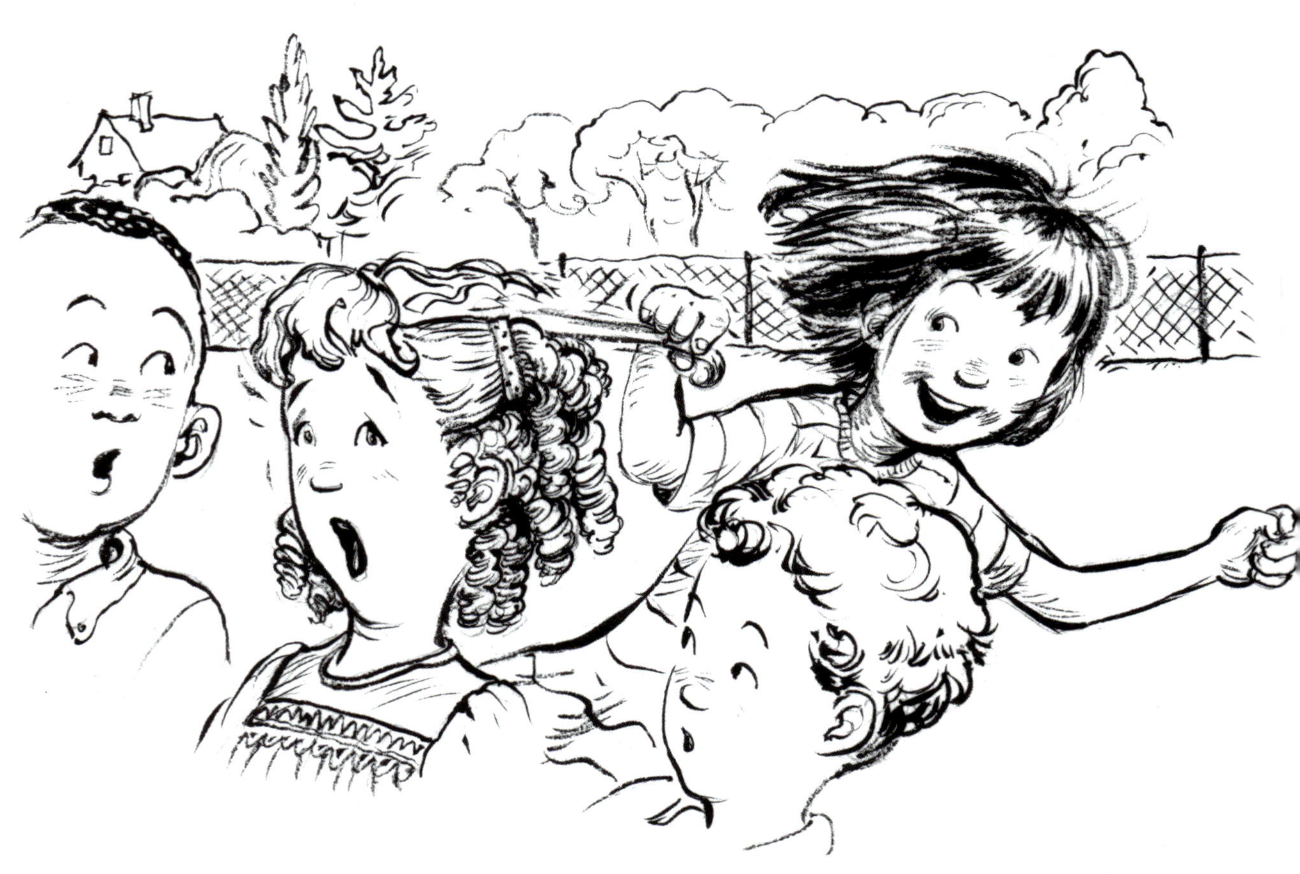

Ramona making trouble from day one.

It's the very first day of school, and already Ramona is seeing something she's never seen before: long, reddish-brown curls that are like springs—and are practically begging to be *boing*ed. These curls will prove irresistible, which Susan, the owner of said curls and already established as a nemesis of Ramona's, does not appreciate. In Rogers's version, the hair is mid-pull. Ramona's face is full of joy, while the expression of Susan, her victim, is open-mouthed shock.

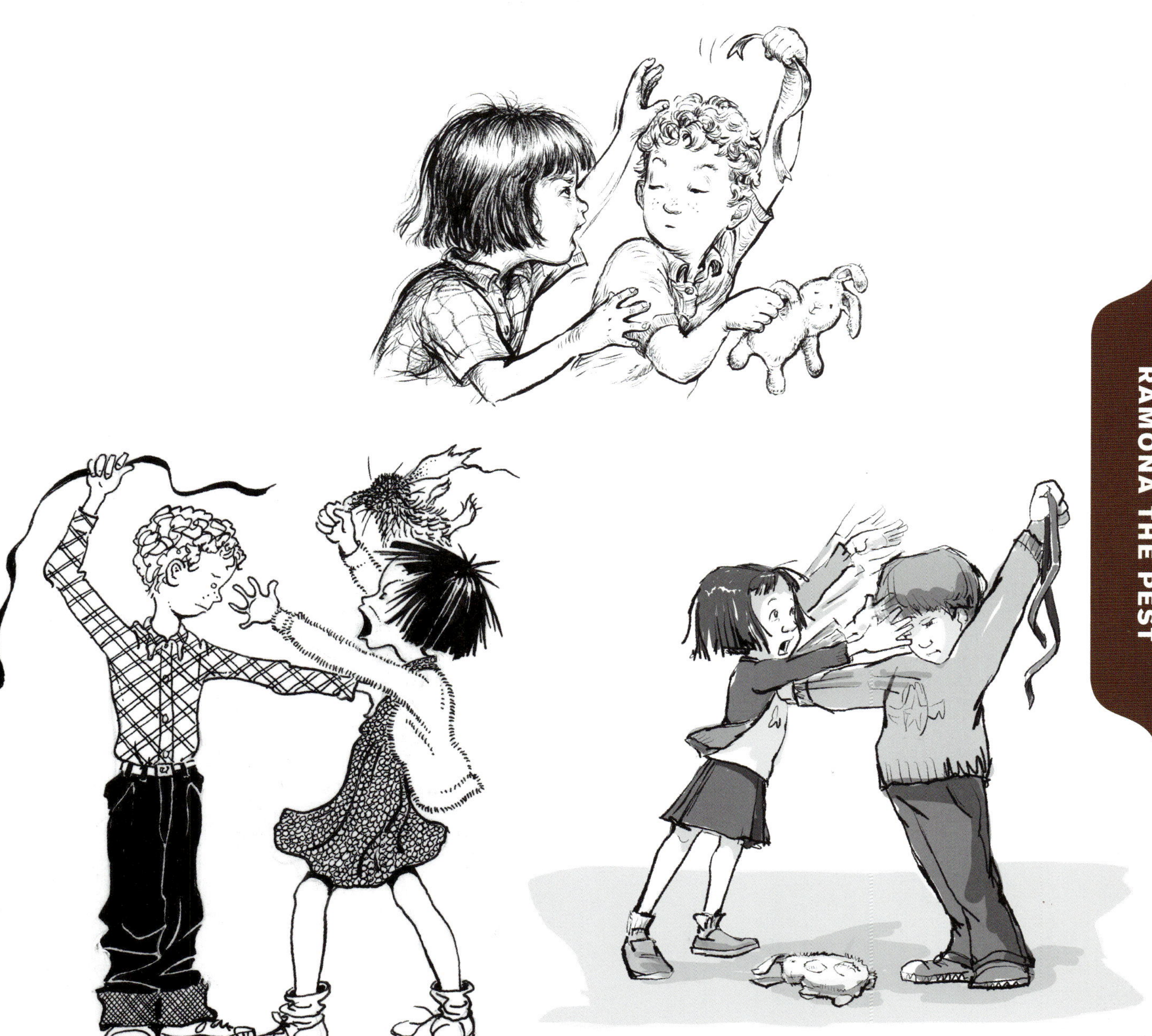

"It isn't yours." Howie showed no excitement, only stubbornness.

Howie's behavior drove Ramona wild. She wanted him to get excited. She wanted him to get angry. "It is too mine!" she shrieked, and at last the mothers turned around.

OPPOSITE: JACQUELINE ROGERS. ABOVE, CLOCKWISE FROM TOP: JACQUELINE ROGERS, TRACY DOCKRAY, AND LOUIS DARLING.

The second day of kindergarten proves just as melodramatic as the first. Howie's mother makes him bring Ramona's old stuffed bunny to Show and Tell. Here, Howie and Ramona fight over the red ribbon that Miss Binney tied around the bunny's neck. Each of the illustrators plainly show Howie's infuriating calmness in the face of Ramona's distress. Rogers's Howie is particularly smug. Can we really blame Ramona for losing her cool?

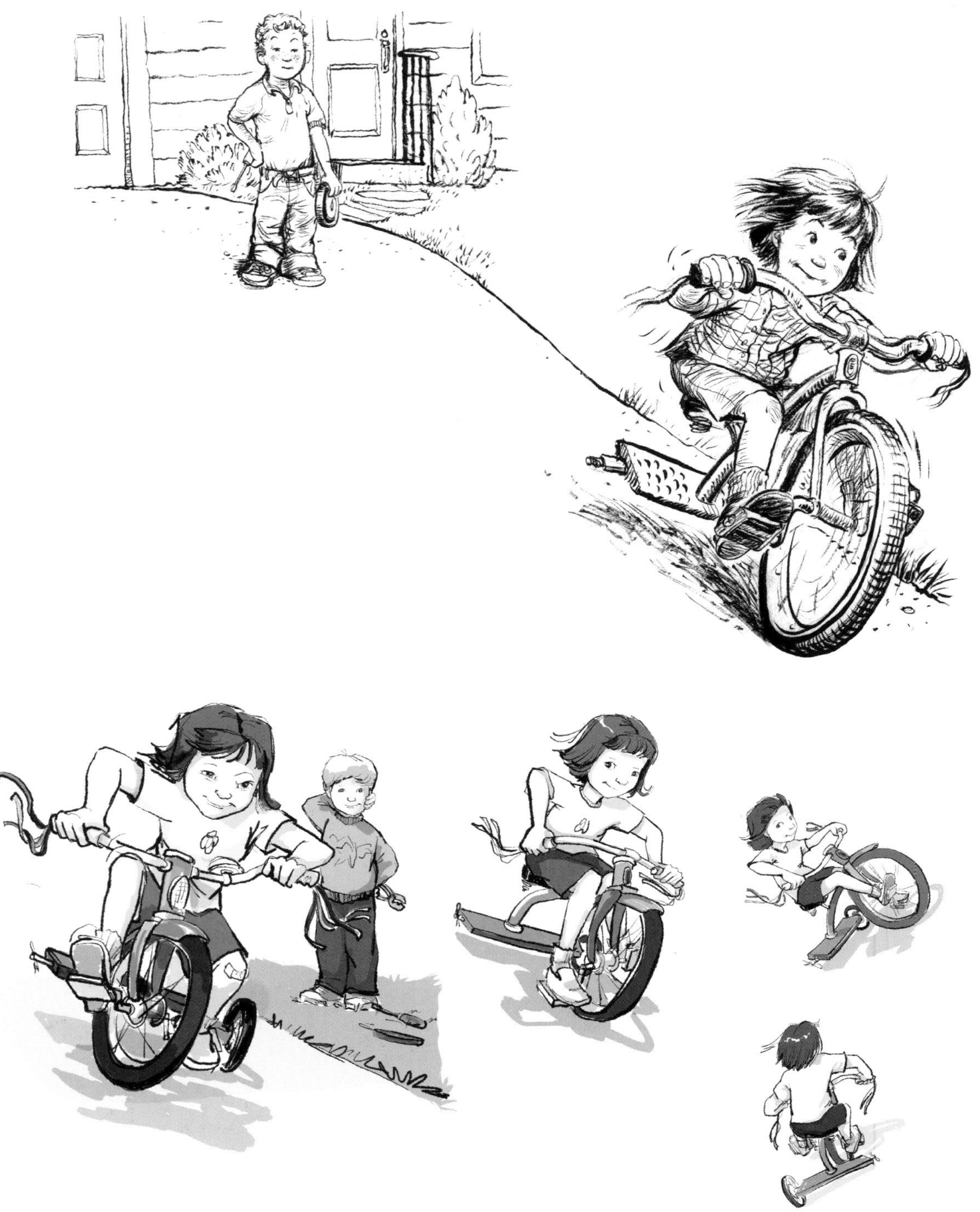

Howie and Ramona make peace.

Ramona lets handyboy Howie convert her tricycle to a two-wheeler; in exchange, Howie gives up ownership of the red ribbon. Darling depicts the two-wheeling Ramona, in dress and fuzzy sweater, with Howie in the background. Dockray extends this moment, showing Ramona, leaning to the side and with the wind in her hair, from multiple angles as she tests out her new makeshift bicycle. From Rogers, we see Howie looking satisfied about a job well done, a wrench and the extraneous wheel in hand.

ABOVE: JACQUELINE ROGERS (TOP) AND TRACY DOCKRAY (BOTTOM). OPPOSITE: LOUIS DARLING.

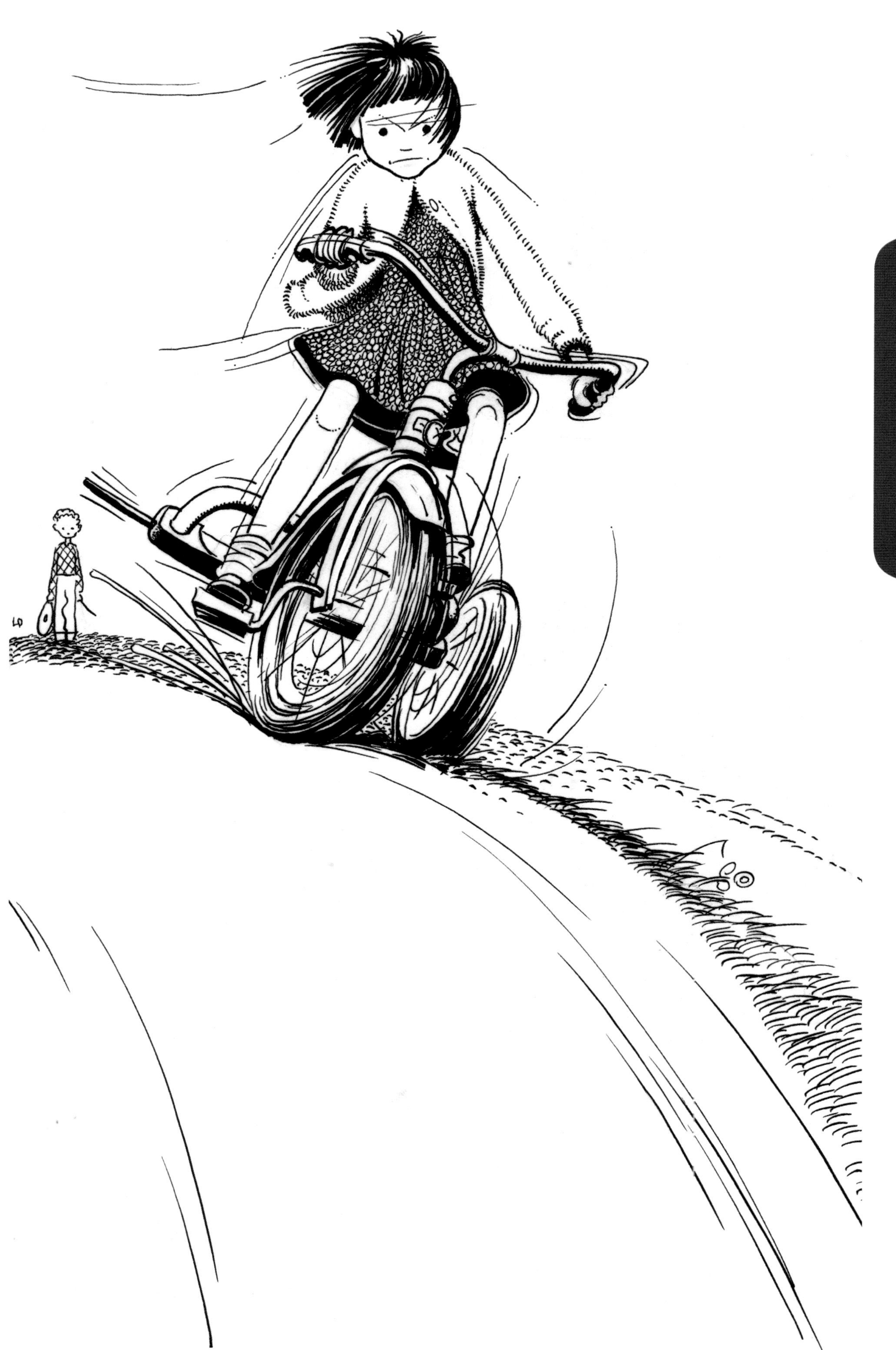

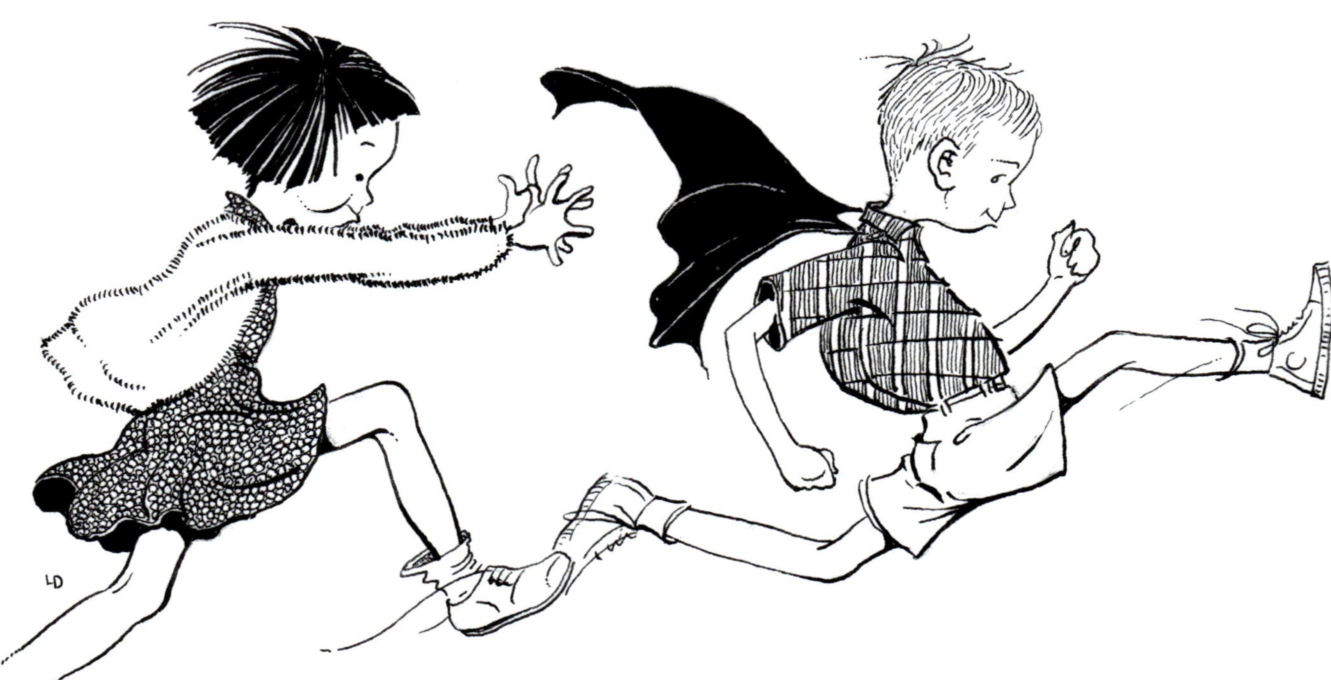

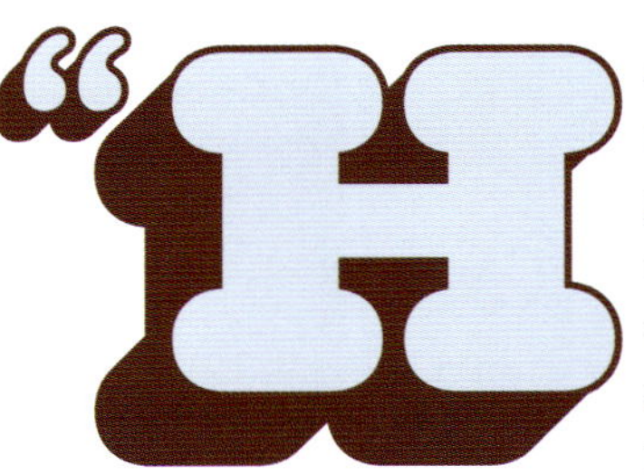

“Here comes Ramona!” the other boys and girls shouted, when they saw Ramona walking down the street. “Run, Davy! Run!”

And Davy ran with Ramona after him. Round and round the playground they ran while the class cheered Davy on.

“That kid ought to go out for track when he gets a little older,” Ramona heard one of the workmen across the street say one day.

Once Ramona came near enough to grab Davy’s clothes, but he jerked away, popping the buttons off his shirt. For once Davy stopped running. “Now see what you did!” he accused. “My mother is going to be mad at you.”

Ramona stopped in her tracks. “I didn’t do anything,” she said indignantly. “I just hung on. You did the pulling.”

“Here comes Miss Binney,” someone called out, and Ramona and Davy scurried to get in line by the door. After that Davy stayed farther away from Ramona than ever, which made Ramona sad because Davy was such a nice boy and she did so long to kiss him. However, Ramona was not so sad that she stopped chasing Davy. Round and round they went every morning until Miss Binney arrived.

LOUIS DARLING (ABOVE AND OPPOSITE).

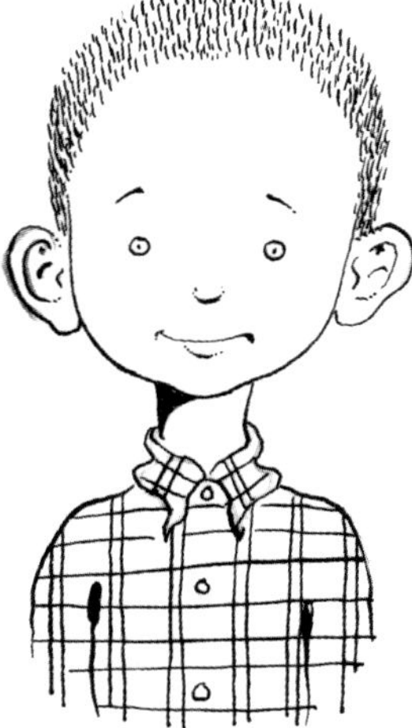

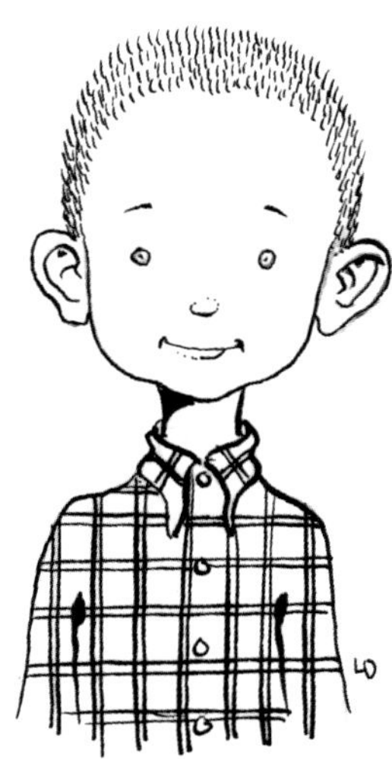

Eric J. and Eric R.

Because there are two Erics in the class, they get “an extra letter followed by a dot” after their first name. In this drawing, they appear to have much in common beyond their shared name. A differentiating feature is the more robust plaid on Eric R.’s shirt.

The Erics’ special treatment seems unfair to Ramona, so even though she’s the only one named Ramona in the class, she asks Miss Binney if she, too, can have a letter with a little dot. Unsurprisingly, she adds some glam by drawing in whiskers and ears along with the Q’s natural tail to make it look like a cat. This is the second sample of Ramona’s writing, after the library card scribble in *Beezus and Ramona*. Later in the book, she will use her new skill to identify herself with a handmade sign at the Halloween parade.

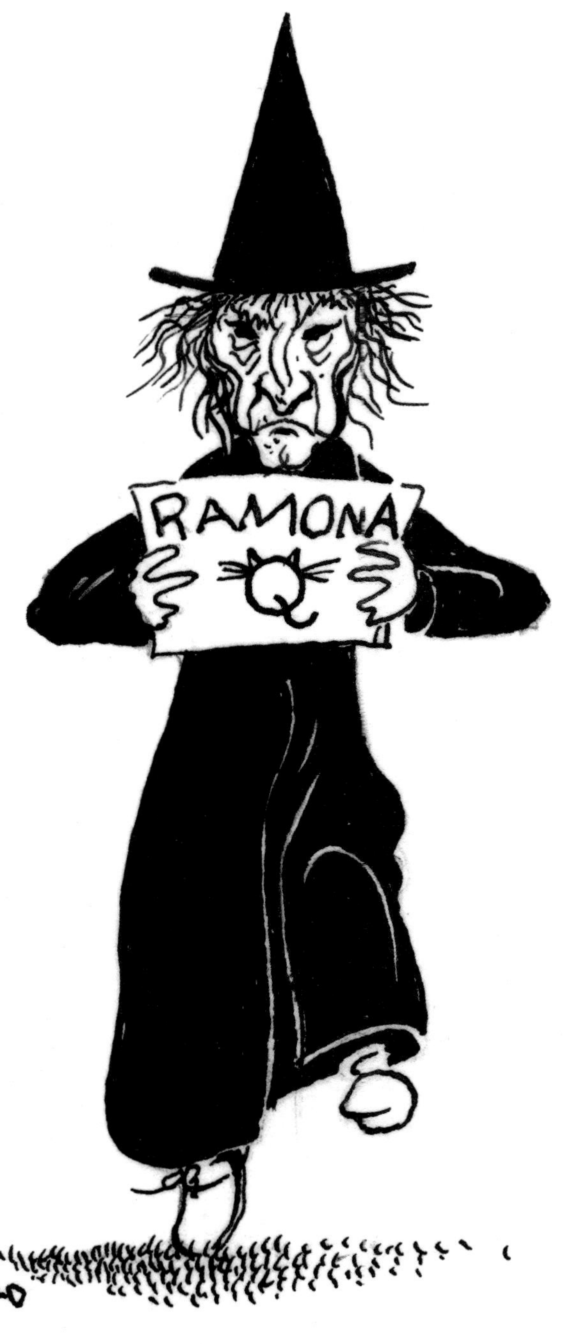

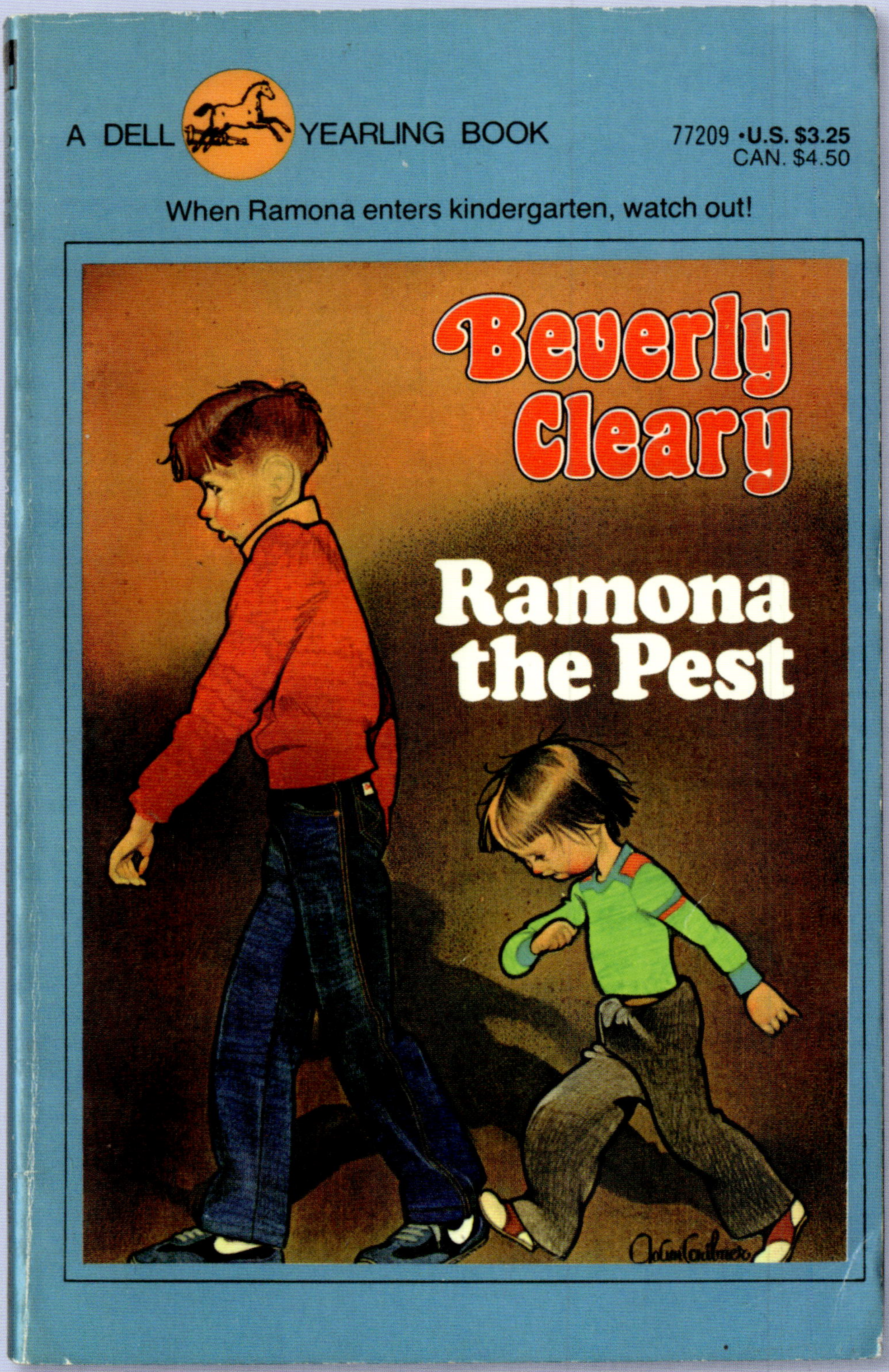

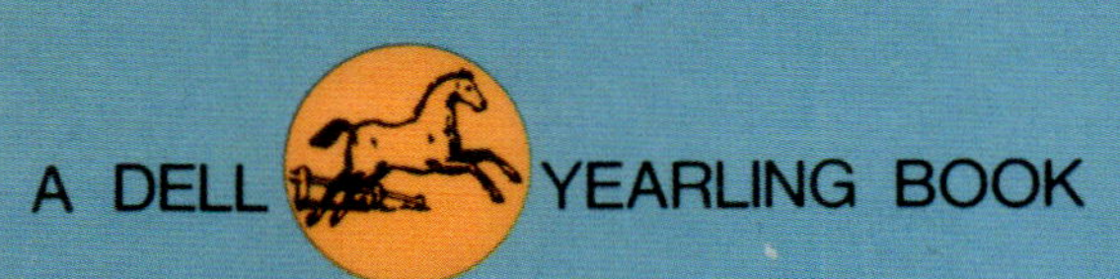
A DELL YEARLING BOOK
77209 •U.S. $3.25
CAN. $4.50
When Ramona enters kindergarten, watch out!
Beverly Cleary
Ramona the Pest

Ramona marched behind Henry, stepping as close to his sneakers as she could.

Awarded the big responsibility of walking herself to school, Ramona decides to push the limits even further by stepping off the crosswalk curb, just to see what Henry Huggins, the traffic boy on duty, will do. He dares to tell her to step back, leaving her no choice but to torment him. In Darling's illustration for the first 1968 edition, Henry wears some kind of official cap and a scowl, and is accompanied by his shaggy companion, Ribsy. Ramona's patterned dress and bobby socks are as cute as can be; the expression on her face is pure malevolence. The book was reissued in 1982 with Joanne Scribner's cover art depicting the same moment, and the two characters are dressed in late 1970s style. Note what appear to be blue Nike sneakers on Henry's feet, and Ramona's brown-and-white saddle shoes and colorful long-sleeved T-shirt.

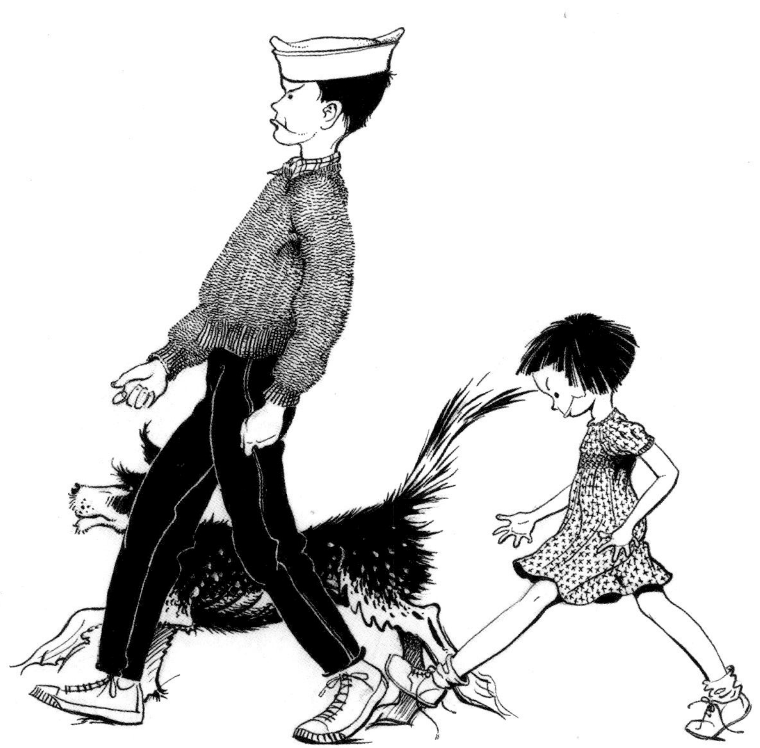

JOANNE SCRIBNER (OPPOSITE) AND LOUIS DARLING (ABOVE).

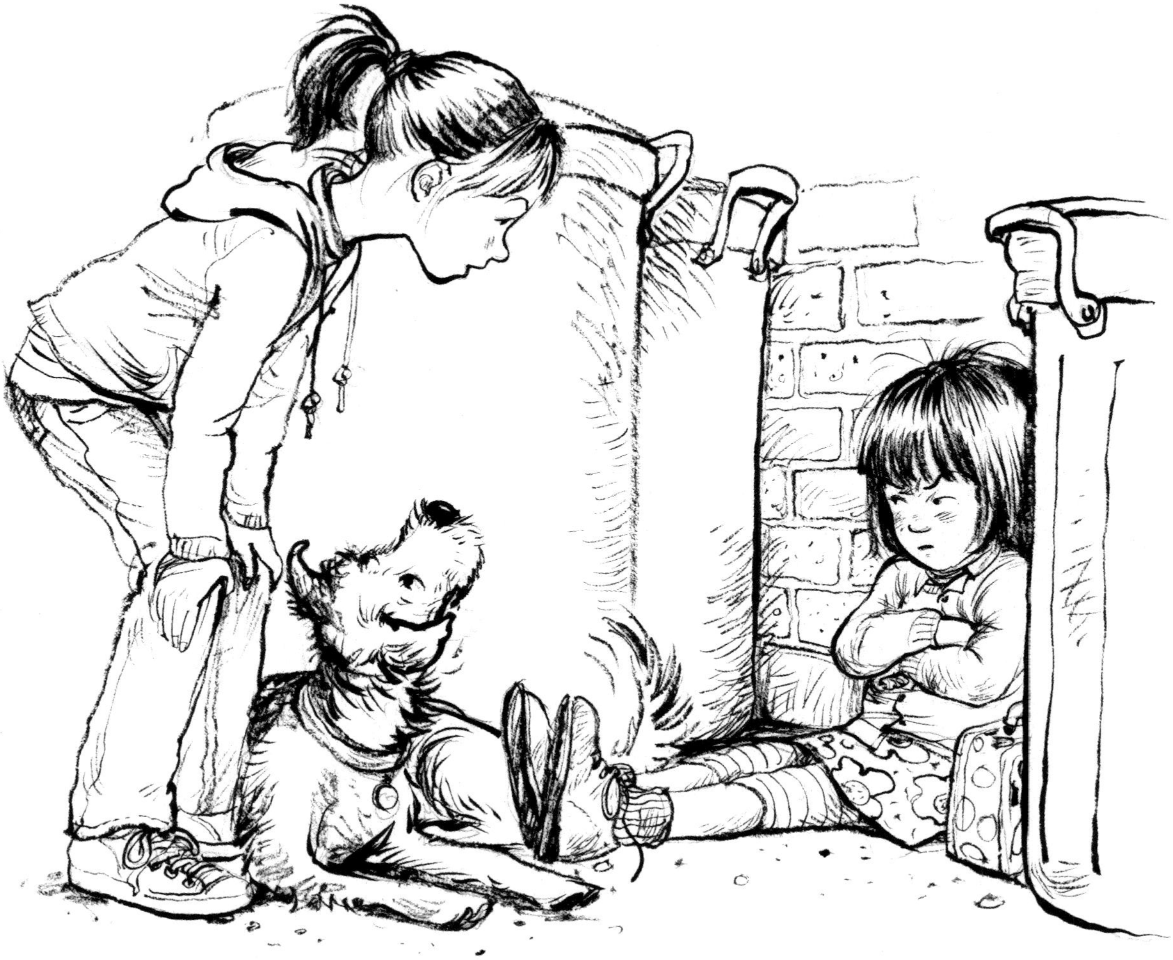

Ramona hides.

At school, Ramona and the other children discover that a stranger has taken Miss Binney's place. After the initial surprise, the majority of the class adjusts and heads inside but, for Ramona, the only sensible thing to do is hide between the trash cans and the red-brick wall. Ribsy, who often waits for Henry during the day, joins her. After what feels like a thousand hours, Ramona's cold and lonely hideout is uncovered, and Beezus is sent for. The elder sister is embarrassed, but in Rogers's illustration she still manages to look concerned. In Dockray's drawing, Beezus stands next to two lookie-loos and wears an expression of exasperation.

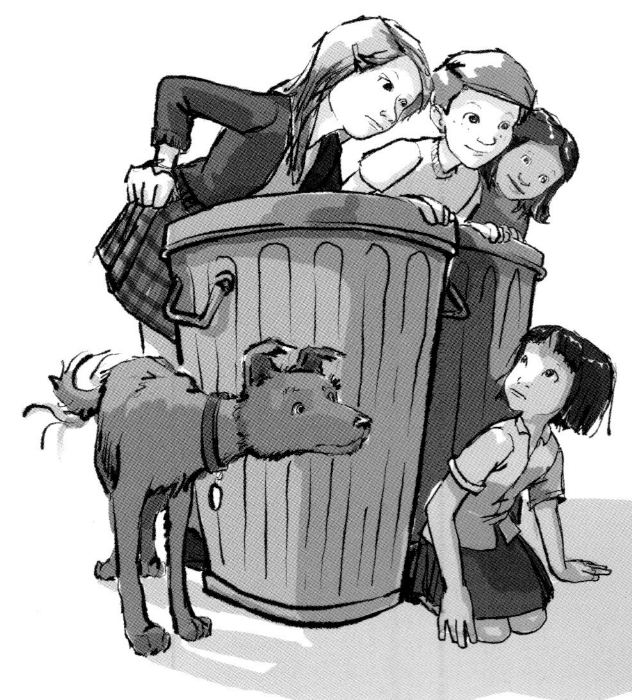

ABOVE: JACQUELINE ROGERS (TOP) AND TRACY DOCKRAY (BOTTOM). OPPOSITE: TRACY DOCKRAY (LEFT) AND JACQUELINE ROGERS (RIGHT).

Ramona wanted to stay close to her sister, but Beezus walked out of the office, leaving her alone with the principal, the most important person in the whole school.

Dockray's illustration clarifies the tension of the moment, with a tentative Ramona pausing on the threshold to the school's inner sanctum. In Rogers's illustration, the surprisingly friendly Miss Mullen takes the girl's hand to lead her back to class, where she will introduce her to the substitute teacher who is covering for Miss Binney while she's out sick with a sore throat. Ramona's endearing self-pity is emphasized with a button nose and sad puppy-dog eyes.

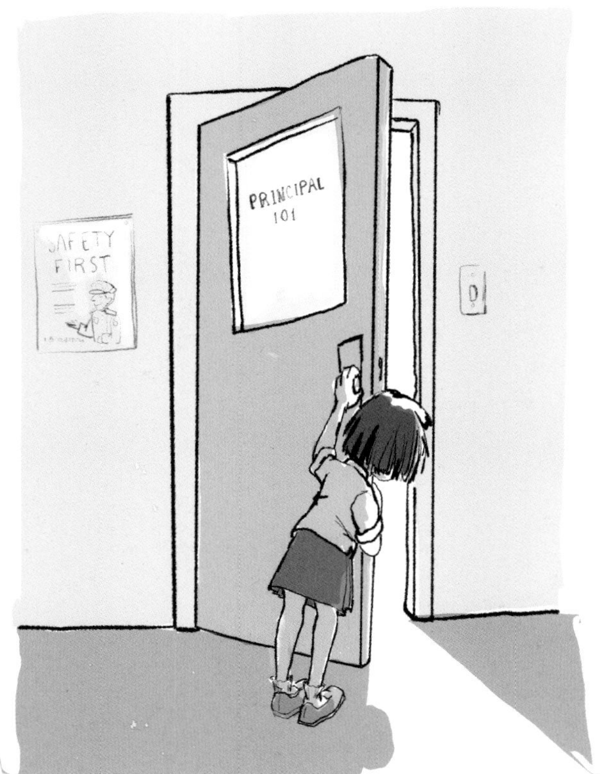

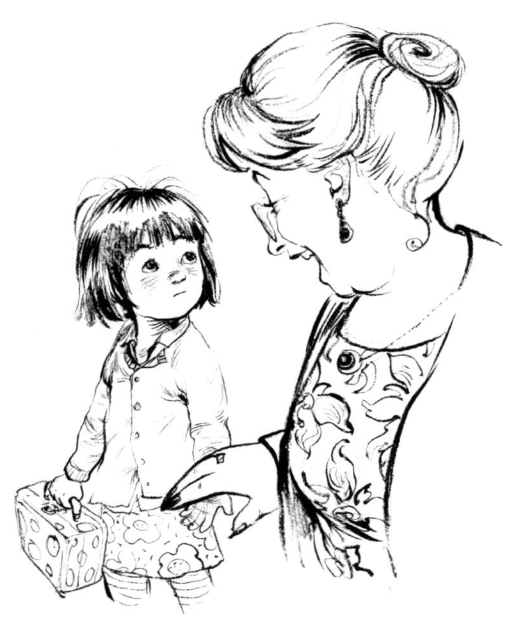

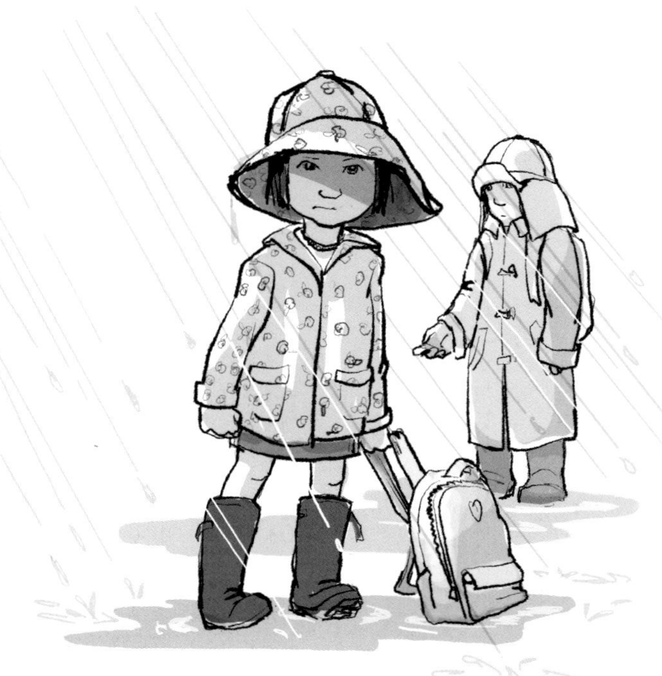

Because she loves kindergarten more than she hates those old ugly hand-me-down brown boots—and because her mother said so—Ramona heads out into quintessential Portland weather. Even her new flowered plastic raincoat and hat can't cheer her up. Howie, the previous owner of the boots, hovers in the background in a yellow raincoat big enough to grow into.

With the encouragement of the kindly shoe man at the shoe store, Mrs. Quimby gives in and buys Ramona a pair of beautiful never-worn-before red boots. Girl's boots. In the parking lot of the market being built across from the school, she tests how her boots work in the mud. They work great! Until they get stuck.

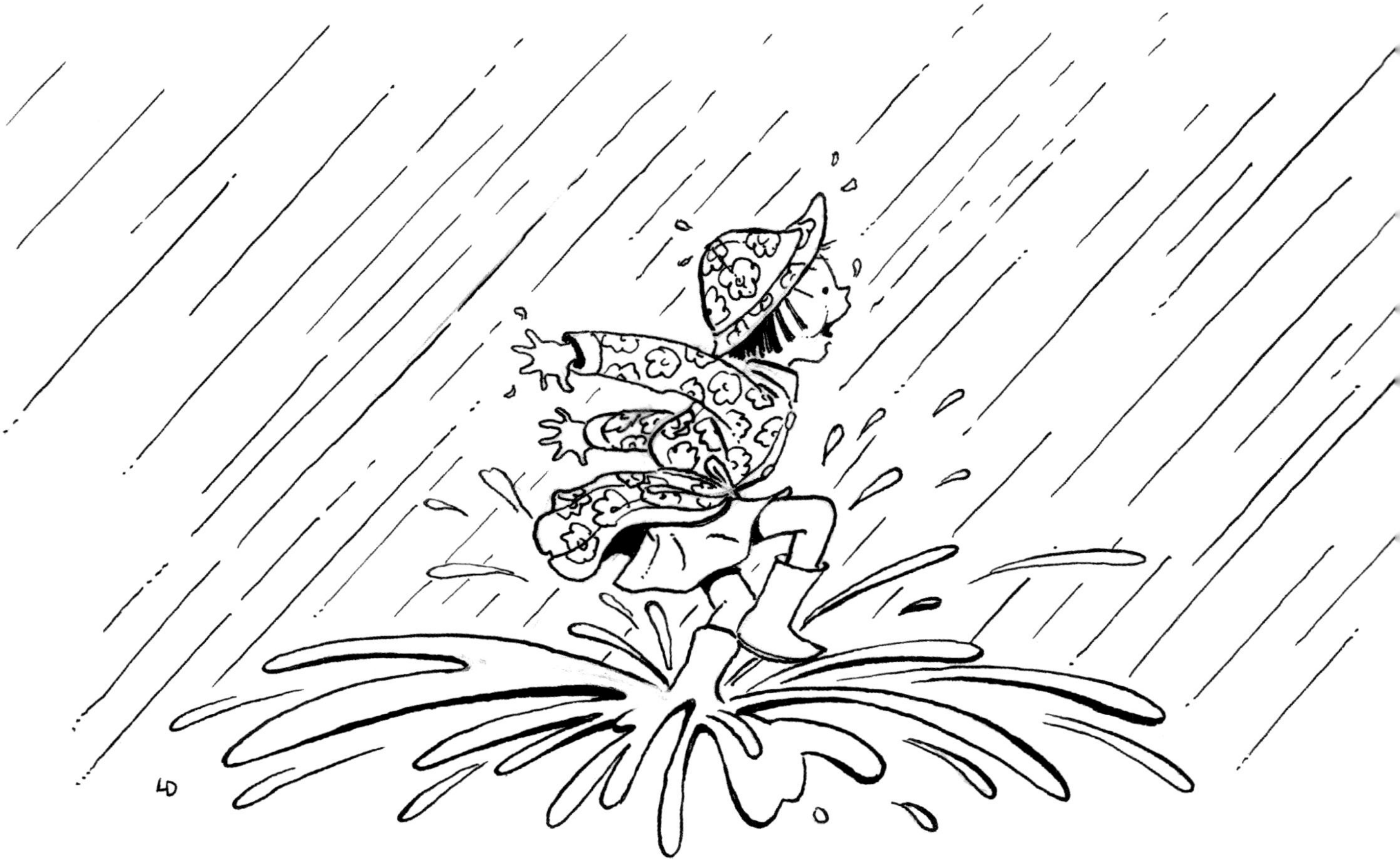

ABOVE: TRACY DOCKRAY (TOP) AND LOUIS DARLING (BOTTOM). OPPOSITE: LOUIS DARLING (TOP) AND JACQUELINE ROGERS (BOTTOM).

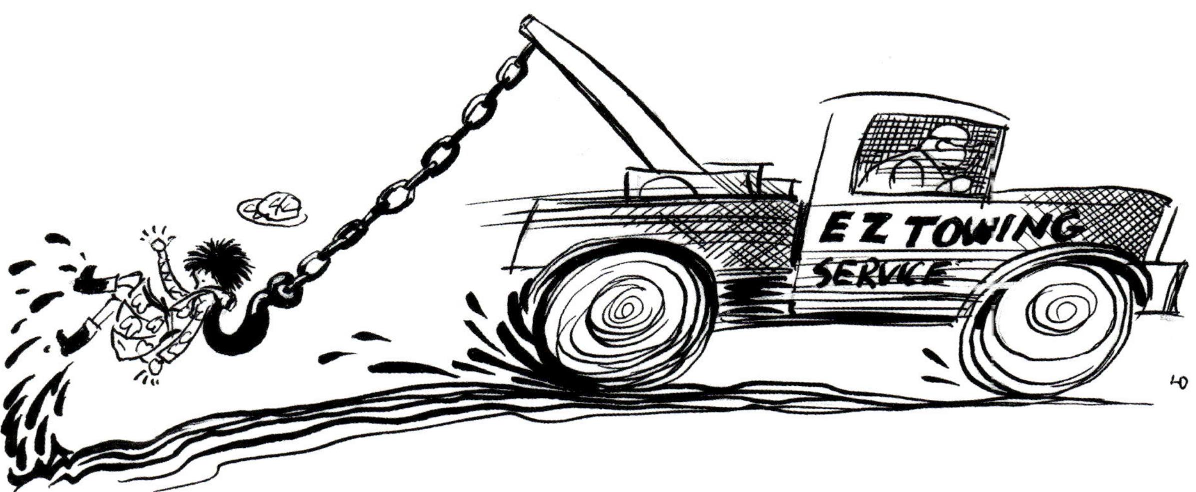

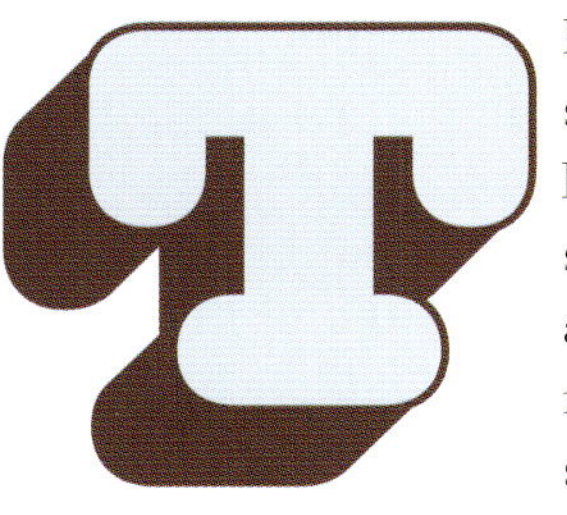

The first bell rang. Ramona sobbed harder. Now Miss Binney would have to go into school and leave her out here alone in the mud and the rain and the cold. By now some of the older boys and girls were staring at her from the windows of the big school. "Now don't worry, Ramona," said Miss Binney. "We'll get you out somehow."

Ramona, who wanted to be helpful, knew what happened when a car was stuck in the mud. "Could you call a t-tow t-truck?" she asked with a big sniff. She could see herself being yanked out of the mud by a heavy chain hooked on the collar of her raincoat. She found this picture so interesting that her sobs subsided, and she waited hopefully for Miss Binney's answer.

Darling is the only illustrator who chose to draw this scene playing out in Ramona's imagination. Somehow, in this illustration, the idea doesn't seem so outlandish.

Of course, what really happens is much more straightforward. Here, Henry Huggins frees Ramona from the mud—and from her boots. In gratitude, Ramona proposes marriage.

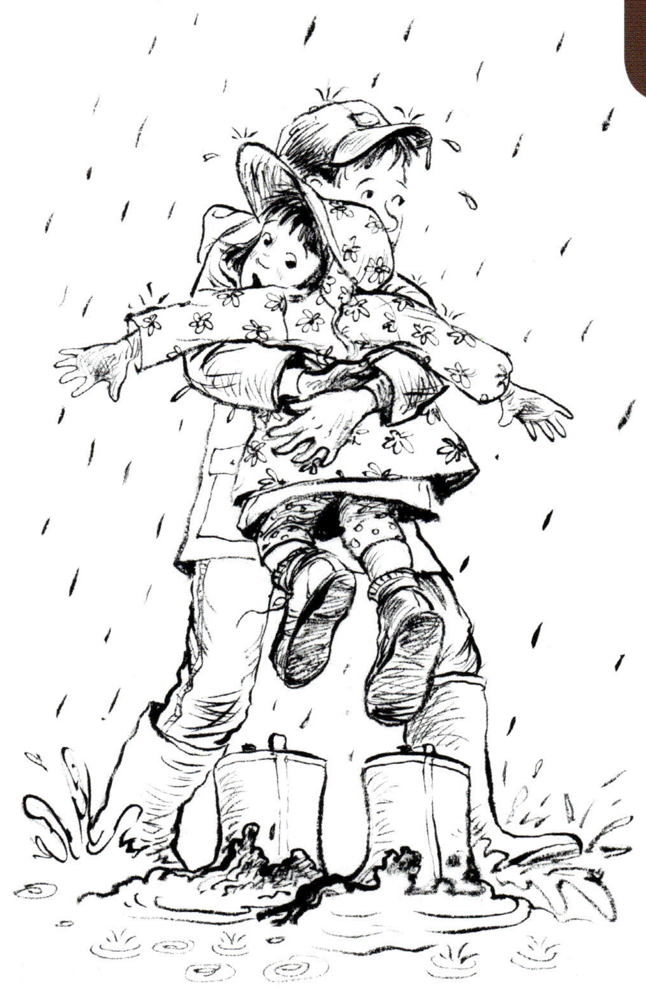

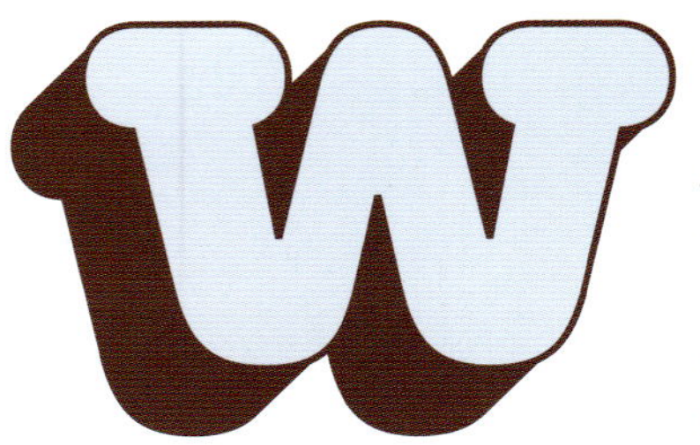

When they were in sight of the playground, Ramona saw that it was already swarming with both the morning and the afternoon kindergartens in their Halloween costumes. . . .

Ramona ran screaming onto the playground. "Yah! Yah! I'm the baddest witch in the world!" Nobody paid any attention, because everyone else was screaming, too. The noise was glorious. Ramona yelled and screamed and shrieked and chased anyone who would run. She chased tramps and ghosts and ballerinas. Sometimes other witches in masks exactly like hers chased her, and then she would turn around and chase the witches right back. She tried to chase Howie, but he would not run. He just stood beside the fence holding his broken tail and missing all the fun.

Ramona discovered dear little Davy in a skimpy pirate costume from the dime store. She could tell he was Davy by his thin legs. At last! She pounced and kissed him through her rubber mask. Davy looked startled, but he had the presence of mind to make a gagging noise while Ramona raced away, satisfied that she finally had managed to catch and kiss Davy.

Then Ramona saw Susan getting out of her mother's car. As she might have guessed, Susan was dressed as an old-fashioned girl with a long skirt, an apron, and pantalettes. "I'm the baddest witch in the world!" yelled Ramona, and ran after Susan, whose curls bobbed daintily about her shoulders in a way that could not be disguised. Ramona was unable to resist. After weeks of longing she tweaked one of Susan's curls, and yelled, "*Boing!*" through her rubber mask.

"You stop that," said Susan, and smoothed her curls.

"Yah! Yah! I'm the baddest witch in the world!" Ramona was carried away. She tweaked another curl and yelled a muffled, "*Boing!*"

A clown laughed and joined Ramona. He too tweaked a curl and yelled, "*Boing!*"

The old-fashioned girl stamped her foot. "You stop that!" she said angrily.

"*Boing! Boing!*" Others joined the game. Susan tried to run away, but no matter which way she ran there was someone eager to stretch a curl and yell, "*Boing!*" Susan ran to Miss Binney. "Miss Binney! Miss Binney!" she cried. "They're teasing me! They're pulling my hair and boinging me!"

"Who's teasing you?" asked Miss Binney.

"Everybody," said Susan tearfully. "A witch started it."

"Which witch?" asked Miss Binney.

Susan looked around. "I don't know which witch," she said, "but it was a bad witch."

That's me, the baddest witch in the world, thought Ramona.

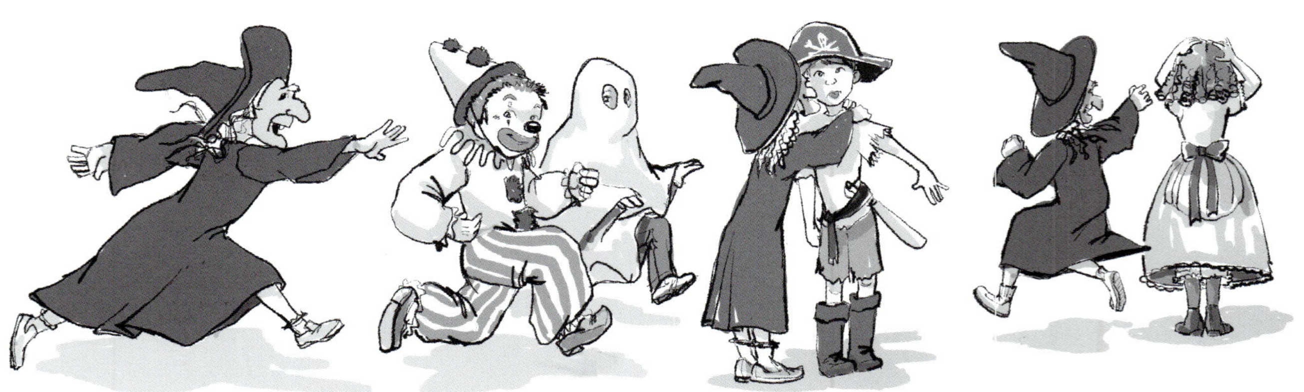

TRACY DOCKRAY (ABOVE) AND LOUIS DARLING (OPPOSITE).

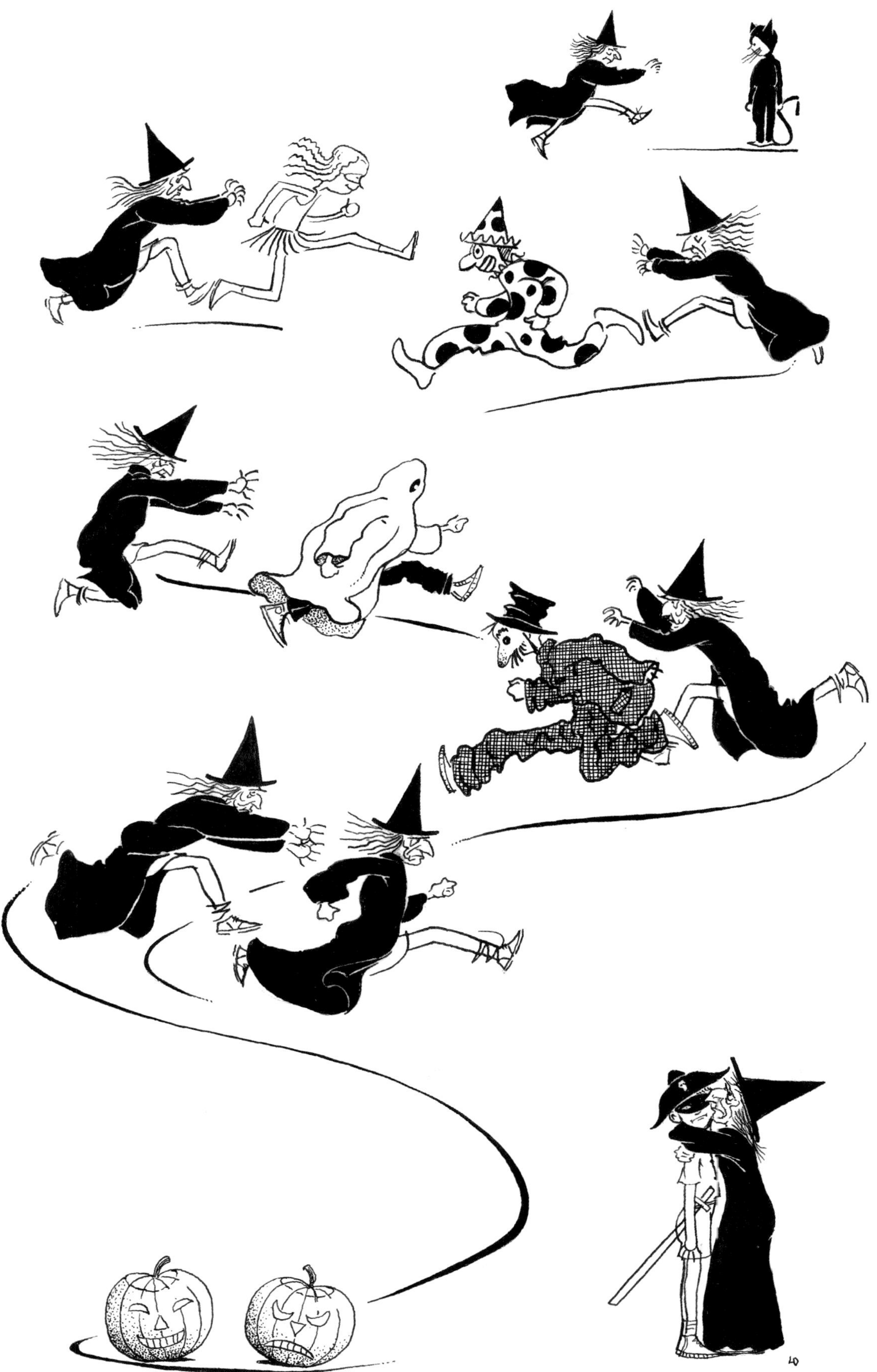

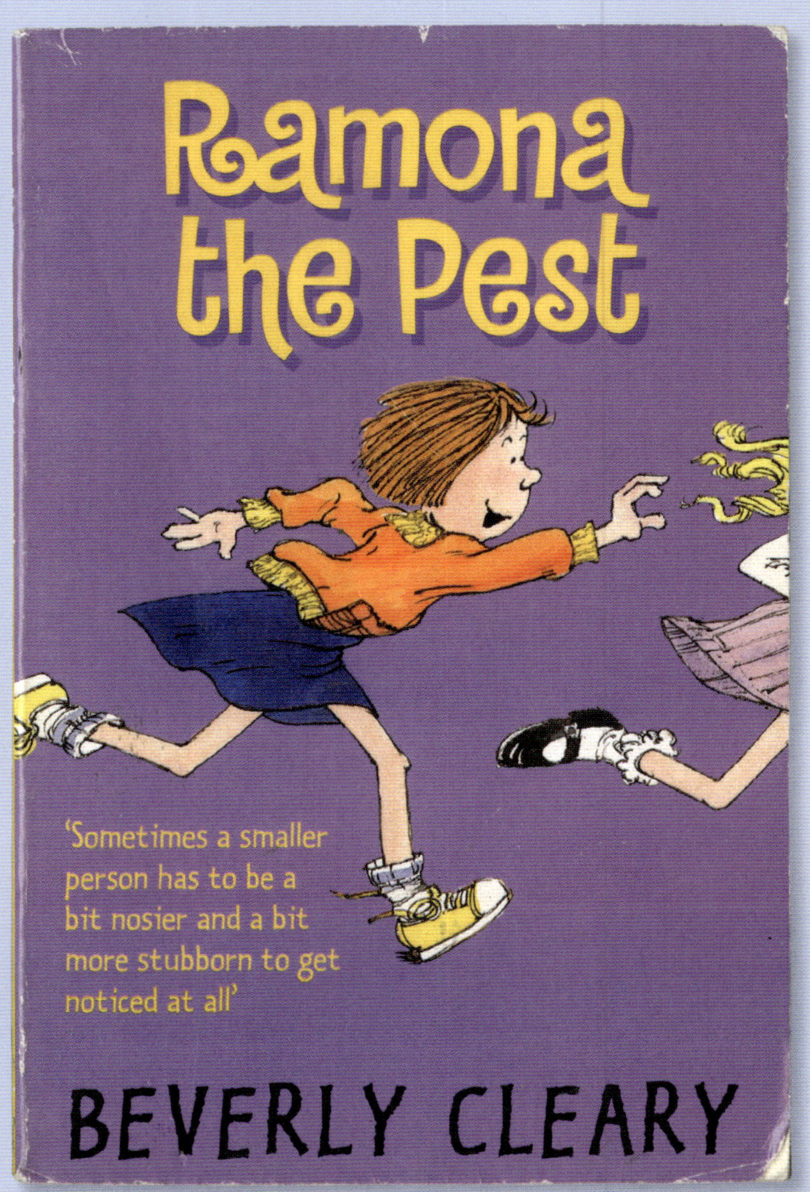

The final *boing.*
Having escaped being identified as the witch who'd started it on Halloween, and filled with the glory of losing her first tooth, Ramona runs around the jungle gym under a shining sun and big blue sky. Her elation causes her to forget her manners, and once again she boings Susan's curl.

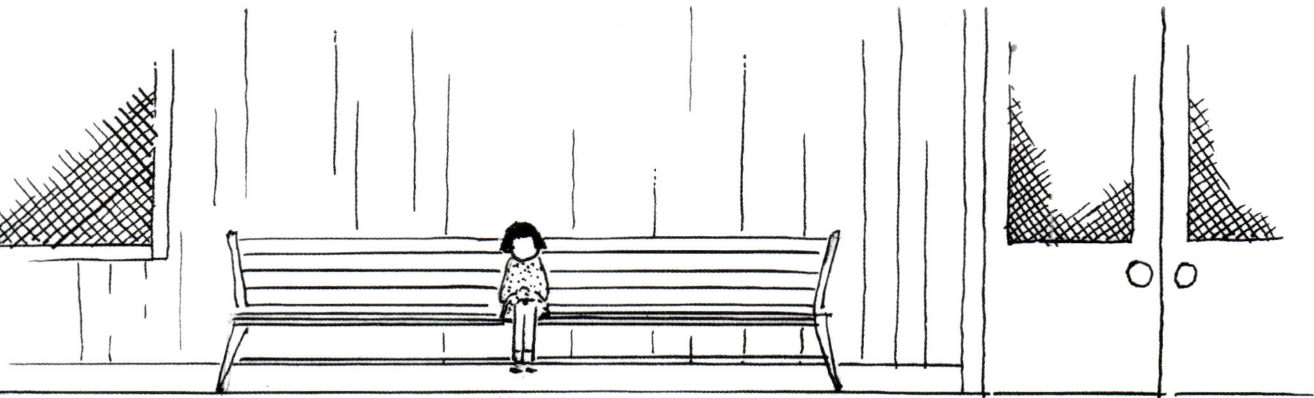

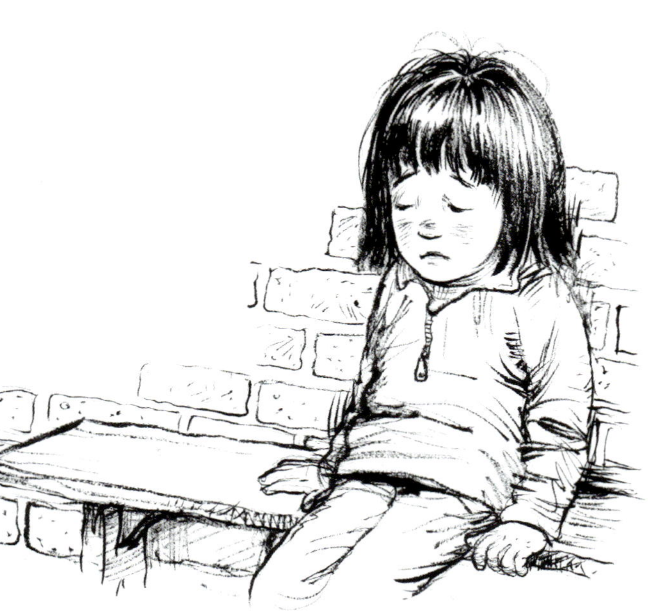

Ramona gets benched.

Ramona, unable to guarantee that she'll never pull Susan's hair again, is sent outside by a cruel and indifferent Miss Binney. In Rogers's illustration, a close-up reveals the most downtrodden girl the world has ever known. Darling's illustration pulls us back to reveal a tiny child all alone on a great big bench, conveying the social isolation that Ramona feels after being sent away.

OPPOSITE: ALAN TIEGREEN. ABOVE: LOUIS DARLING (TOP) AND JACQUELINE ROGERS (BOTTOM).

She was a terrible, wicked girl! Being such a bad, terrible, horrid, wicked girl made her feel good!

After a day in which everything goes wrong, the last thing she needs is a sister who is always right or her parents' patronizing sympathy. She is *not* upset, and she is *not* a little girl! In Darling's illustration, Ramona, wearing a dress, lies on her frilly bedspread and extends an arm for extra leverage as she pounds her heels against the wall, leaving marks on the somewhat indistinct pattern of the wallpaper. Dockray drew two bold legs and a series of after-shadows to show the motion of her kicking legs, the thumps lifting the framed drawing of a castle off the wall. Ramona's toys are strewn about the floor; the lamp has fallen over.

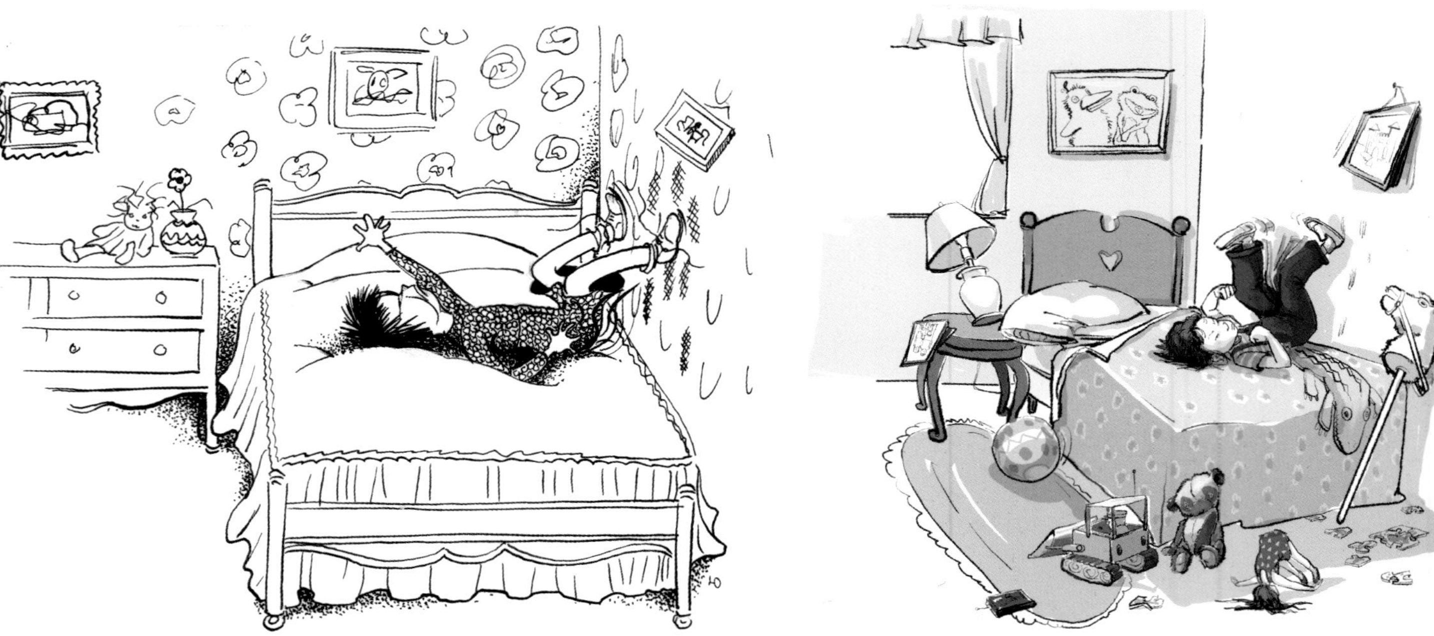

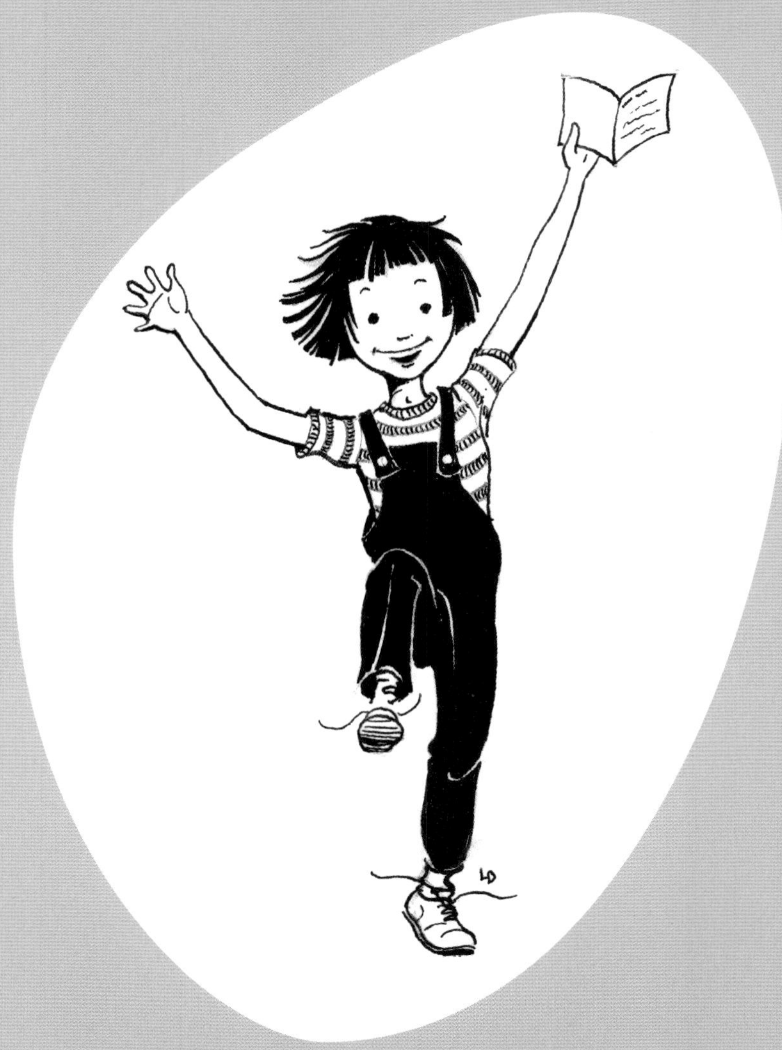

After one week of being a kindergarten dropout, Ramona decides to return to school.

All it took was a nice letter—with Ramona's first lost tooth attached—from Miss Binney, delivered by Howie to the Quimbys' door. This portrait of a little girl skipping with joy would be Darling's last drawing of Ramona.

OPPOSITE: LOUIS DARLING (LEFT) AND TRACY DOCKRAY (RIGHT). ABOVE: LOUIS DARLING.

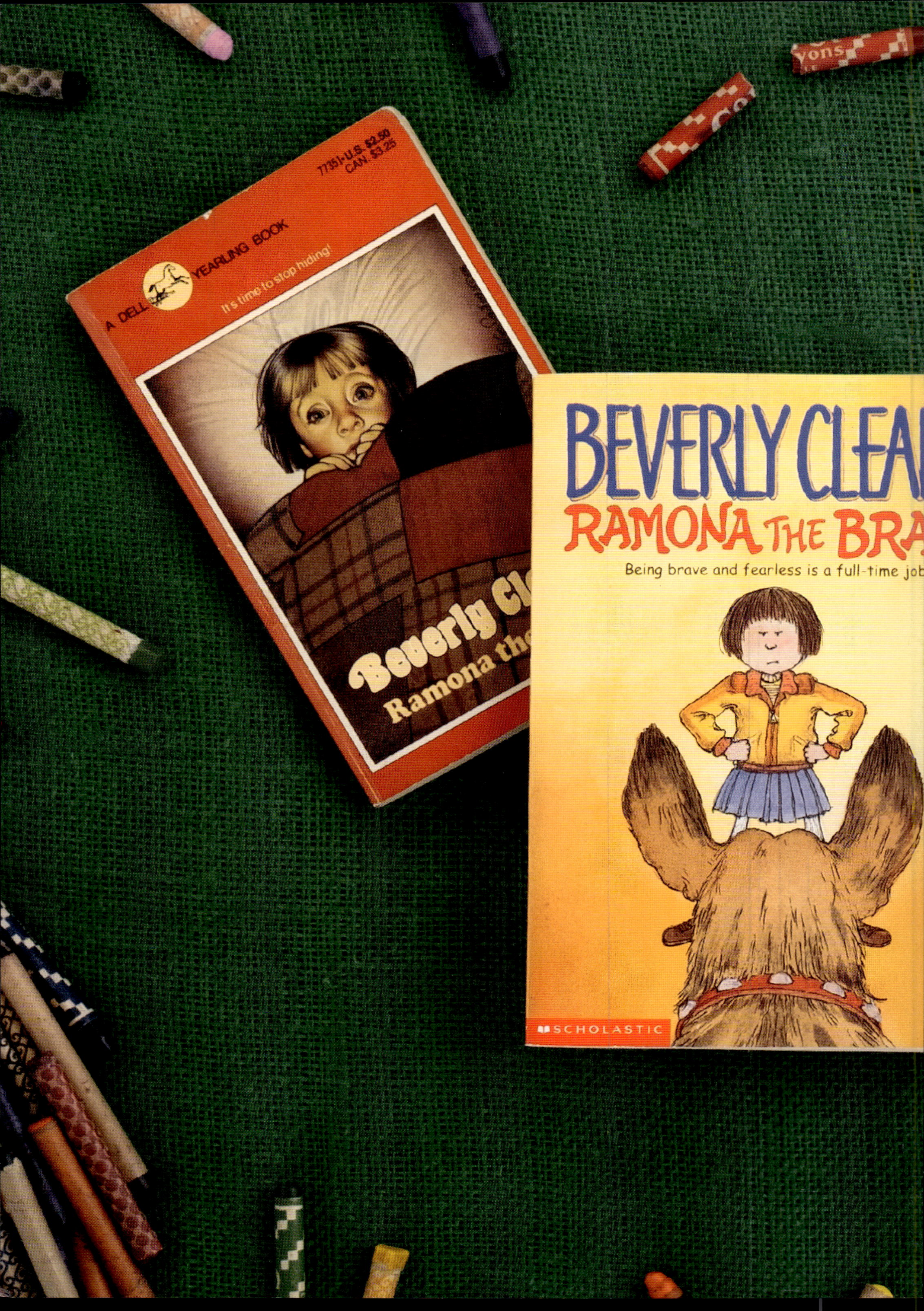
A DELL YEARLING BOOK
77351-U.S. $2.50
CAN. $3.25
It's time to stop hiding!
SCHOLASTIC

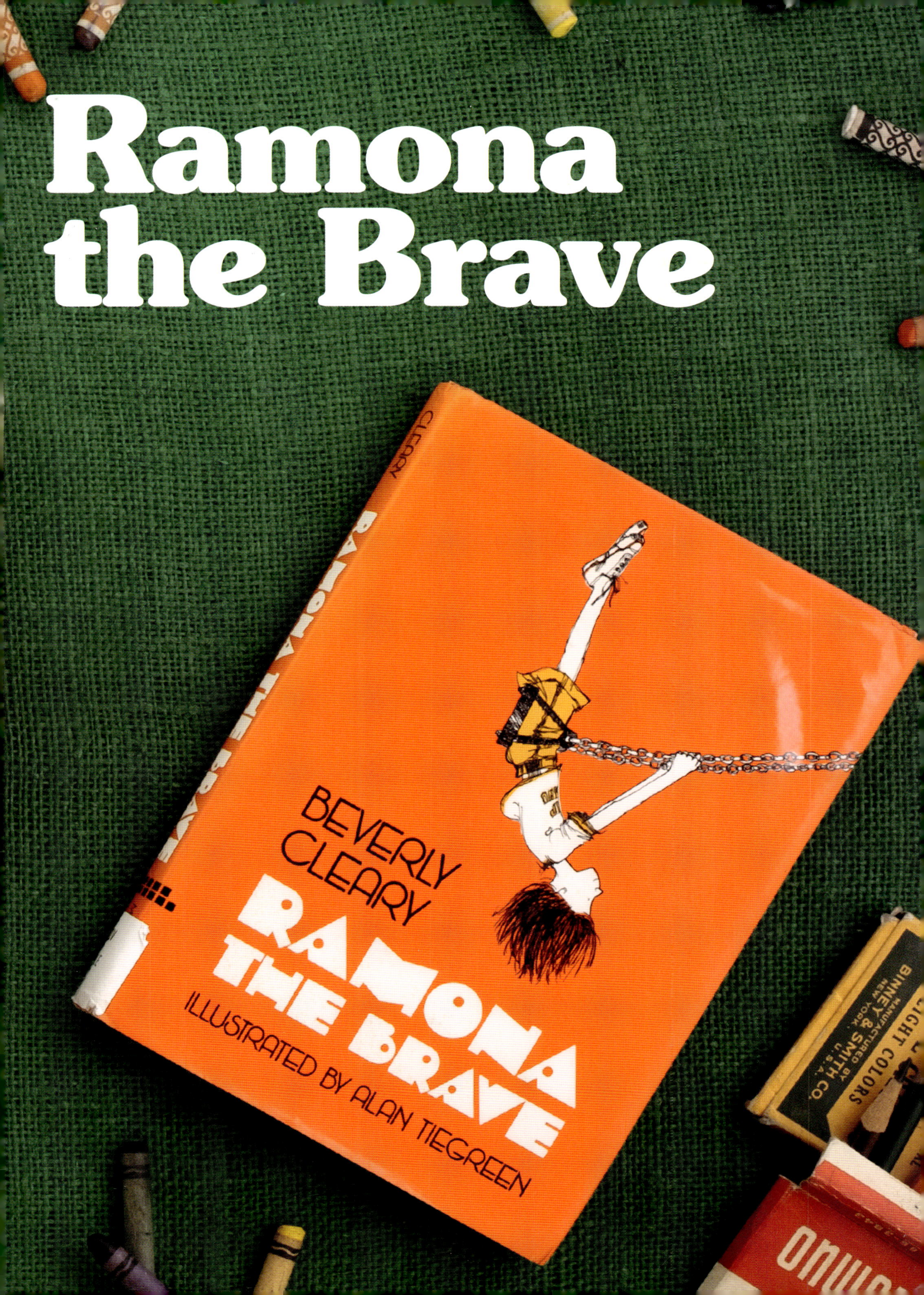
Ramona the Brave
CLEARY
RAMONA THE BRAVE
BEVERLY CLEARY
RAMONA THE BRAVE
ILLUSTRATED BY ALAN TIEGREEN
BINNEY & SMITH CO.
MANUFACTURED BY
NEW YORK, U.S.A.
IGHT COLORS

Ramona the Brave

Chapter Three

"Oh, Mother!" Beezus was all enthusiasm . . . "Just think! You're going to be liberated!"

Seven years have passed since the release of the previous Ramona Quimby book, in 1968, yet Ramona has aged but a year. Still, she can no longer rely on the slack given to babyish kindergarteners; the time has come for her to take on the more grown-up responsibilities of a first-grader.

But Ramona is not the only one dealing with change. It was 1975 at the time of *Ramona the Brave*'s publication, and the women's liberation movement was in full swing. So it makes sense that Cleary chose this book for Mrs. Quimby's entrance into the workforce outside the home. (It could also have been a coincidence, given that both daughters are now in school and therefore their mother is freed from having to provide all-day childcare).

Mrs. Quimby gets a part-time job to pay for the construction of a new room, so that each of the girls can have their own bedroom. Though a solid strategy for putting an end to the tension that comes from one neat girl and one messy girl sharing a space, this will put Ramona's nighttime bravery to the test.

While Mrs. Quimby is venturing out into the professional world, Ramona is entering the classroom of Mrs. Griggs, a less charming and more authoritative teacher than the lovely kindergarten teacher Miss Binney. The newly minted first-grader has always been a creative and energetic girl whose confidence stems from her own belief in her bravery, but now she'll be forced to learn some nuance. Yes, she is brave. But sometimes behaving in a way *she* considers brave, like defending her big sister from some mean boys at the park, is actually just, well, embarrassing. Or scrunching up Susan's copycatted paper owl—that was just impulsive. Other times, like when she throws her shoe at a growling German shepherd she meets on the way to school, bravery is just that: bravery.

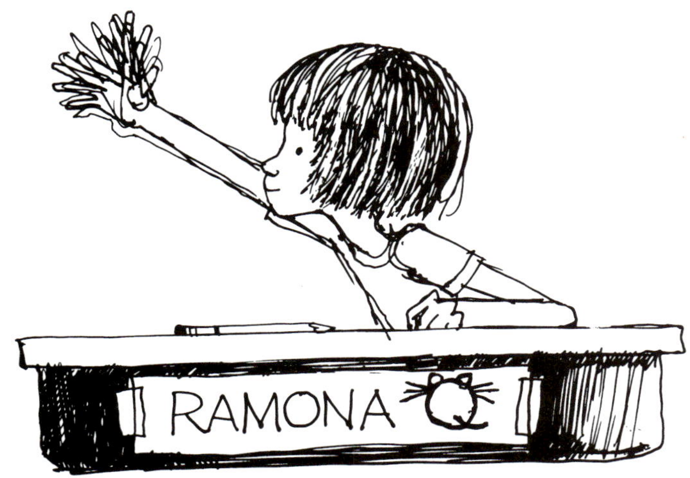

ALAN TIEGREEN

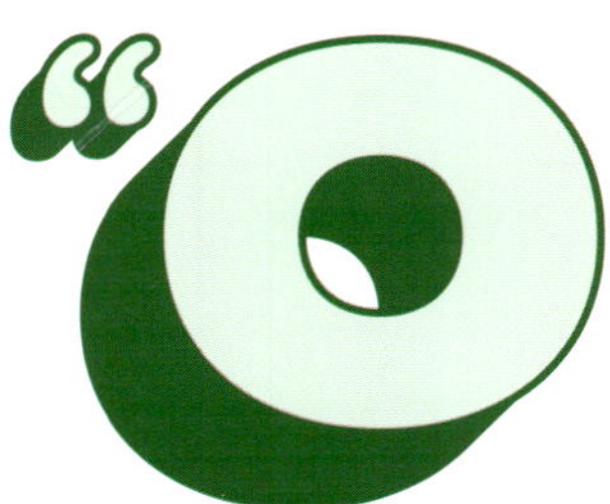

"Oh, Mama, it was just awful. It was terrible. All those big awful boys! They kept saying, 'Jesus, Beezus' and 'Beezus, Jesus.' I jumped out of the swing, and I told them—"

Beezus interrupted. Anger once more replaced tears. "And then Ramona had to get into the act. Do you know what she did? She jumped out of the swing and preached a sermon! Nobody wants a little sister tagging around preaching sermons to a bunch of boys. And they weren't that big either. They were just trying to act big."

Ramona was stunned by this view of her behavior. How unfair of Beezus when she had been so brave. And the boys had seemed big to her.

Mrs. Quimby spoke to Beezus as if Ramona were not present. "A sermon! You must be joking."

Ramona tried again. "Mama, I—"

Beezus was not going to give her little sister a chance to speak. "No, I'm not joking. And then Ramona stuck her thumbs in her ears, waggled her fingers, and stuck out her tongue. I just about died, I was so embarrassed."

Ramona was suddenly subdued. She had thought Beezus was angry at the boys, but now it turned out she was angry with her little sister, too. Maybe angrier. Ramona was used to being considered a little pest, and she knew she sometimes was a pest, but this was something different. She felt as if she were standing aside looking at herself. She saw a stranger, a funny little six-year-old girl with straight brown hair, wearing grubby shorts and an old T-shirt, inherited from Beezus, which had Camp Namanu printed across the front. A silly little girl embarrassing her sister so much that Beezus was ashamed of her. And she had been proud of herself because she thought she was being brave.

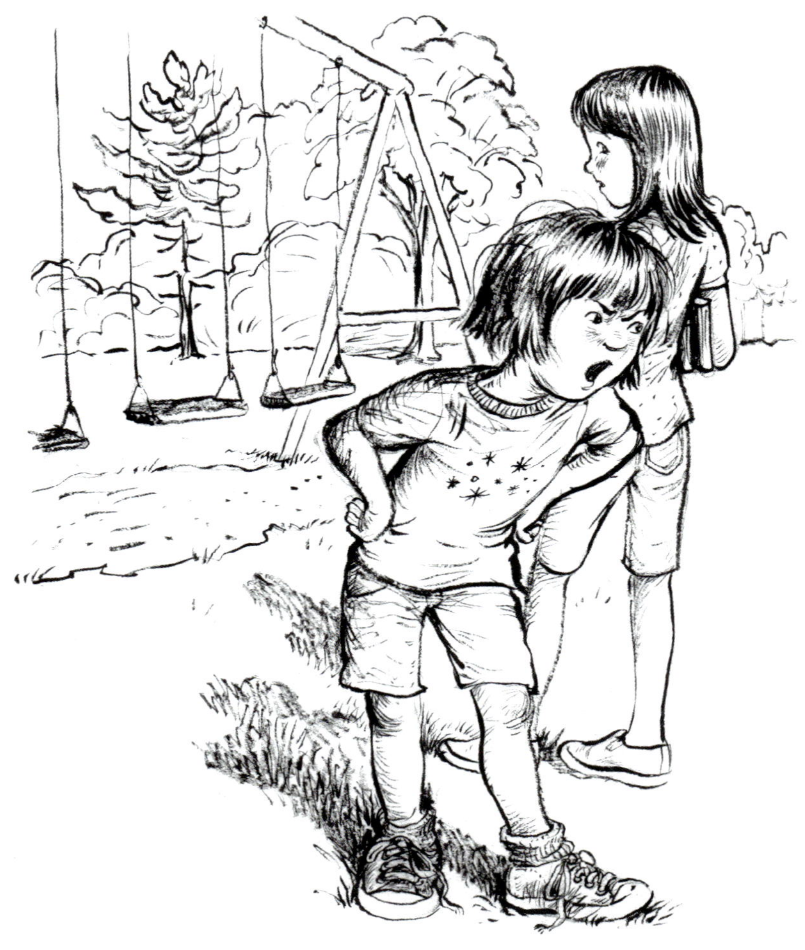

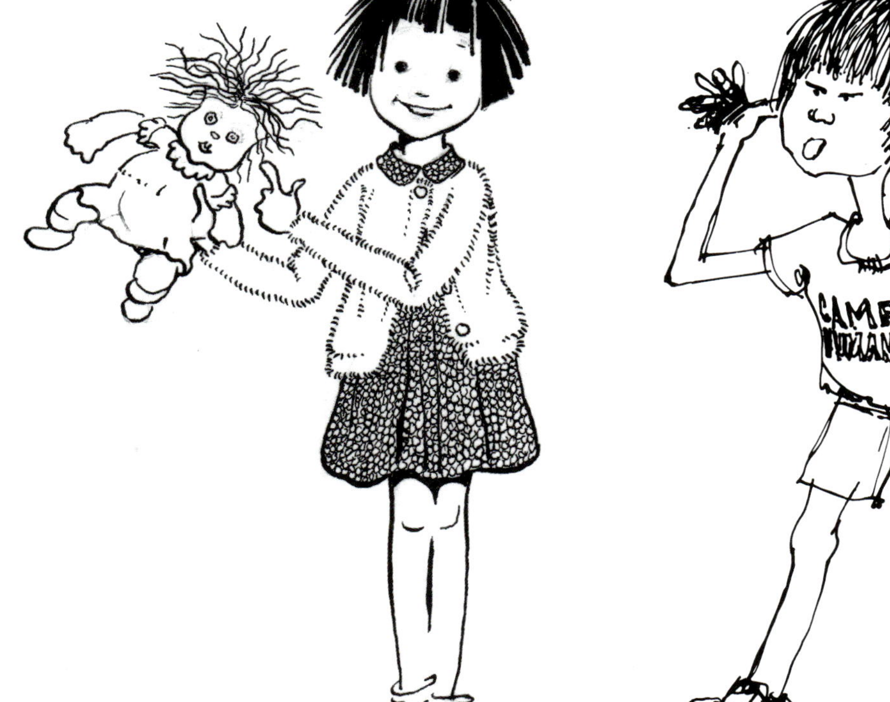

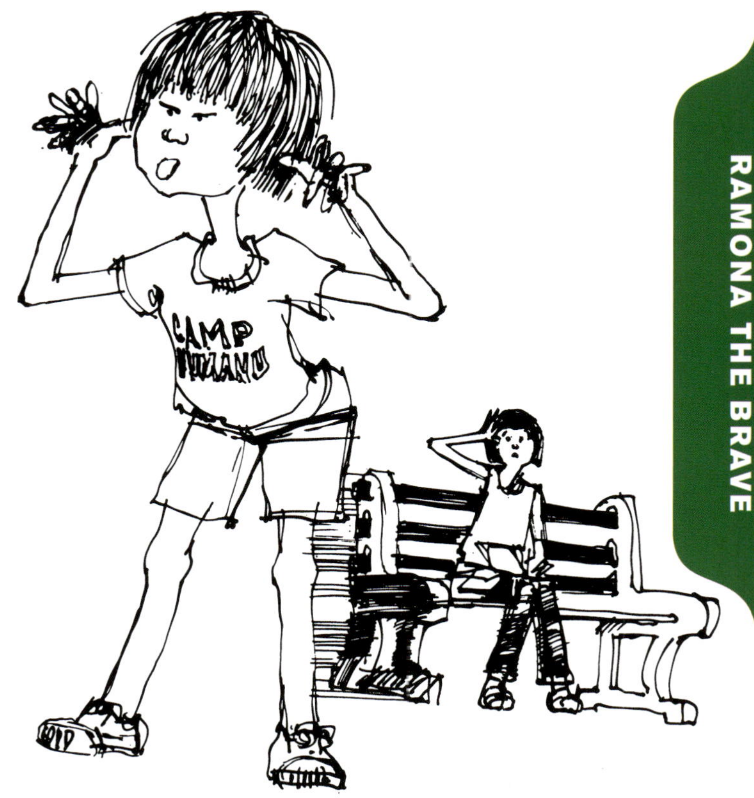

Ramona 2.0

Louis Darling died in 1970, at the age of fifty-three. Alan Tiegreen took over the job for the third book of the series, released five years later. Darling's Ramona, pictured here showing her doll Chevrolet for Show and Tell in *Ramona the Pest*, had an open face with wide-set eyes and a wide smile. When not in dungarees and bunny ears, she wore dresses, sweaters, bobby socks, and saddle shoes. Tiegreen's Ramona took on a more modern look, with an updated pageboy hairstyle, a more cartoonish face with close-set eyes and a mushroom nose, and a T-shirt and shorts or jacket and skirt.

OPPOSITE: JACQUELINE ROGERS. ABOVE: LOUIS DARLING (LEFT) AND ALAN TIEGREEN (RIGHT).

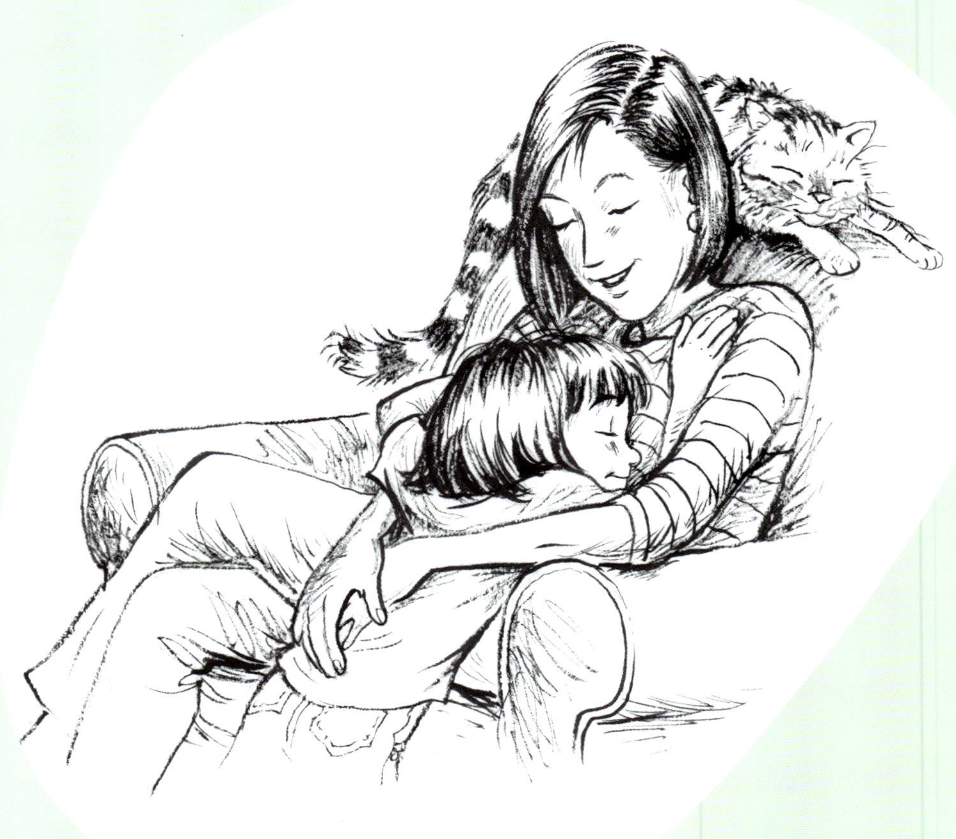

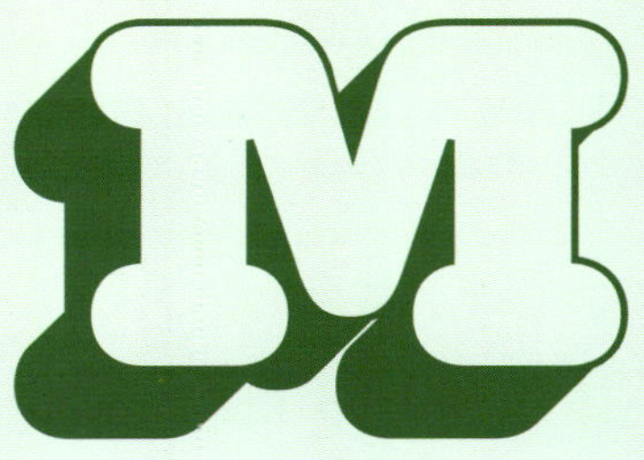

rs. Quimby smiled a different smile, exasperating and mysterious. "Sh-h-h," she said, her finger on her lips. "It's a secret, and wild horses couldn't drag it out of me."

Ramona found secrets hard to bear. "Tell me, Mama! Mama, please tell me." She threw her arms around her mother, who had a good smell of clean clothes and perfumed soap. "Please, please, please!"

Like in any good mystery, *Ramona the Brave* introduces a secret early on for the protagonist to solve. Why has Ramona's mother gotten a haircut and put on a touch of eye shadow before going on an errand this afternoon?

JACQUELINE ROGERS (ABOVE) AND TRACY DOCKRAY (OPPOSITE).

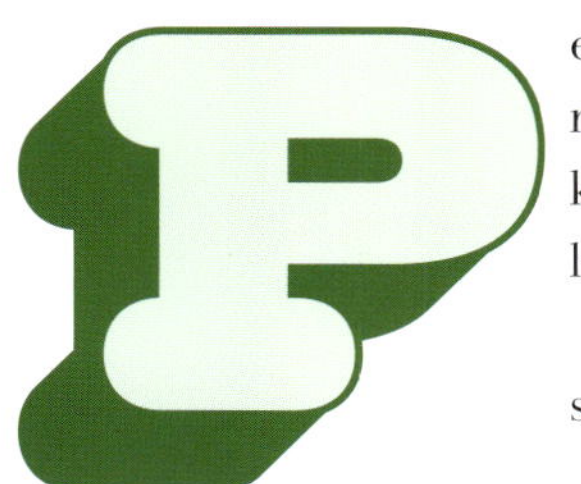

Peace between the sisters could not last. Ramona saw the broken remains of her red crayon lying in the middle of her bed.

"Who broke my crayon?" she demanded.

"You shouldn't leave your crayon on other people's beds where it can get sat on." Beezus did not even bother to look up from her book.

Ramona found this answer most annoying. "You should look where you sit," she said, "and you don't have to be so bossy."

"This is my bed." Beezus glanced at her sister. "You have your own half of the room."

"I don't have anyplace to put anything."

"Pooh," said Beezus. "You're just careless and messy."

Ramona was indignant. "I am not careless and messy!" Picky-picky woke up, leaped from Beezus's bed, and departed, tail held straight. Picky-picky often made it plain he did not care for Ramona.

"Yes, you are," said Beezus. "You don't hang up your clothes, and you leave your toys all over."

"Just because the clothes bar is easy for you to reach," said Ramona, "and you think you're too big for toys." To show her sister that she did pick up her things, she laid the pieces of her broken crayon in her drawer on top of her underwear. She had lost interest in crayoning. She did not want to color boots with the rough ends of a broken crayon.

"Besides," said Beezus, who did not like to be interrupted when she was deep in a good book, "you're a pest."

Pest was a fighting word to Ramona, because it was unfair. She was not a pest, at least not all the time. She was only littler than anyone else in the family, and no matter how hard she tried, she could not catch up. "Don't you call me a pest," she shouted, "or I'll tell Mama you have a lipstick hidden in your drawer."

Beezus finally laid down her book. "Ramona Geraldine Quimby!" Her voice and manner were fierce. "You're nothing but a snoop and a tattletale!"

Ramona had gone too far. "I wasn't snooping. I was looking for a safety pin," she explained, adding, as if she were a very good girl, "and anyway I haven't told Mama yet."

Beezus gave her sister a look of disgust. "Ramona, grow up!"

Ramona lost all patience. "Can't you see I'm trying?" she yelled at the top of her voice.

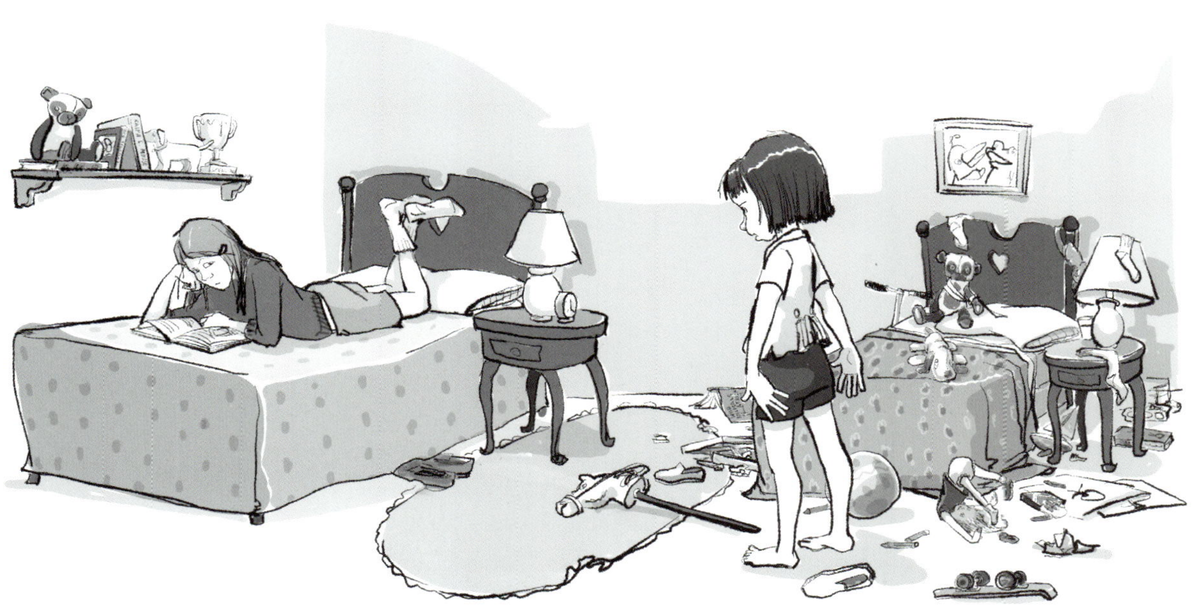

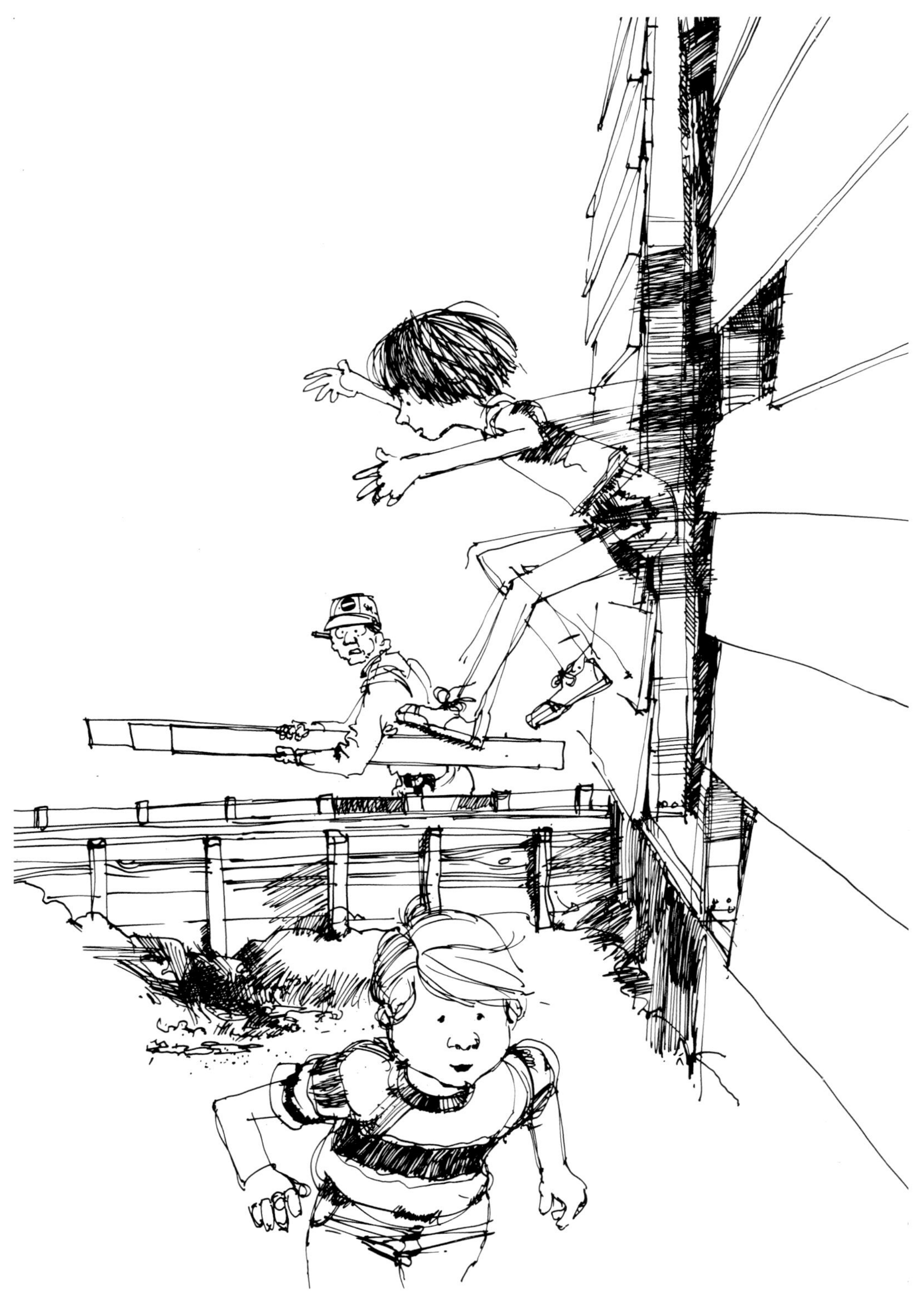

Construction has begun, and in this scene Ramona and Howie jump through the hole in the house that will eventually lead to Ramona's new bedroom. The illustrators portray this moment of joyful flight from different angles. Tiegreen adds a sense of danger by making the distance from the ground to the hole nearly as high as Howie is tall and placing a dismayed contractor, mouth agape, in the background. Rogers uses perspective to make the readers feel as though they are following right behind the two daring first-graders, about to jump without knowing how far they'll fall.

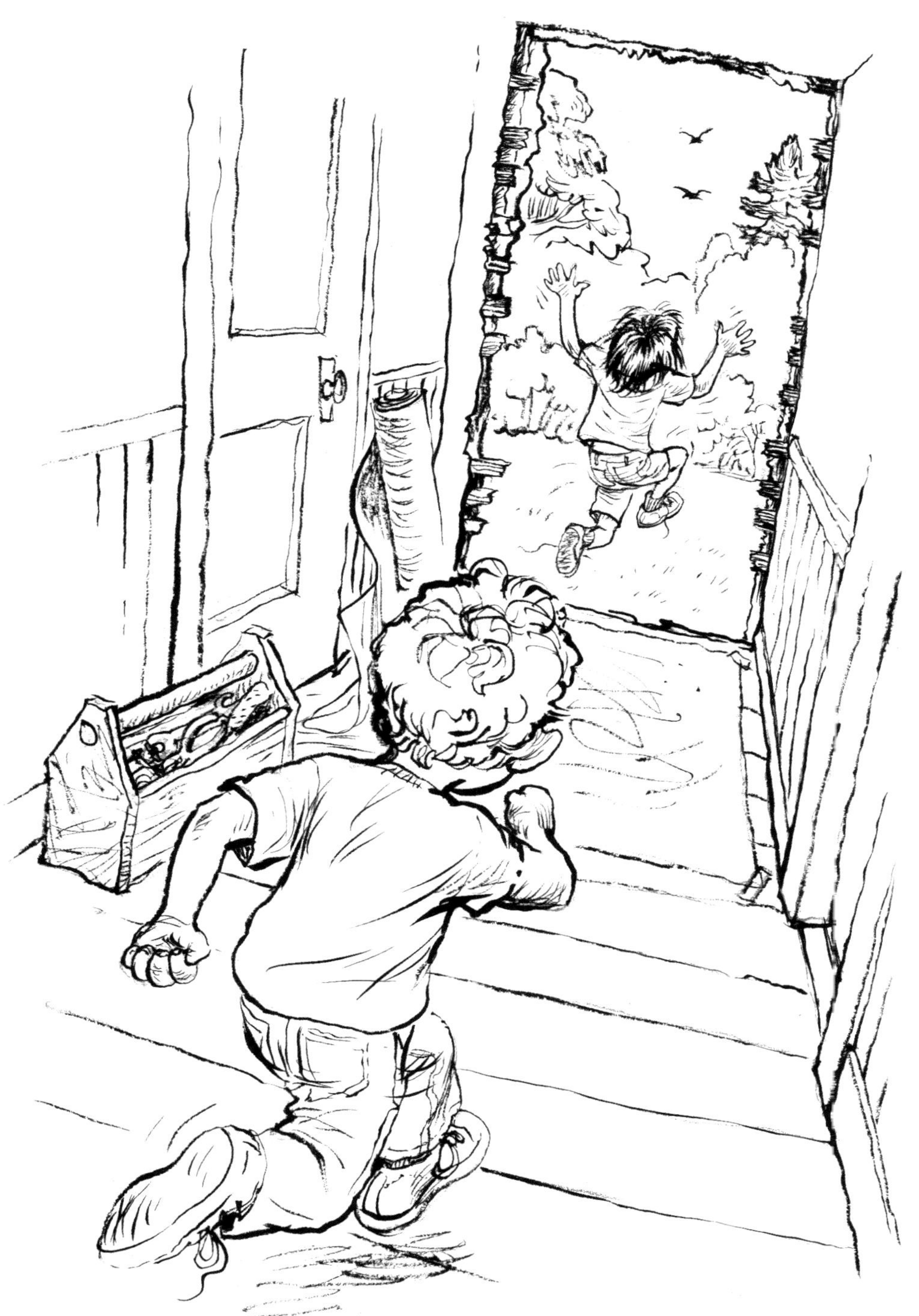

ALAN TIEGREEN (OPPOSITE) AND JACQUELINE ROGERS (ABOVE).

Here it was, the first half of the first morning of the first day of school, and already the first grade was spoiled for her.

Ramona tells the class that some men came and chopped a great big hole in her house, but her classmates don't believe her. Howie, the forlorn boy seated farthest to the right, has not backed up her story, due to a technicality—later he informs her that they didn't "chop a hole in her house," they pried siding off the house with a crowbar. Ramona, determined to be the grown-up first-grader that she is, doesn't kick Howie, instead directing her frustration at the wall.

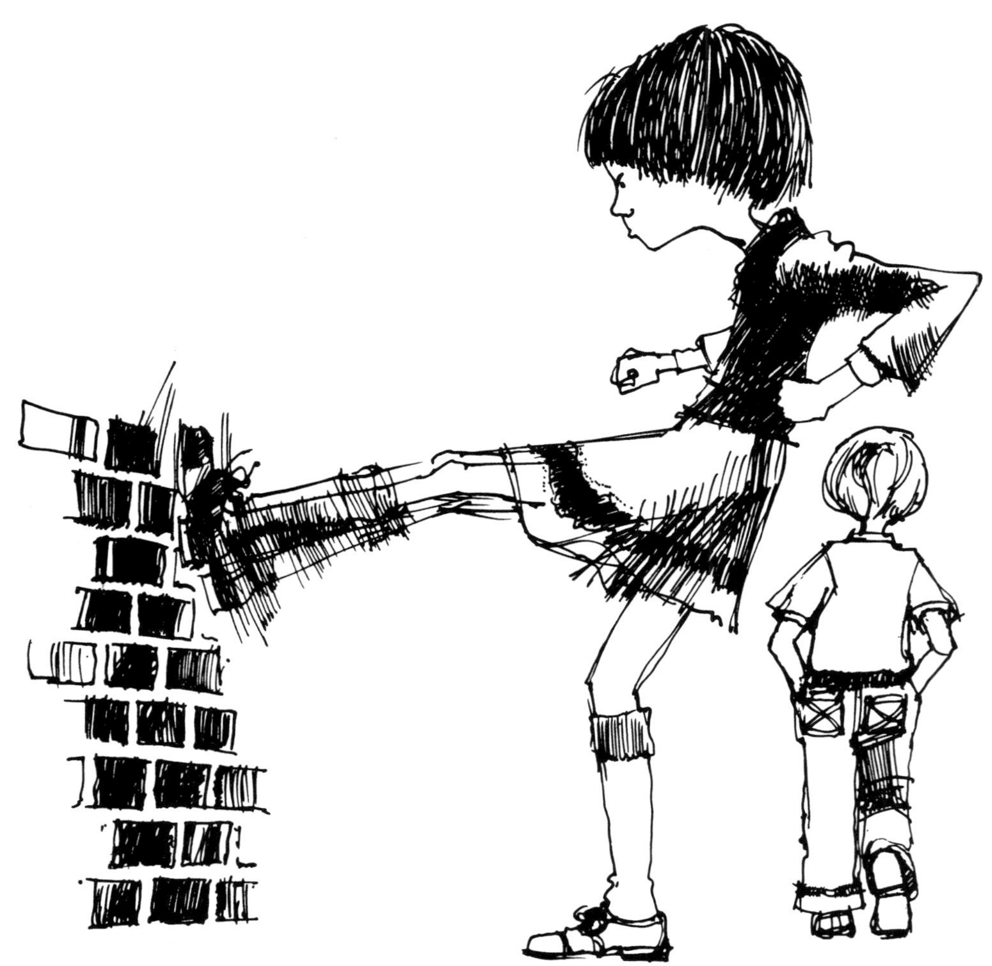

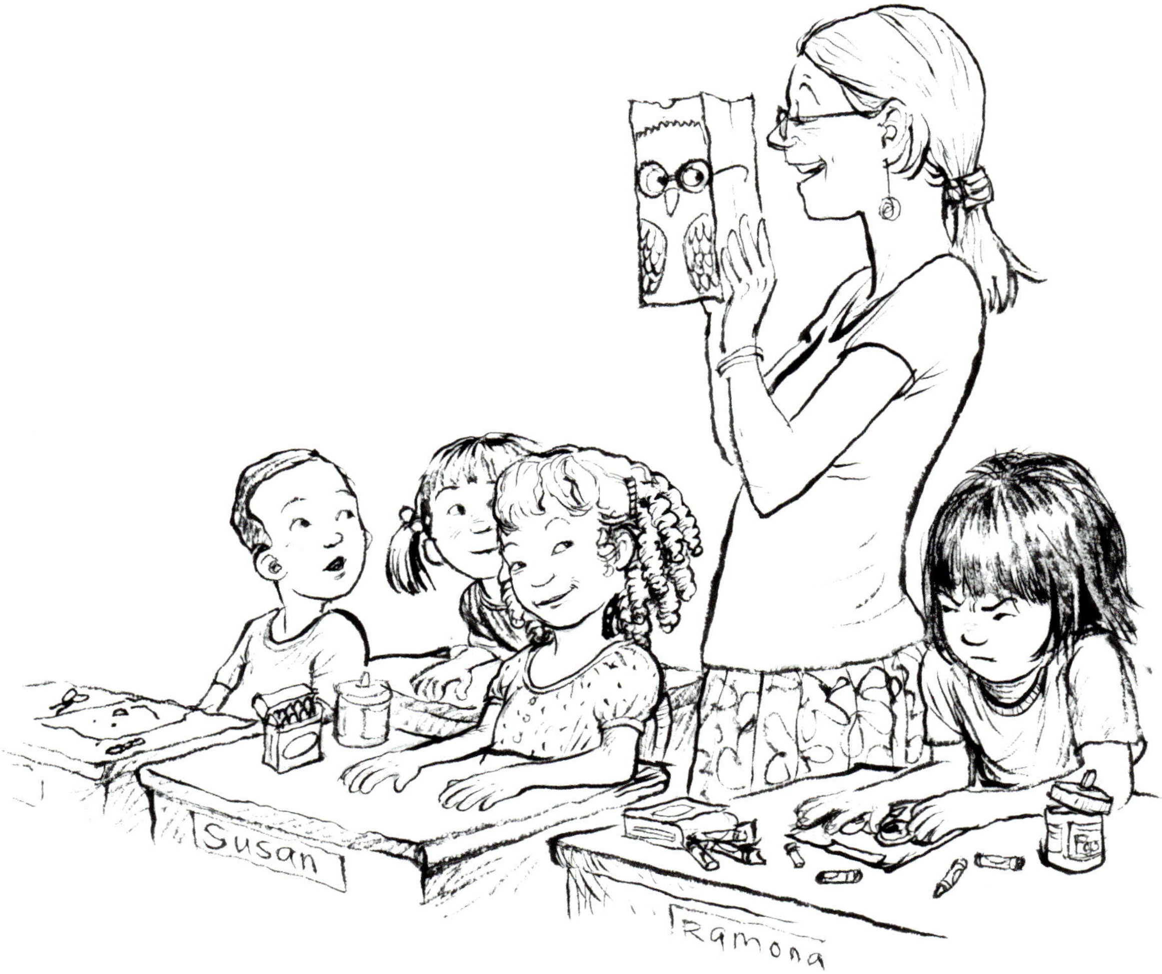

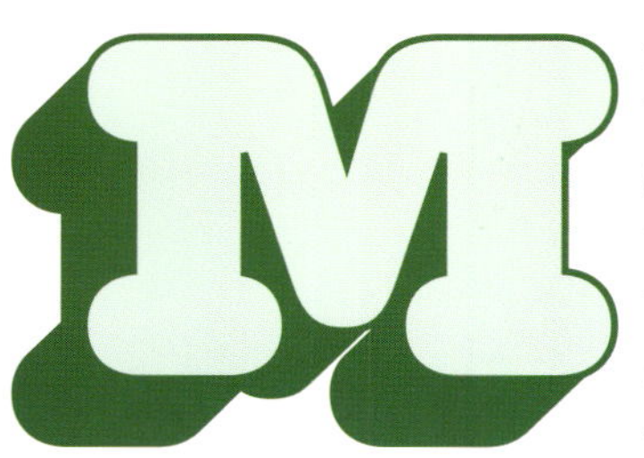

Mrs. Griggs paused between Ramona's and Susan's desks. Ramona bent over her owl, because she wanted to surprise Mrs. Griggs when it was finished. "What a wise old owl Susan has made!" Mrs. Griggs held up Susan's owl for the class to see while Susan tried to look modest and pleased at the same time. Ramona was furious. Susan's owl had wings and feathers exactly like her owl. Susan had peeked! Susan had copied! She scowled at Susan and thought, Copy-cat, copycat! She longed to tell Mrs. Griggs that Susan had copied, but she knew what the answer would be. "Ramona, nobody likes a tattletale."

ALAN TIEGREEN (OPPOSITE) AND JACQUELINE ROGERS (ABOVE).

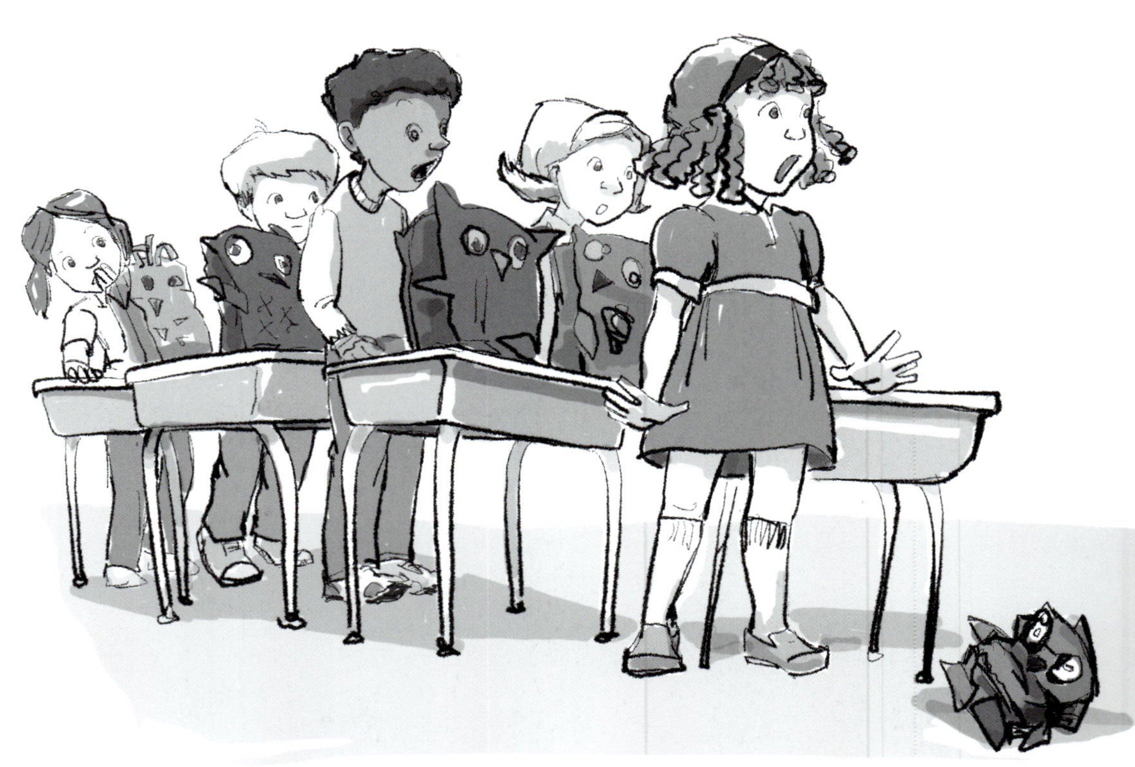

Ramona scrunches Susan's owl.
Even a brave girl can only take so much.

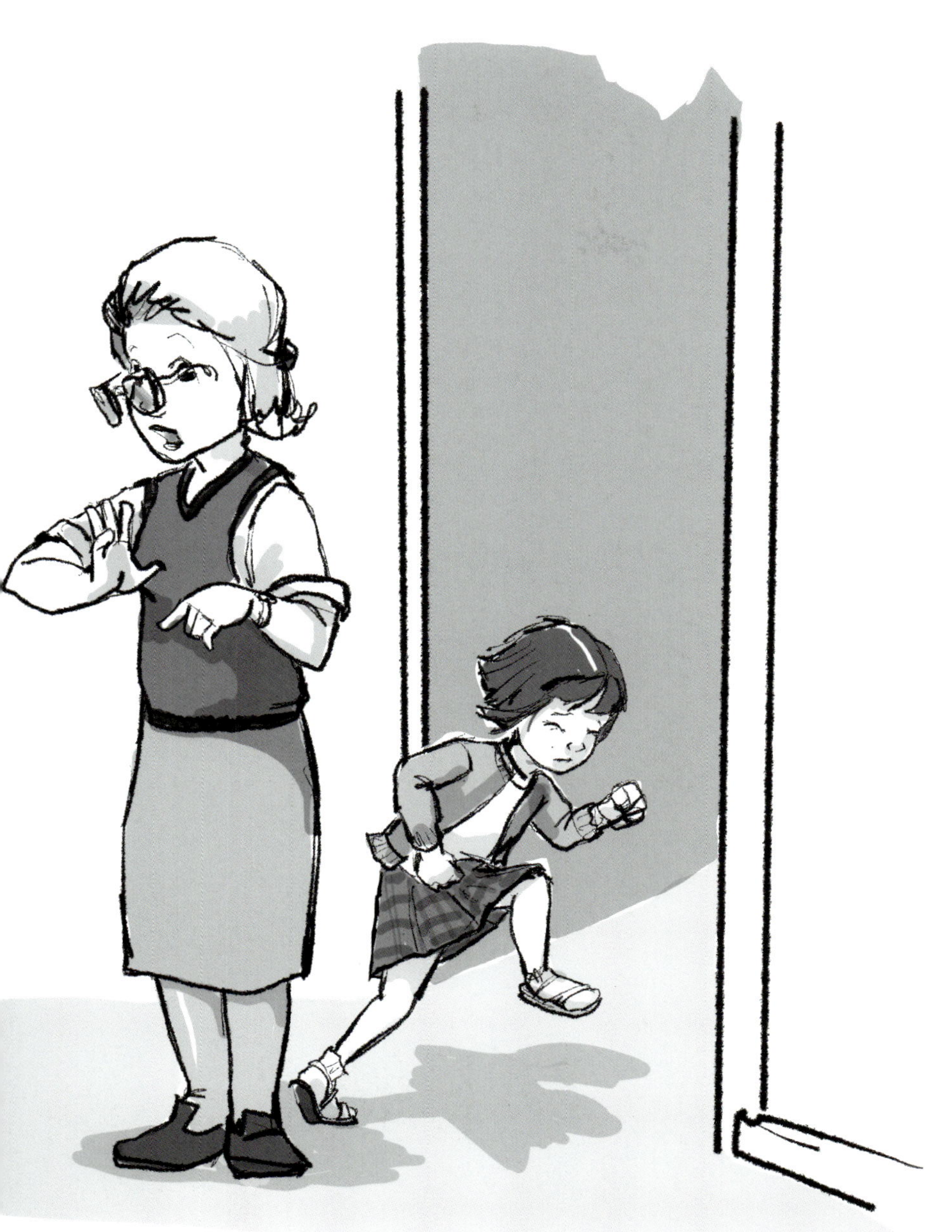

While Mr. and Mrs. Quimby are at Parents' Night at Glenwood School, Ramona reckons with her conscience and the fear that they'll be disappointed in her when they find out she scrunched Susan's owl. Hoping to get ahead of the scandal as well as impress her parents, she writes this note. This is the first image of Ramona's writing beyond her name.

TRACY DOCKRAY (ABOVE) AND JACQUELINE ROGERS (RIGHT).

Come here Moth
er. Come here
to me.

Ramona apologizes.

Just as expected, Mrs. Griggs ratted out Ramona. Even worse, the teacher insists that Ramona get up in front of the class to say she's sorry to Susan. Tiegreen zooms in on Ramona, more dressed up than usual and with crossed ankles and hands clasped behind her back in a gesture of abashment. Dockray and Rogers both chose to include the class, perhaps to emphasize the publicness of this humiliation. Suffice it to say, Susan and Ramona are now mortal enemies.

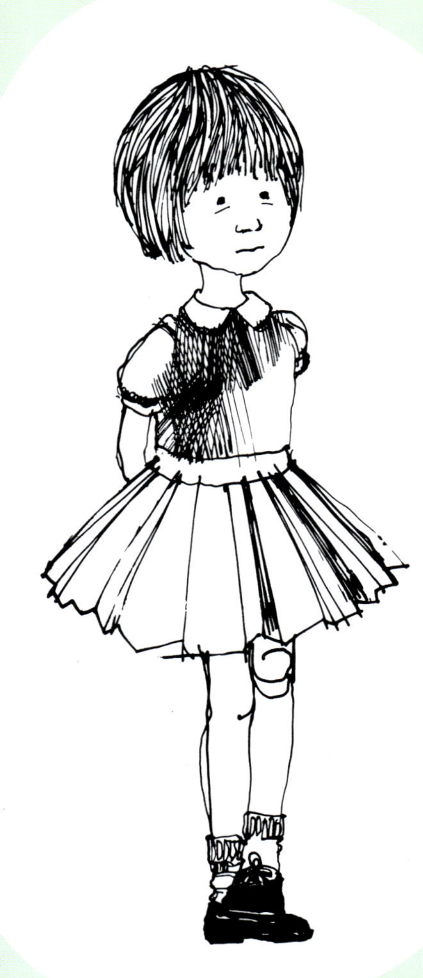

ABOVE: ALAN TIEGREEN. OPPOSITE: TRACY DOCKRAY (TOP) AND JACQUELINE ROGERS (BOTTOM).

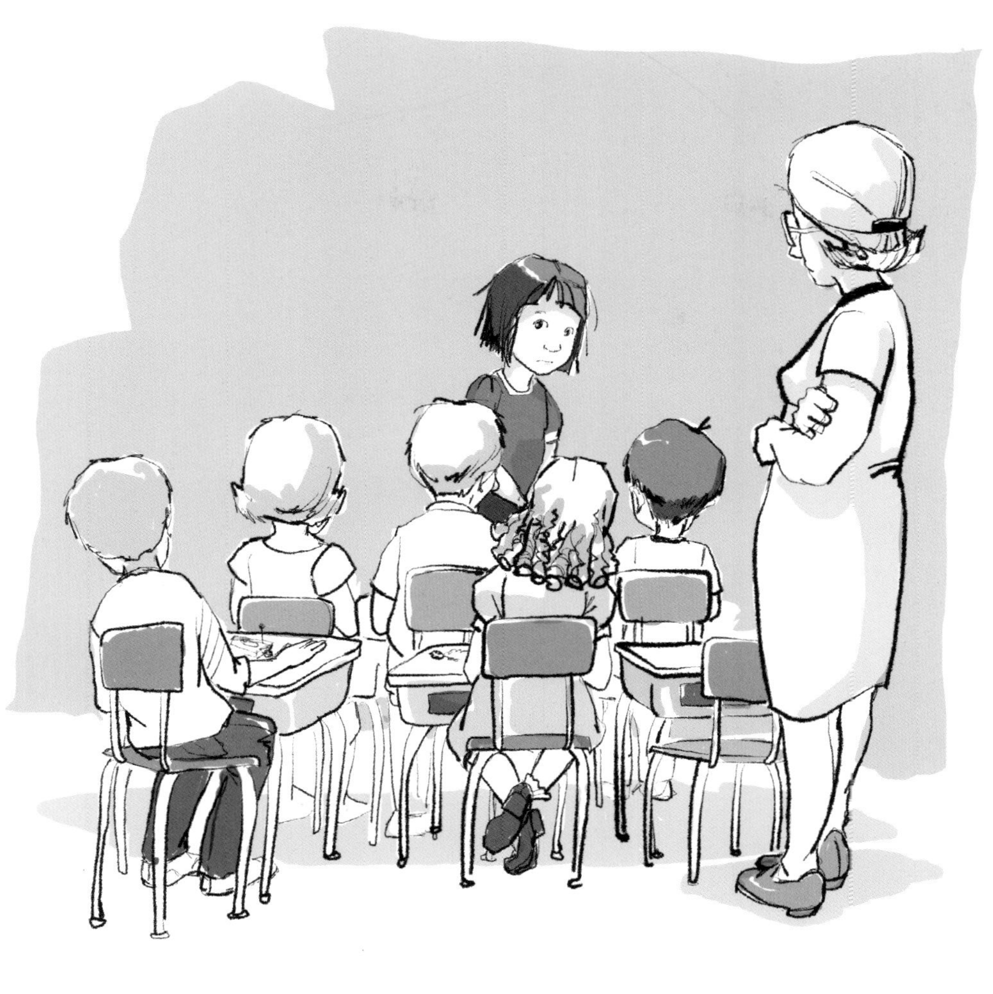

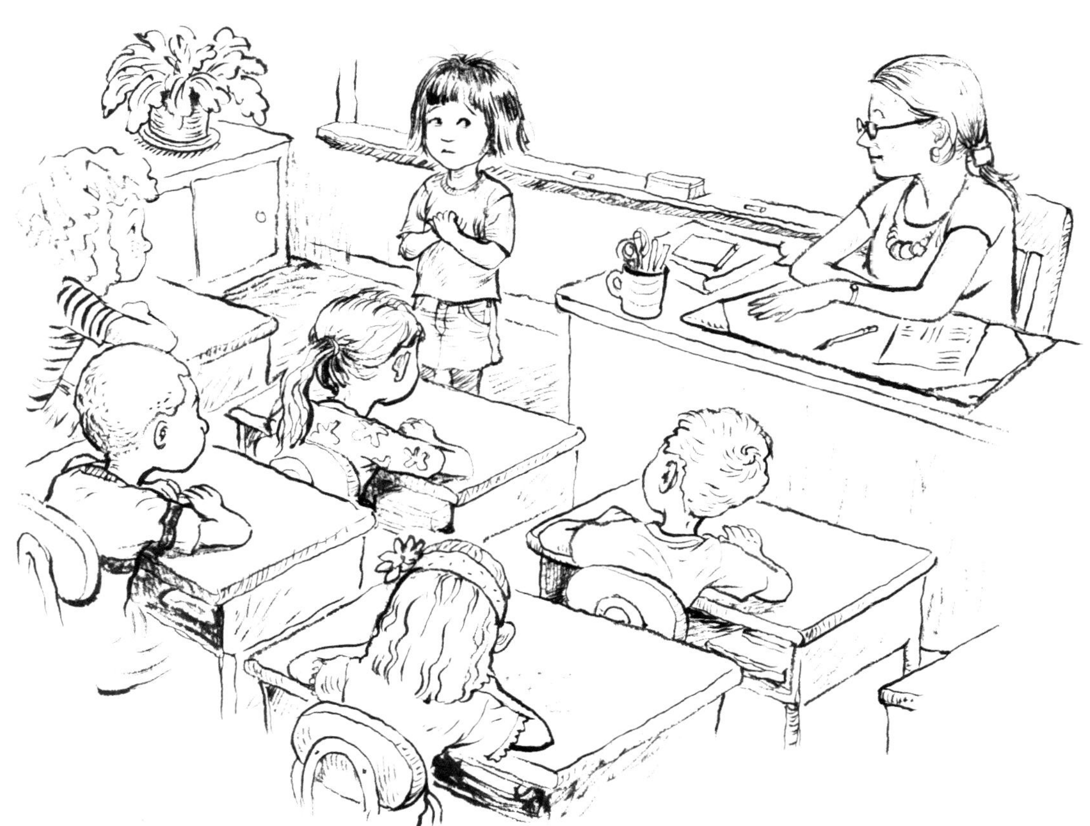

The moment Ramona dreaded had come. There was no one awake to protect her. Ramona tried to lie as flat and as still as a paper doll so that Something slithering under the curtains and slinking around the walls would not know she was there. She kept her eyes wide open. She longed for her father to come home; she was determined to stay awake until morning.

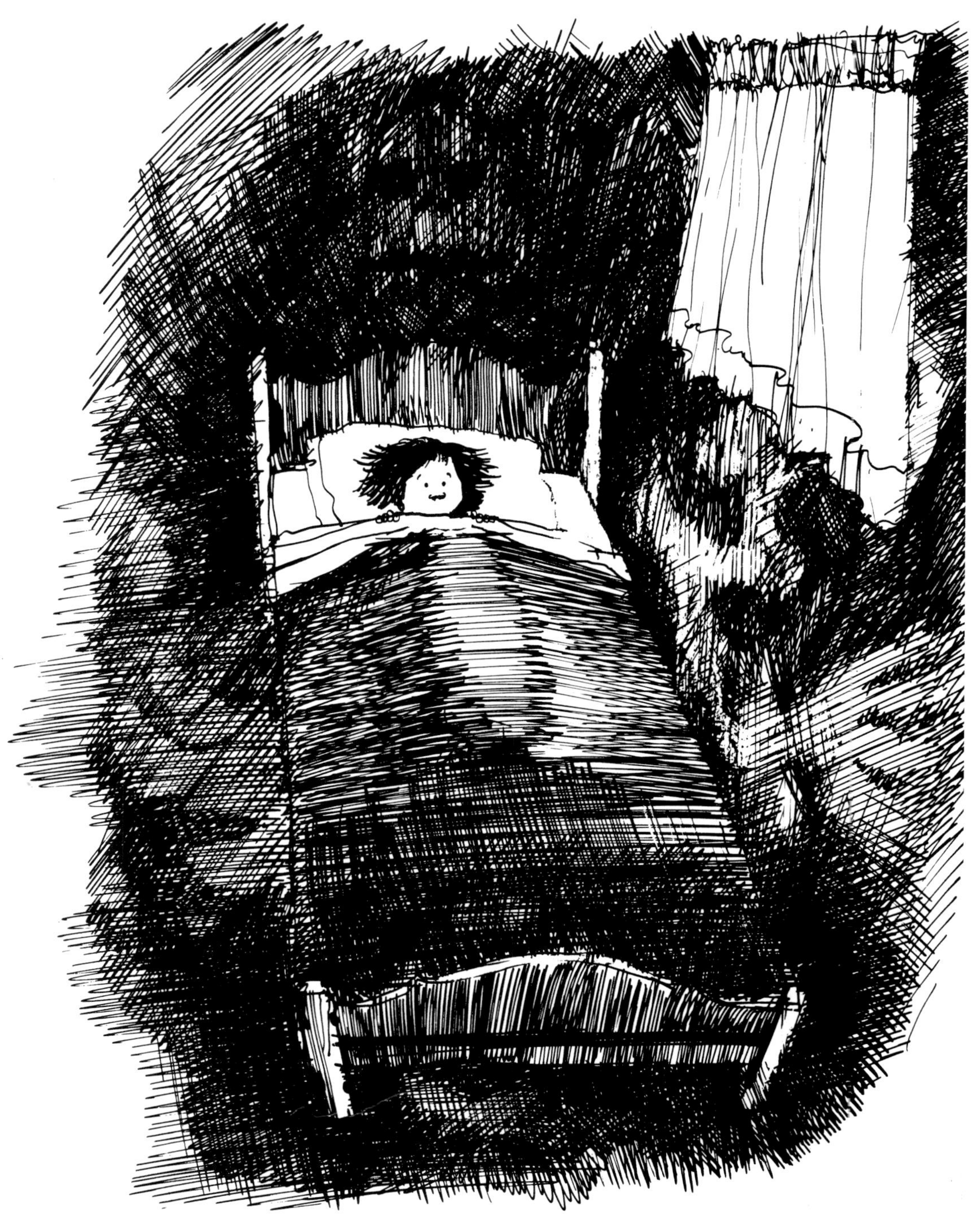

Her days at school are hard enough, but now that Ramona has her own room—the very room that she and Beezus dreamt of and fought over—her nights are even harder. With careful crosshatching, Tiegreen has captured the lonely, fearsome darkness. Is that a ghostly face looming over the bed, and terrible hands reaching out to grab her?

ALAN TIEGREEN

Ramona takes a moment to collect herself.

Still reeling from the night before, Ramona takes momentary refuge at the foot of the stairs leading up to the upper grades. Tiegreen's version, with a tiny Ramona huddled in the bottom right-hand corner of a seemingly miles-long stairway, emphasizes the girl's exhaustion and desperation. Rogers chose to depict the scene a few moments later, when her sister's beloved seventh-grade teacher, Mr. Cardoza, manages to cheer her up.

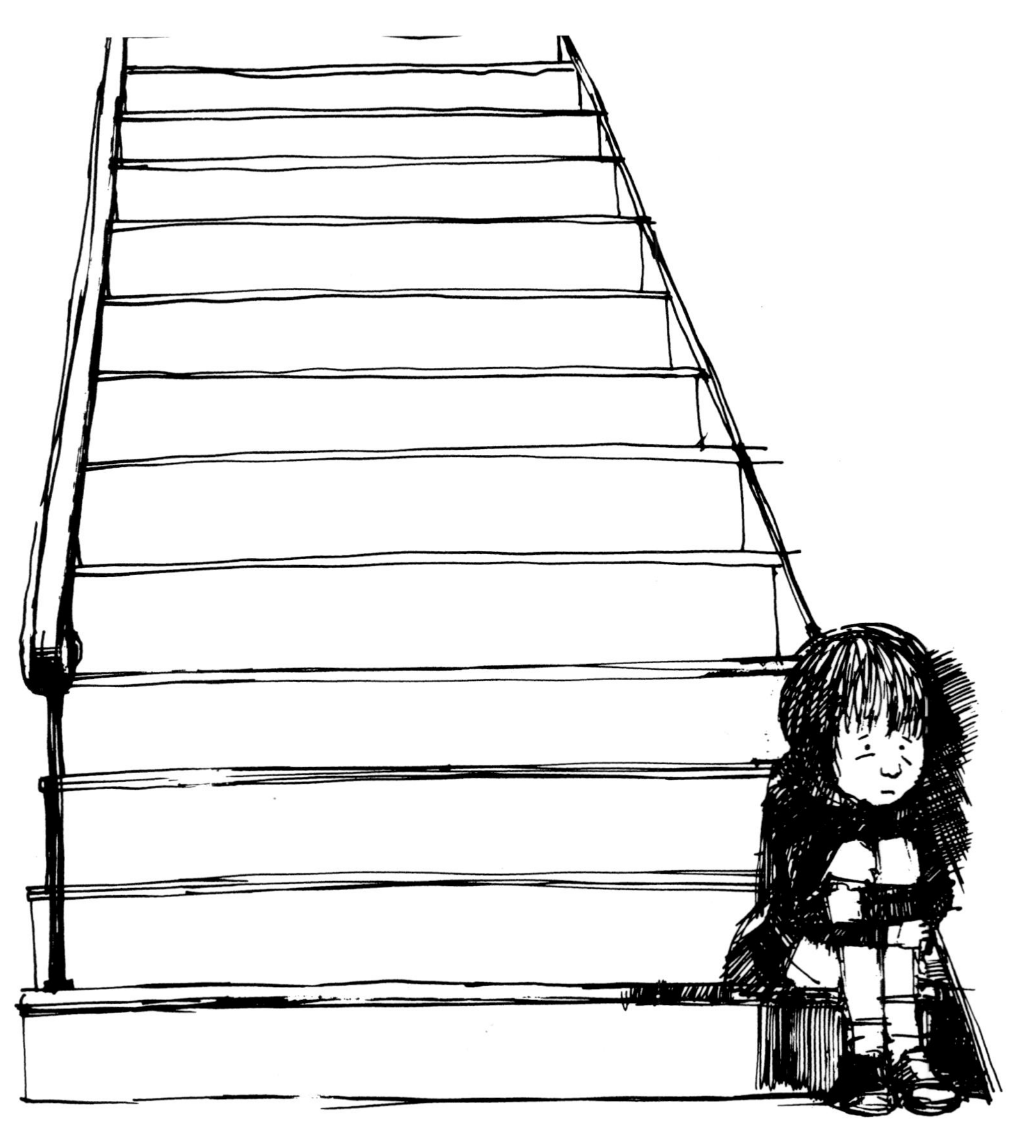

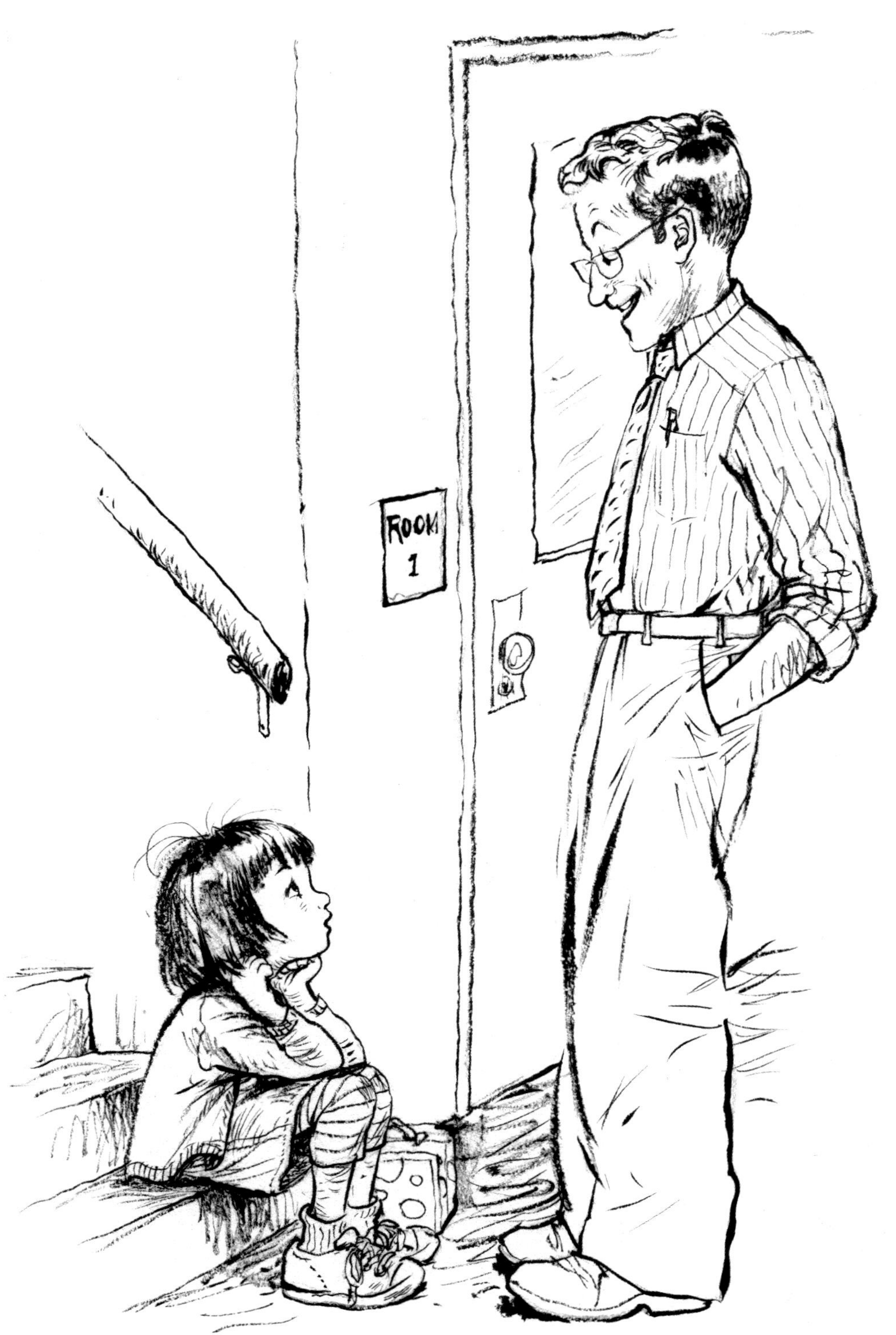

ALAN TIEGREEN (OPPOSITE) AND JACQUELINE ROGERS (ABOVE).

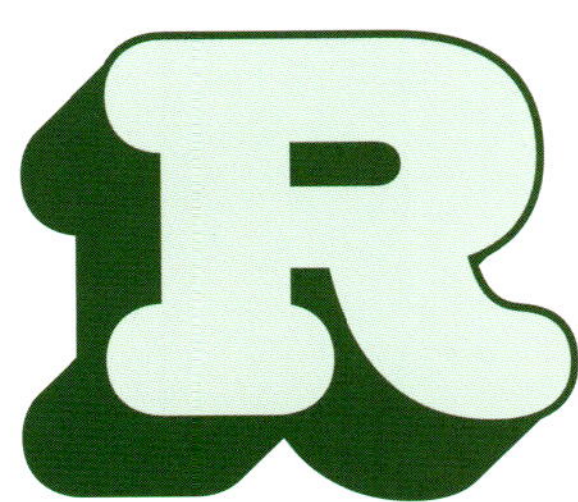amona had had enough. She had been miserable the whole first grade, and she no longer cared what happened. She wanted to do something bad. She wanted to do something terrible that would shock her whole family, something that would make them sit up and take notice. "I'm going to say a bad word!" she shouted with a stamp of her foot.

That silenced her family. Picky-picky stopped washing and left the room. Mr. Quimby looked surprised and—how could he be so disloyal?—a little amused. This made Ramona even angrier. Beezus looked interested and curious. After a moment Mrs. Quimby said quietly, "Go ahead, Ramona, and say the bad word if it will make you feel any better."

Ramona clenched her fists and took a deep breath. "Guts!" she yelled. "Guts! Guts! Guts!" There. That should show them.

Unfortunately, Ramona's family was not shocked and horrified as Ramona had expected. They laughed. All three of them laughed. They tried to hide it, but they laughed.

"It isn't funny!" shouted Ramona. "Don't you dare laugh at me!" Bursting into tears, she threw herself facedown on the couch. She kicked and she pounded the cushions with her fists. Everyone was against her. Nobody liked her. Even the cat did not like her. The room was silent, and Ramona had the satisfaction of knowing she had stopped their laughing. She heard responsible old Beezus go to her room to do her responsible old homework. Her parents continued to sit in silence, but Ramona was past caring what anyone did. She cried harder than she ever had cried in her life. She cried until she was limp and exhausted.

Then Ramona felt her mother's hand on her back. "Ramona," she said gently, "what are we going to do with you?"

With red eyes, a swollen face, and a streaming nose, Ramona sat up and glared at her mother. "Love me!"

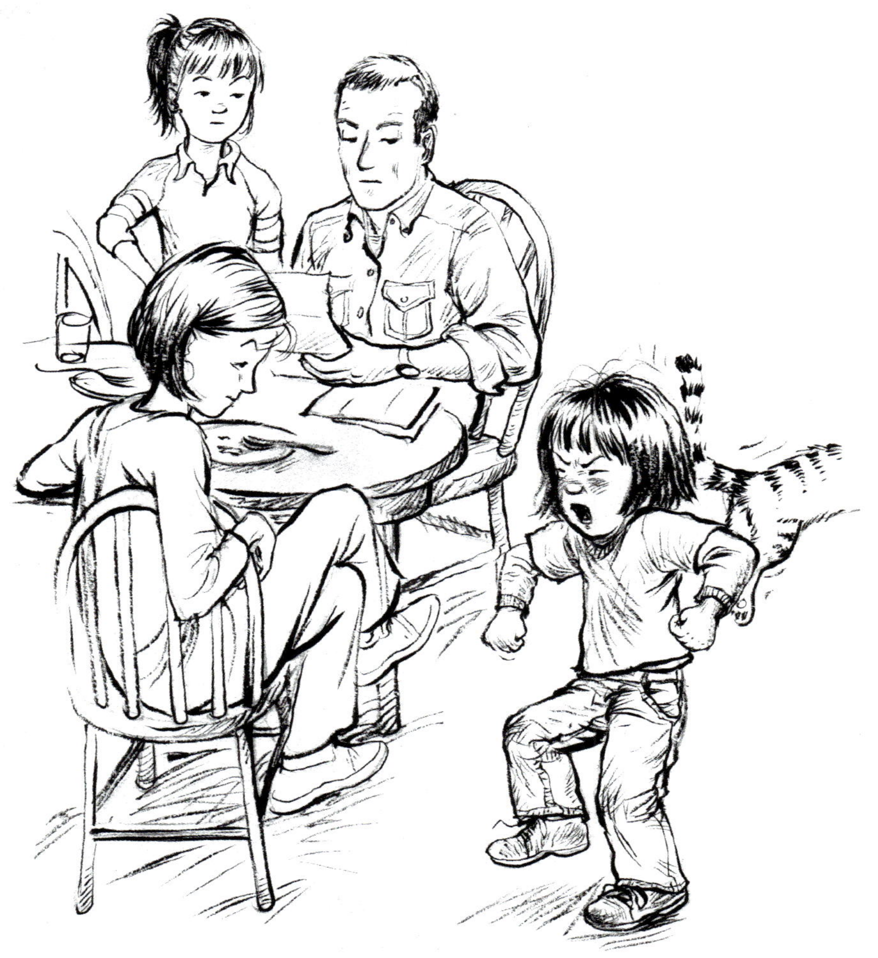

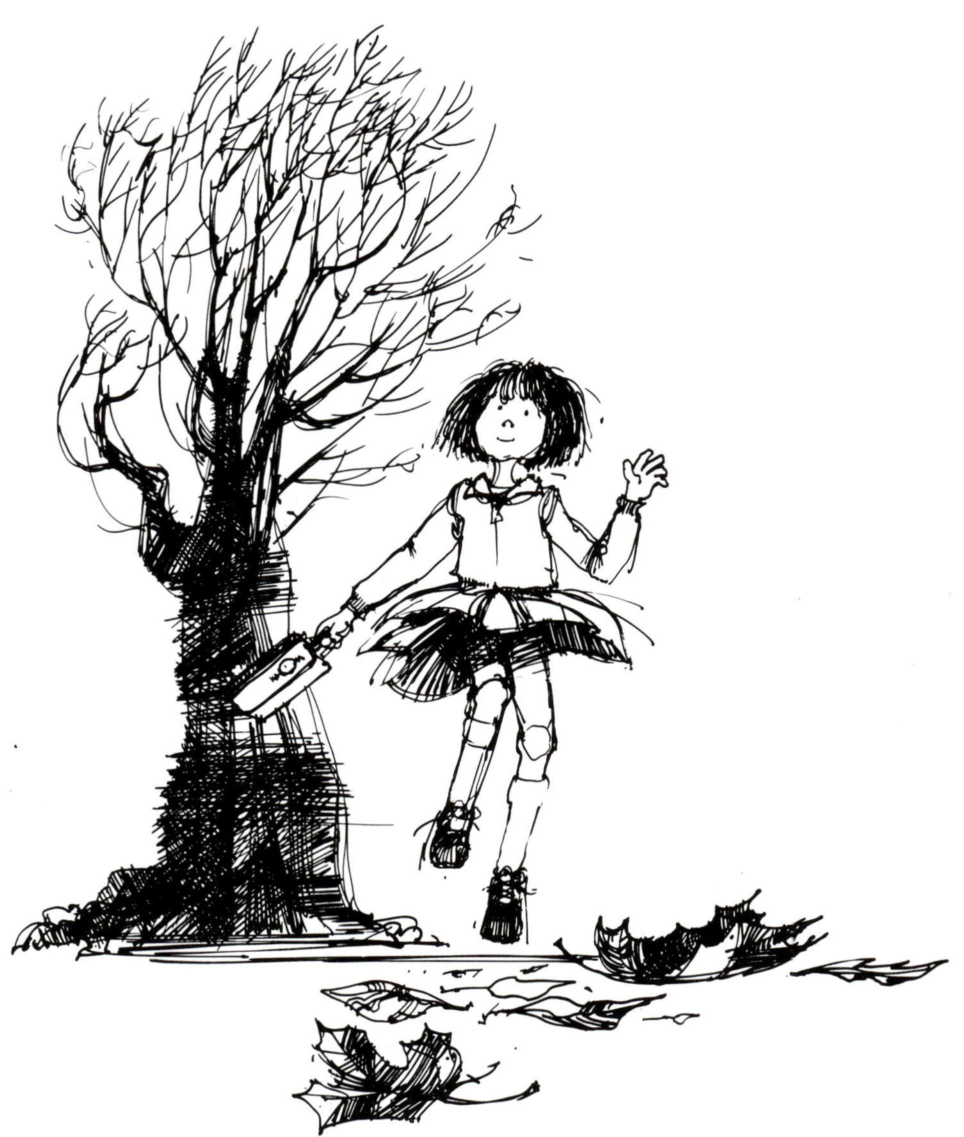

The big feelings of the previous evenings have reached their peak and, due to the curative powers of good parenting and a good cry, dissipated. Once again, Ramona is her father's spunky girl, so filled with spirit and pluck that she is inspired to take a new route to school. Tiegreen faces the frame head-on, with Ramona mid-skip, a bare-limbed tree in the background and a few scattered autumn leaves in the foreground.

JACQUELINE ROGERS (OPPOSITE) AND ALAN TIEGREEN (ABOVE).

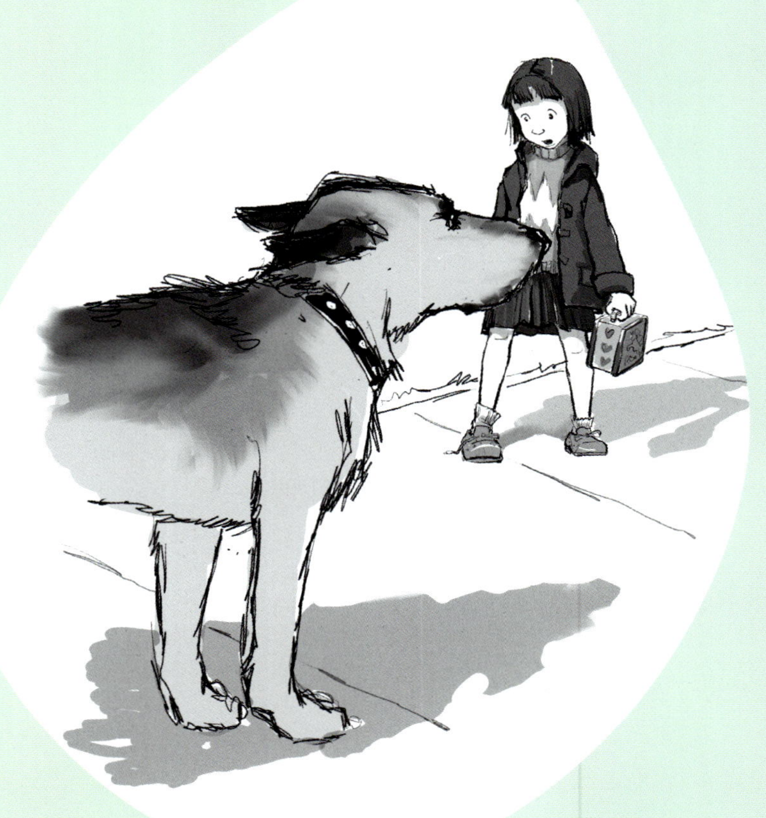

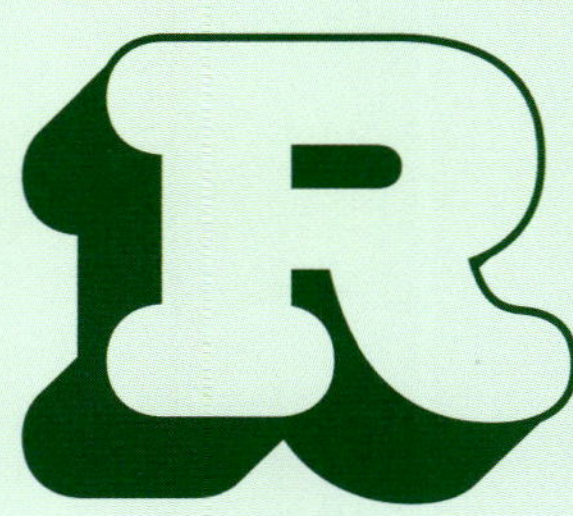

amona turned the second corner, and as she hippity-hopped down the unfamiliar street past three white houses and a tan stucco house, she enjoyed a feeling of freedom and adventure. Then as she passed a gray shingle house in the middle of the block, a large German shepherd dog, license tags jingling, darted down the driveway toward her. Terrified, Ramona stood rooted to the sidewalk. She felt as if her bad dream had come true. The grass was green, the sky was blue. She could not move; she could not scream.

Each of the illustrators again chose a slightly different angle from which to catch this frightening moment. In Dockray's illustration, we see Ramona almost from the dog's point of view, while Rogers's depicts the dog's approach and Ramona standing her ground. Tiegreen's version captures the scene a few moments later, when Ramona has removed her shoe to throw in case of attack. Ultimately, the dog decides he'd rather gnaw on her brown oxford than on her.

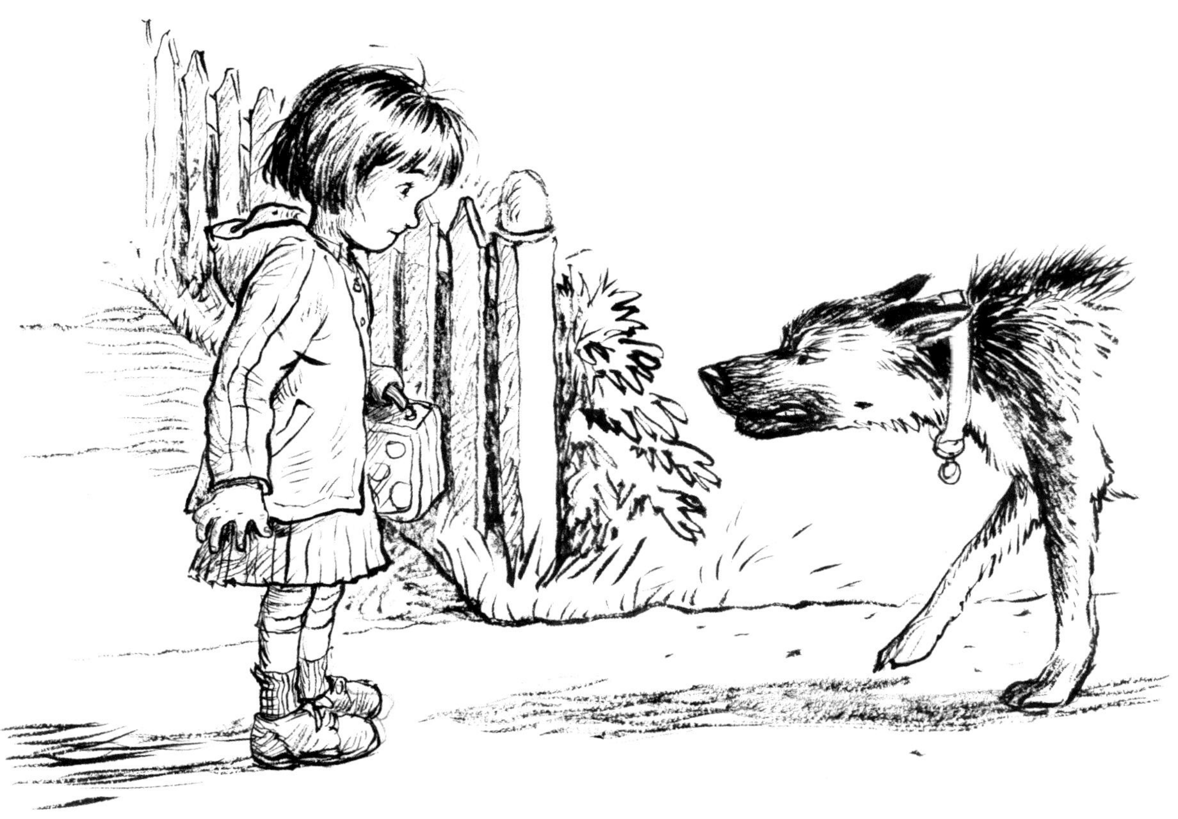

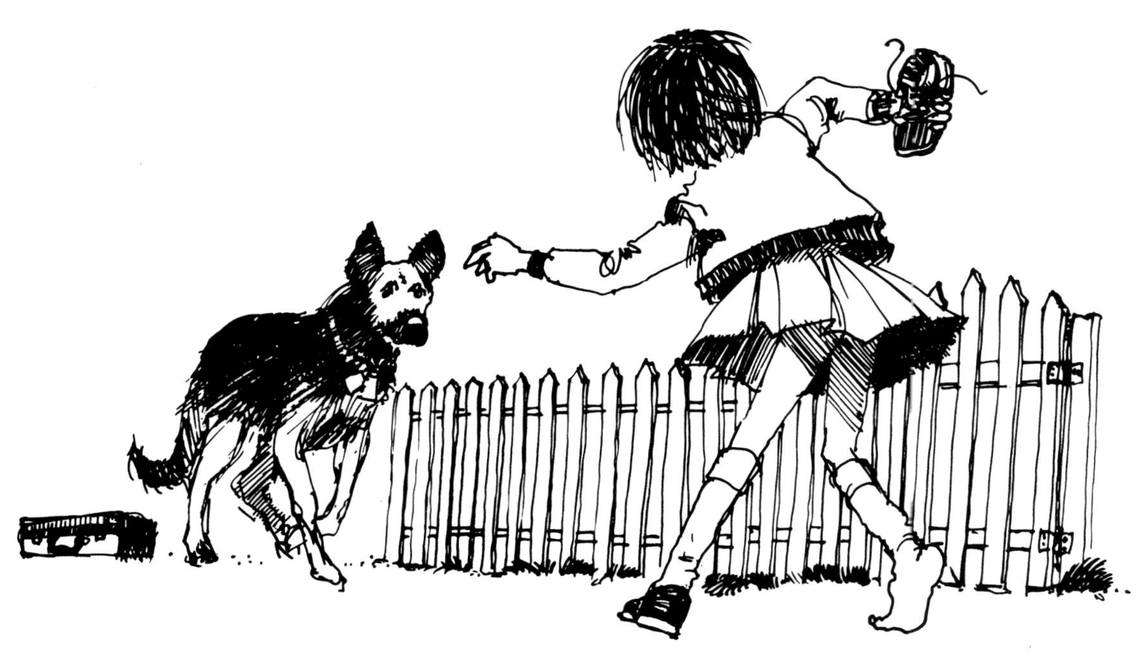

OPPOSITE: TRACY DOCKRAY. ABOVE: JACQUELINE ROGERS (TOP) AND ALAN TIEGREEN (BOTTOM).

Ramona refused to let her courage fail her. She remembered her manners and asked, "May I please borrow your stapler? I can use it right here in the hall, and it will only take a minute."

Finally, after much anticipation, Mrs. Griggs calls on Ramona to lead the flag salute. Only now just so happens to be the worst possible time, given that our heroine only has one shoe. And when the teacher notices, she tells her to borrow an ugly old brown boot from the cloakroom. Yuck! Ramona will have to get creative to find a better solution.

Rather than wear some dumb old boot, Ramona decides to make a shoe out of paper towels. Mr. Cardoza had gained Ramona's trust just as he'd gained Beezus's, and so it is to his classroom she goes when looking for a stapler to complete the project. See a perplexed Beezus in the background.

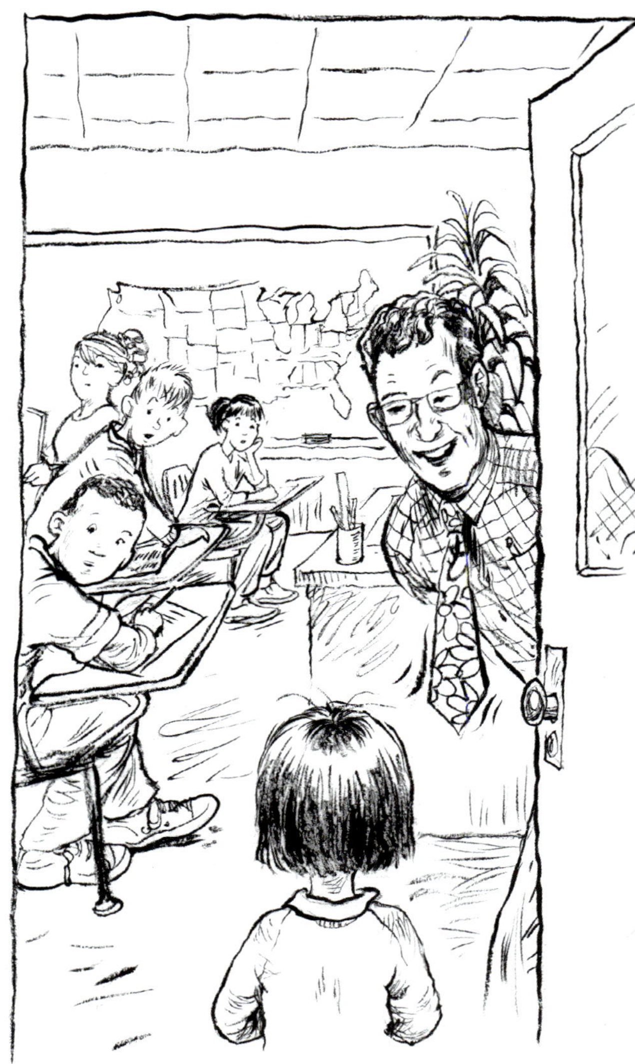

JACQUELINE ROGERS (RIGHT) AND TRACY DOCKRAY (OPPOSITE).

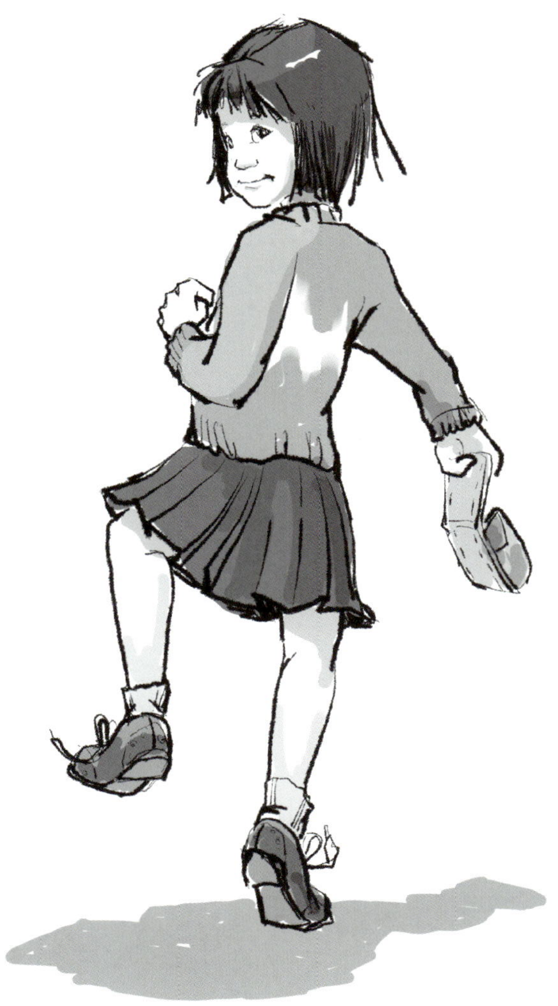

Ramona is the bravest girl in the first grade.

And so Ramona gets her groove back. In less than twenty-four hours, she has said a bad word ("guts"), had a much-needed row with her parents, scared off a mean dog, ventured up the stairs to the big kids' classrooms and asked Mr. Cardoza for a stapler, and built herself a neat paper shoe. Now she's won not just the respect of her teacher, the school secretary, and her peers, but the self-respect she'd nearly lost. Ramona is indeed brave!

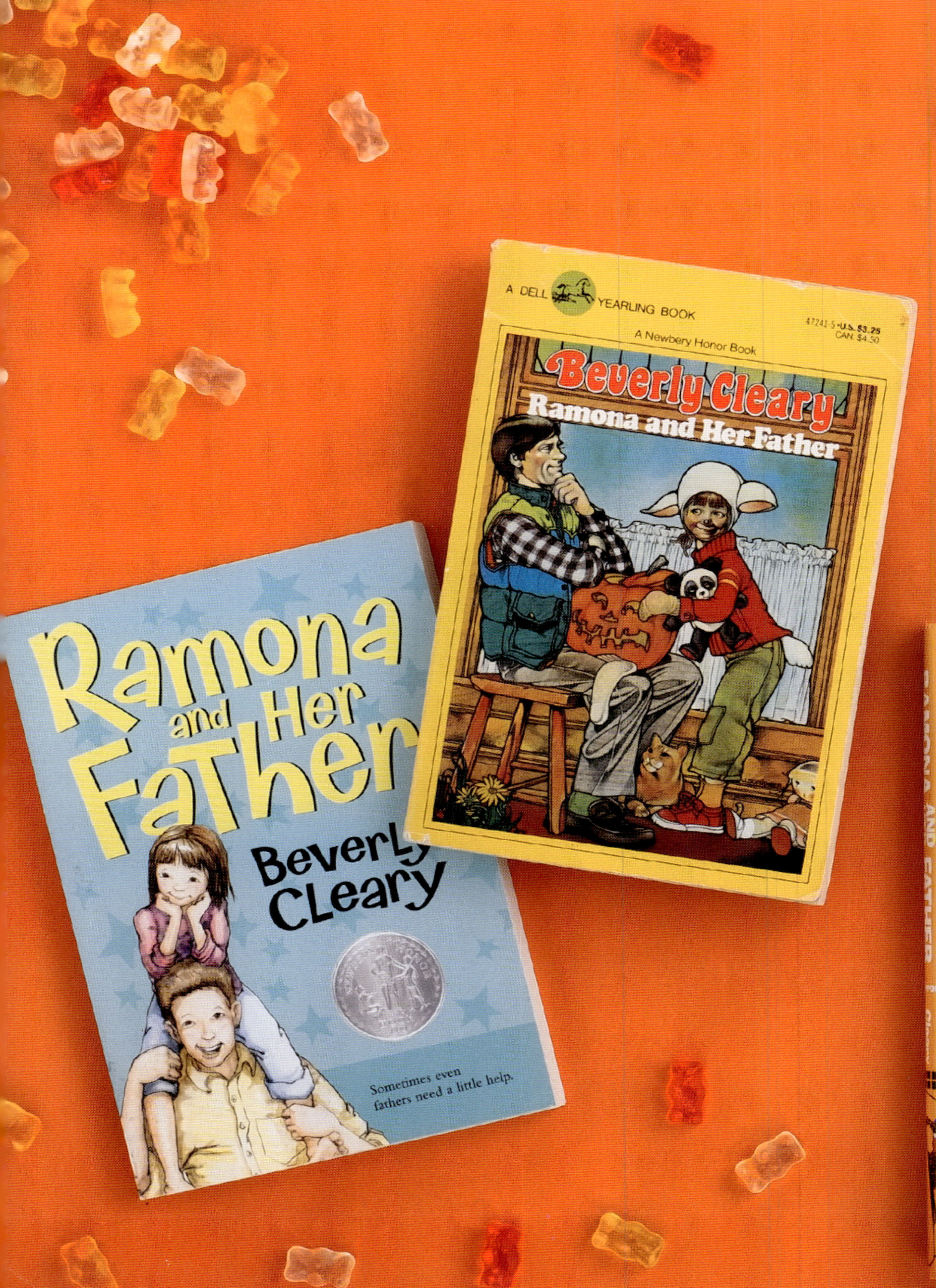
Ramona and Her Father
Beverly Cleary
Sometimes even fathers need a little help.
A DELL YEARLING BOOK
47241-5 U.S. $3.25
CAN. $4.50
A Newbery Honor Book
Beverly Cleary
Ramona and Her Father

Ramona and Her Father

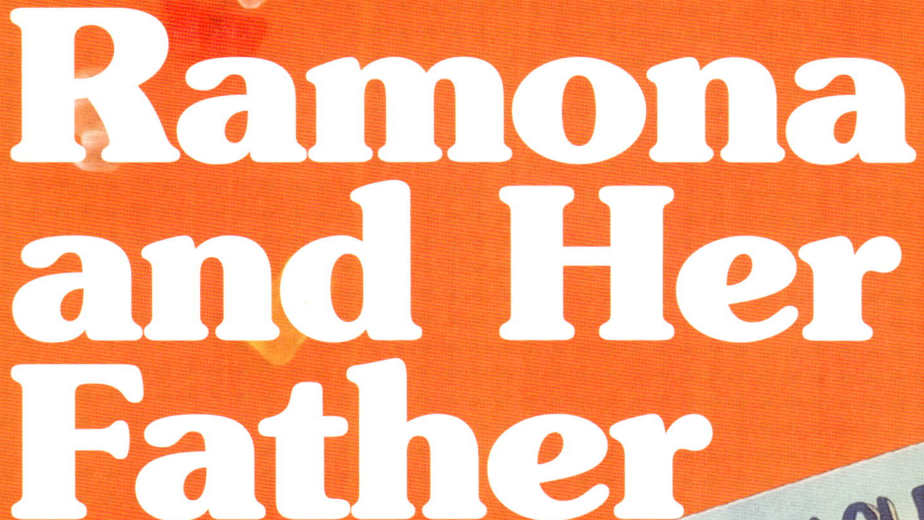

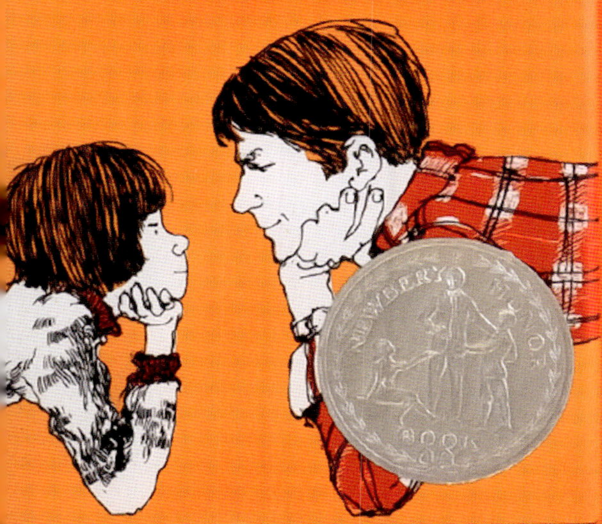

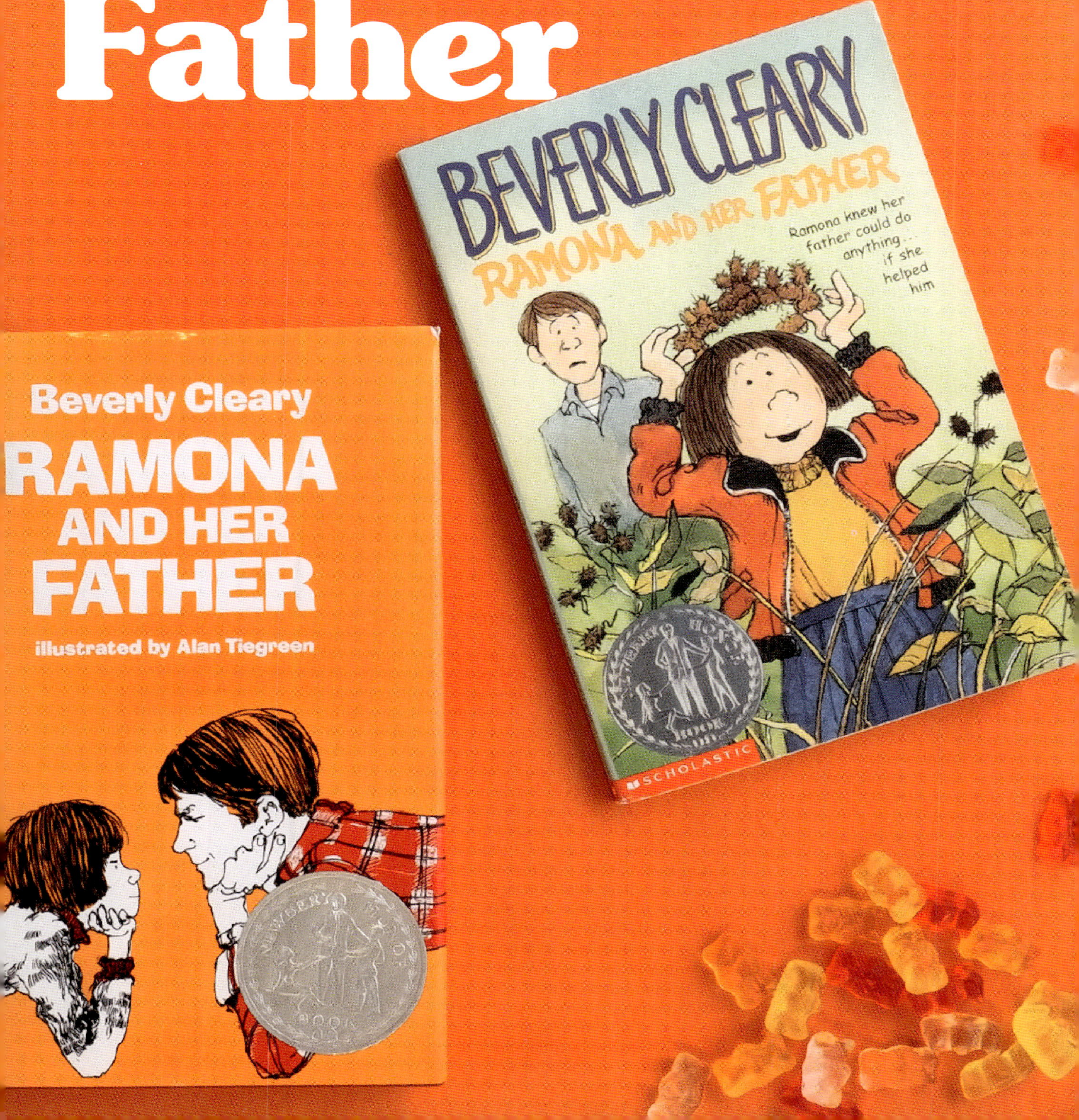

Chapter Four

Ramona and Her Father

Ramona wished she had a million dollars so her father would be fun again.

In 1977, when *Ramona and Her Father* was published, the United States was reeling from the recessions of the early 1970s and the continued stagflation that kept both prices and unemployment rising. Beverly Cleary, as a child of the Great Depression, knew all too well the anxiety associated with familial financial strain, so perhaps she was especially qualified to write for all those readers whose parents were struggling to make ends meet.

Though the working-class Quimbys have always been frugal, in this book they must "scrimp and pinch" even more when Mr. Quimby loses his job. For the first time, Ramona, now in second grade, becomes aware of and affected by her parents' worry and the larger forces at play, forces against which she is helpless.

With little to do beyond waiting by the phone, Mr. Quimby takes up smoking with a vengeance. This book just so happened to coincide with the expansion of the anti-smoking movement in the United States. The World Health Organization took a public position against smoking in the 1970s; in 1971, advertising for cigarettes was banned from television and radio; in 1972 the Civil Aeronautics Board implemented the (clearly pointless) requirement of separating non-smoking from smoking sections on commercial airplanes; and in 1973 Arizona became the first state to ban smoking in all public places. So, on top of the stress of unemployment, Mr. Quimby has to reckon with the stress of his children protesting his primary method of stress relief.

For the first time in the series, the readers see the Quimbys struggling and unhappy, fighting in a way that is less contained and more complex than before. For the first time, Ramona feels truly afraid. For the first time, she worries that her father might tire of his worry and his worrisome family and simply leave. Like most children (and adults), she takes her family's unhappiness personally and shoulders the burden of curing it.

Each of the covers shows a pleasant scene of Ramona with her father. Those moments exist in the book, too. (And, anyway, who wants to see an unemployed father nervously smoking a cigarette on the cover of a children's book?) Though the book does have a happy ending, the path there is fraught. But of course, it wouldn't be a Ramona Quimby book without Cleary's signature warmth, humor, and deep respect for Ramona and her family.

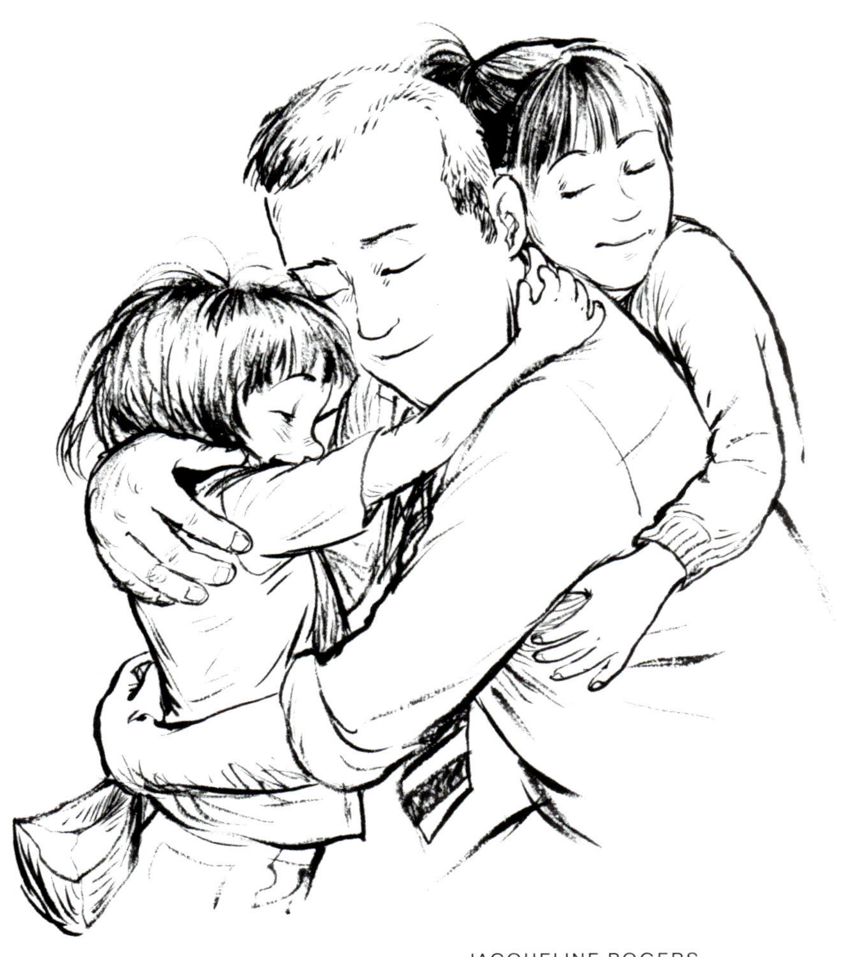

JACQUELINE ROGERS

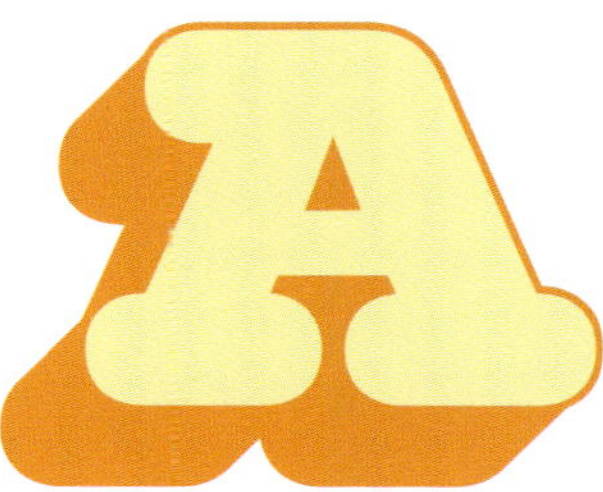A contented silence fell over the house as three members of the family looked forward to supper at the Whopperburger, where they would eat, close and cozy in a booth, their food brought to them by a friendly waitress who always said, "There you go," as she set down their hamburgers and French fries.

Ramona had decided to order a cheeseburger when she heard the sound of her father's key in the front door. "Daddy, Daddy!" she shrieked, scrambling down from the chair and running to meet her father as he opened the door. "Guess what?" Beezus, who had come from her room, answered before her father had a chance to guess. "Mother said maybe we could go to the Whopperburger for dinner!"

Mr. Quimby smiled and kissed his daughters before he held out a small white paper bag. "Here, I brought you a little present." Somehow he did not look as happy as usual. Maybe he had had a hard day at the office of the van-and-storage company where he worked.

His daughters pounced and opened the bag together. "Gummybears!" was their joyful cry. The chewy little bears were the most popular sweet at Glenwood School this fall. Last spring powdered Jell-O eaten from the package had been the fad. Mr. Quimby always remembered these things.

"Run along and divide them between you," said Mr. Quimby. "I want to talk to your mother."

"Don't spoil your dinner," said Mrs. Quimby.

The girls bore the bag off to Beezus's room, where they dumped the gummybears onto the bedspread. First they divided the cinnamon-flavored red bears, one for Beezus, one for Ramona. Then they divided the orange bears and the green, and as they were about to divide the yellow bears, both girls were suddenly aware that their mother and father were no longer talking. Silence filled the house. The sisters looked at one another. There was something unnatural about this silence. Uneasy, they waited for some sound, and then their parents began to speak in whispers. Beezus tiptoed to the door to listen.

Ramona bit the head off a red gummybear. She always ate toes last. "Maybe they're planning a big surprise," she suggested, refusing to worry.

"I don't think so," whispered Beezus, "but I can't hear what they are saying."

"Try listening through the furnace pipes," whispered Ramona.

"That won't work here. The living room is too far away." Beezus strained to catch her parents' words. "I think something's wrong."

Ramona divided her gummybears, one heap to eat at home, the other to take to school to share with friends if they were nice to her.

"Something is wrong. Something awful," whispered Beezus.

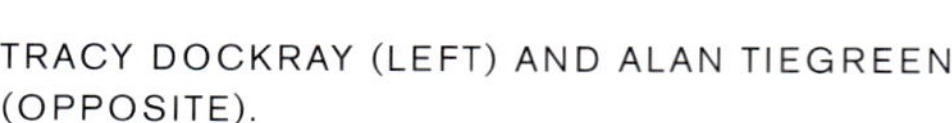

TRACY DOCKRAY (LEFT) AND ALAN TIEGREEN (OPPOSITE).

Mr. Quimby gives Ramona and Beezus a present.

To bring home candy after getting laid off speaks volumes about Mr. Quimby's character. He probably also knew that the process of dividing up the gummybears would distract his daughters long enough for him to deliver the bad news to Mrs. Quimby. Tiegreen captures the moment of gummybear-induced excitement, while Rogers (see page 109) shows the hug that Mr. Quimby must have sorely needed.

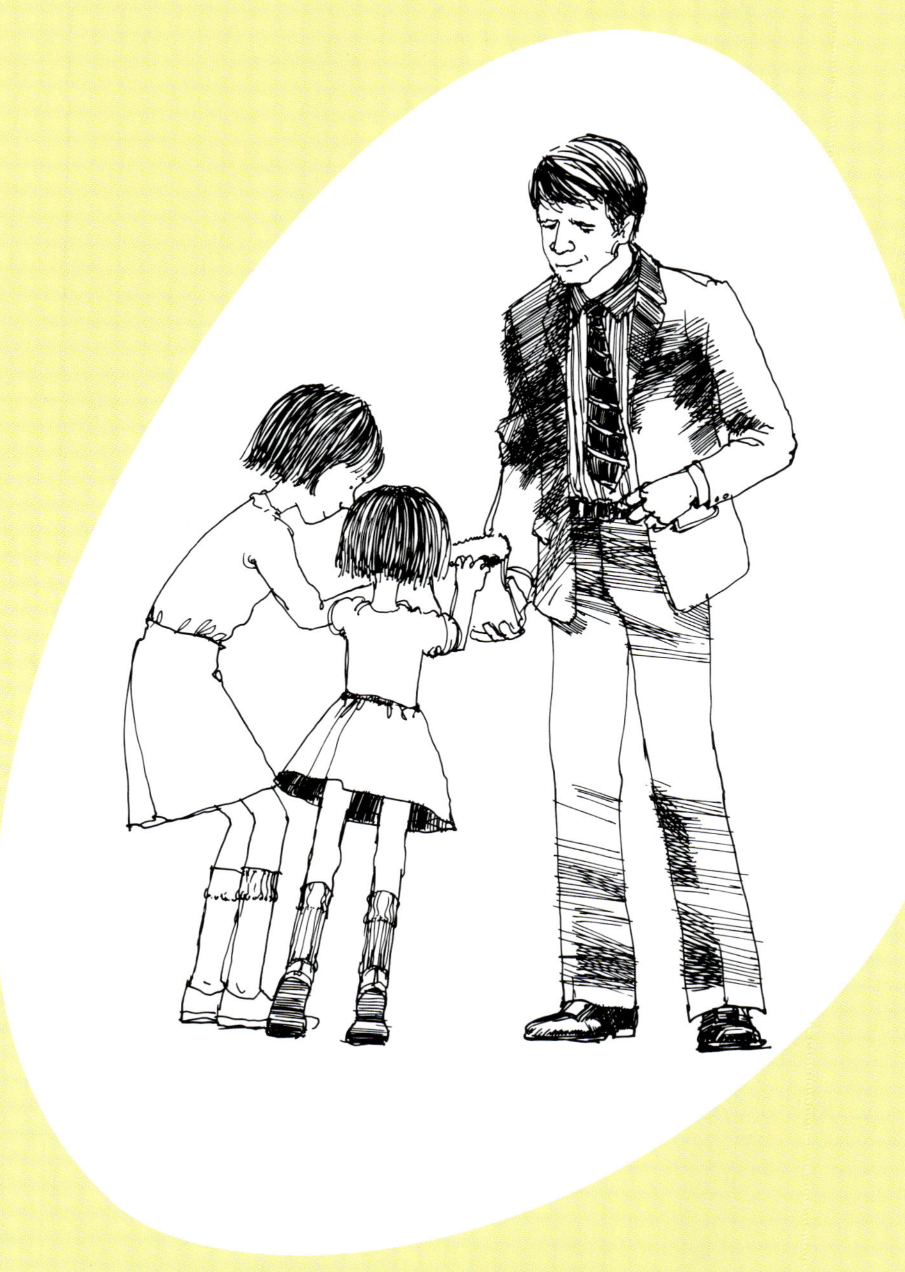

"That kid must be earning a million dollars." Mr. Quimby snuffed out his cigarette in a loaded ashtray. "He's singing that commercial every time I turn on the television."

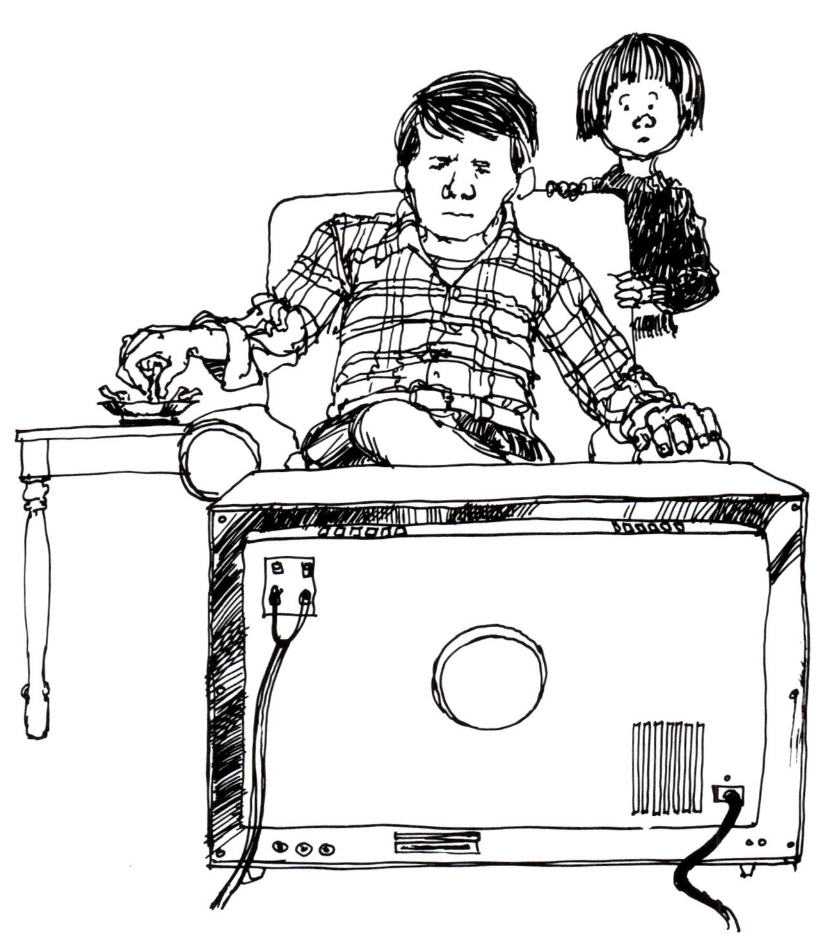

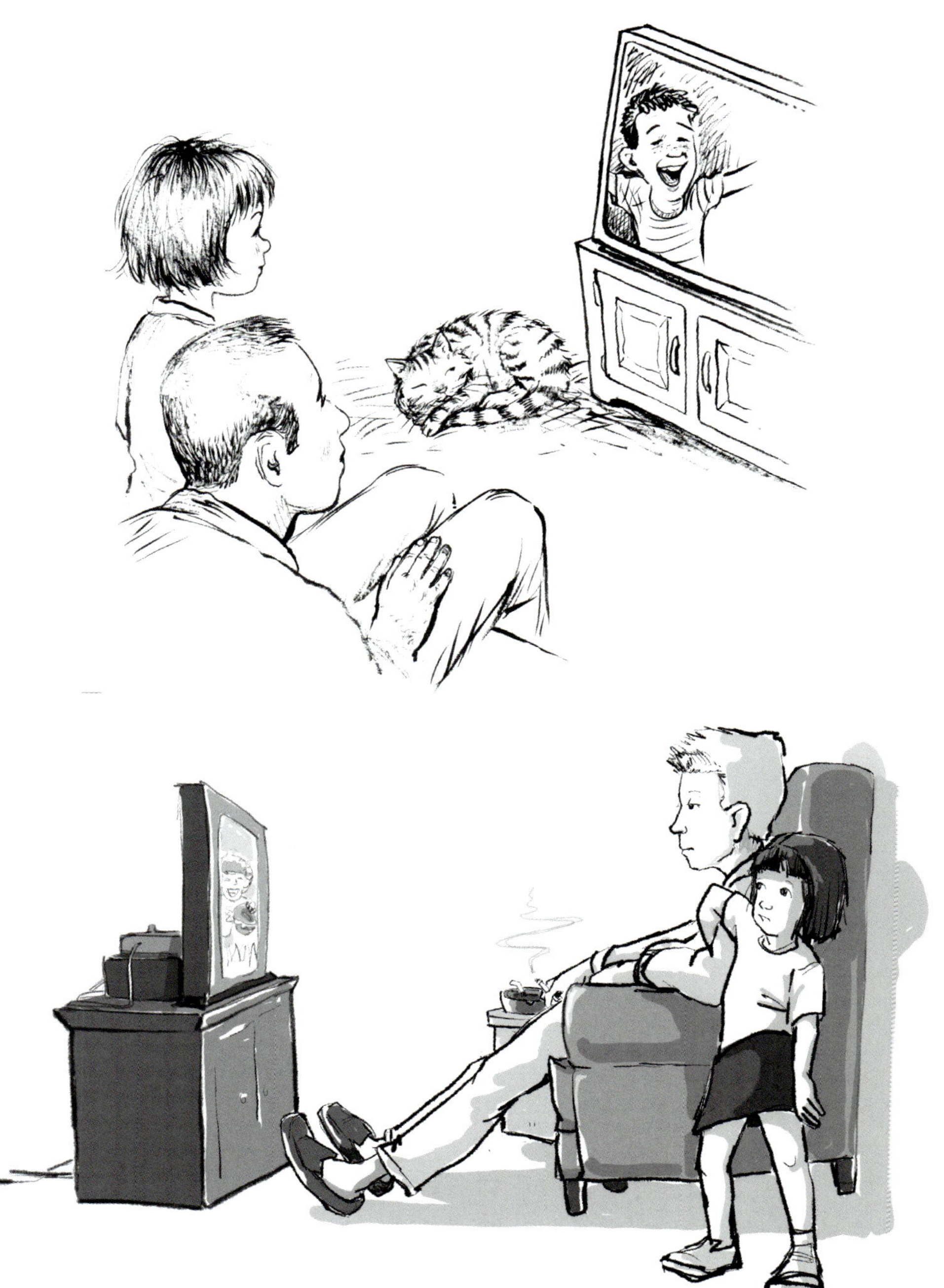

Her father's offhand remark gives Ramona an idea about how she might be able to make a million dollars so her parents won't have to worry, and so the family can eat in a restaurant every day if they wanted.

Put together, these three illustrations provide a panoramic view of this prosaic yet inspiring moment: a TV commercial, a dad watching from a sofa chair, a daughter nearby. Tiegreen's Ramona stands behind the chair in the upper right corner of the frame, while Mr. Quimby extinguishes his cigarette, a slight furrow to his brow. She looks worried, and the back of the television occupies the foreground. Dockray shows this scene from the side, and Ramona strikes a much cozier pose, leaning up against her father, one arm flung back and over his shoulder. In Rogers's illustration, the reader can see what Ramona and Mr. Quimby see: the kid on TV singing his heart out for a big payout. Even Picky-picky looks toward the screen with a half-open eye, giving it an amount of attention significant for a cat.

OPPOSITE: ALAN TIEGREEN. ABOVE: JACQUELINE ROGERS (TOP) AND TRACY DOCKRAY (BOTTOM).

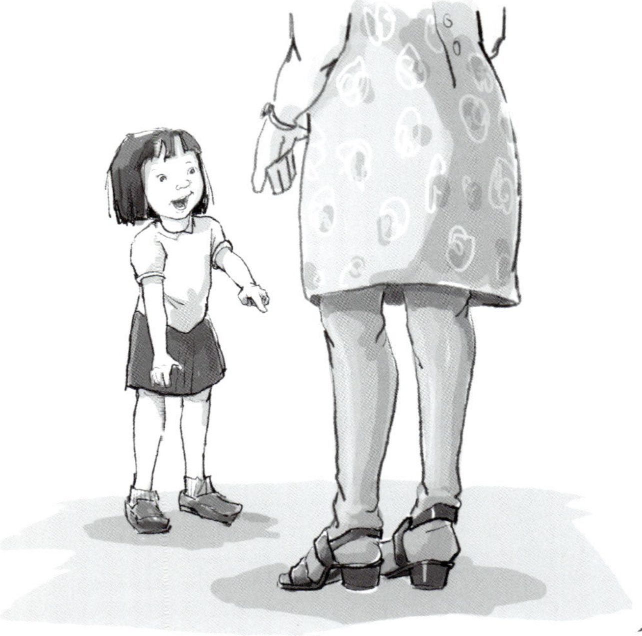

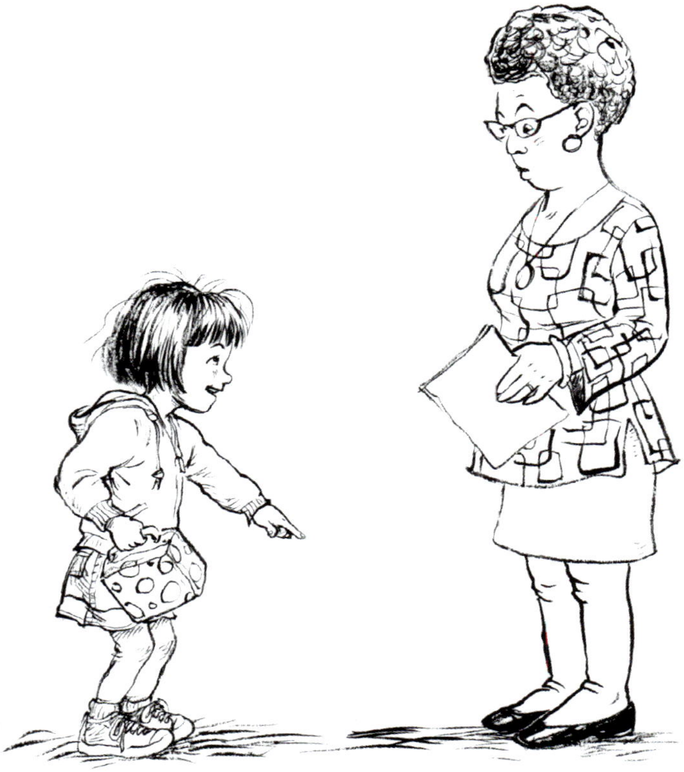

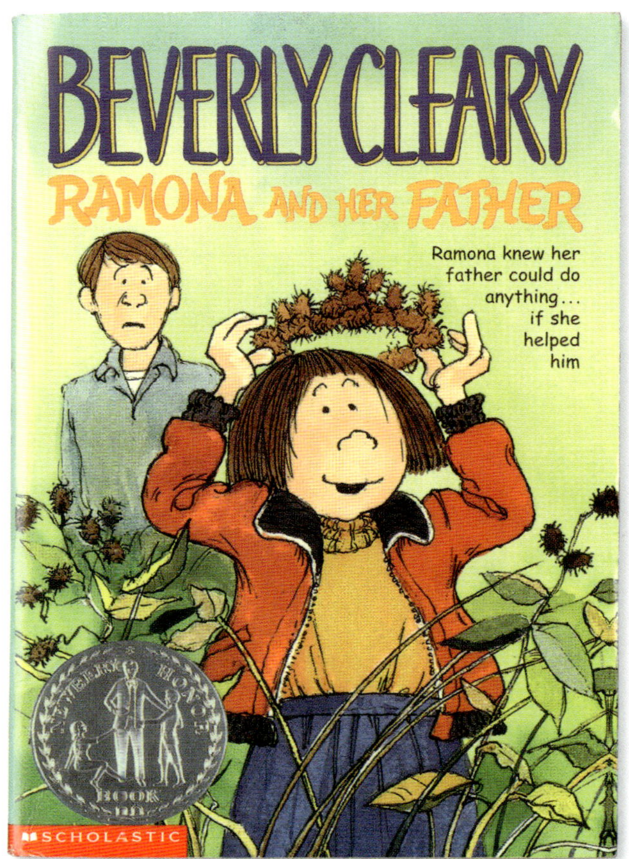

Ramona tells Mrs. Rogers that her pantyhose are wrinkled like an elephant's legs. Somehow, this doesn't have the same effect as when the curly-haired girl said the same thing to her mother in the pantyhose commercial on TV. Dockray's illustration focuses on Ramona attempting to be adorable and includes just the teacher's legs, whereas Rogers shows the teacher in her entirety, including her less-than-amused expression.

Now that he's unemployed and Mrs. Quimby is working full time, it's up to Mr. Quimby to attend the parent-teacher conference. While he's meeting with Mrs. Rogers, Ramona gets swept up into fantasy land, imagining herself as a commercial actor on television and making a crown like a boy wore in a margarine commercial. For this cover, Tiegreen plays with the timeline, bringing Mr. Quimby out early to discover Ramona among the burdock plants across the street from the school, coronating herself.

ABOVE, CLOCKWISE FROM TOP LEFT: JACQUELINE ROGERS, TRACY DOCKRAY, AND ALAN TIEGREEN. OPPOSITE: JACQUELINE ROGERS.

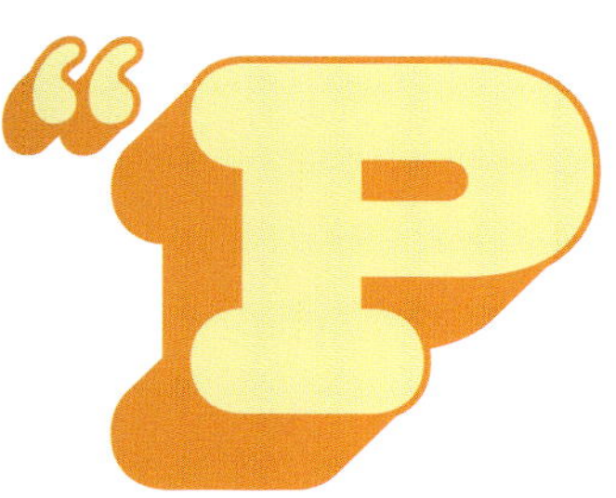

“Please pass the tommy-toes,” said Ramona, hoping to make someone in the family smile. She felt good when her father smiled as he passed her the bowl of stewed tomatoes. He smiled less and less as the days went by and he had not found work. Too often he was just plain cross. Ramona had learned not to rush home from school and ask, “Did you find a job today, Daddy?” Mrs. Quimby always seemed to look anxious these days, either over the cost of groceries or money the family owed. Beezus had turned into a regular old grouch, because she dreaded Creative Writing and perhaps because she had reached that difficult age Mrs. Quimby was always talking about, although Ramona found this hard to believe.

Even Picky-picky was not himself. He lashed his tail and stalked angrily away from his dish when Beezus served him Puss-puddy, the cheapest brand of cat food Mrs. Quimby could find in the market.

All this worried Ramona. She wanted her father to smile and joke, her mother to look happy, her sister to be cheerful, and Picky-picky to eat his food, wash his whiskers, and purr the way he used to.

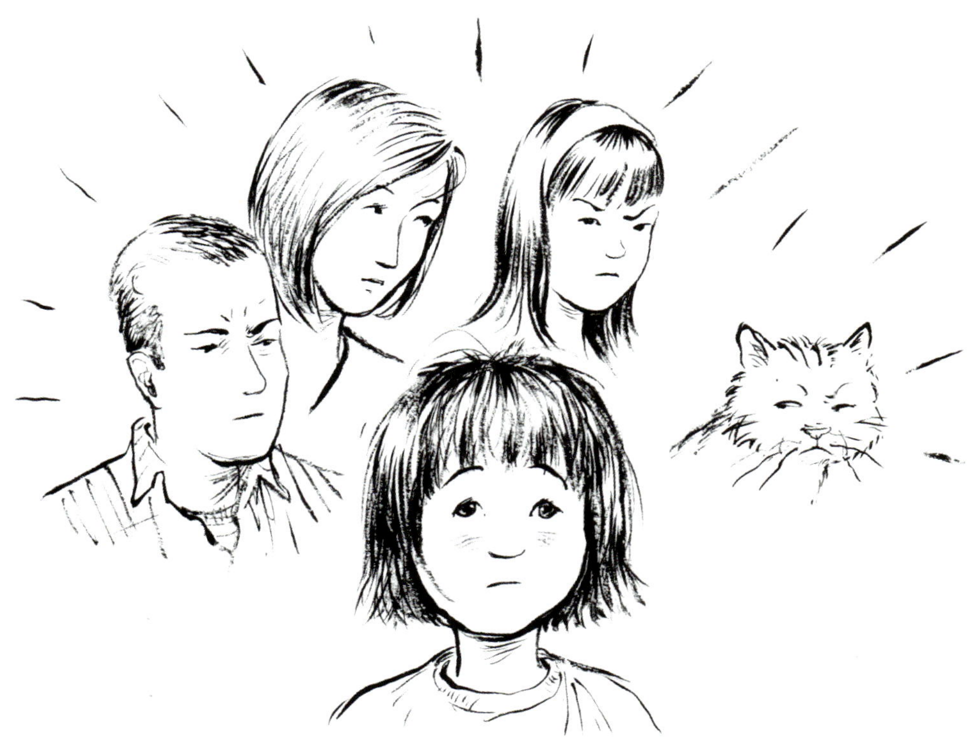

"Oh, Daddy!" Ramona threw her arms around her father. "It's the wickedest jack-o'-lantern in the whole world."

Pumpkin carving gives the Quimby family a momentary respite. In Tiegreen's illustration, Ramona seems to bask in a beam of happiness—and the glow from the candle within the jack-o'-lantern.

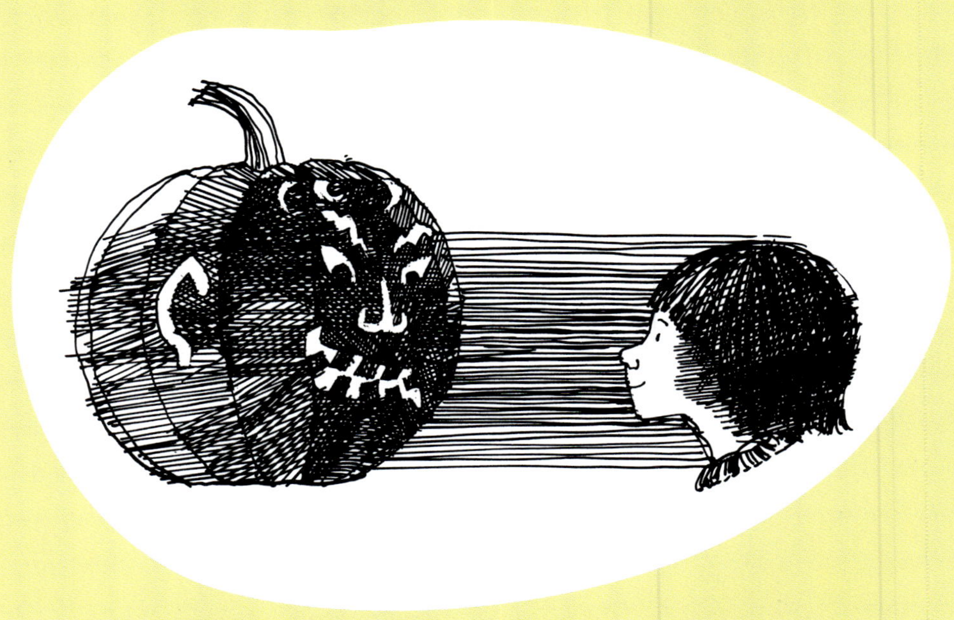

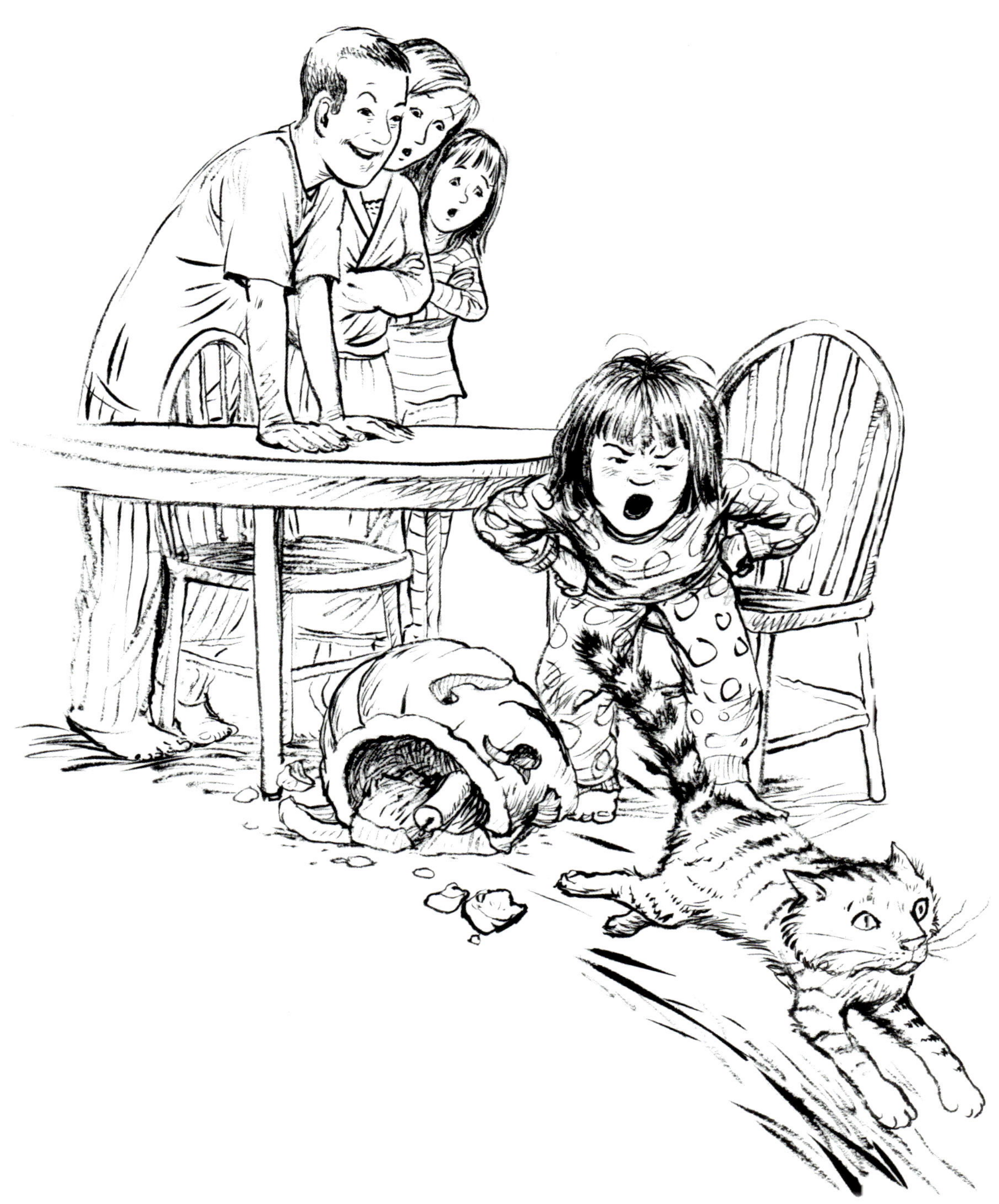

Picky-picky finds an alternative to that awful Puss-puddy.

Ramona couldn't be angrier when Picky-picky eats the pumpkin for a late-night snack. Beezus adds fuel to the fire by using the cat's bad behavior as an opportunity to bring up her father's smoking. If the family can't afford to buy the more expensive food that Picky-picky likes, then how can they afford Mr. Quimby's cigarettes? And cigarettes kill!

ALAN TIEGREEN (OPPOSITE) AND JACQUELINE ROGERS (ABOVE).

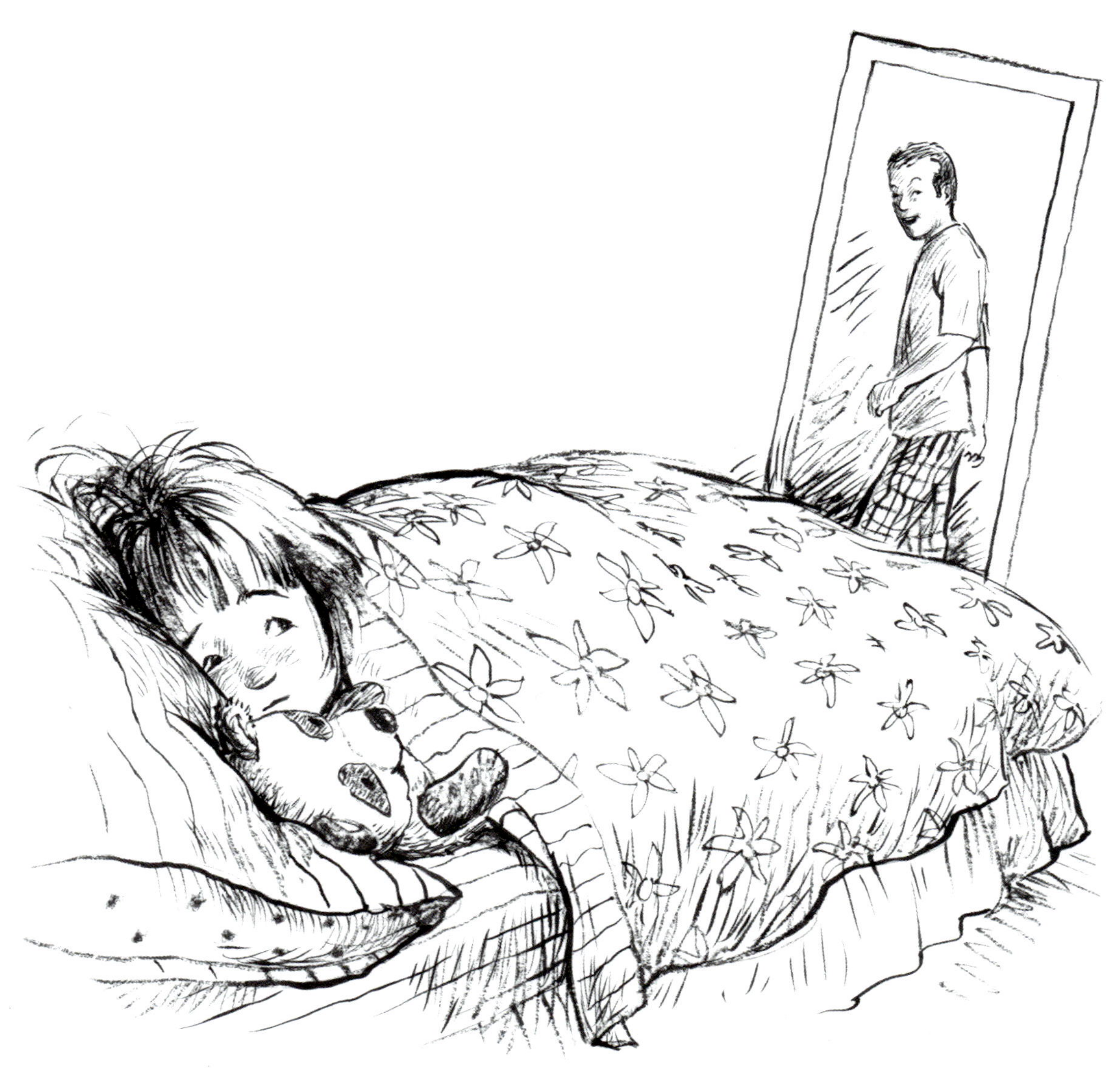

Another worry added to Ramona's long list of worries: her father's blackening lungs.

After the pumpkin fiasco, Ramona pulls her old panda bear out from under her bed for comfort. In Rogers's illustration, Mr. Quimby promises his daughter that they'll get another pumpkin, unaware that this is not Ramona's primary concern. Dockray shows the comforting light from the hallway shining on Ramona's bed, while Tiegreen drew a close-up of Ramona and the old panda bear, all alone.

ABOVE: JACQUELINE ROGERS. OPPOSITE: ALAN TIEGREEN (TOP) AND TRACY DOCKRAY (BOTTOM).

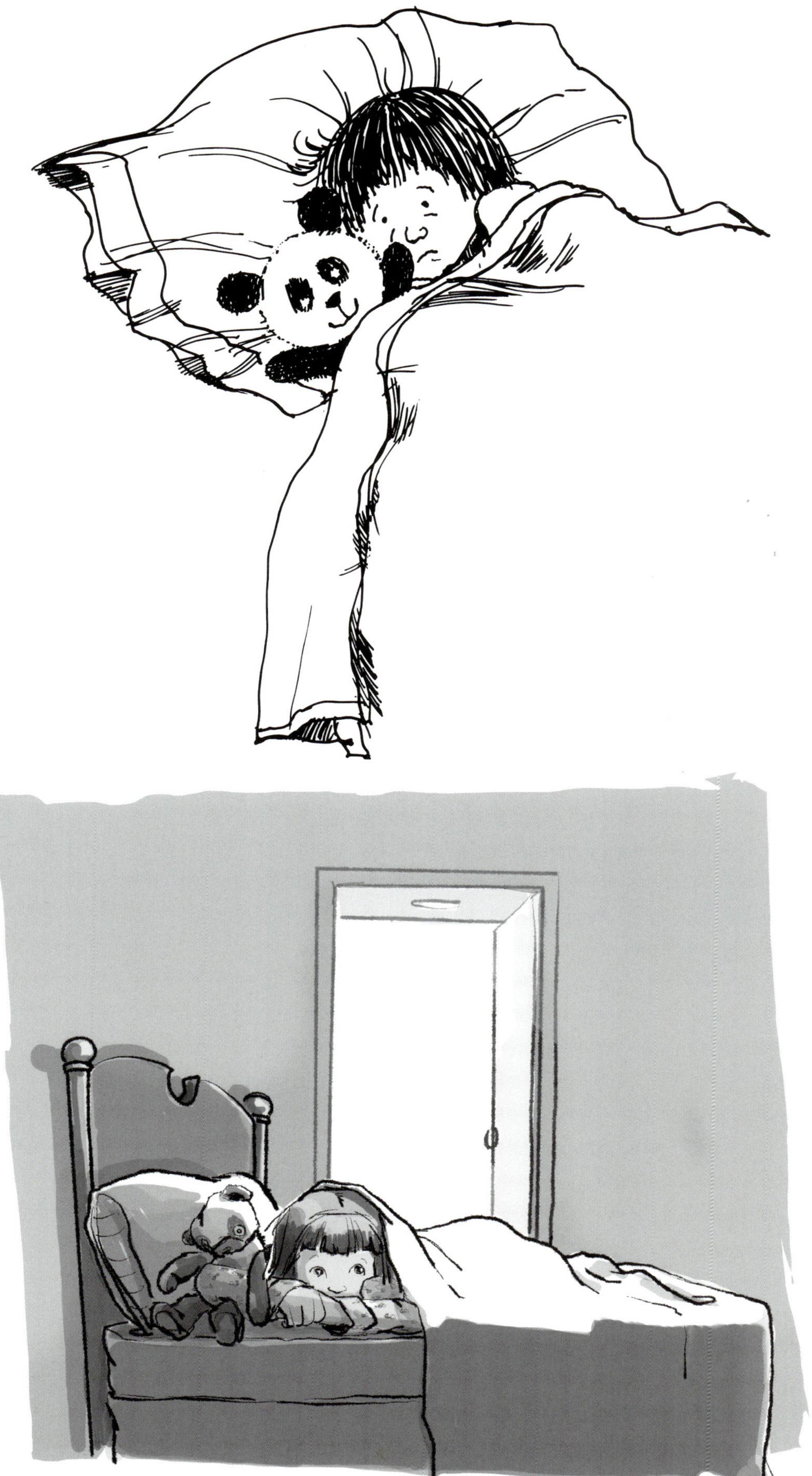

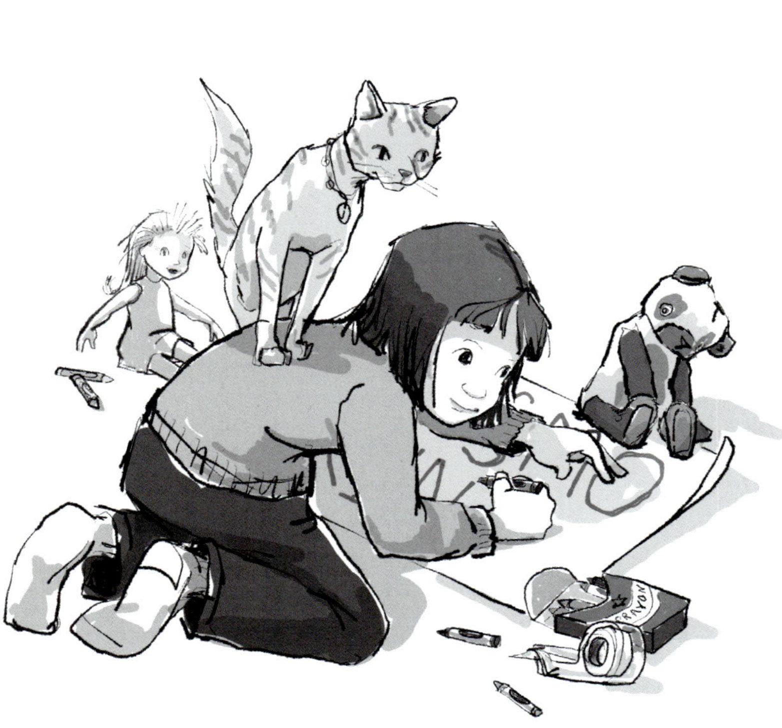

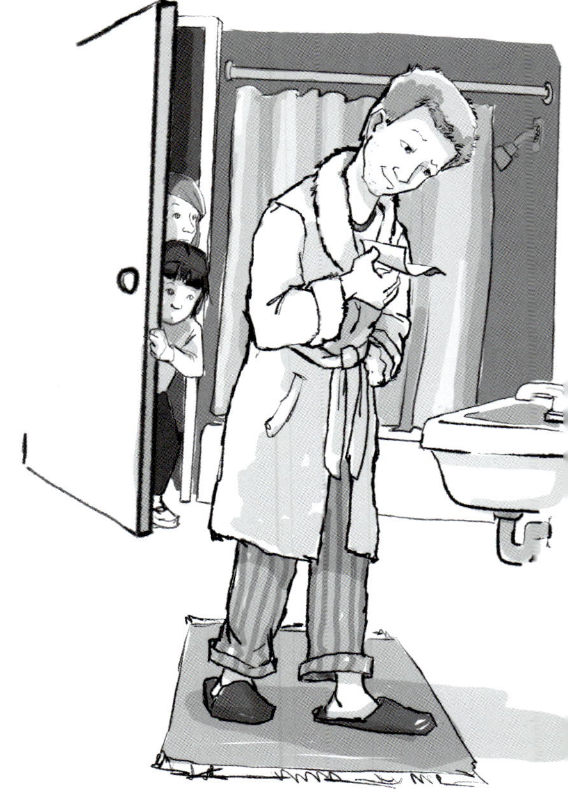

During a particularly boring day at school, Ramona decides to take the matter of saving her father's life into her own hands. Back at home, she draws a No Smoking sign but forgets to plan ahead and so is forced to finish the second word on another line. In Dockray's illustration, the old panda and a doll provide company, and Picky-picky offers his creative input.

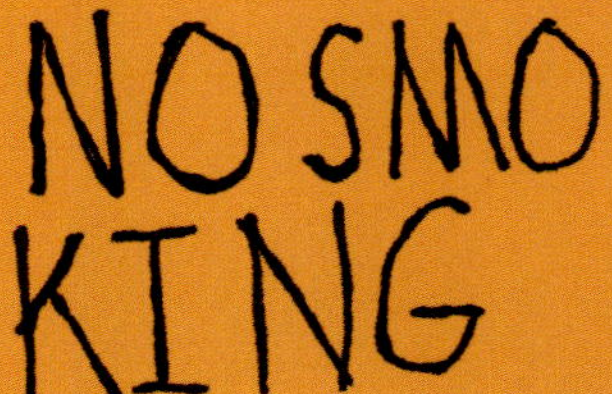

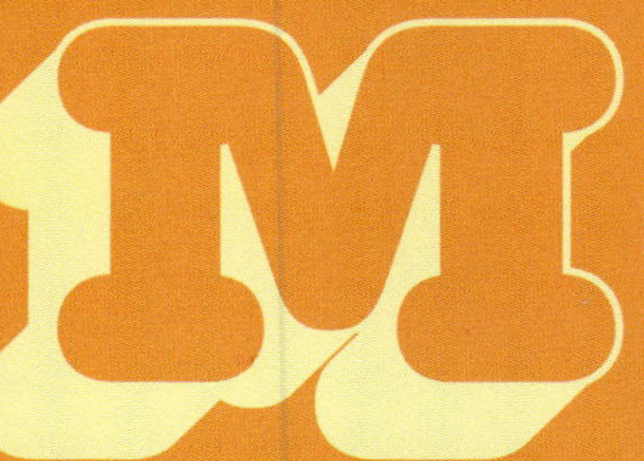

r. Quimby, although he must have seen the sign, said nothing until after dinner when he had finished his pumpkin pie. He asked for an ashtray and then inquired, "Say, who is this Mr. King?"

"What Mr. King?" asked Ramona, walking into his trap.

"Nosmo King," answered her father without cracking a smile.

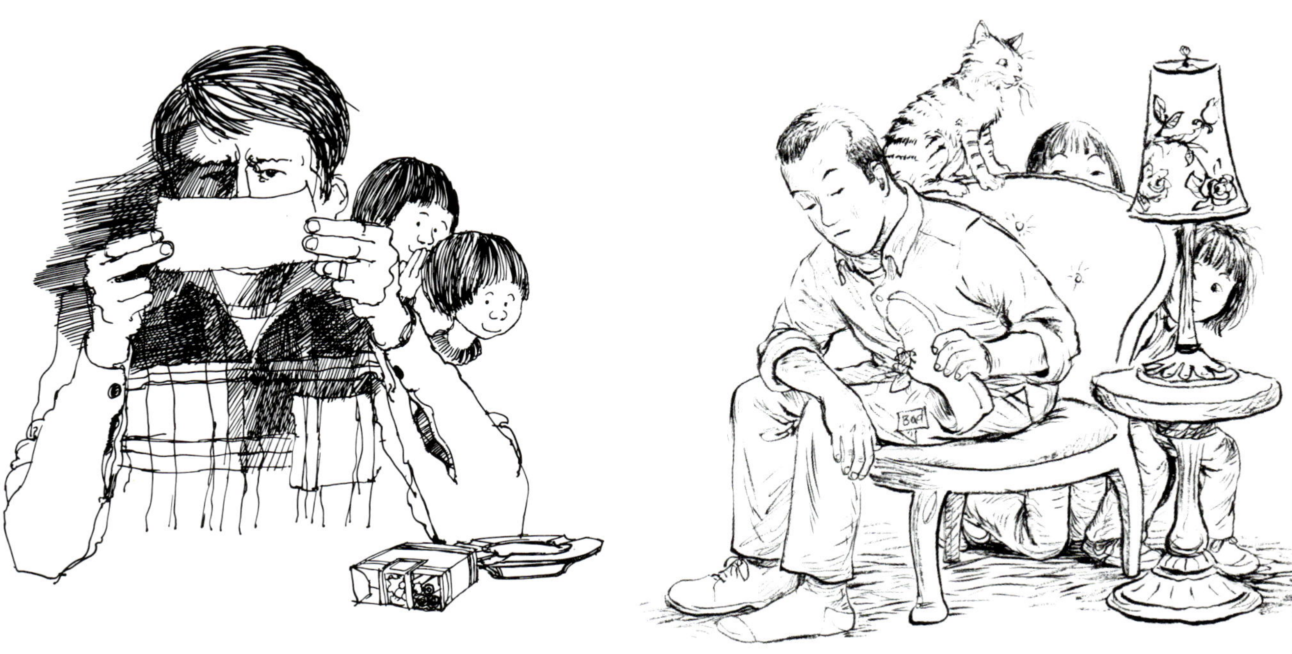

Ramona and Beezus escalate their anti-smoking offensive.

After her first failed attempt to sway her father with the Nosmo King sign, Ramona tapes a drawing of a cigarette with a big black *X* and the word *BAD* to the refrigerator door. Beezus contributes her spelling expertise for bigger words like *pollution*, and together the girls tape more signs to the mantel, the dining-room curtains, and the door of the hall closet. Mr. Quimby ignores them, and so they are forced to escalate yet again. In these illustrations, Mr. Quimby finds tiny signs in increasingly unlikely spots.

OPPOSITE: TRACY DOCKRAY. ABOVE: ALAN TIEGREEN (LEFT) AND JACQUELINE ROGERS (RIGHT).

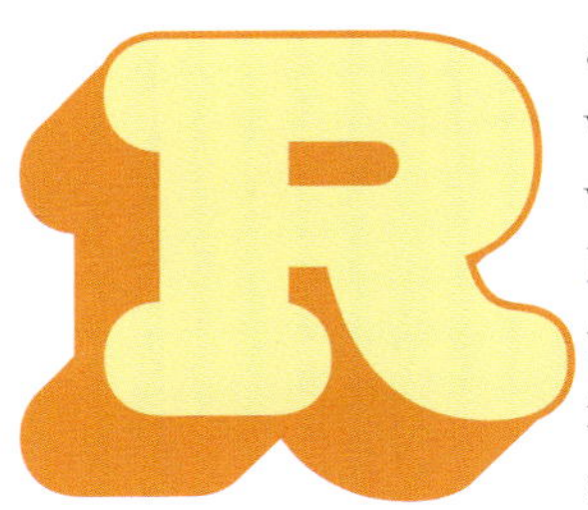

amona's insides tightened with fear. Maybe her father was angry with her. Maybe he had gone away because she tried to make him stop smoking. She thought she was saving his life, but maybe she was being mean to him. Her mother said she must not annoy her father, because he was worried about being out of work. Maybe she had made him so angry he did not love her anymore. Maybe he had gone away because he did not love her. She thought of all the scary things she had seen on television—houses that had fallen down in earthquakes, people shooting people, big hairy men on motorcycles—and knew she needed her father to keep her safe.

Arriving home after school, Ramona finds the door locked and no one home to answer her knock. Tiegreen's wide-angle drawing shows the bigness of the world and how scared and small Ramona feels in this moment.

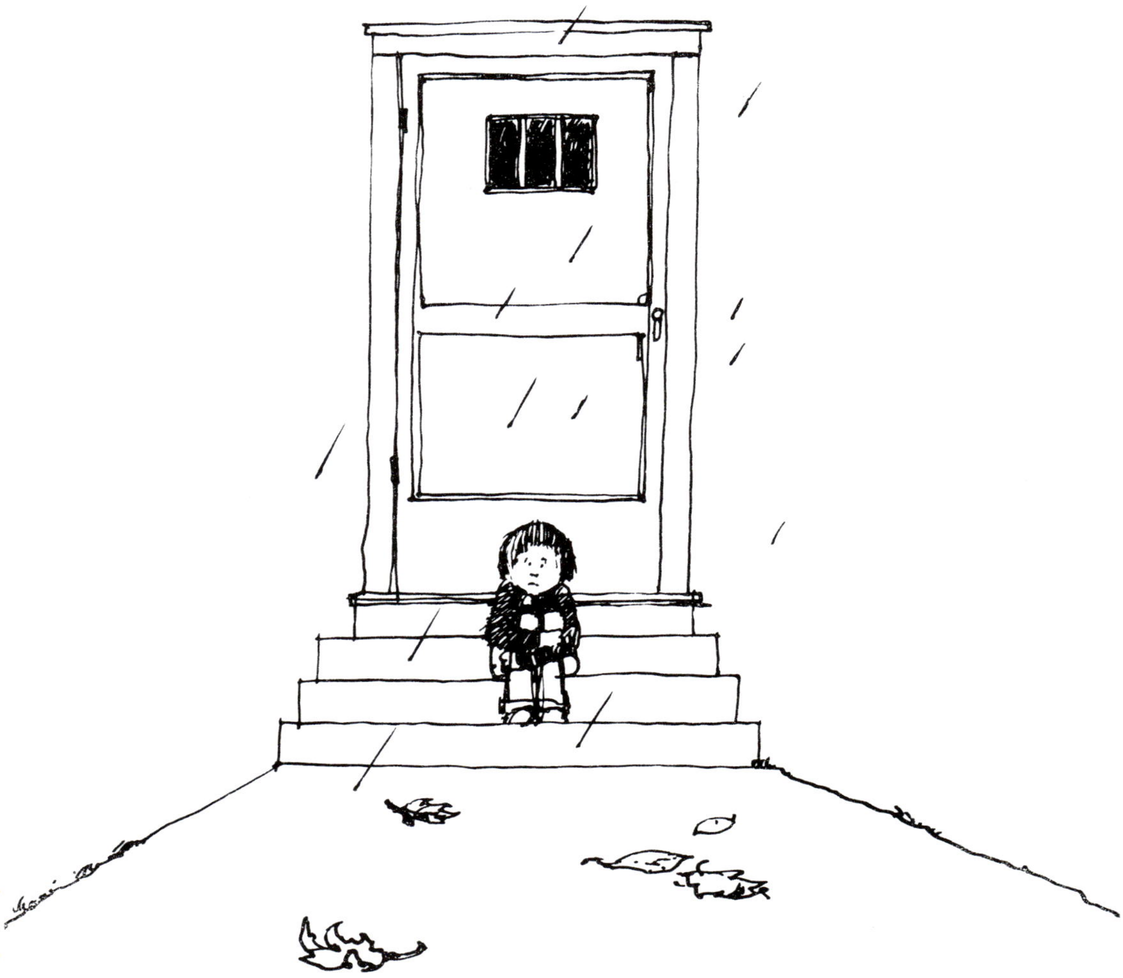

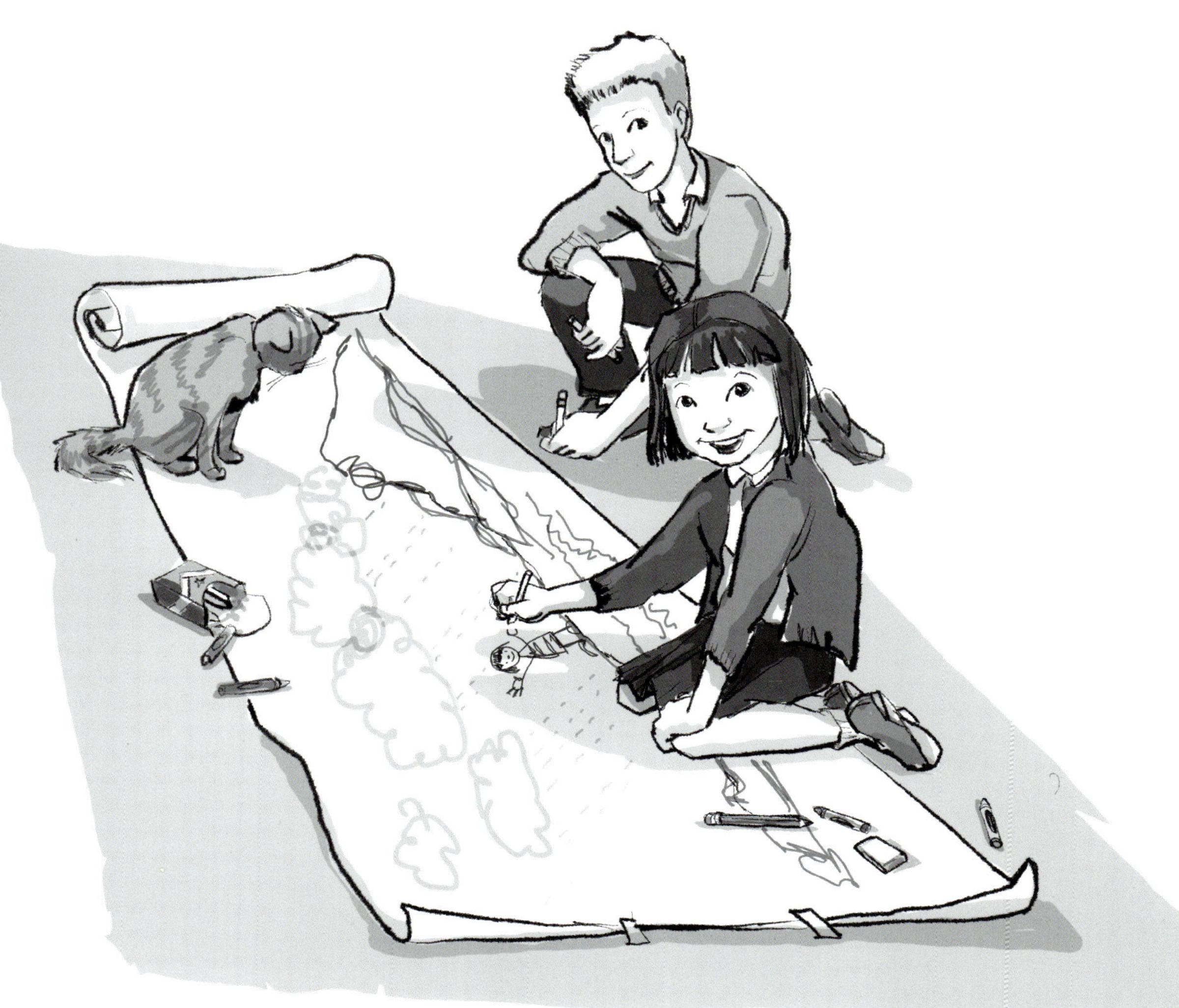

Mr. Quimby comes home.

Of course, Ramona's father did not abandon her. He was merely waiting in a long line to collect his unemployment insurance. Here they draw the longest picture in the world, with the Interstate Bridge between Oregon and Washington State over the Columbia River, Mount Hood in the distance. Ramona has a big smile on her face—Daddy is home, and everything is all right with the world.

ALAN TIEGREEN (OPPOSITE) AND TRACY DOCKRAY (ABOVE).

Beezus faces another dreaded creative assignment.

Despite Mrs. Swink's terrible polyester pantsuit, Beezus (who recently had grown critical of clothing) works up the nerve to interview her for a school project. Ramona is in tow and ready to be entertained. The neighborhood will rue the day that the Quimbys' neighbor reveals the secret to building DIY tin-can stilts.

BELOW: TRACY DOCKRAY. OPPOSITE: ALAN TIEGREEN (TOP) AND JACQUELINE ROGERS (BOTTOM).

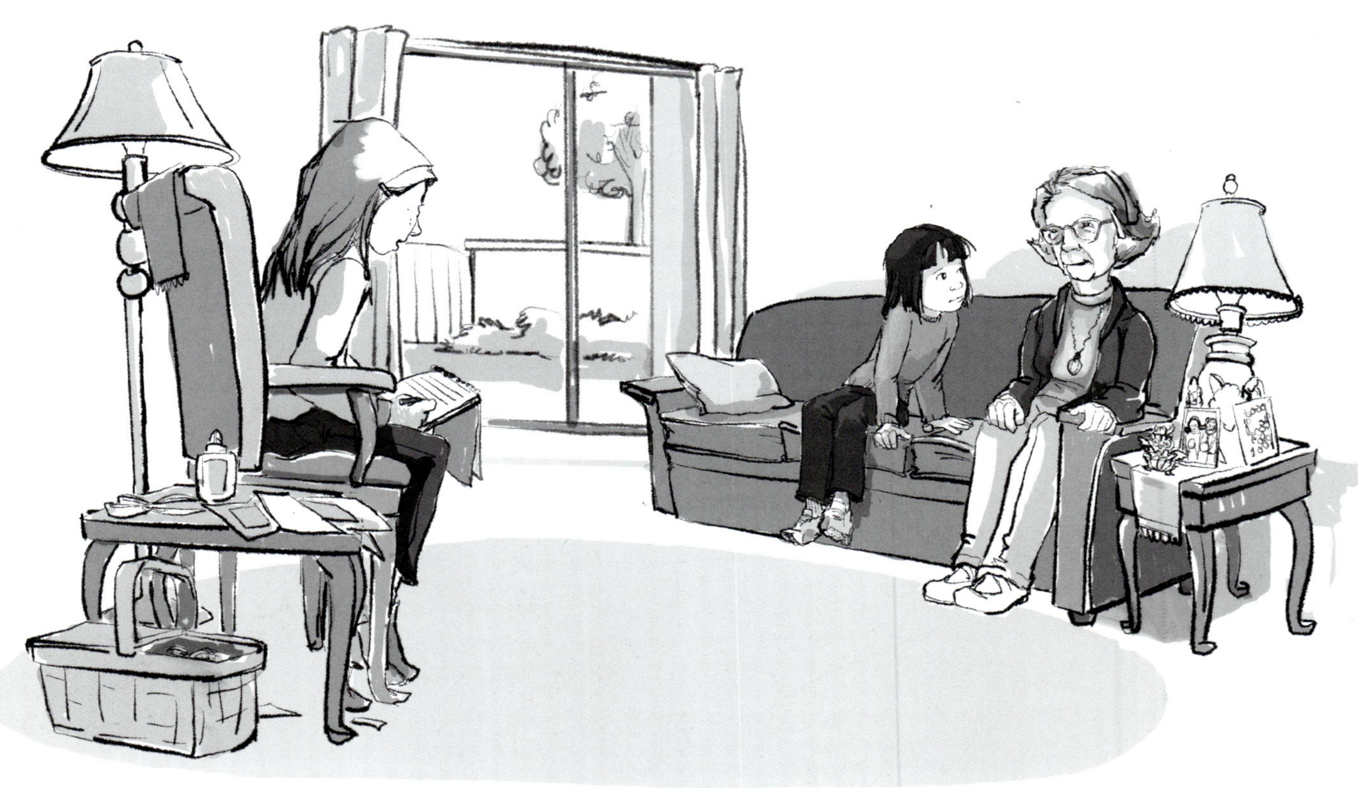

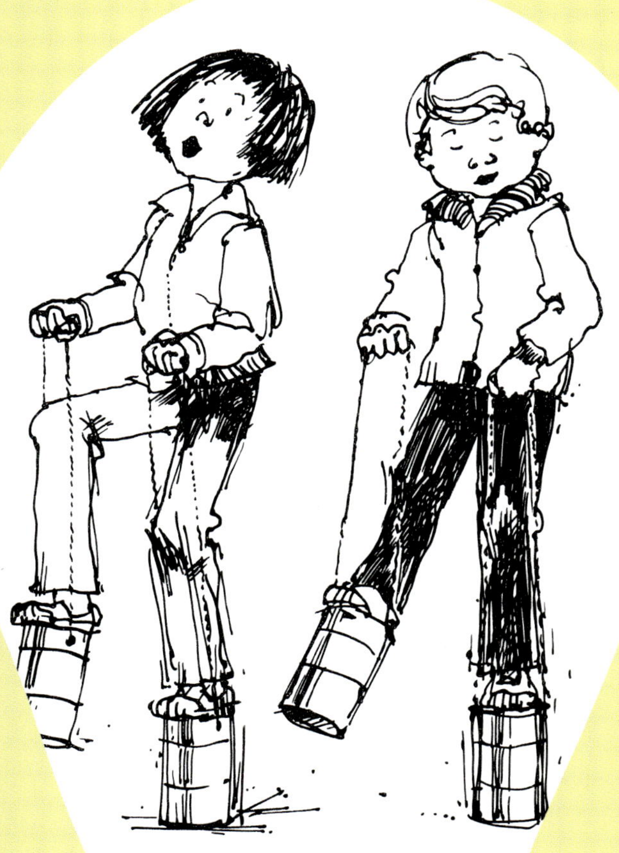

Leave it to handyboy Howie to turn the tin-can stilt dream into a reality—finally, something to relieve Ramona's second-grade ennui. Perhaps, in Tiegreen's illustration, Ramona and her friend are just warming up, while in Rogers's version they are full-on belting out a drinking song.

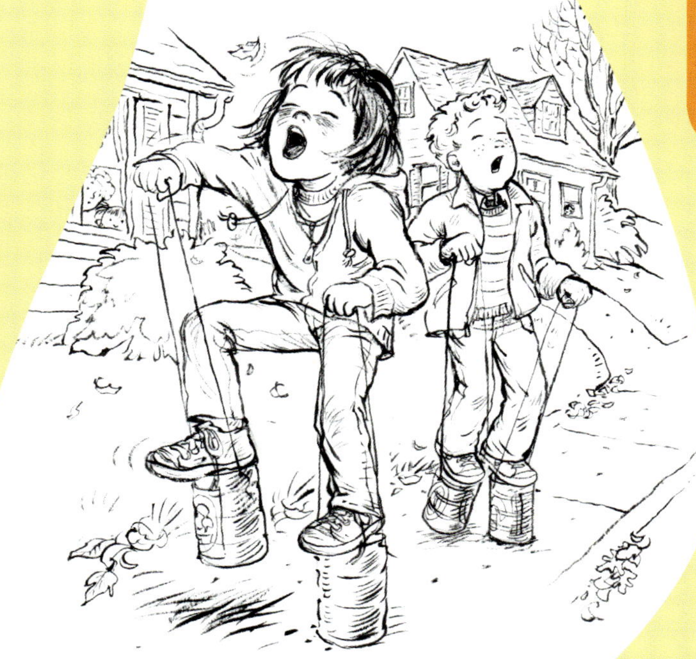

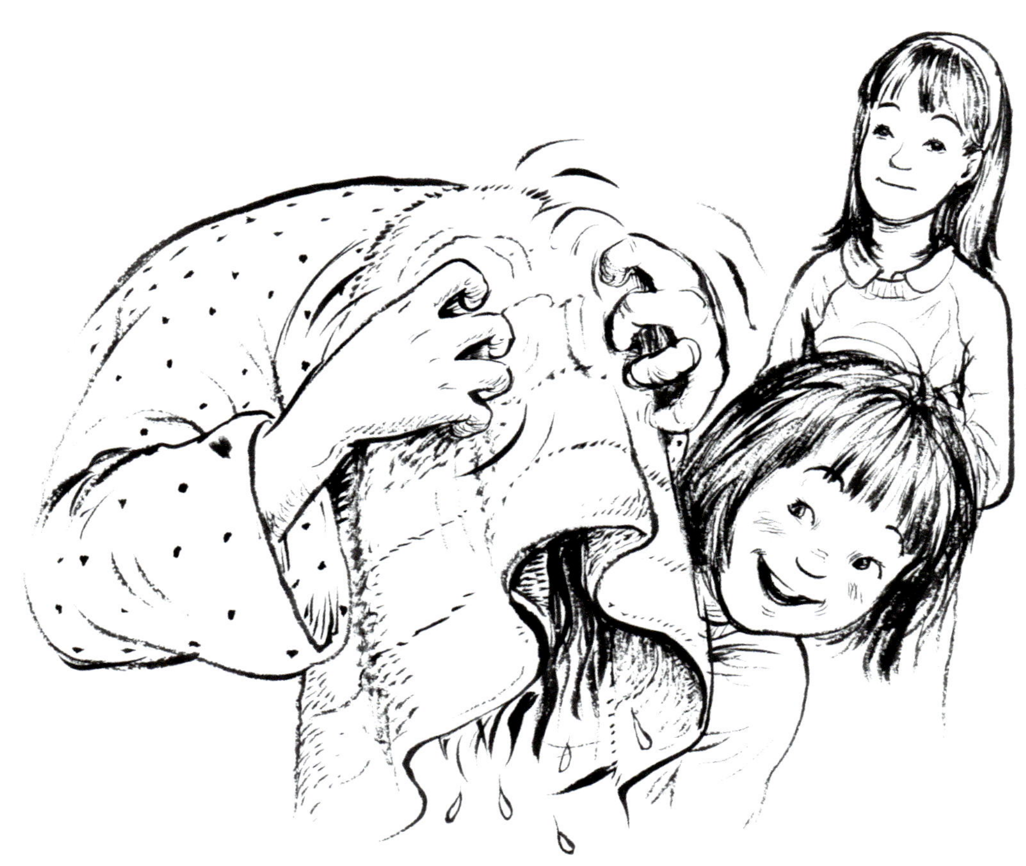

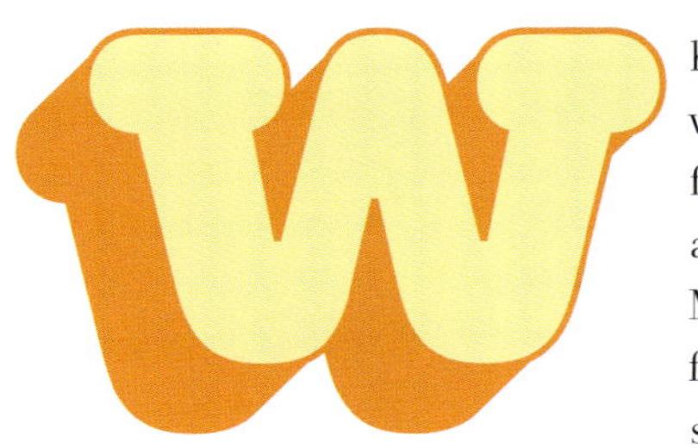

hen Sunday school was over, Beezus found Ramona and asked, "Where's Mother going to find time to make a sheep costume?"

"After work, I guess." This problem was something Ramona had not considered.

Knowing that her working mother might not welcome an additional obligation, Ramona waits until Mrs. Quimby is drying her hair with a bath towel to break the news that she's volunteered her to help with the Nativity scene at the Christmas pageant.

JACQUELINE ROGERS (ABOVE) AND ALAN TIEGREEN (OPPOSITE).

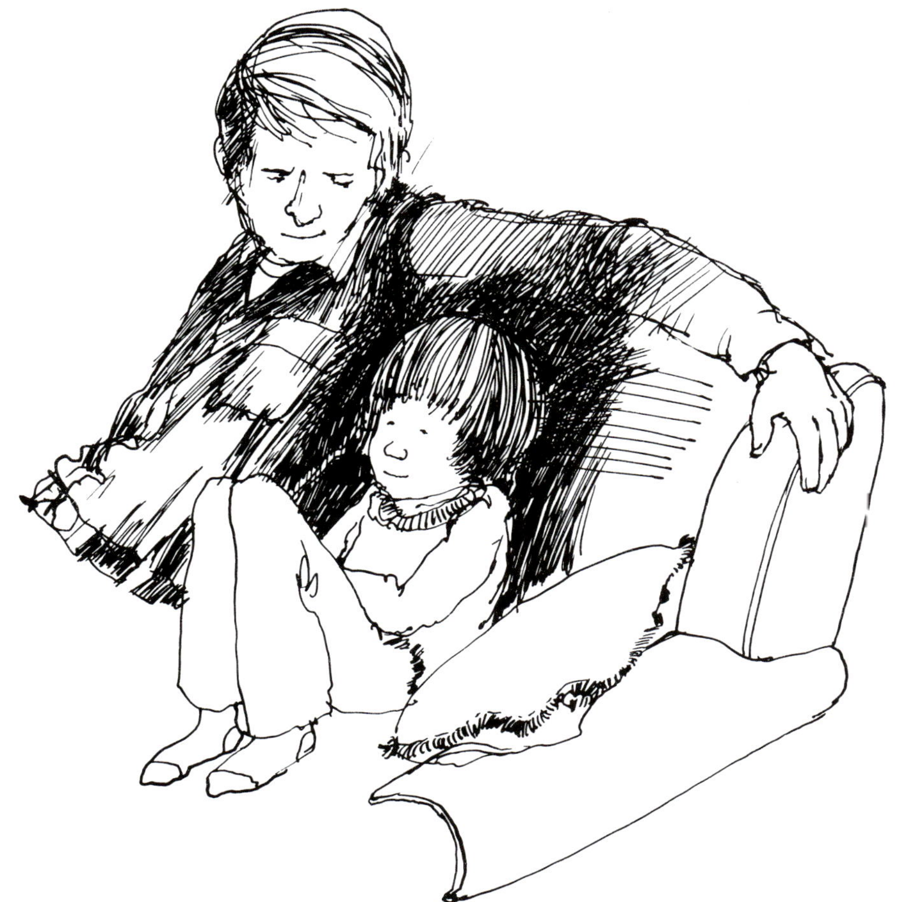

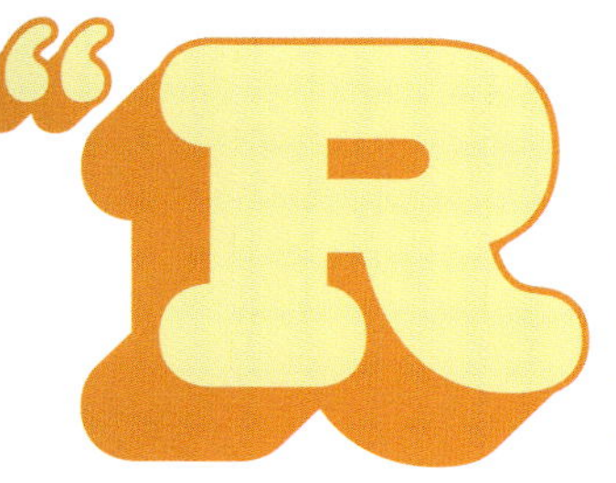

"Ramona," he said, "it isn't easy to break a bad habit. I ran across one cigarette, an old stale cigarette, in my raincoat pocket and thought it might help if I smoked just one. I'm trying. I'm really trying."

Hearing her father speak this way, as if she really was a grown-up, melted the last of Ramona's anger. She turned into a seven-year-old again and climbed on the couch to lean against her father. After a few moments of silence, she whispered, "I love you, Daddy."

He tousled her hair affectionately and said, "I know you do. That's why you want me to stop smoking, and I love you, too."

"Even if I'm a brat sometimes?"

"Even if you're a brat sometimes."

Ramona thought awhile before she sat up and said, "Then why can't we be a happy family?"

For some reason Mr. Quimby smiled. "I have news for you, Ramona," he said. "We are a happy family."

"We are?" Ramona was skeptical.

"Yes, we are." Mr. Quimby was positive. "No family is perfect. Get that idea out of your head. And nobody is perfect either. All we can do is work at it. And we do."

Ramona tried to wiggle her toes inside her shoes and considered what her father had said. Lots of fathers wouldn't draw pictures with their little girls. Her father bought her paper and crayons when he could afford them. Lots of mothers wouldn't step over a picture that spread across the kitchen floor while cooking supper. Ramona knew mothers who would scold and say, "Pick that up. Can't you see I'm trying to get supper?" Lots of big sisters wouldn't let their little sister go along when they interviewed someone for creative writing. They would take more than their fair share of gummybears because they were bigger and . . .

Ramona decided her father was probably right, but she couldn't help feeling they would be a happier family if her mother could find time to sew that sheep costume. There wasn't much time left.

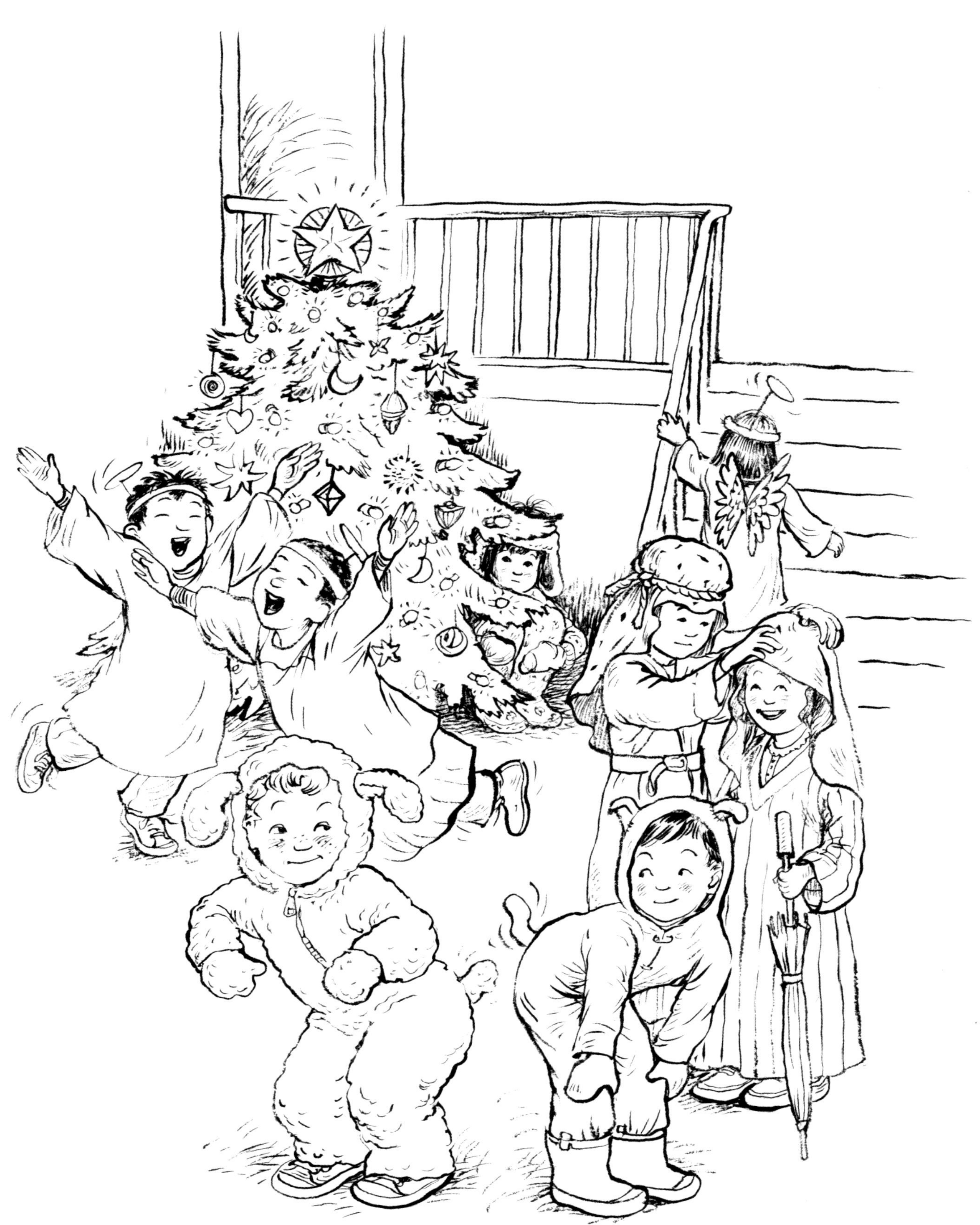

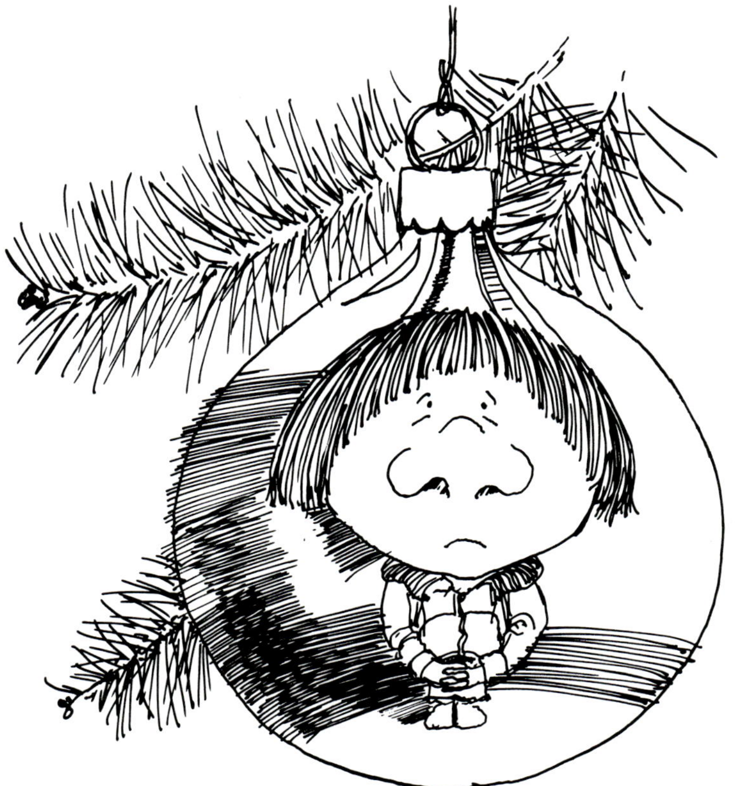

Despite her promise, Mrs. Quimby did not have time to make Ramona's sheep costume after all. In Rogers's illustration, Ramona sits hunched in the corner behind the Christmas tree in the church basement while the other children prepare themselves for the Nativity scene. Tiegreen brings the view way in, showing the misery on her face in the distorted reflection from a green Christmas ornament. Nobody understands.

ALAN TIEGREEN (ABOVE) AND JACQUELINE ROGERS (OPPOSITE)

Christmas miracles.

With the encouragement of the Three Wise Persons—three kind eighth-grade girls—and their application of contraband mascara to Ramona's nose to make her look like a sheep, the younger girl takes her place in the Christmas program behind the kindergarten angels. More miraculous even than Ramona getting over her stubbornness is the blessed phone call that came a few days earlier with news that Mr. Quimby's new job starts the morning after New Year's Day. Now that Ramona is feeling the holiness of the holiday, she remembers that the perpetual worried frown has disappeared from her mother's face, that her family loves her, and that she loves them too. Even Beezus.

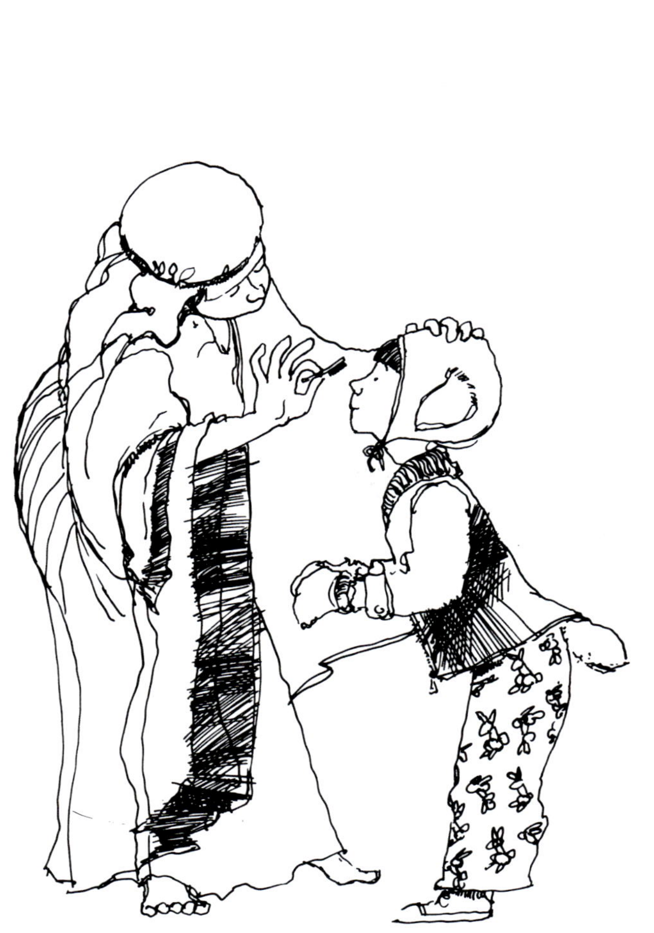

ALAN TIEGREEN (LEFT) AND TRACY DOCKRAY (RIGHT).

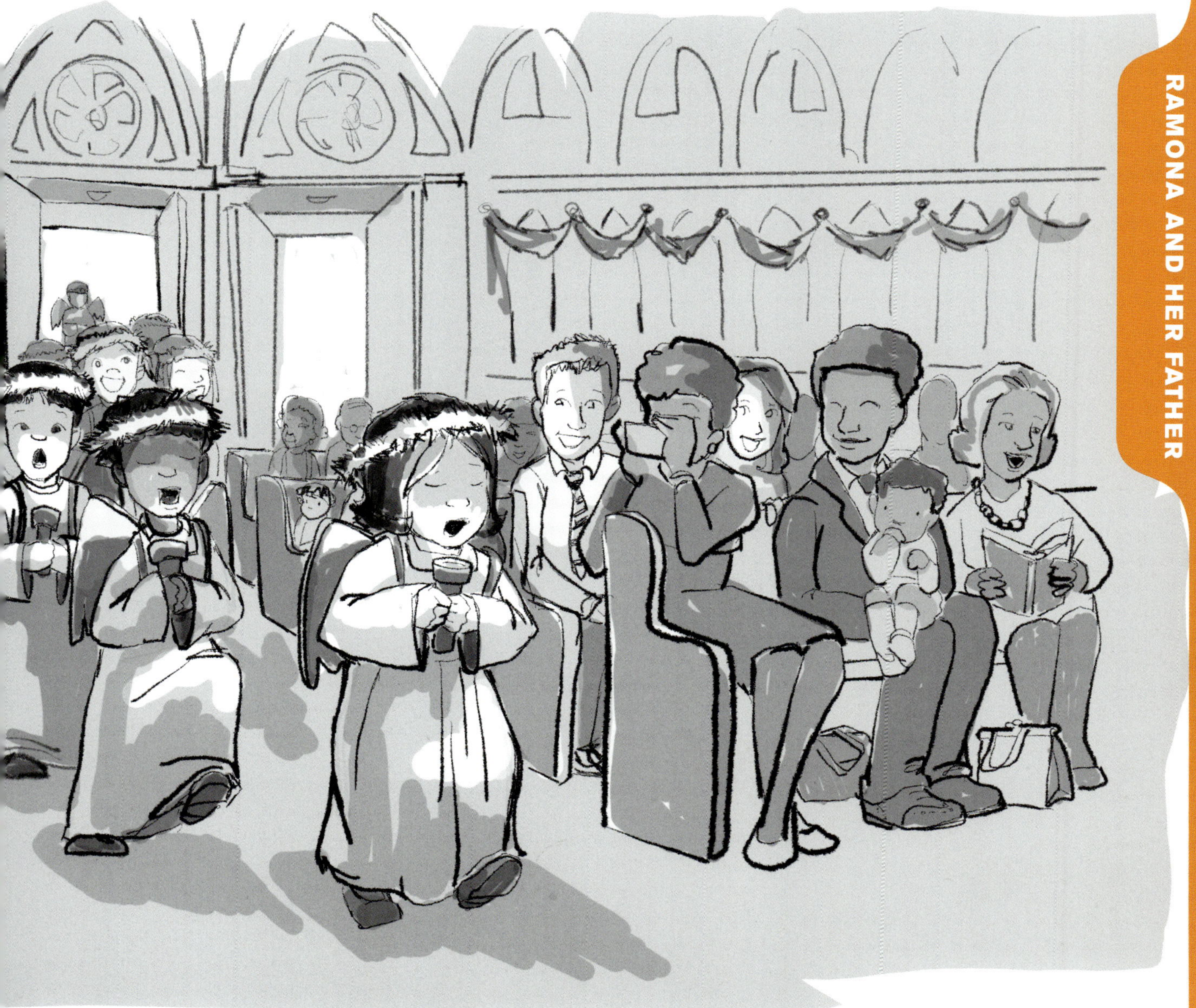

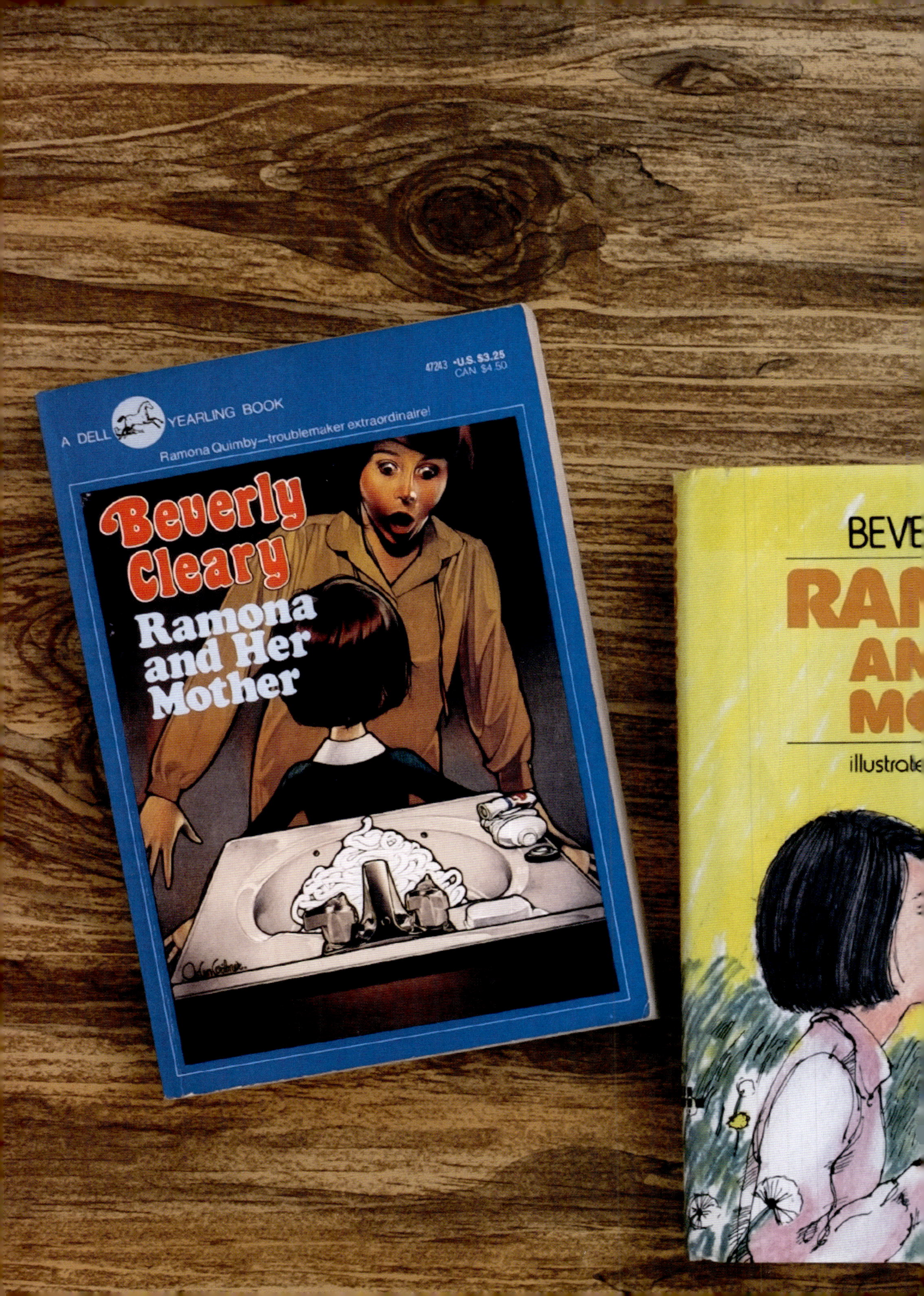

47243 •U.S. $3.25
CAN $4.50
A DELL YEARLING BOOK
Ramona Quimby—troublemaker extraordinaire!
Beverly Cleary
Ramona and Her Mother

Ramona and Her Mother

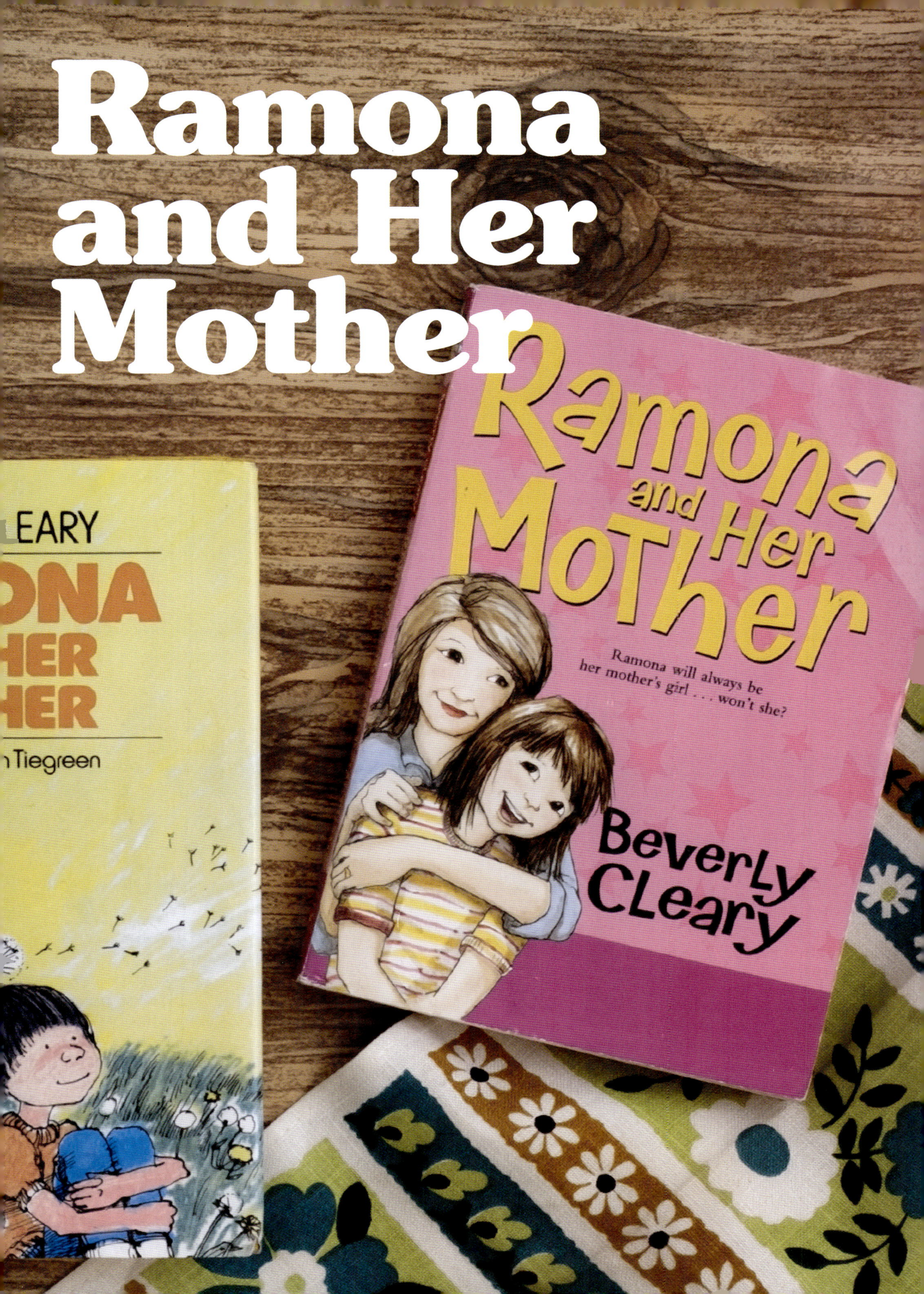

Ramona and Her Mother

Chapter Five

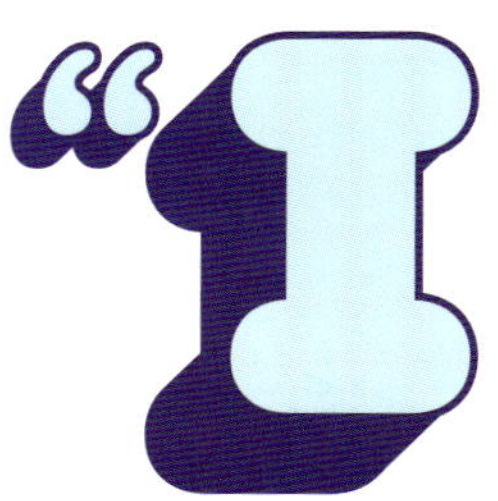

'm going to wash my hair," announced Beezus.

"Again?" inquired Mrs. Quimby. "You washed it only the day before yesterday."

"But it's so oily," complained Beezus.

"Don't worry, it's just your age," reassured Mrs. Quimby. "You'll outgrow it."

"Yes," said Beezus gloomily. "In about a million years when I'm too old to care."

"You'll never be that old," said Mrs. Quimby. "I promise."

The girls are growing up, and Mr. and Mrs. Quimby are taking on new dimensions, beyond their roles simply as Mom and Dad—they are, in fact, humans too. Even more surprising is that Ramona's position as the primary pest has been usurped by Willa Jean. And so the pest becomes the pestered.

Ramona and Her Mother **and the previous book,** ***Ramona and Her Father*****, were published two years apart, in 1979 and 1977, respectively. Ramona is still in second grade, though Mrs. Rogers has gone on maternity leave and been replaced by Mrs. Rudge. Mr. Quimby has found employment as a cashier at a grocery store; after months of unemployment, he appreciates the paycheck but doesn't enjoy the work itself.**

Having two full-time working parents and a seventh-grade sister is not without its challenges. Ramona is growing up fast, but no matter how fast she grows, Beezus always seems to maintain the same distance ahead of her. And now an adolescent, Beezus is going through her own growing pains, which begin to ripple out into the family. (A home haircut, for example, will no longer cut it, and Beezus will go shaggy as a sheepdog to make her point.) After their parents' long workdays, the little attention left over goes to the elder girl, and the younger daughter starts to doubt her mother's love.

JACQUELINE ROGERS (OPPOSITE).

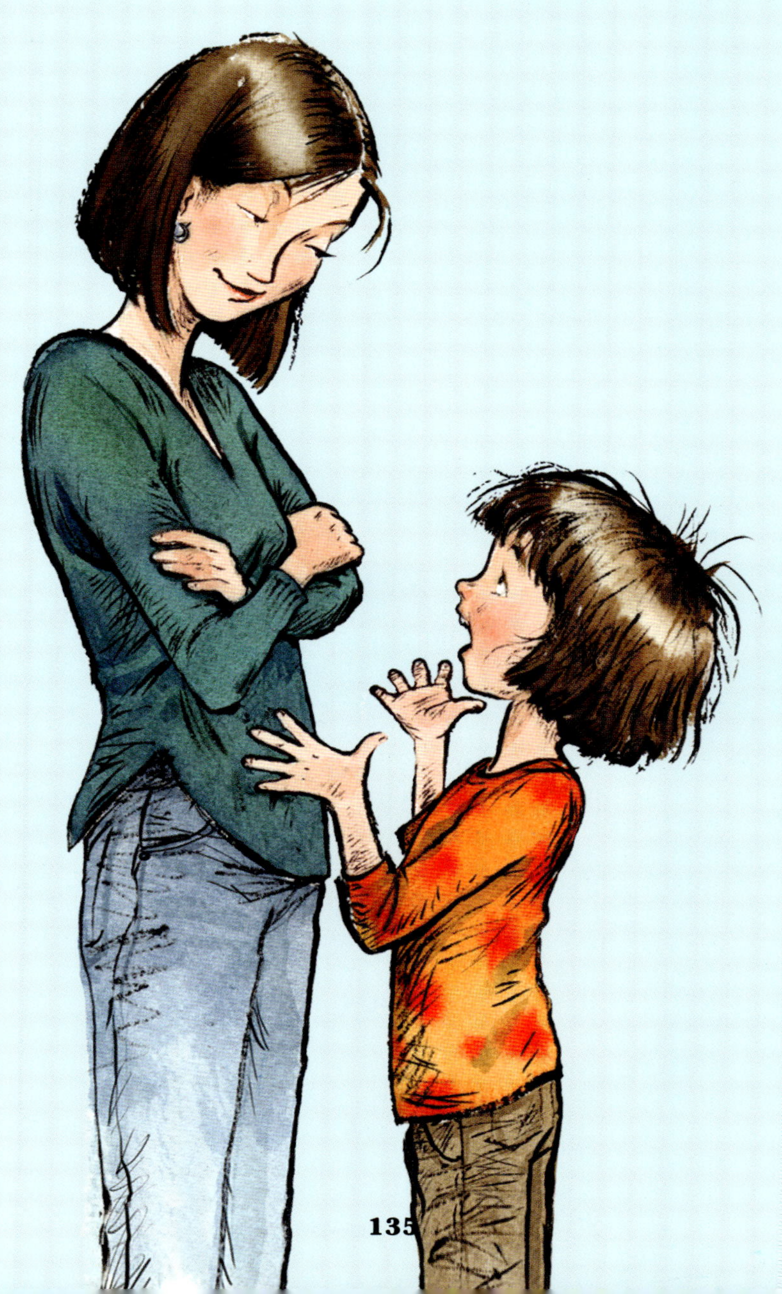

Ramona helps out.

To celebrate both the New Year and Mr. Quimby's new job at the ShopRite Market, the Quimbys host a brunch for some neighbors, including the Kemp family. Ramona has been given the duty of dusting, but in her excitement she can't help but spin and twirl. In Dockray's illustration, she nearly knocks over the lamp while her father looks on in consternation. Tiegreen's Ramona is still, with cloth in hand. Perhaps she has already been scolded for her inattention, or she's been told by her mother, for the zillionth time, to be nice to Willa Jean.

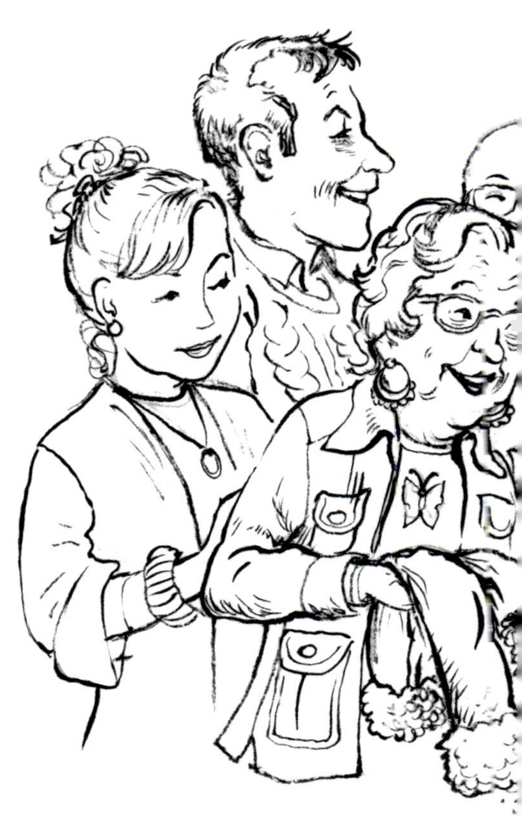

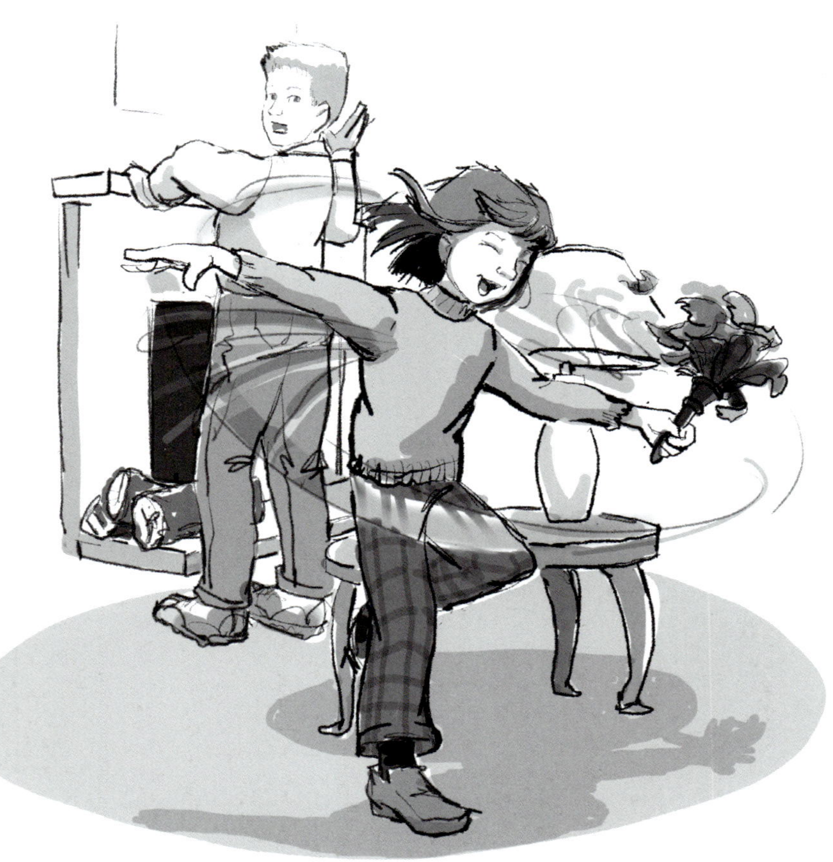

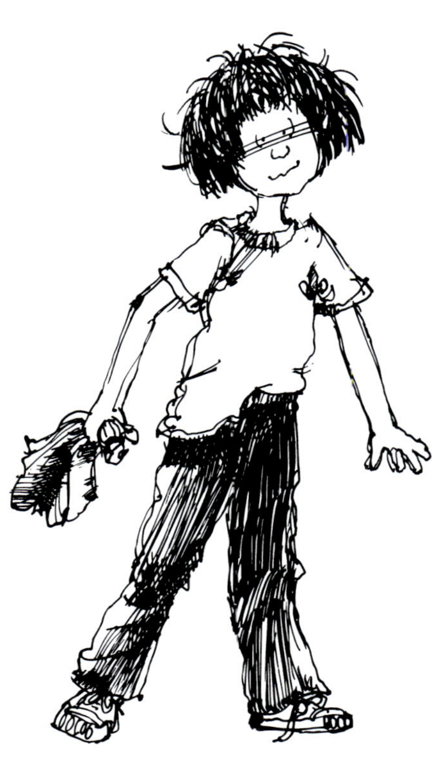

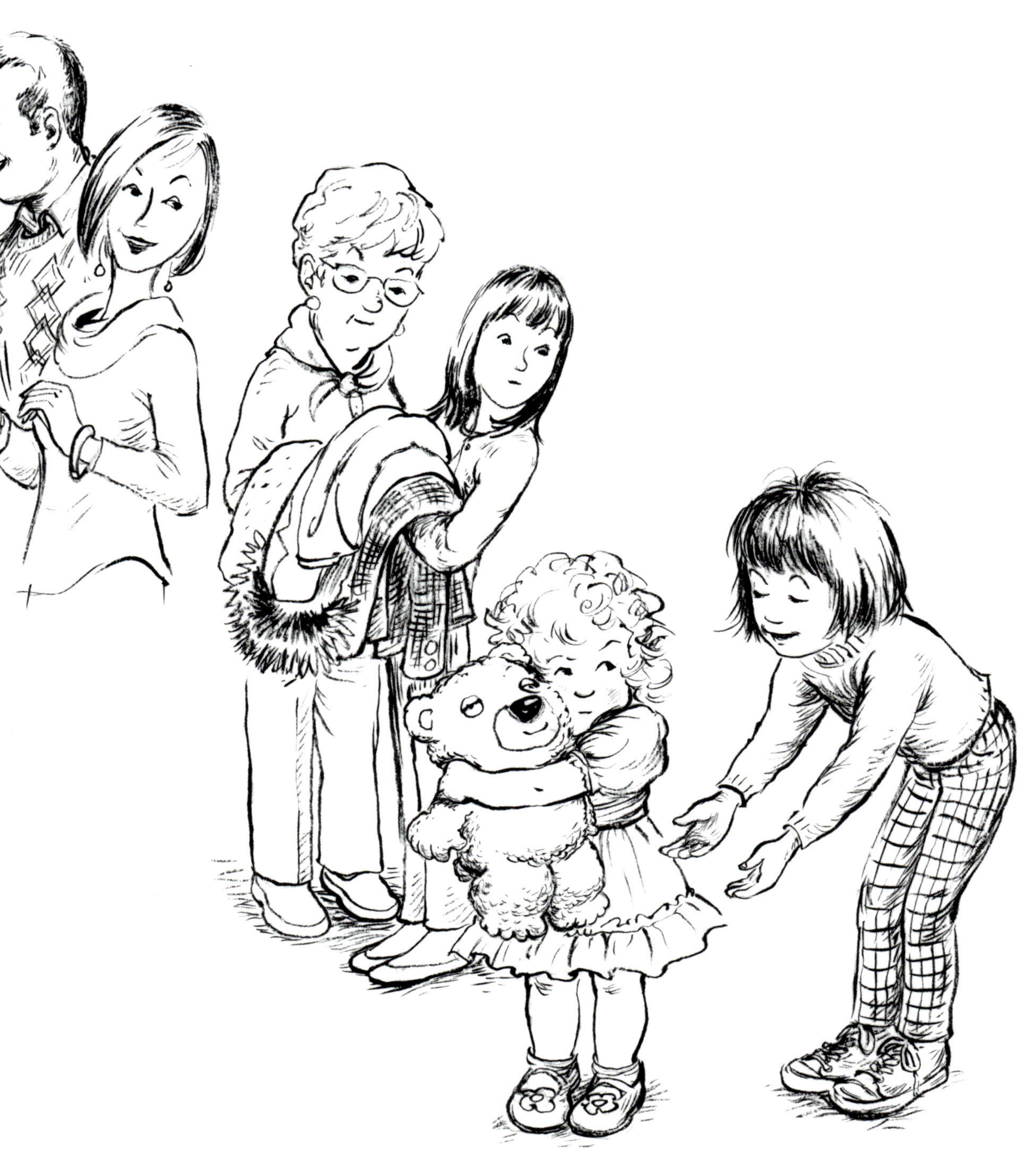

Ramona tries to be nice.

As instructed, Ramona goes out of her way to be nice to the youngest Kemp, kindly offering to hold the teddy bear Woger. Willa Jean is having none of it.

OPPOSITE: TRACY DOCKRAY (LEFT) AND ALAN TIEGREEN (RIGHT). ABOVE: JACQUELINE ROGERS.

“See me!” Willa Jean ordered the grown-ups as she ran around pulling and flinging Kleenex all over the room.

A very grown-up Beezus is just as shocked as the adults at the little girl's behavior. In Tiegreen's illustration, Ramona takes a back-seat to the action, appalled too but also a little bit jealous—she's always wanted to pull out a whole box of tissues one sheet at a time. She stands front and to the right of the little hellion in Dockray's illustration, a tissue on her head. Willa Jean is becoming less and less cute by the second.

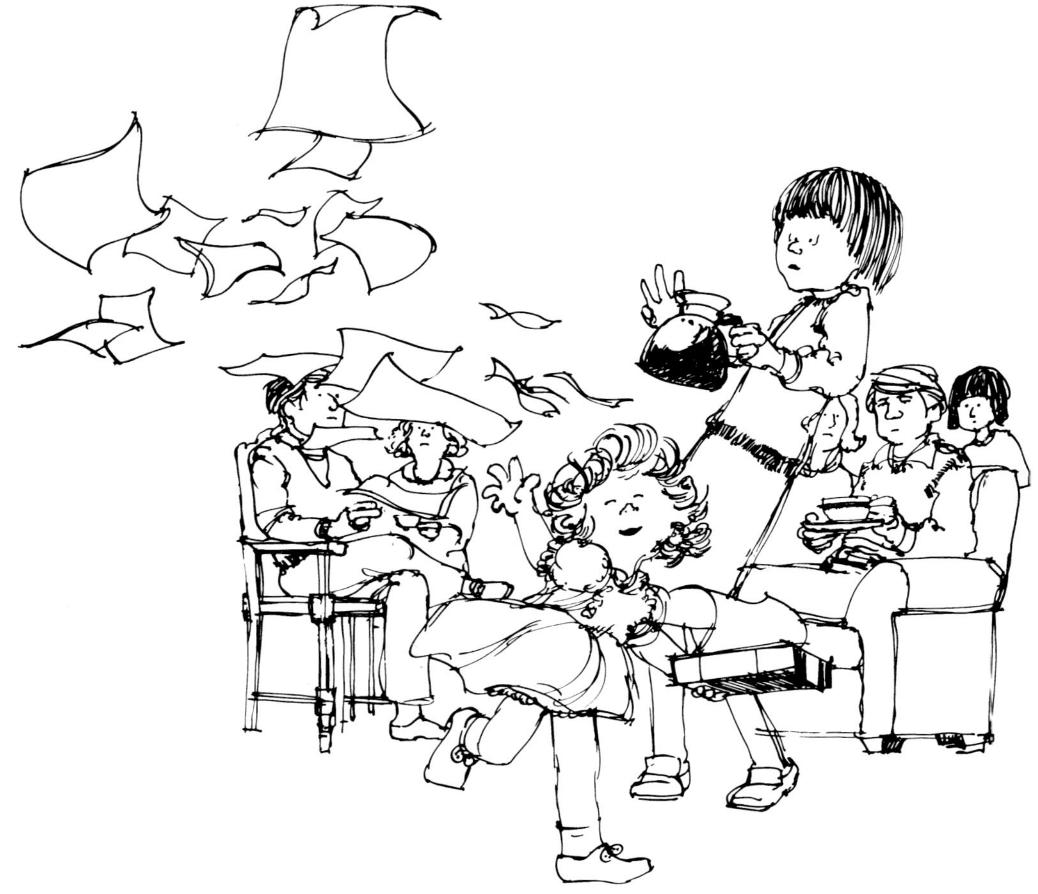

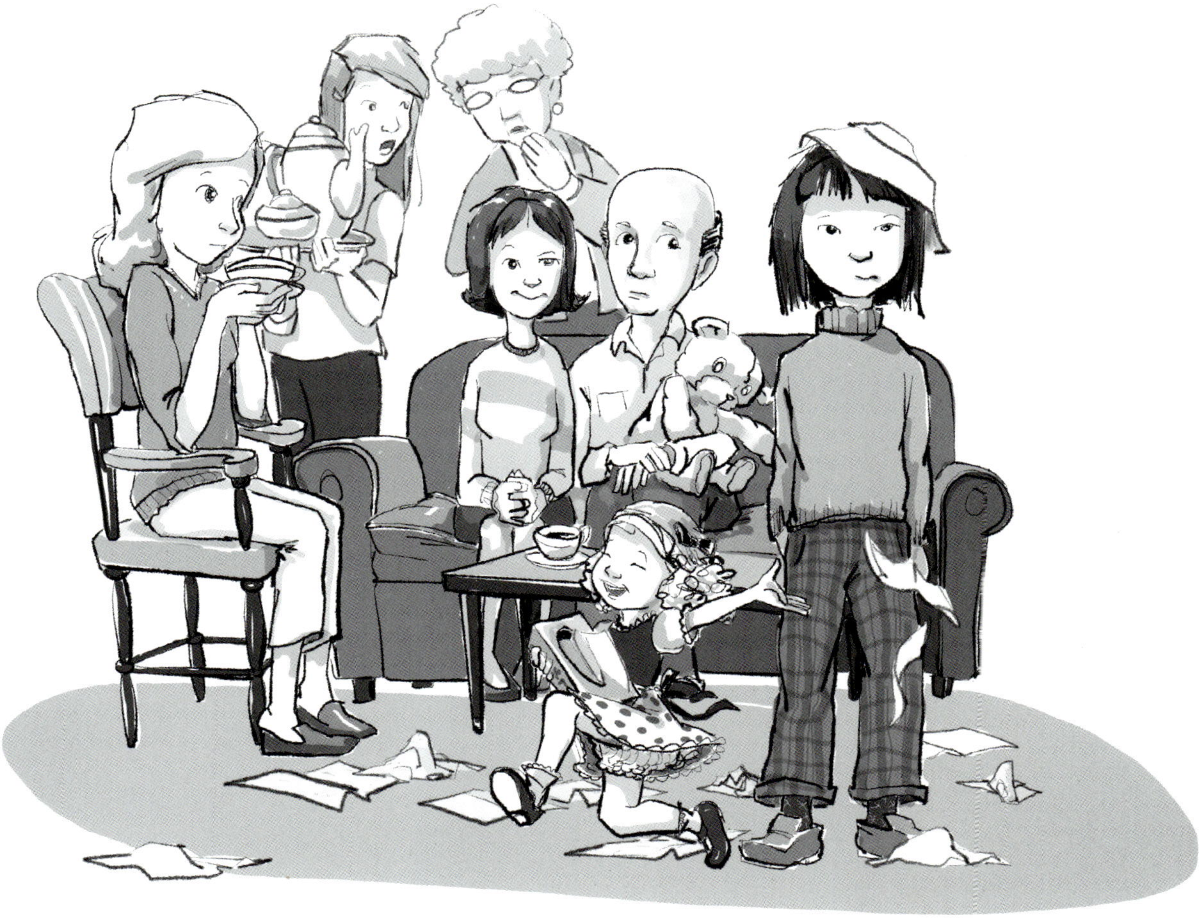

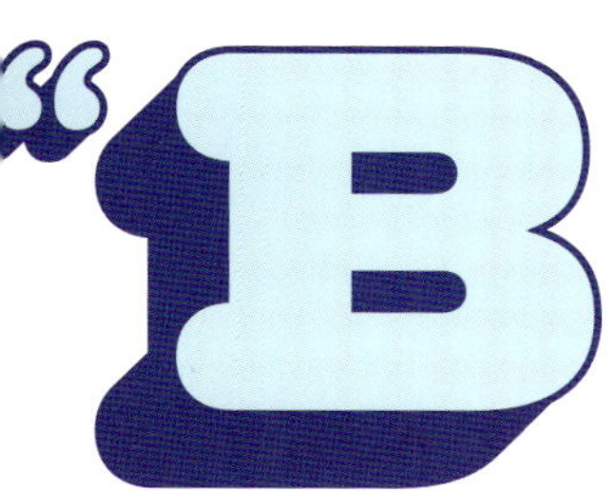

"Bye-bye," said Willa Jean prettily as her father carried her and Woger out the door. Other guests were telling Mr. and Mrs. Quimby how much they had enjoyed the brunch. Beezus was standing beside them as if it had been her party, too. Mrs. McCarthy smiled. "I can see you are your mother's girl," she said.

"I couldn't get along without her," Mrs. Quimby replied generously.

I never was as awful as Willa Jean, Ramona told herself as she went to work collecting two hundred and fifty pieces of scattered pink Kleenex. I just know I wasn't. She followed the trail of Kleenex back to her bedroom, and when the two hundred and fiftieth piece was stuffed in the bag, she leaned against her dresser to study herself in the mirror.

How come nobody ever calls me my mother's girl? Ramona thought. How come Mother never says she couldn't get along without me?

ALAN TIEGREEN (OPPOSITE) AND TRACY DOCKRAY (ABOVE).

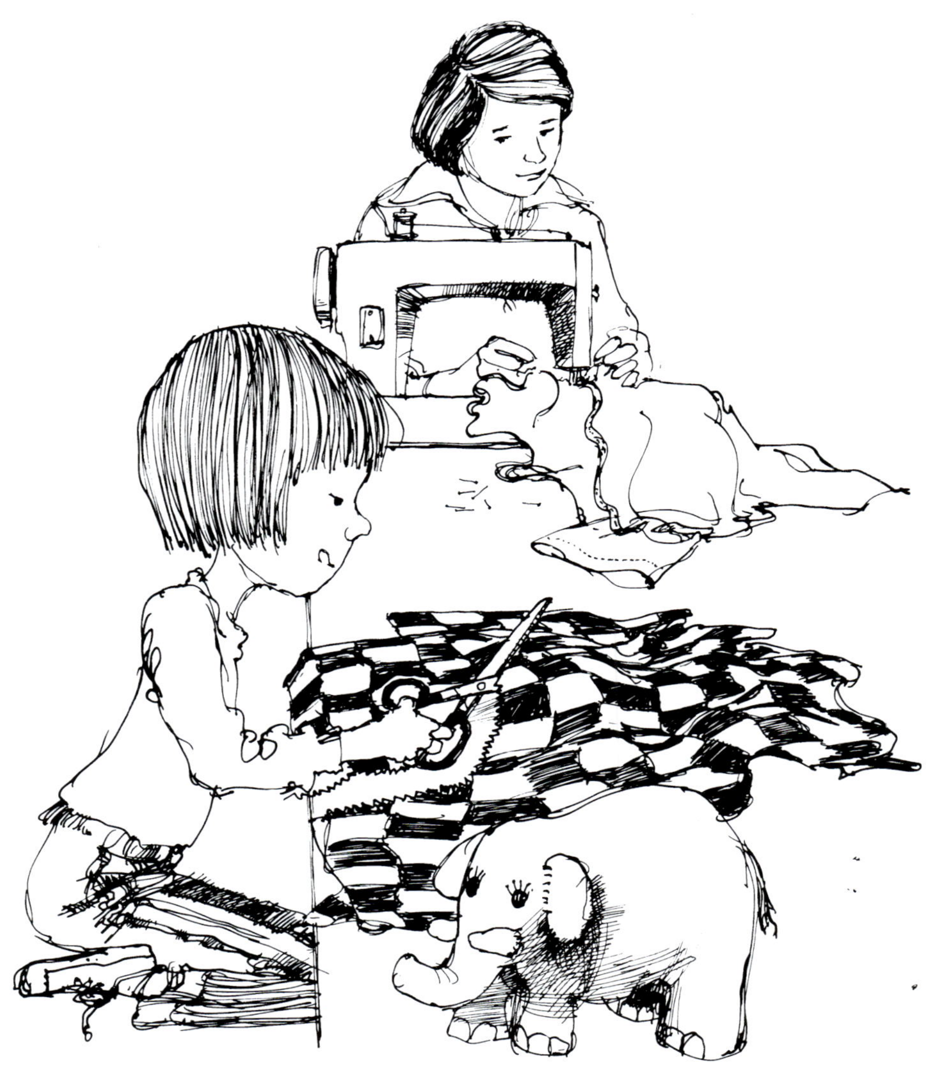

A cozy Saturday with Mother and Beezus.

Perhaps inspired by Willa Jean's Woger, Ramona takes Ella Funt out of retirement in order to sew her a pair of slacks while Mrs. Quimby finishes a blouse and Beezus works on a skirt. Mrs. Quimby allows her youngest to use the sewing machine for the first time but hints that sewing pants for an elephant won't be easy. Ramona is undeterred.

ALAN TIEGREEN (ABOVE) AND TRACY DOCKRAY (OPPOSITE).

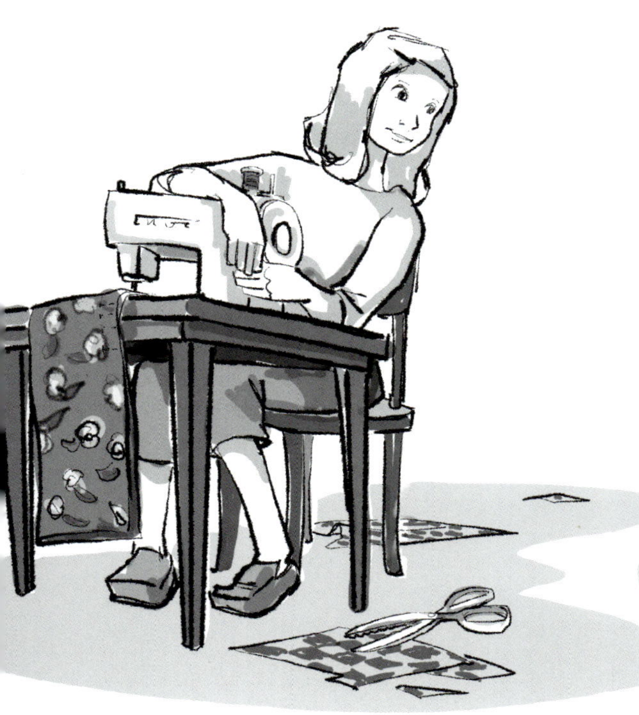

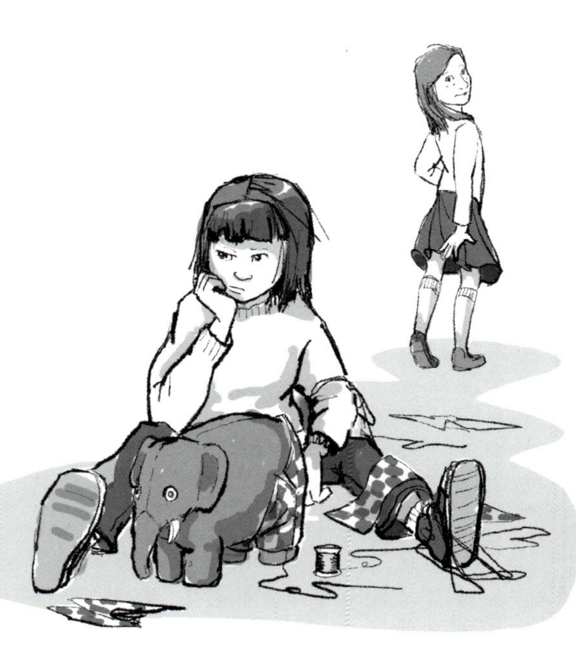

Ramona tugged and tugged at Ella Funt's slacks, but no matter how hard she tugged she could not make them come up to the elephant's waist, or to what she guessed was the elephant's waist. Ella Funt's bottom was too big, or the slacks were too small. At the same time, the front of the slacks seemed way too big. They bunched under Ella Funt's paunch. Ramona scowled.

Just after bragging to Beezus about being able to use the sewing machine too, Ramona must acknowledge that her mother was correct about the difficulty of the project. In the background, Beezus admires her own handiwork on a skirt, probably just to be intentionally annoying, then suggests that Ramona make Ella Funt a skirt. This does not improve Ramona's mood.

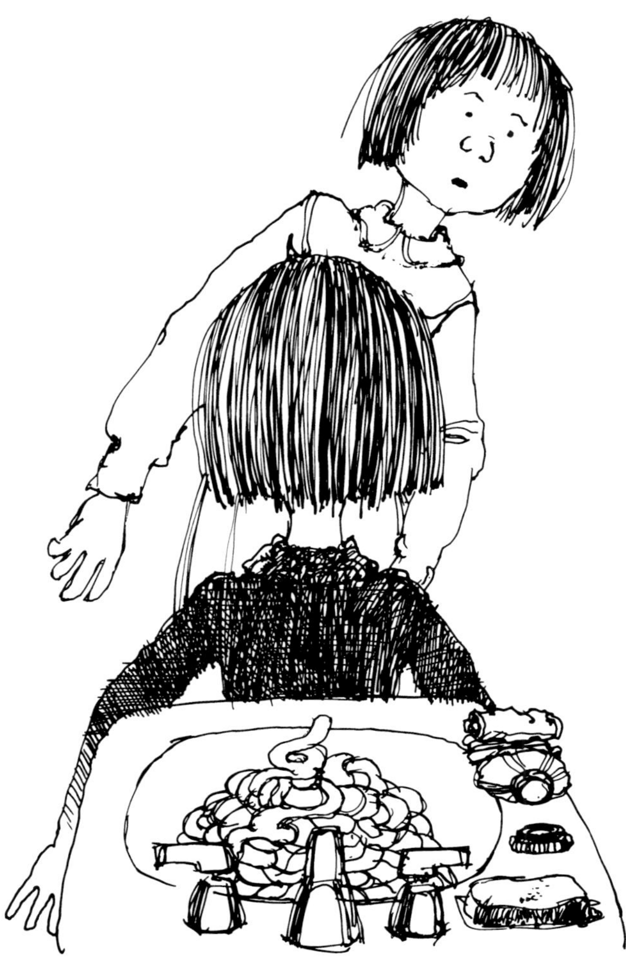

Ramona takes out her feelings on the family's tube of toothpaste.

To Ramona, the failure to sew Ella Funt a proper pair of slacks is not just one of life's little disappointments, as her mother claimed. It is a very big disappointment, and she knows the difference! The second-grader is used to being disappointed, what with never being able to find a tricycle license plate with her name on it. And then there was that time she'd found only two little crushed chocolate eggs on the Easter Egg hunt in the park, and also there's having to go to bed every night at eight-thirty and miss the ending of every movie on television! It's a lot for a seven-year-old to bear. What is a disappointed girl to do?

It is while crying in the bathroom that Ramona notices the brand-new economy-size tube of toothpaste next to the sink. Surely, she reasons to herself, just one little squeeze would make her feel better. Tiegreen drew this scene for the book's interior, while Scribner chose this same moment for her full-color cover. Many of the illustrations' details are identical—the location of the tube of toothpaste and cap, the bar of soap, the general shape of the disgorged toothpaste in the sink, Ramona's position, the composition of the drawing as a whole. Tiegreen's illustration features Beezus in the initial moment of discovery while Ramona attempts to hide the minty mound. The elder sister has a perplexed look on her face and, of course, she immediately tattles to their mother. In Scribner's version, Mrs. Quimby has arrived on the scene and seems more appalled than perplexed. In this drawing, the cartoonishness of the toothpaste contrasts with the more realistic rendering of the faucet in the foreground and Mrs. Quimby in the background, as per Scribner's style—the illustrator believed that the realism and vividness of the people on the book cover was the best way to attract readers.

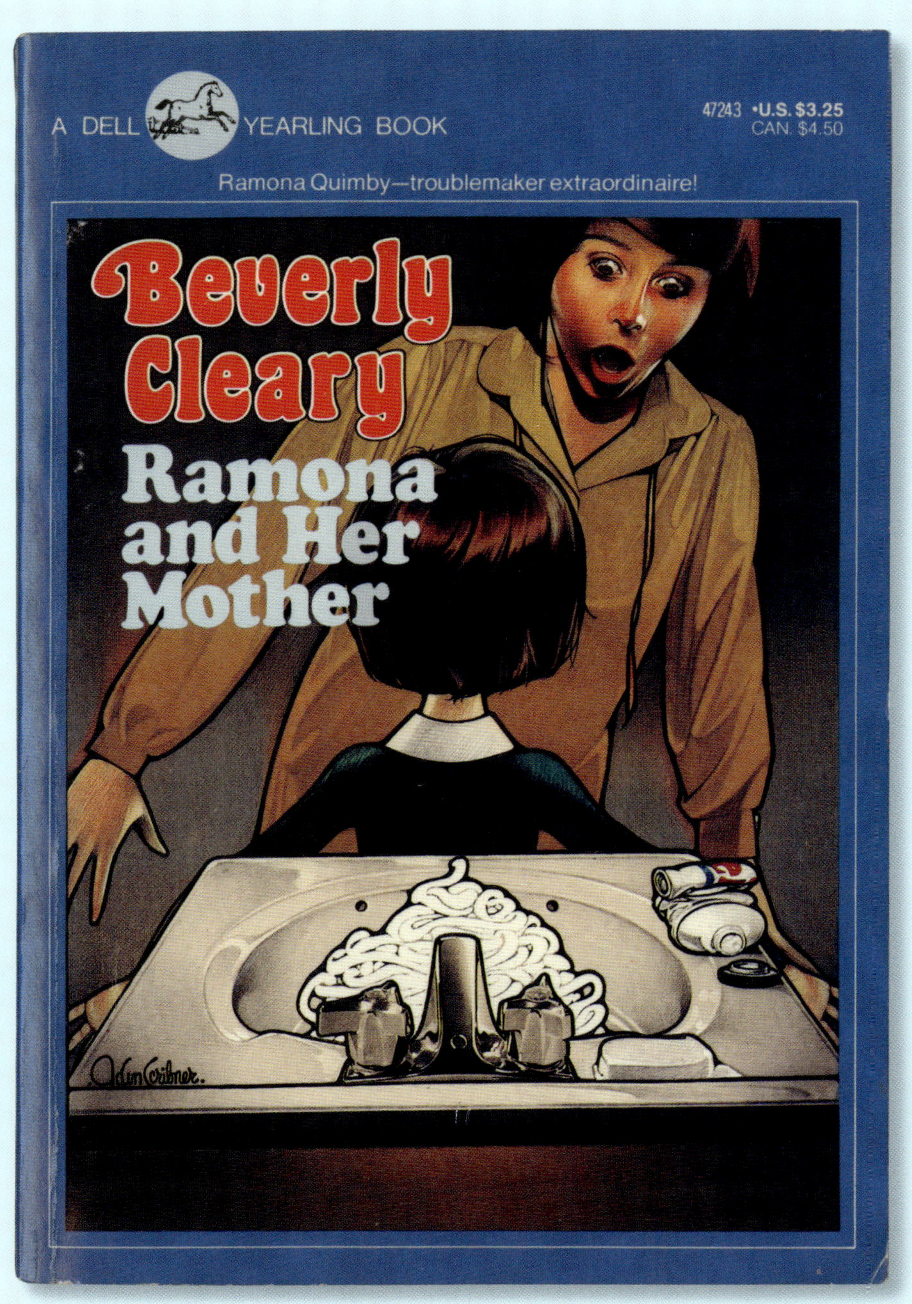

ALAN TIEGREEN (OPPOSITE) AND JOANNE SCRIBNER (ABOVE).

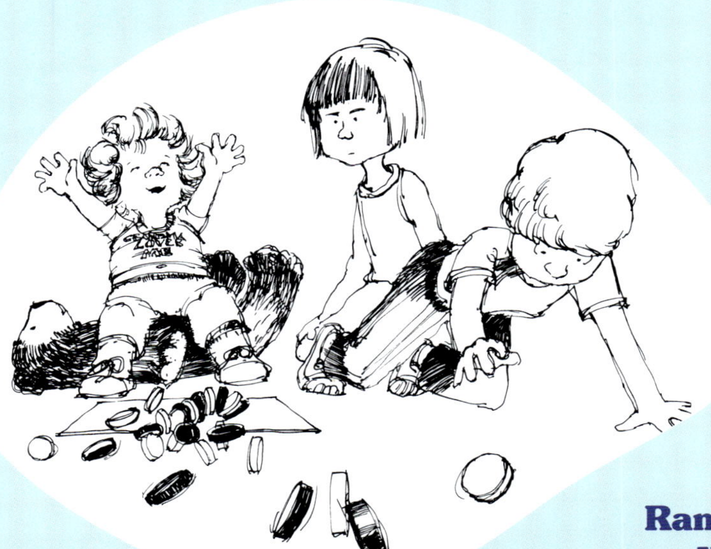

Ramona was never a such a pest as Willa Jean.

Or was she? In Louis Darling's cover art for *Beezus and Ramona* (page 28), a bunny-eared four-year-old Ramona crashes into Beezus and Henry Huggins's checkers game. In Tiegreen's illustration for *Ramona and Her Mother*, Willa Jean intrudes on Ramona and Howie's game in, some might argue, a less disruptive fashion. At least there's no tricycle involved.

The boat floated. Howie and Ramona stirred up a storm at sea to make things interesting and watched their boat ride the waves. As it bobbed up and down, Ramona happened to glance up at a shelf above the laundry tub. There she spotted a blue plastic bottle with the picture of a nice old-fashioned lady's face on the label. Bluing!

Ramona knew all about bluing because her mother had used it to make white washing look whiter back in the days before she had gone to work. "If we could get that bottle, we could turn the water blue like a real ocean," she suggested. "It only takes a little bit."

To escape Willa Jean, Howie and Ramona go down to the basement to build a boat. Rogers shows the first optimistic phase of the climb to get the bluing bottle, with Howie assisting Ramona by holding her knees. Tiegreen provides a bird's-eye view of the scene some moments later when the cap to the bottle of bluing comes loose. Dockray depicts the blue-handed and blue-footed second-graders facing the consequences of their actions.

ABOVE: ALAN TIEGREEN. OPPOSITE, CLOCKWISE FROM TOP RIGHT: ALAN TIEGREEN, TRACY DOCKRAY, AND JACQUELINE ROGERS.

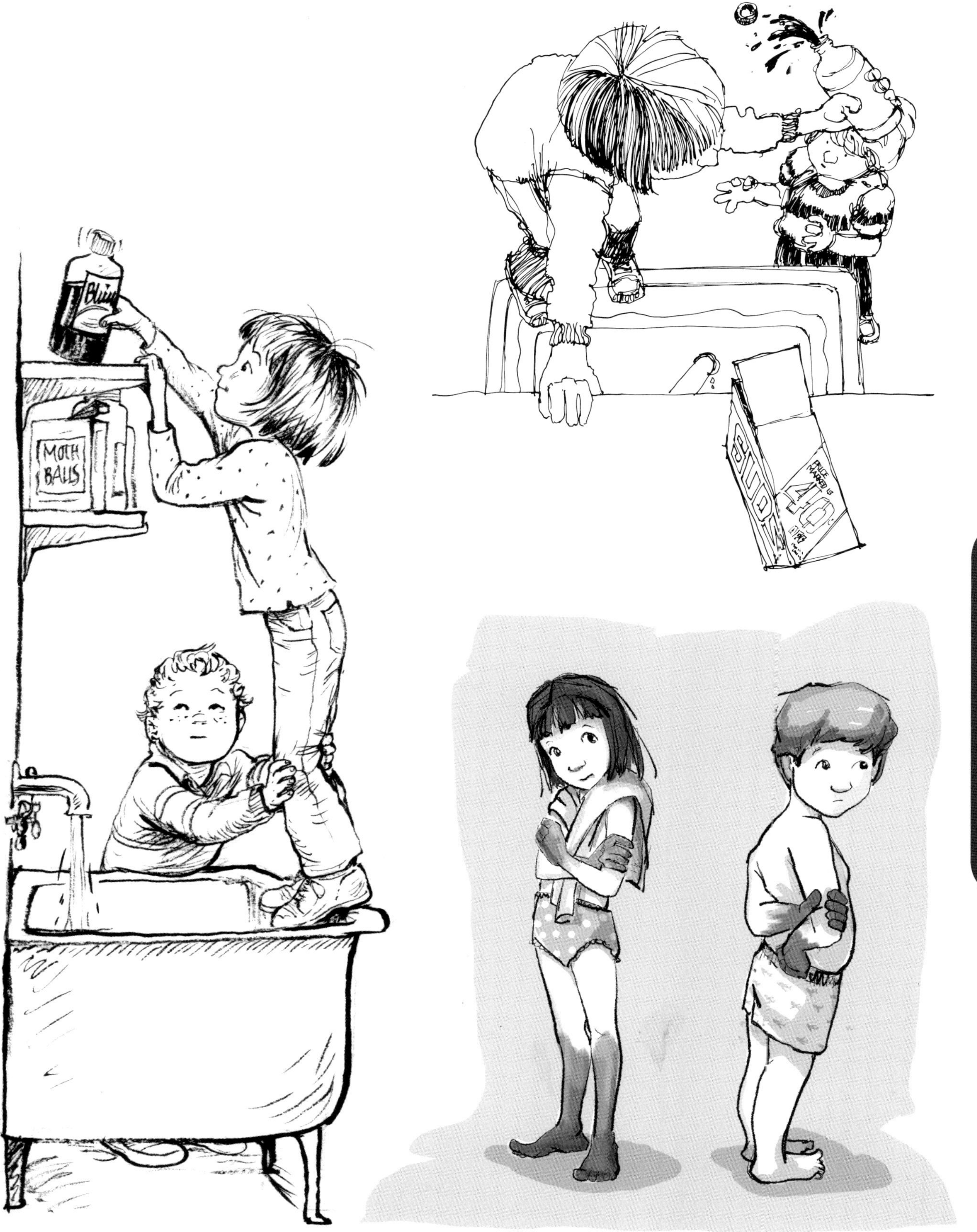
MOTH BALLS
SUDS

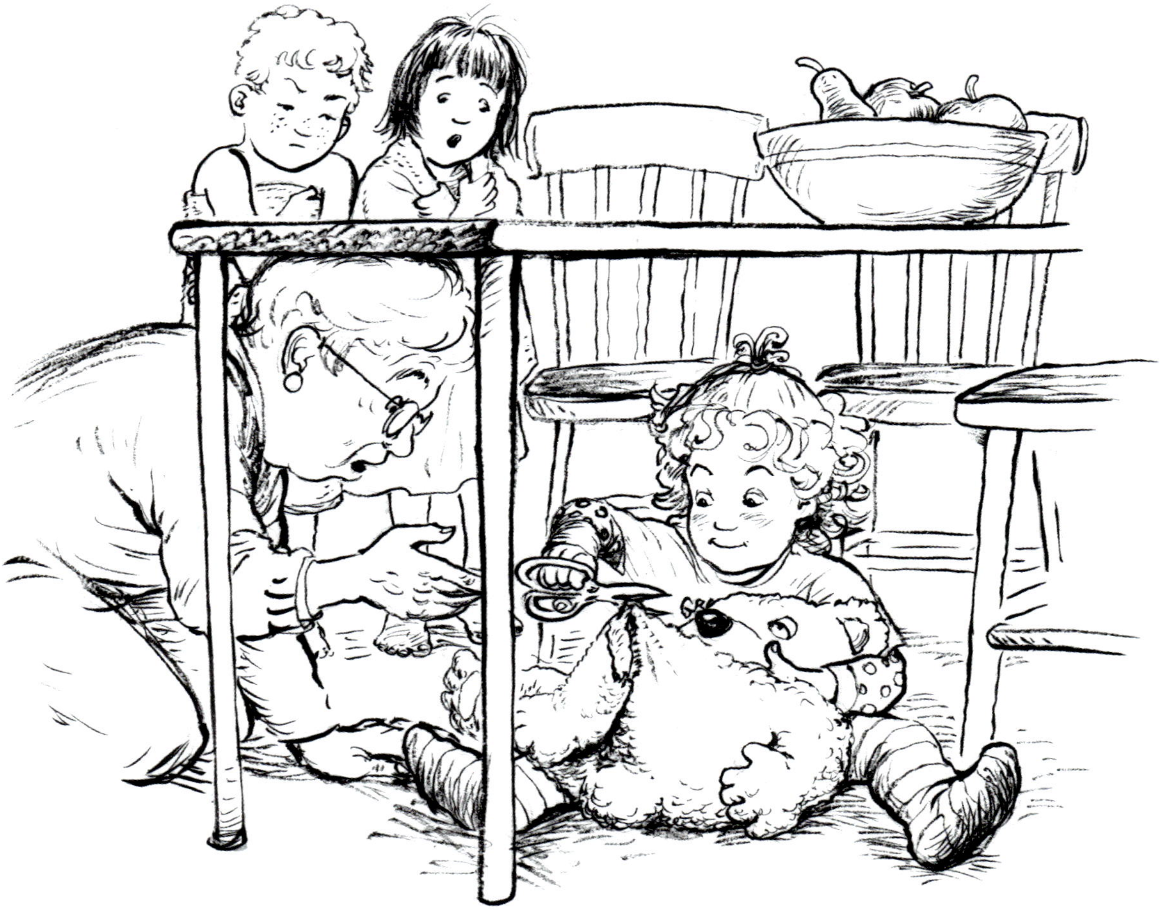

uddenly Mrs. Kemp missed Willa Jean. "Oh, my goodness!" she cried, and dashed up the stairs. Ramona and Howie, careful not to look at one another, followed. What Ramona saw made tears come to her eyes. There sat Willa Jean under the dining-room table holding a pair of scissors, sharp scissors, and Woger, who now had only one leg. Willa Jean had cut off Woger's leg! That lovable bear. How could Willa Jean do such a terrible thing? Ramona felt like crying, she loved Woger so.

"Give Grandma the scissors," coaxed Mrs. Kemp. "We don't want the scissors to hurt Willa Jean."

"Boy, Willa Jean." Howie was disgusted. "What did you have to go and do a dumb thing like that for?"

Willa Jean looked as if her brother had said something unkind. "I wanted to see if Woger had bones," she said.

How could this terrible day get any worse?

The terrible day gets worse.

Mrs. Quimby's bus was late, and when she finally got to the garage she found that the mechanics hadn't finished fixing the car. After waiting for them to do so, she went to pick up Mr. Quimby, then Beezus, then Ramona, who'd had to sit on the Kemps' couch while the family ate dinner.

The Quimbys were all looking forward to getting home to the nice warm stew that had been cooking in the Crock-Pot all day. The only problem, they soon discovered, was that someone forgot to turn on the Crock-Pot. Here, Mrs. Quimby lifts the lid to find a pot full of raw meat and cold vegetables. Tired and hangry, with two starving children looking on, the parents try to figure out who is to blame. "I suppose you think turning on a Crock-Pot is woman's work," Mrs. Quimby says to her husband. And so the quarrel of all quarrels begins. In Dockray's illustration, the whole family gathers around the unappetizing sight.

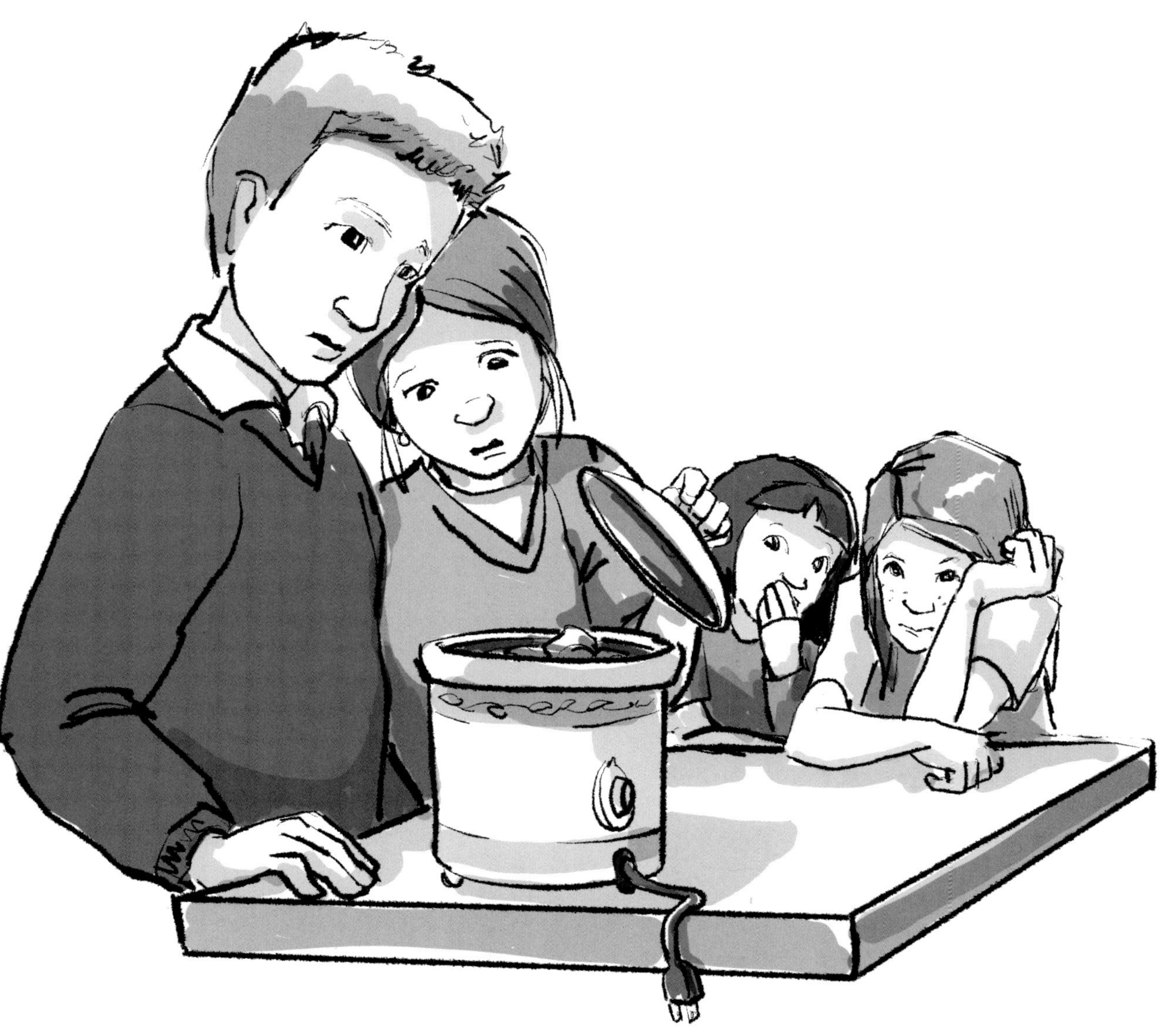

JACQUELINE ROGERS (OPPOSITE) AND TRACY DOCKRAY (ABOVE).

RAMONA AND HER MOTHER

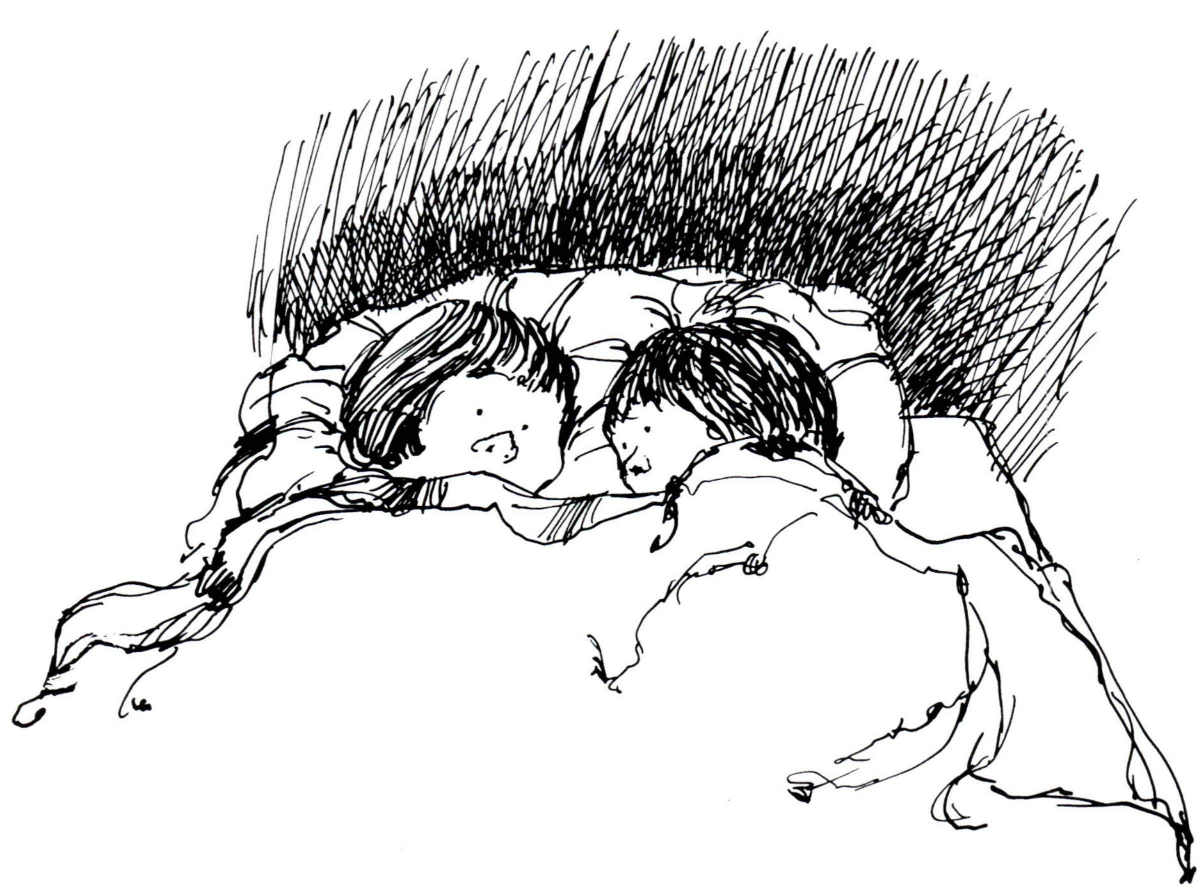

After a terrible day, Ramona slips into bed with her sister.

Huddled under the blankets in the dark, the two girls discuss divorce. Who will take care of Ramona if their parents split up? Beezus thinks it over, then tells her little sister that she'll try, even though she herself isn't really grown-up enough yet. Before falling asleep, Ramona prays that her parents will no longer fight. Tiegreen captures the fear and insecurity of the moment, just as he did in *Ramona the Brave*, when Ramona slept alone for the first time in her new room. It's a sweet moment in which the sisters comfort each other.

ALAN TIEGREEN (ABOVE AND OPPOSITE).

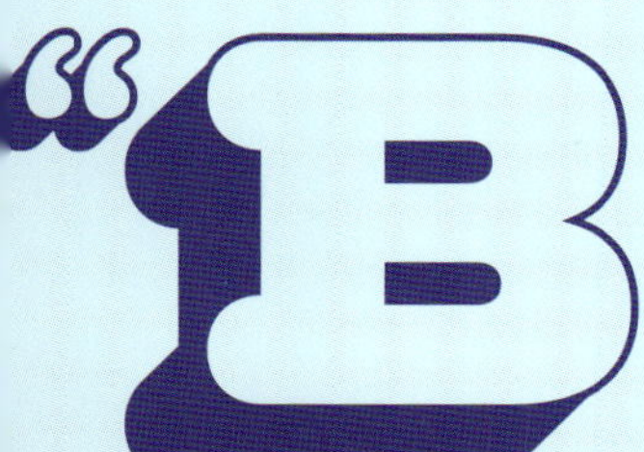

“Be sensible,” said Mrs. Quimby.

Beezus scowled. “I’ve been good old sensible Beezus all my life, and I’m tired of being sensible.” She underlined this announcement by adding, “Ramona can get away with anything, but not me. No. I always have to be good old sensible Beezus.”

“That’s not so.” Ramona was indignant. “I never get away with anything.”

After a thoughtful moment, Mrs. Quimby spoke. “So am I tired of being sensible all the time.”

Both sisters were surprised, Ramona most of all. Mothers were supposed to be sensible. That was what mothers were for.

Mrs. Quimby continued. “Once in a while I would like to do something that isn’t sensible.”

“Like what?” asked Beezus.

“Oh—I don’t know.” Mrs. Quimby looked at the breakfast dishes in the sink and at the rain spattering against the windows. “Sit on a cushion in the sunshine, I guess, and blow the fluff off dandelions.”

Beezus looked as if she did not quite believe her mother. “Weeds don’t bloom this time of year,” she pointed out.

Ramona felt suddenly close to her mother and a little shy. “I would like to sit on a cushion and blow dandelion fluff with you,” she confided, thinking what fun it would be, just the two of them, sitting in warm sunshine, blowing on the yellow blossoms, sending dandelion down dancing off into the sunlight. She leaned against her mother, who put her arm around her and gave her a little hug. Ramona twitched her nose with pleasure.

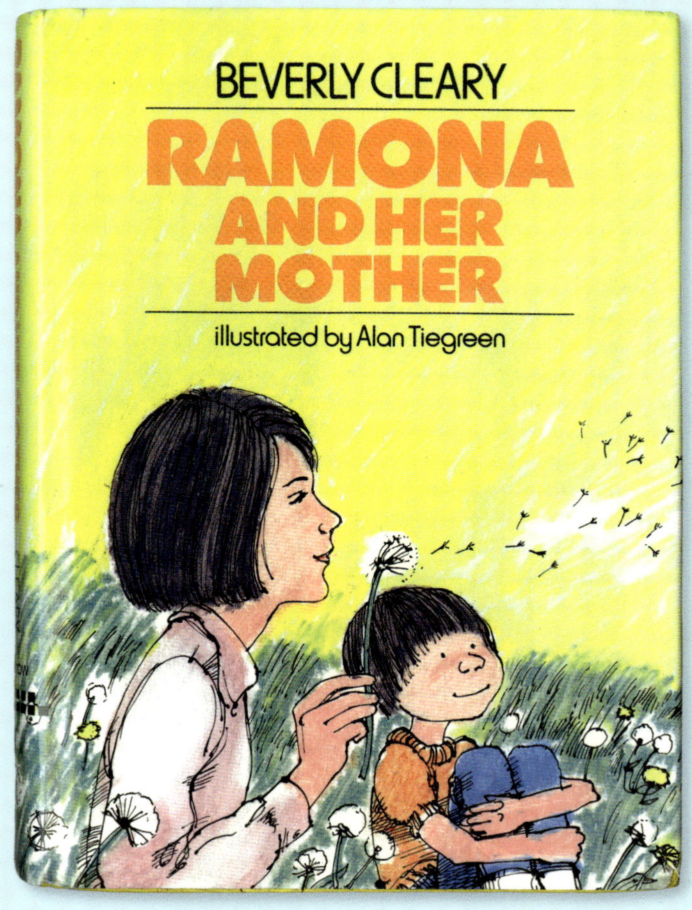

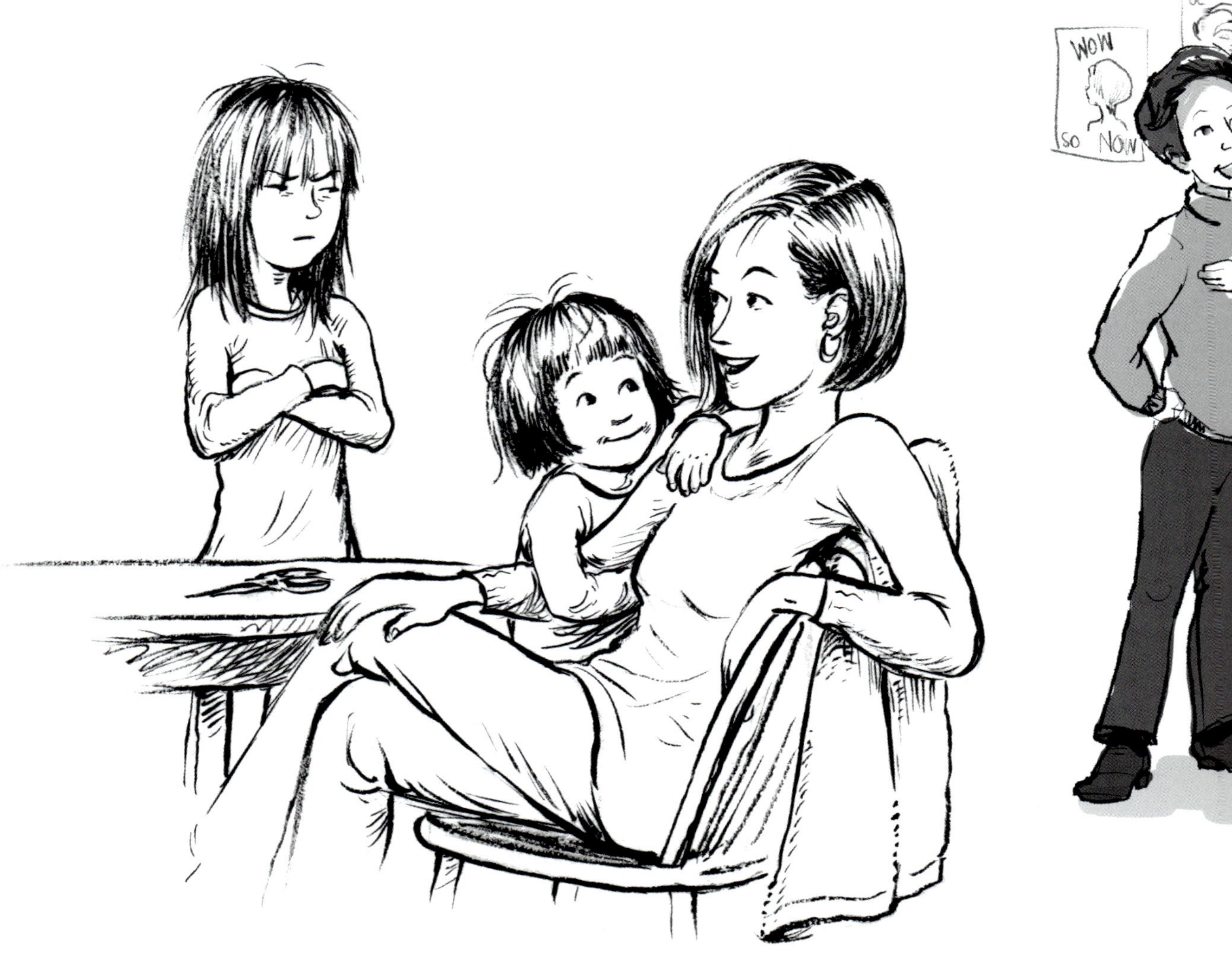

Shaggy Beezus needs a haircut.

This is the first, but certainly not the last, big fight between mother and elder adolescent daughter. Never before has Beezus minded her home haircut, but now, as a seventh-grader, she's desperate for a beauty shop haircut like all the other girls have. And she'll refuse the scissors until she gets what she wants. For once, Ramona is the good girl—or, according to Beezus, a goody-goody and a little twerp. See how the youngest Quimby revels in this rare moment while her scowling sister, arms crossed, stands her ground.

ABOVE, LEFT TO RIGHT: JACQUELINE ROGERS, TRACY DOCKRAY, AND ALAN TIEGREEN.

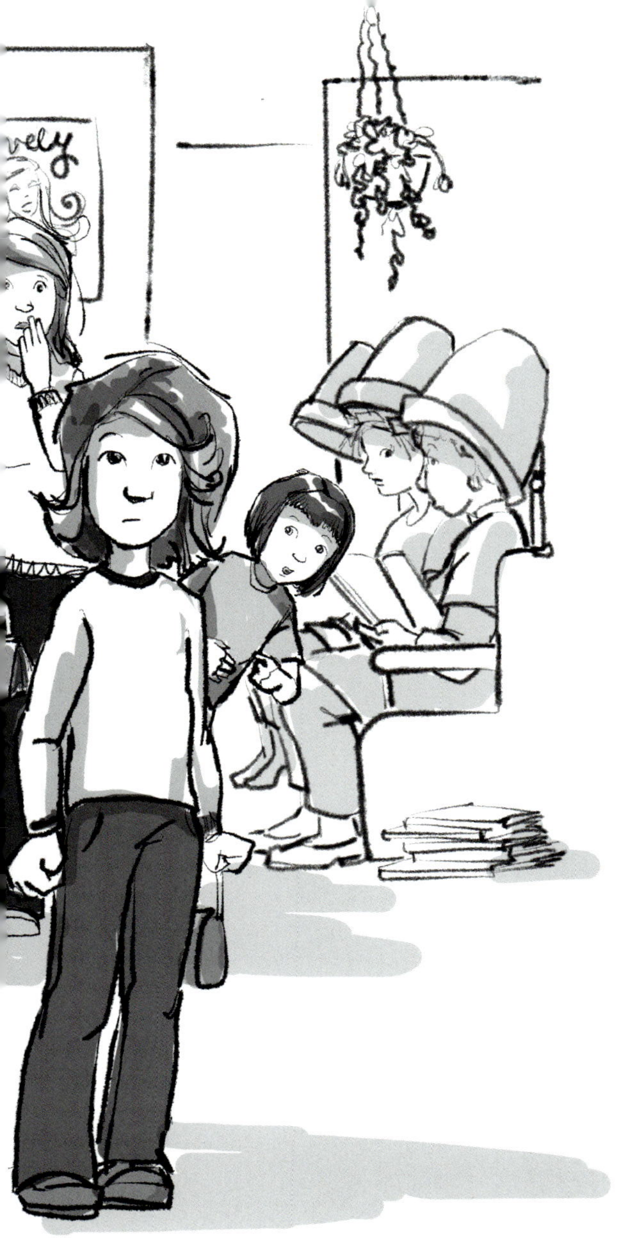

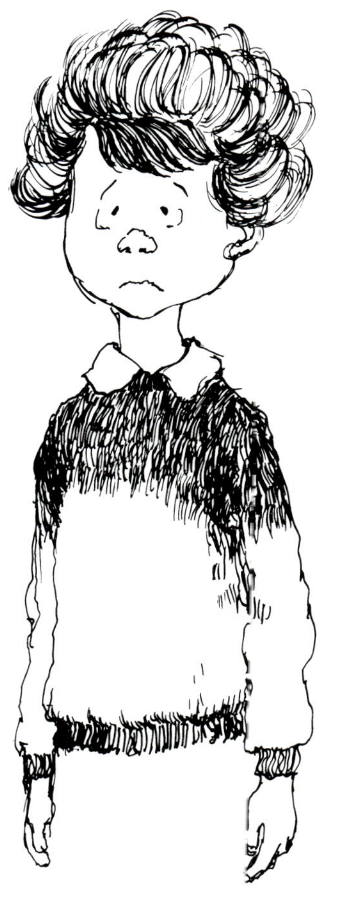

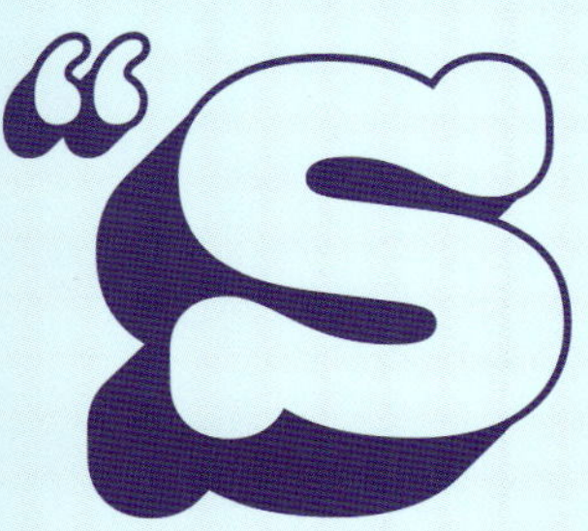

“Some of the girls at school get their hair cut at Robert's School of Hair Design. People who are learning to cut hair do the work, but a teacher watches to see that they do it right. It doesn't cost as much as a regular beauty shop. I've saved my allowance, and there's this lady named Dawna who is really good and can cut hair so it looks like that girl who ice skates on TV. You know, the one with the hair that sort of floats when she twirls around and then falls in place when she stops. Please, Mother, I have enough money saved.”

Beezus is likely referring to Dorothy Hamill, a 1976 Olympic and world-champion figure skater, and her signature wedge cut. (This book was published three years later, in 1979, so the skater and her hair were hot news at the time of its writing.) Unfortunately, Dawna has recently graduated from Robert's School of Hair Design, and the new student who takes over isn't quite able to pull off the look. In Dockray's illustration, Mrs. Quimby and Ramona—as well as a couple of other customers, now worried—stand behind Beezus and her atrocious haircut, biting their tongues. In Tiegreen's version, we see Beezus and the horror of her hair all alone.

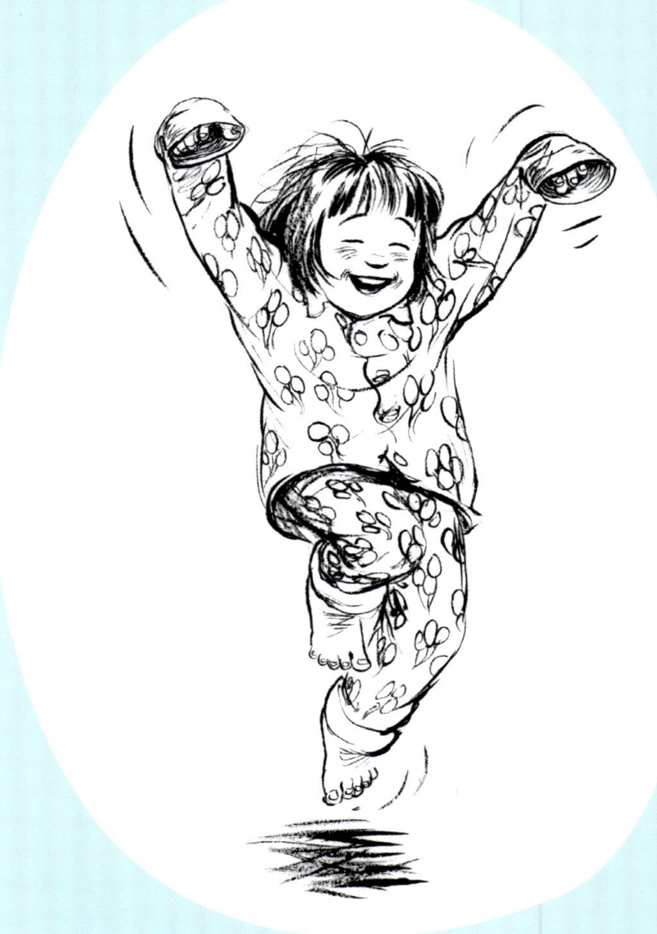

Ramona gets new pajamas.

These big pajamas—which are *not* hand-me-downs from Beezus and not too tight like the ones that Ramona had previously been wearing—make hopping around like a little rabbit so much easier.

JACQUELINE ROGERS (ABOVE) AND TRACY DOCKRAY (OPPOSITE).

"Your cheeks are very pink," said Mrs. Rudge. "I think you had better go to the office and ask Mrs. Miller to take your temperature."

So comfortable is Ramona in her new fuzzy pajamas that she decides to wear them to school, underneath her clothing, a decision she'll soon regret. Here, a hot and sweaty Ramona sits in the office with a thermometer in her mouth. In Dockray's illustration, we can see Ramona's pajamas poking out at the ankles, wrists, and waist, and sweaty hair sticking to her face. She also includes a desktop computer, which had been invented but wasn't in mainstream use at the time of the first edition's release in 1979.

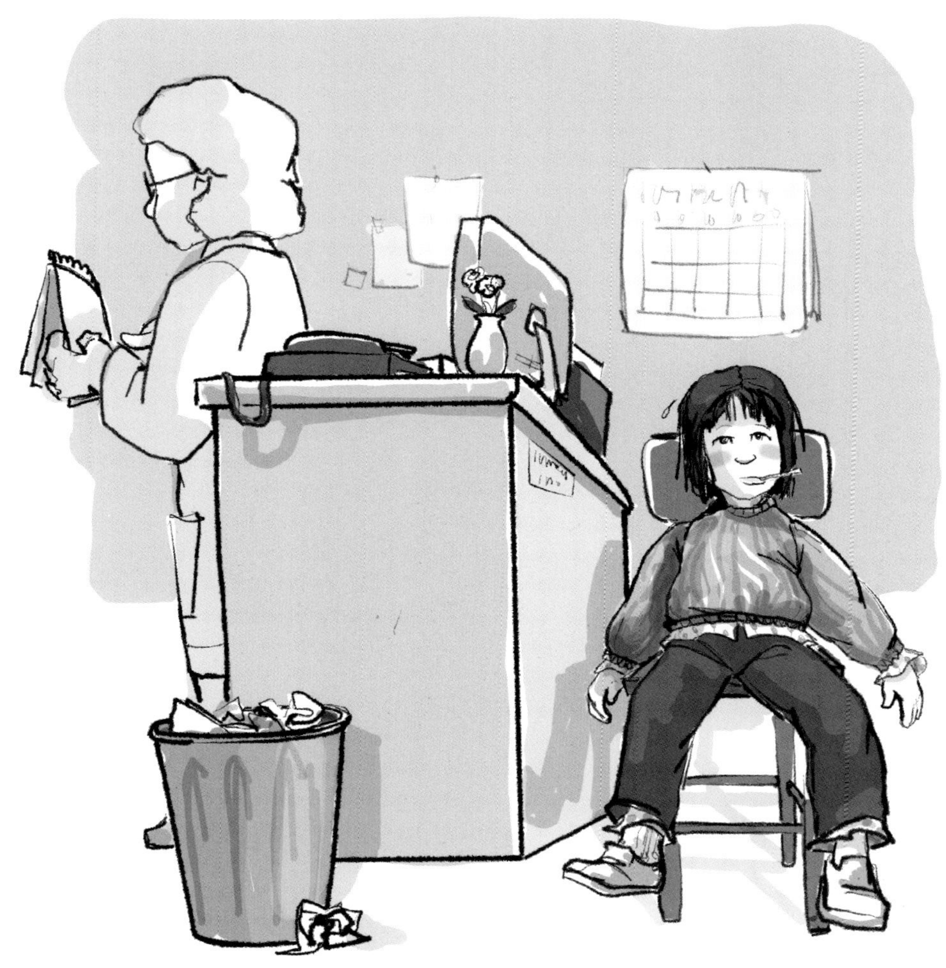

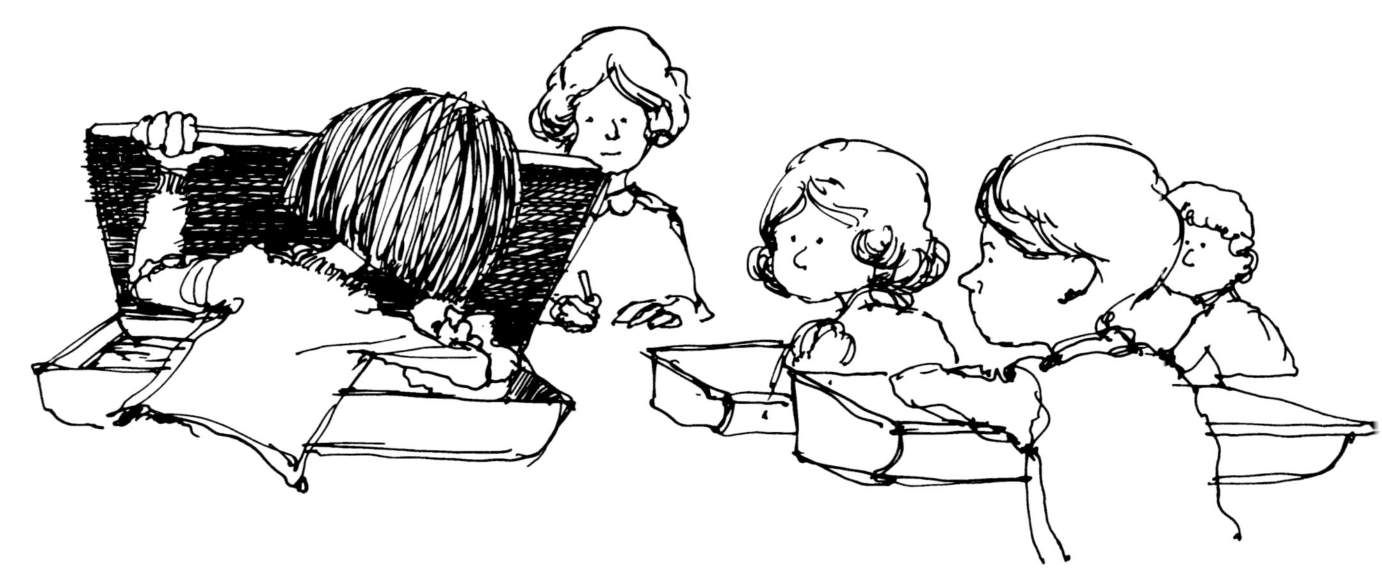

Ramona hides her sweaty pajamas.

After Mrs. Rudge finally gets Ramona to admit to the problem, the teacher suggests that she go and take off her pajamas in the bathroom and then hide them in her desk. Mrs. Rudge promises that she won't tell Ramona's mother.

ALAN TIEGREEN (ABOVE) AND JACQUELINE ROGERS (OPPOSITE).

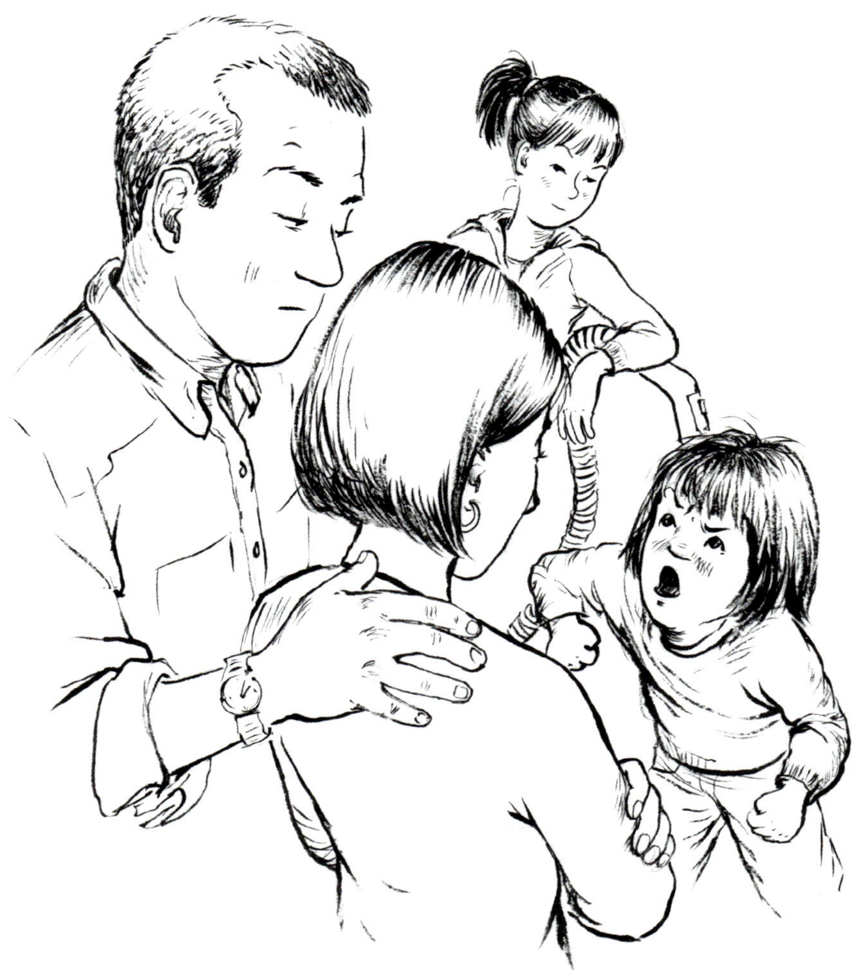

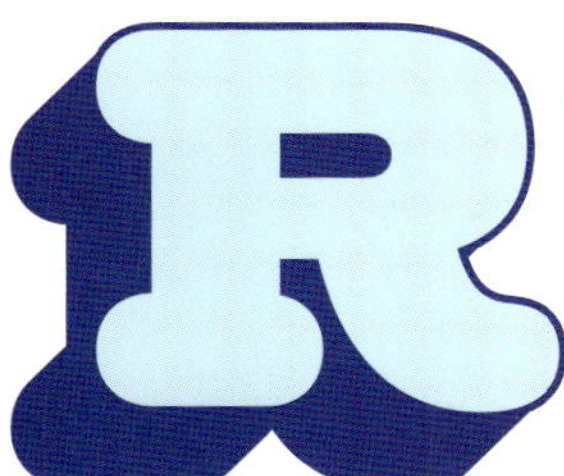

amona faced her mother. "Mrs. Rudge told!" she shouted. "And she promised she would never tell. And then you had to go and laugh!"

"Now calm down." Mrs. Quimby plucked a fluff of dust from Ramona's sleeve.

"I won't calm down!" yelled Ramona so loud her father came down the hall to see what was going on. "I hate Mrs. Rudge! She's a tattletale. She doesn't love me and she tells fibs!" Ramona saw her mother and father exchange a familiar look that said, Which of us is going to handle this one?

"Hate is a strong word, Ramona," said Mrs. Quimby quietly.

"Not strong enough," said Ramona.

"This looks like nine on the Richter scale," said Mr. Quimby, as if Ramona were an earthquake.

"And you and Daddy talk about me in your room at night," Ramona stormed at her mother.

"Someday, Ramona," said her father, "you are going to have to learn that the world does not revolve around you."

"I don't care what Mrs. Rudge says," shouted Ramona. "I didn't leave my pajamas at school on purpose. I forgot." Mrs. Quimby looked astonished. "Left your pajamas—what on earth are your pajamas doing at school?" She was plainly trying to stifle a laugh.

Ramona was both surprised and bewildered. If her mother did not know about her pajamas, what could Mrs. Rudge have said?

"What on earth are your pajamas doing at school?" Ramona's mother asked again.

The whole story—her feeling that the flannel was as soft as bunny fur and how she pretended to be a fireman so she wouldn't have to take her pajamas off—flashed through Ramona's mind and embarrassed her. "I won't tell," she said, folding her arms defiantly.

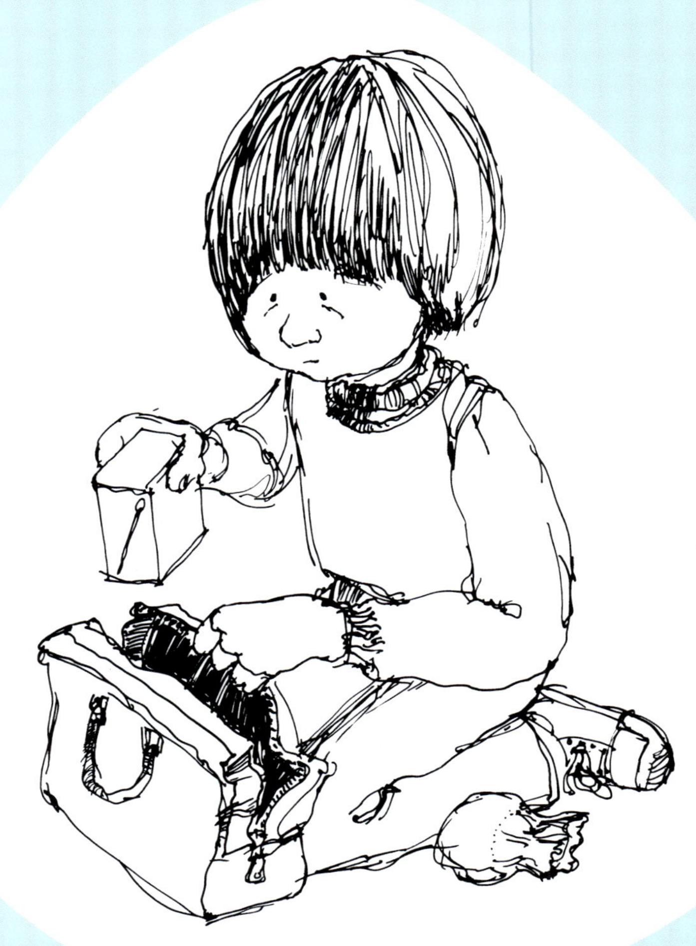

Ramona prepares to run away.

Ramona packs the Q-tips box that contains all the money she has in the world: forty-three cents. Why is no one coming to beg her to stay?

ABOVE: ALAN TIEGREEN. OPPOSITE: TRACY DOCKRAY (TOP) AND ALAN TIEGREEN (BOTTOM).

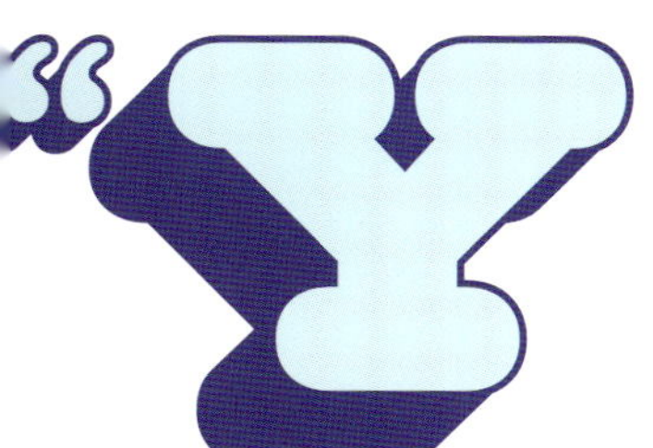

ou tricked me!” cried Ramona. “You made the suitcase too heavy on purpose. You don’t want me to run away!”

“I couldn’t get along without my Ramona,” said Ramona’s mother. She held out her arms. Ramona ran into them. Her mother had said the words she had longed to hear. Her mother could not get along without her. She felt warm and safe and comforted and oh, how good her mother smelled, so clean and sweet like flowers. Better than any mother in the whole world. Ramona’s tears dampened her mother’s blouse. After a moment Mrs. Quimby handed Ramona a Kleenex. When Ramona had wiped her eyes and nose, she was surprised to discover that her mother had tears in her eyes, too.

As do we all after reading such a heartrending scene. In this moment Mrs. Quimby also tells Ramona that she and Mr. Quimby weren’t, in fact, talking about their youngest in their room at night but rather about Mr. Quimby’s going back to school to finish his degree.

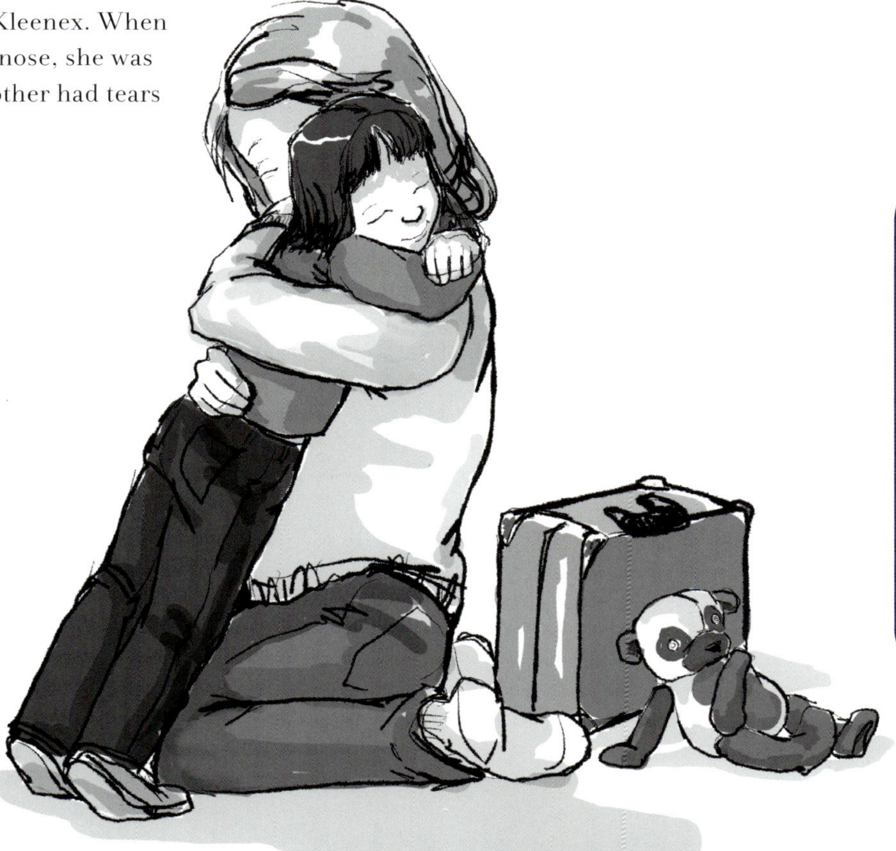

Ramona Quimby

Ramona learns that she was wrong about the purpose of Mrs. Rudge’s phone call to her parents. The teacher described her as “one of those little sparklers” who make teaching interesting. Feeling sparkly, she writes her name, in bold cursive, with a happy sparkler on the end.

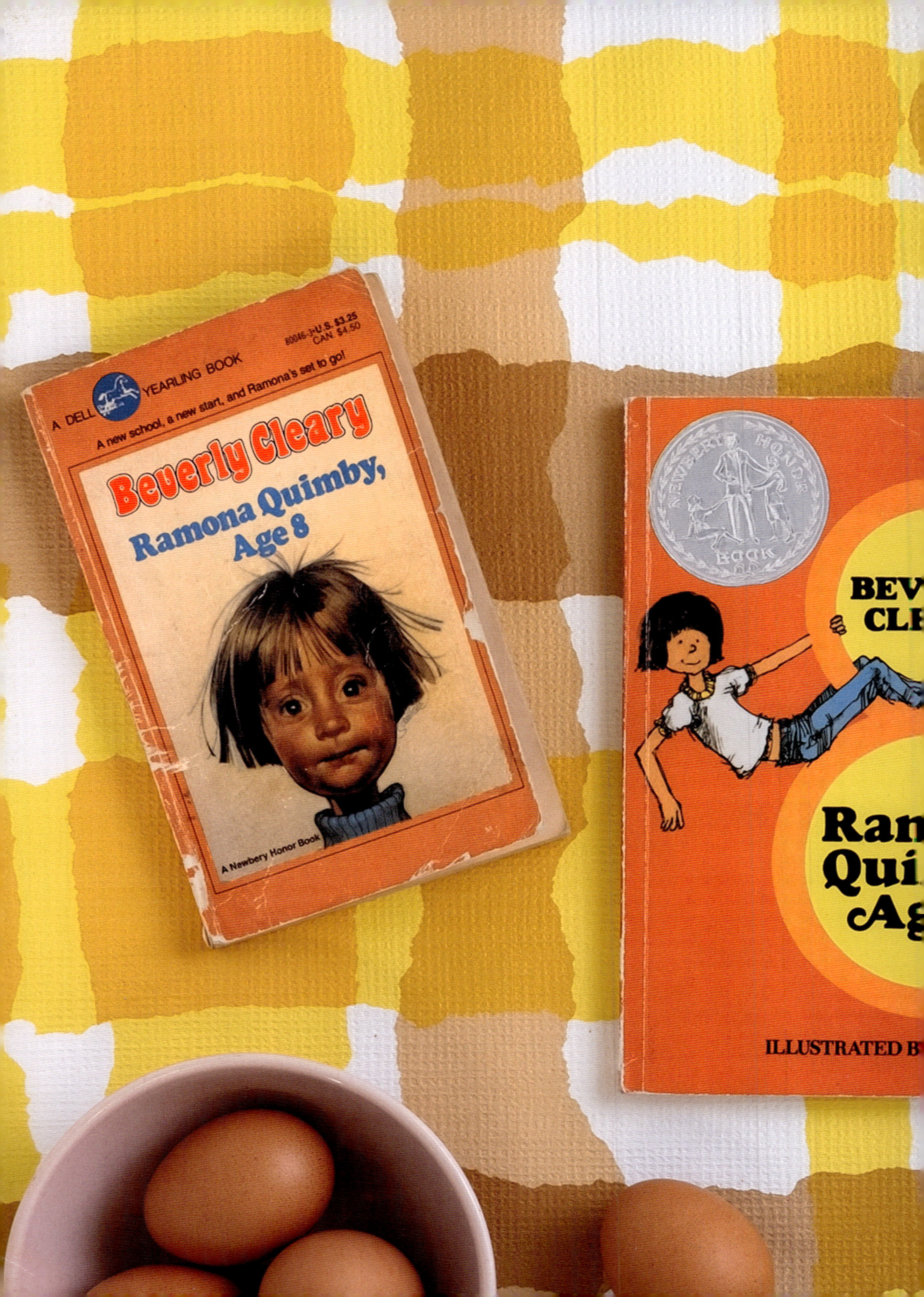
A DELL YEARLING BOOK
80046-3•U.S. $3.25
CAN. $4.50
A new school, a new start, and Ramona's set to go!
Beverly Cleary
Ramona Quimby, Age 8
A Newbery Honor Book

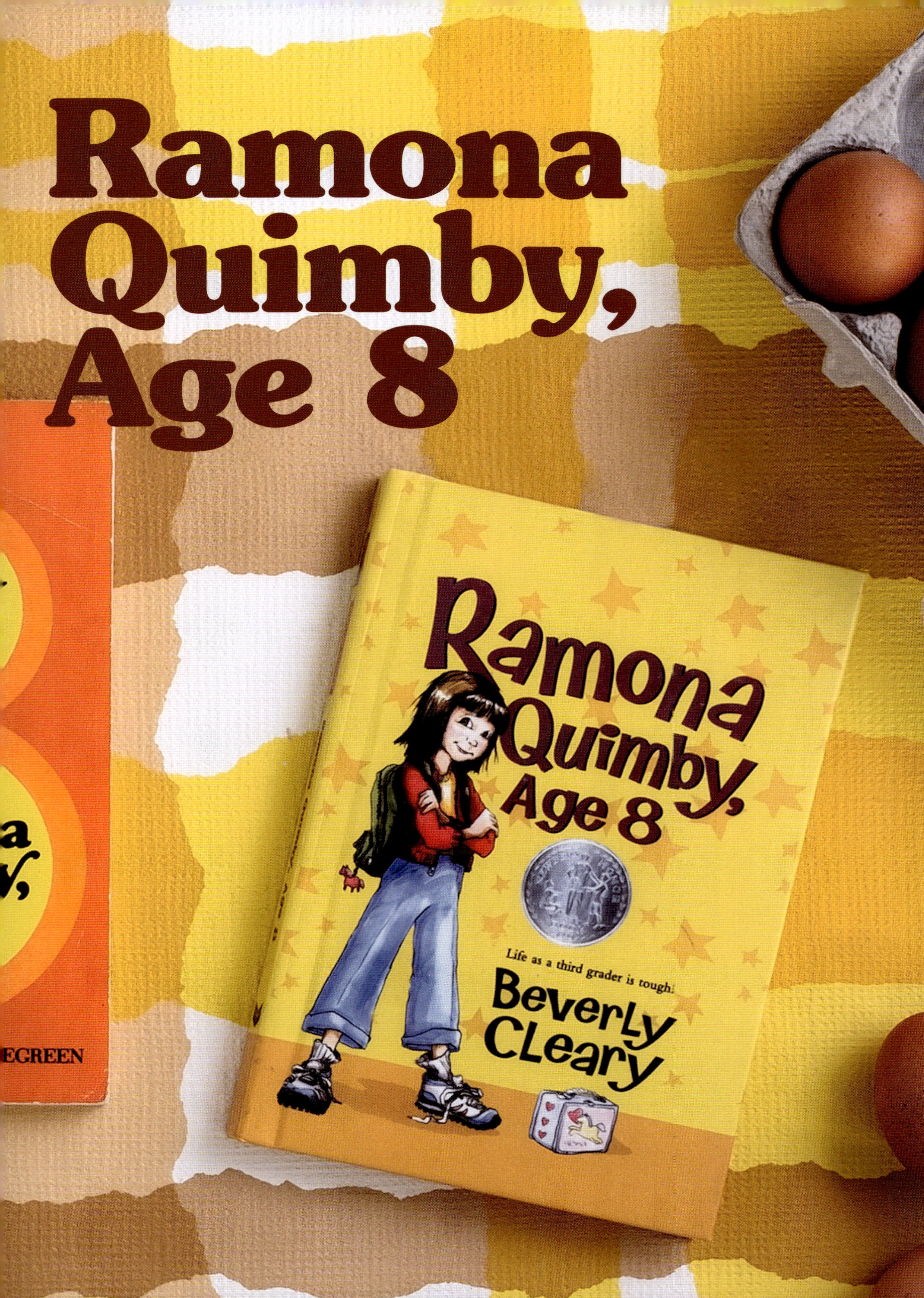
Ramona Quimby, Age 8
Ramona Quimby, Age 8
Life as a third grader is tough!
Beverly Cleary

Chapter Six

Ramona Quimby, Age 8

Third graders were the biggest people—except teachers, of course—at this school. All the little first and second graders running around the playground, looking so young, made Ramona feel tall, grown up, and sort of . . . well, wise in the ways of the world.

Much of *Ramona Quimby, Age 8* focuses on being called a "nuisance," a topic about which Beverly Cleary writes extensively in her first autobiography, *A Girl from Yamhill.* When Cleary was in third grade, all the girls except her and one other were cast in the spring PTA program as dancing lilac blossoms. The reason given for this was that Cleary and the other girl were too short. They could, however, be understudies, in case one of the lilac blossoms got sick. One morning, Cleary noticed that a girl was absent; she found the blossom director in conversation with another teacher in the hallway and asked which of the substitutes would be filling in during rehearsal. As Cleary put it, "The teacher put her hand on my shoulder, turned, and smiled at the other teacher. 'This one,' she said, 'is a nuisance.'"

This terrible pejorative would torment the young Cleary, and in *Ramona Quimby, Age 8*, Ramona has a similar experience and similar struggle. Now, Cleary is adamant that she does not write children's books to teach lessons. She writes to entertain, to make children (and adults) laugh, to make interesting, complex characters in which her readers can see themselves. But it's hard not to find some kind of message here, about the power teachers have and the ease with which their words can hurt the children in their care.

Ramona is now in the third grade and Beezus is in junior high. Because Glenwood has become an intermediate school, Ramona and her classmates start at Cedarhurst Primary School; she is excited to go somewhere new, where she won't have to follow in the long shadow of her perfect sister. Mr. Quimby is also in school, studying to become an art teacher while working part-time driving a forklift in a frozen-foods warehouse. Mrs. Quimby continues to work full-time.

In this 1982 Newbery Honor Book, Ramona uses D.E.A.R. (Drop Everything and Read) to deal with the pest Willa Jean, learns how to write in cursive, and transfers her affections from Davy (who she never could catch on the playground, though not for lack of trying) to a boy whom she nicknames "Yard Ape." He will not only create the kind of trouble that schoolyard crushes always do but provide a subtle kind of support after Ramona overhears her teacher referring to her as a nuisance. The pain this causes is the primary conflict of the book, one that prompts Ramona to grow up just a little bit more.

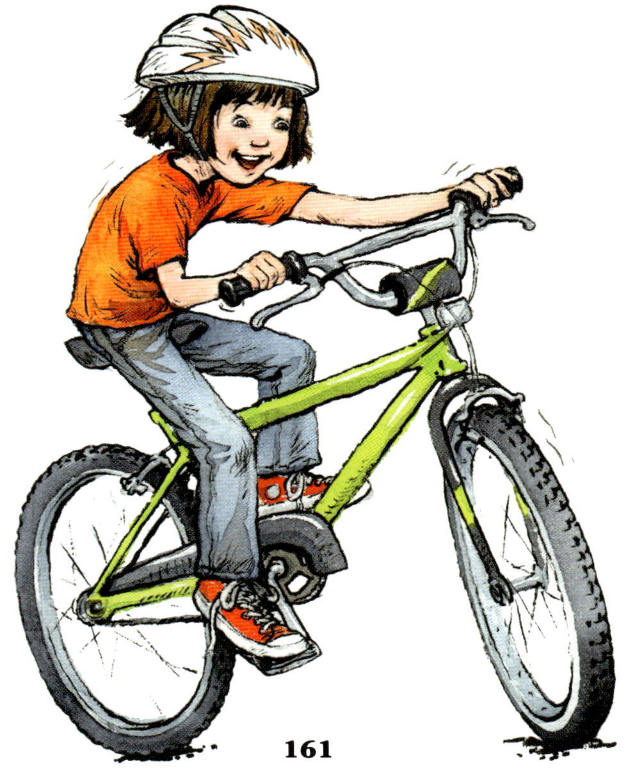

JACQUELINE ROGERS

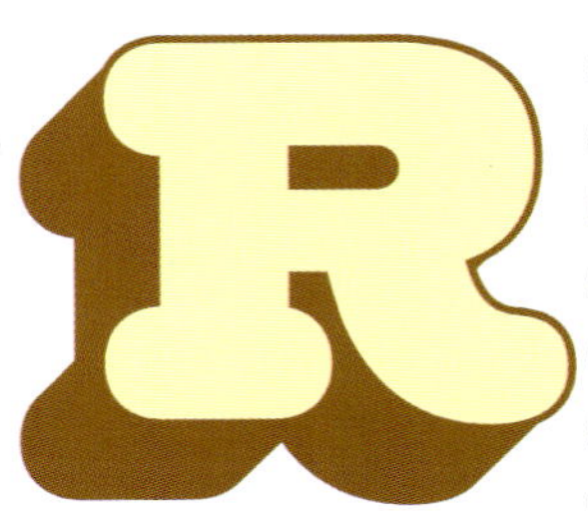

Ramona had reached the age of demanding accuracy from everyone, even herself. All summer, whenever a grown-up asked what grade she was in, she felt as if she were fibbing when she answered, "third," because she had not actually started the third grade. Still, she could not say she was in the second grade since she had finished that grade last June. Grown-ups did not understand that summers were free from grades.

"Ha-ha to both of you," said Mr. Quimby, as he carried his breakfast dishes into the kitchen. "You're not the only ones going to school today." Yesterday had been his last day working at the checkout counter of the ShopRite Market. Today he was returning to college to become what he called "a real, live school teacher." He was also going to work one day a week in the frozen-food warehouse of the chain of ShopRite Markets to help the family "squeak by," as the grown-ups put it, until he finished his schooling.

"Ha-ha to all of you if you don't hurry up," said Mrs. Quimby, as she swished suds in the dishpan. She stood back from the sink so she would not spatter the white uniform she wore in the doctor's office where she worked as a receptionist.

"Daddy, will you have to do homework?" Ramona wiped off her milk moustache and gathered up her dishes.

"That's right." Mr. Quimby flicked a dish towel at Ramona as she passed him. She giggled and dodged, happy because he was happy. Never again would he stand all day at a cash register, ringing up groceries for a long line of people who were always in a hurry.

Ramona slid her plate into the dishwater. "And will Mother have to sign your progress reports?"

Mrs. Quimby laughed. "I hope so."

Beezus was last to bring her dishes into the kitchen. "Daddy, what do you have to study to learn to be a teacher?" she asked.

Ramona had been wondering the same thing. Her father knew how to read and do arithmetic. He also knew about Oregon pioneers and about two pints making one quart.

Mr. Quimby wiped a plate and stacked it in the cupboard. "I'm taking an art course, because I want to teach art. And I'll study child development—"

Ramona interrupted. "What's child development?"

"How kids grow," answered her father.

Why does anyone have to go to school to study a thing like that? wondered Ramona.

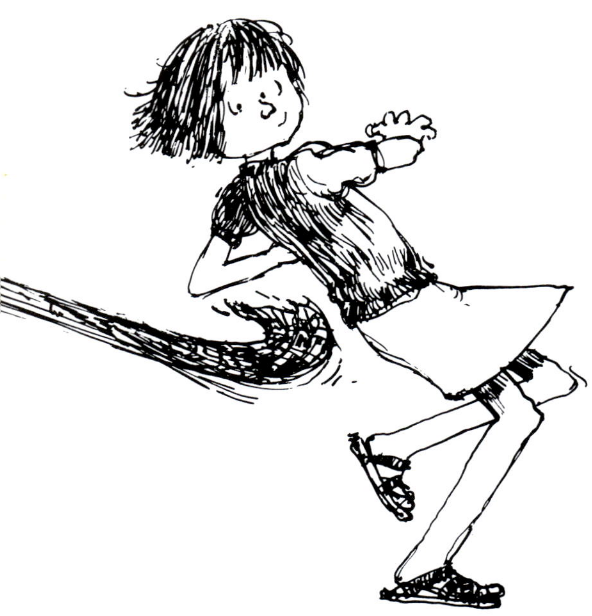

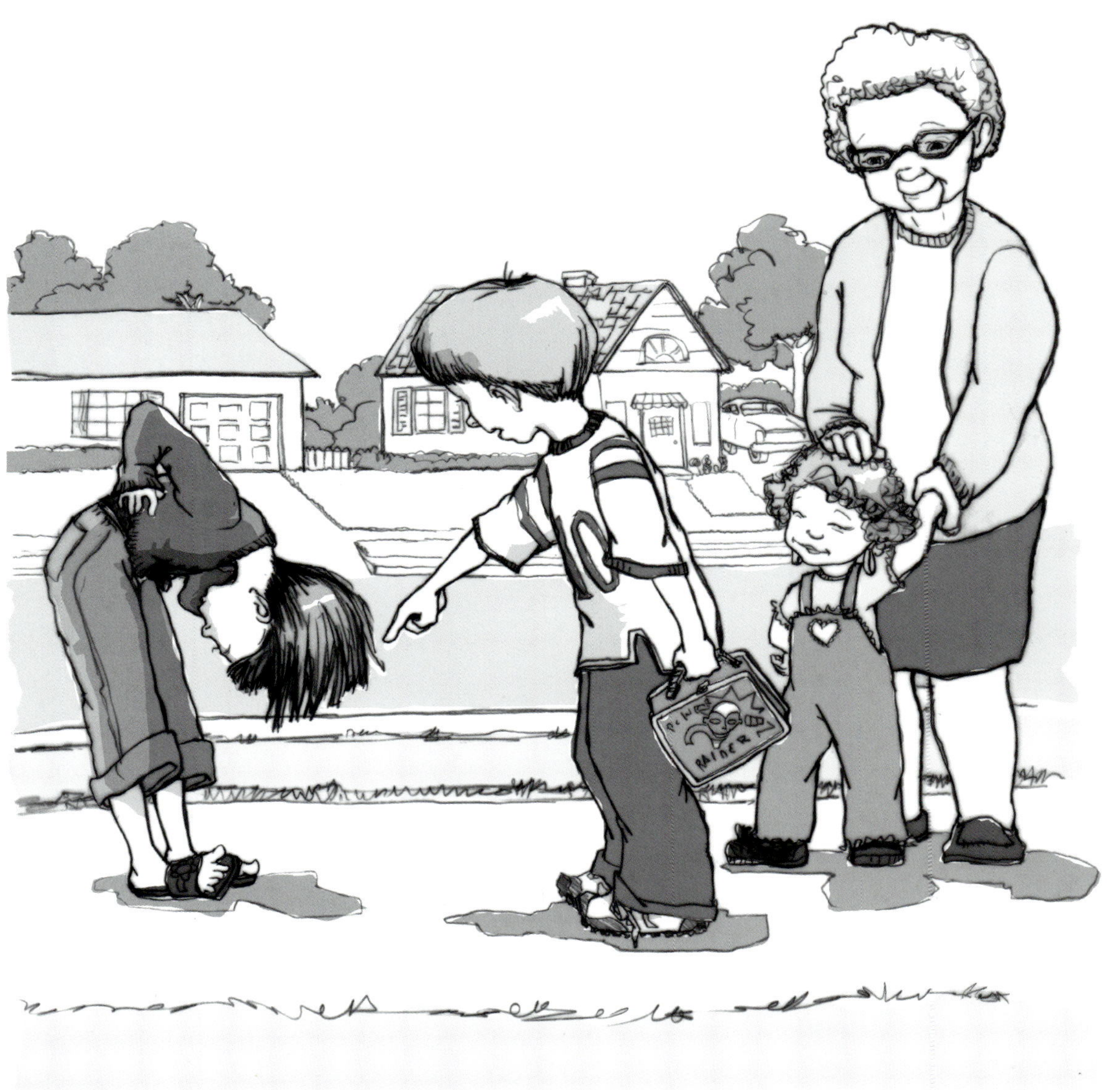

It's the first day of third grade, and Ramona comes upon Howie, Willa Jean, and Mrs. Kemp waiting at the bus stop. Right off the bat, her neighborhood pal tells her that her feet look big in their new sandals. She can't really disagree.

Ramona's full-bodied gesture of examination fits with Dockray's more cartoonish style.

ALAN TIEGREEN (OPPOSITE) AND TRACY DOCKRAY (ABOVE).

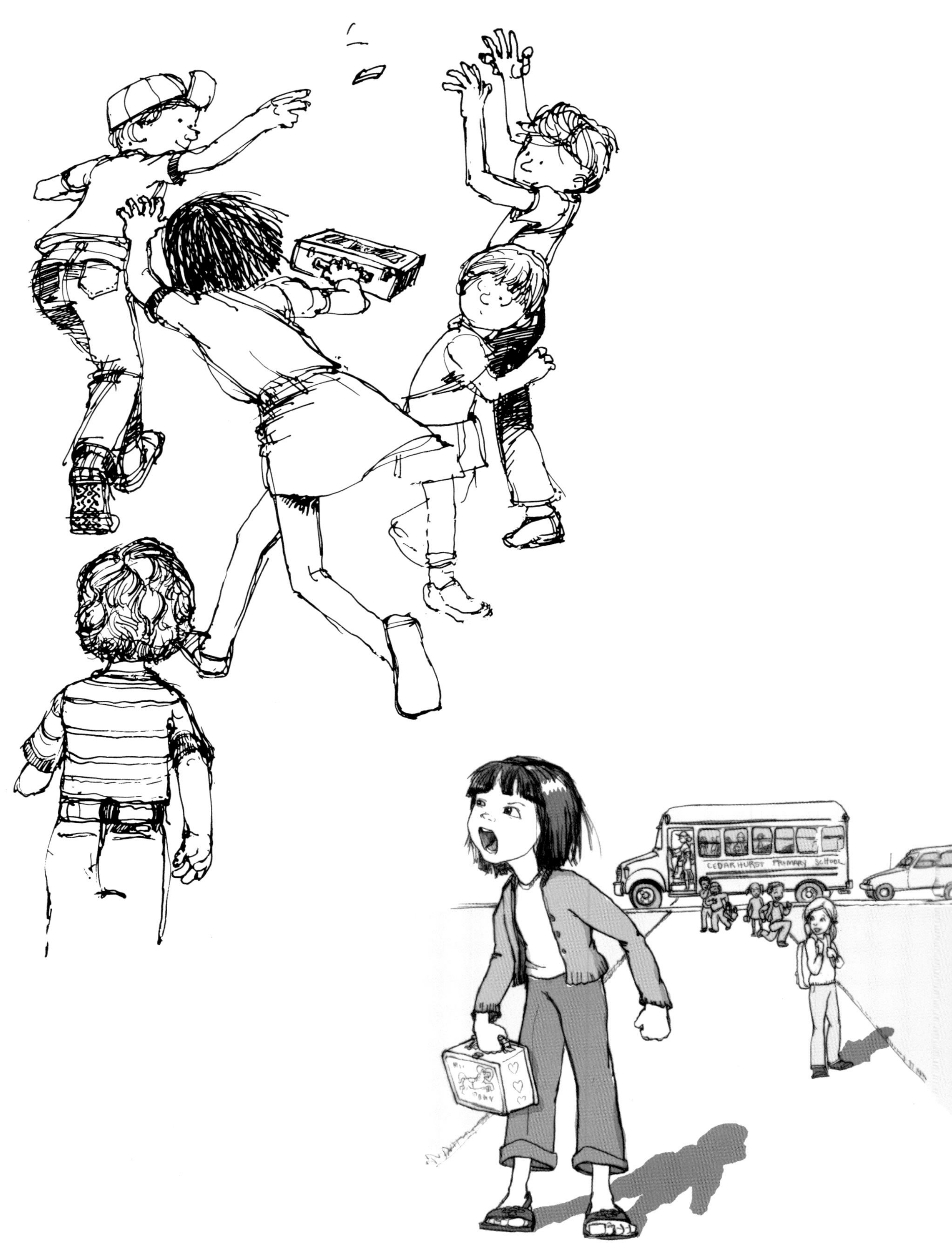

ABOVE: ALAN TIEGREEN (LEFT) AND TRACY DOCKRAY (RIGHT). OPPOSITE: JACQUELINE ROGERS.

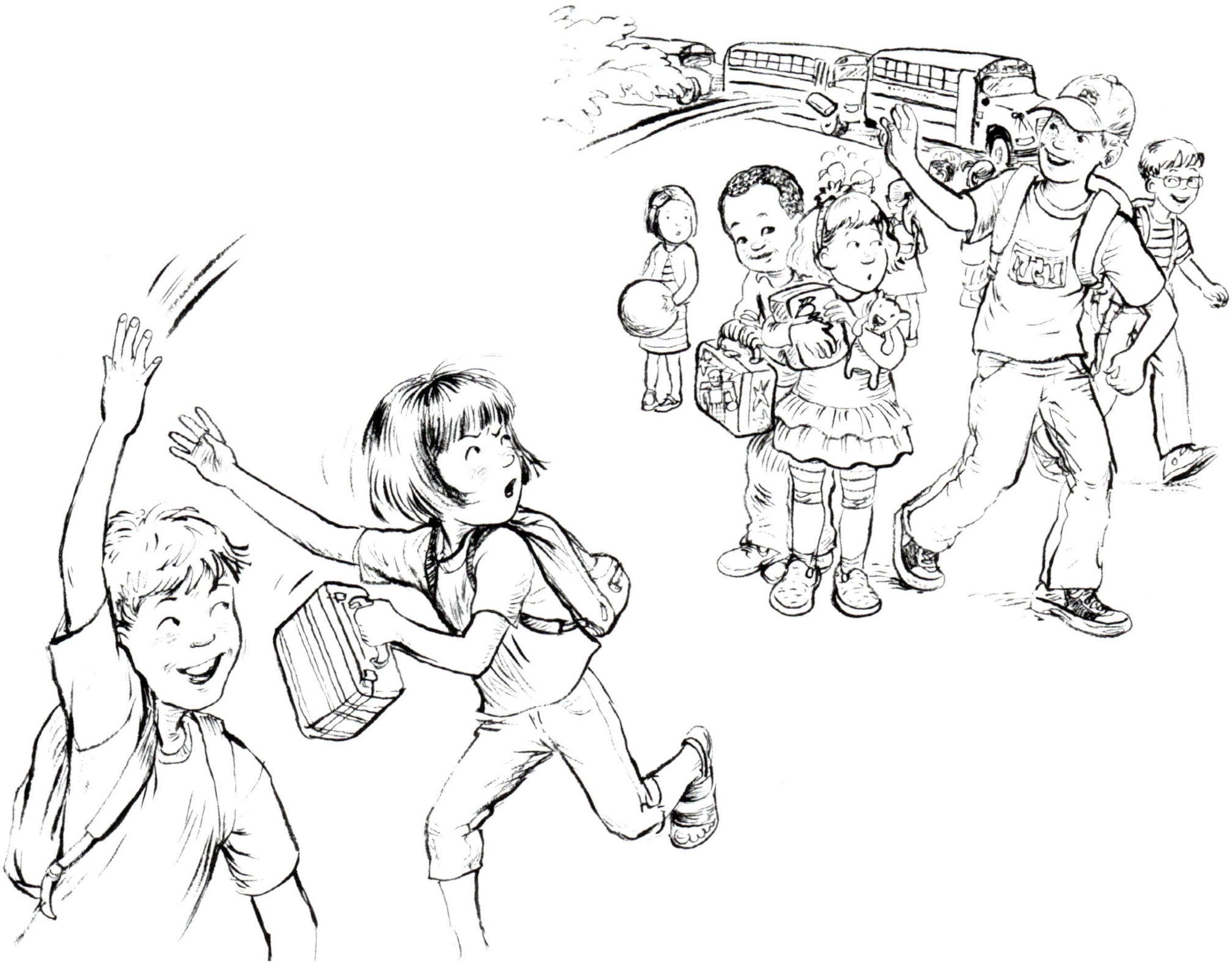

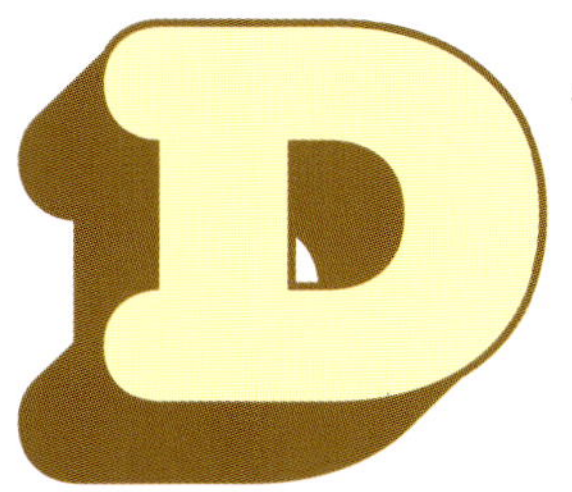

Danny shoved ahead of her. "Catch!" he yelled to another boy. Something small and pink flew through the air and into the second boy's cupped hands. The boy wound up as if he were pitching a baseball, and the eraser flew back to Danny.

"You gimme back my eraser!" Encumbered by her lunch box, Ramona chased Danny, who ran, ducking and dodging, among the first and second graders. When she was about to catch him, he tossed her eraser to the other boy. If her lunch box had not banged against her knees, Ramona might have been able to grab him. Unfortunately, the bell rang first.

"Yard apes!" yelled Ramona, her name for the sort of boys who always got the best balls, who were always first on the playground, and who chased their soccer balls through other people's hopscotch games. She saw her pink eraser fly back into Danny's hands.

"Yard apes!" she yelled again, tears of anger in her eyes. "Yucky yard apes!" The boys, of course, paid no attention.

And so we meet Ramona's newest crush (whose real name is Danny but who is soon to be given the very special nickname of "Yard Ape"). From their first meeting, we learn that this boy has no qualms about teasing poor innocent girls.

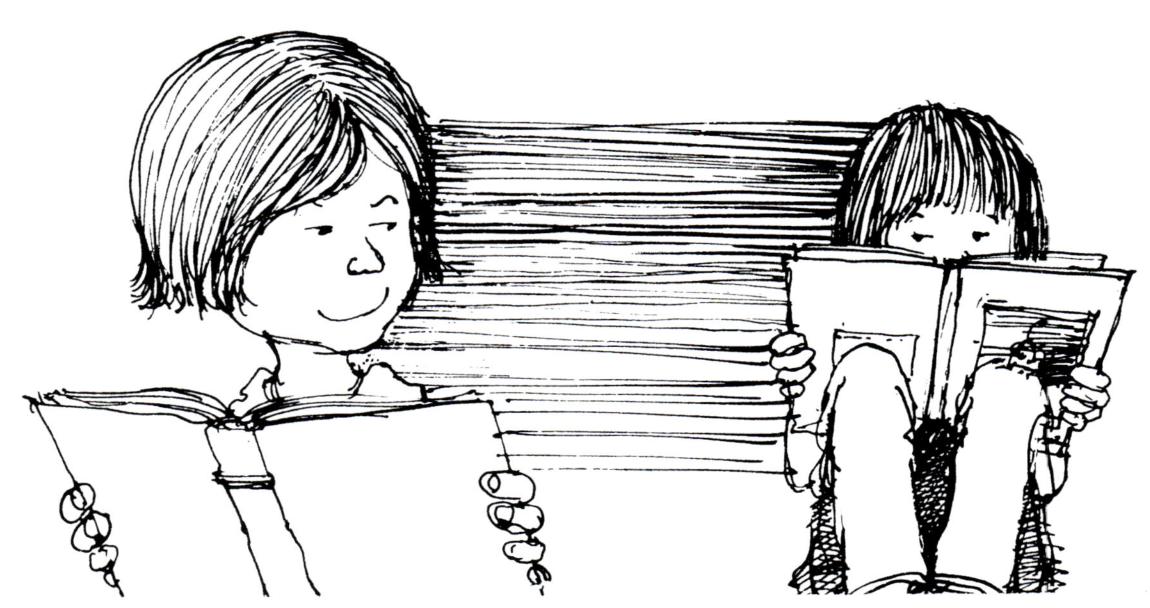

Ramona finally has a good excuse for not playing with Willa Jean.

It just doesn't seem fair. Mr. and Mrs. Quimby pay Mrs. Kemp to watch Ramona, but really all Mrs. Kemp does is watch her stories on TV, leaving Ramona to entertain the babyish Willa Jean, and sometimes her little friend Bruce. Beezus, a junior high schooler, has the excuse of homework, while Howie gets to go ride bikes with his friends. What is Ramona to do?

Fortunately, third-graders have Sustained Silent Reading (or the much less official-sounding D.E.A.R., Drop Everything and Read). That phrase is enough to impress Willa Jean, who's happy bossing Bruce around anyway.

In Rogers's illustration, the two little kids are off to play dress-up, and Ramona is clearly satisfied with her mission accomplished. In Dockray's version, Willa Jean hasn't quite gotten the memo. Tiegreen left the two nursery schoolers out altogether, instead focusing on Beezus and Ramona exchanging a conspiratorial look. Perhaps Beezus already knew about using homework as an excuse to avoid having to entertain younger kids.

ABOVE: ALAN TIEGREEN. OPPOSITE: JACQUELINE ROGERS (TOP) AND TRACY DOCKRAY (BOTTOM).

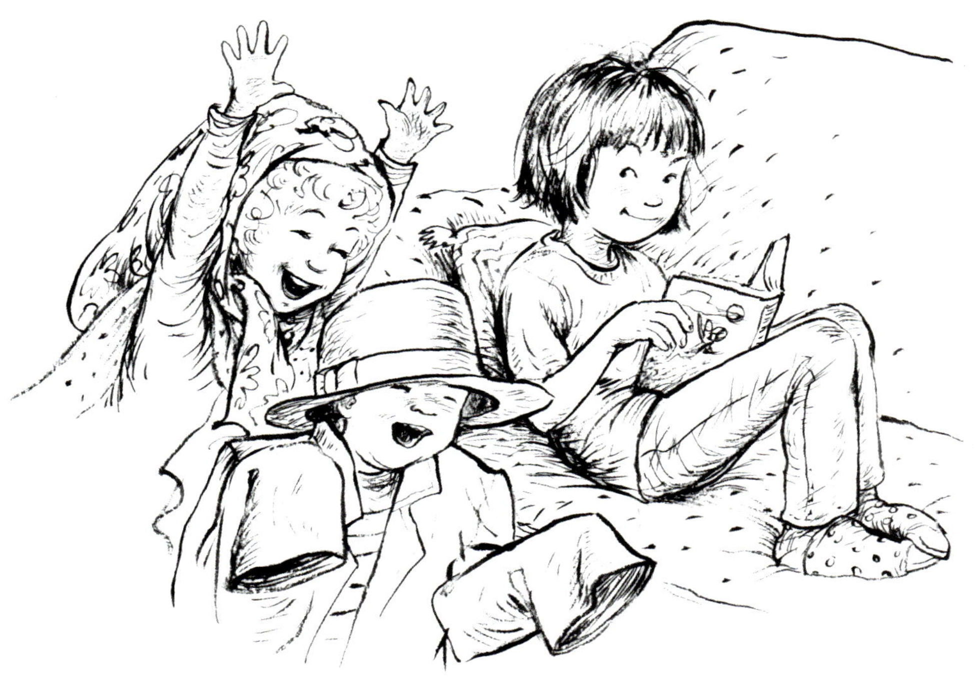

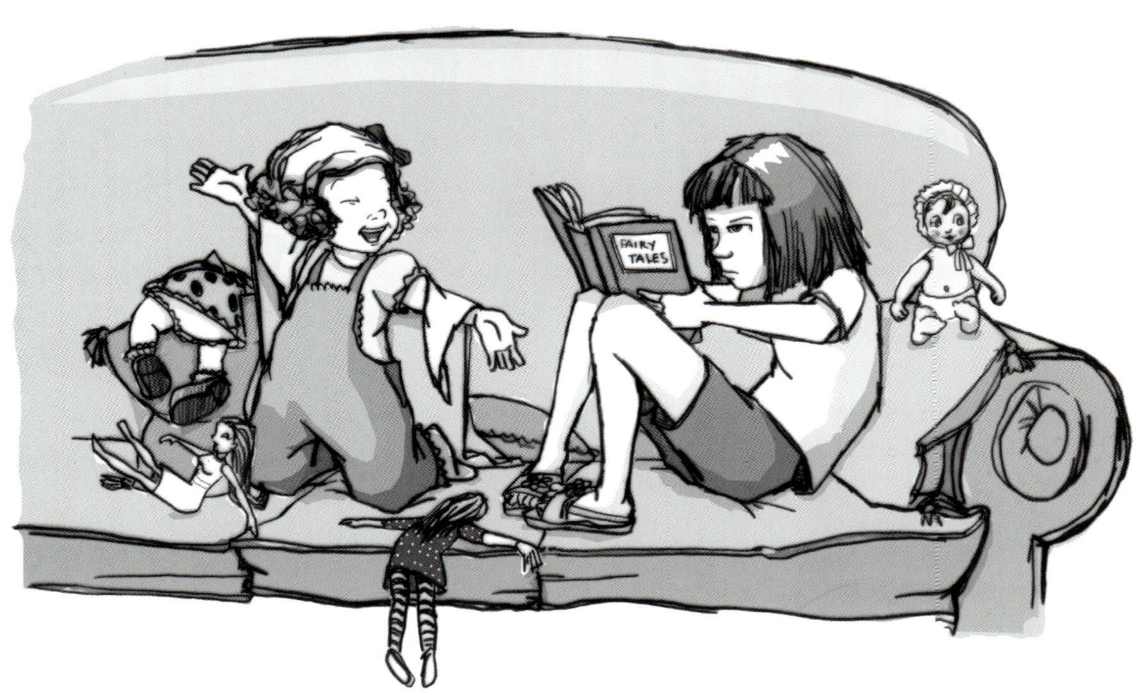
FAIRY TALES

There were a number of ways of cracking eggs. The most popular, and the real reason for bringing an egg to school, was knocking the egg against one's head. There were two ways of doing so, by a lot of timid little raps or by one big whack. Sara was a rapper. Ramona, like Yard Ape, was a whacker.

While both illustrators depict the egg-crushing event, Dockray's Ramona seems to hold the expression of the sheer joy of the whack, while Rogers's Ramona has clearly realized that the egg in her lunch was raw, not hard-boiled.

TRACY DOCKRAY (TOP) AND JACQUELINE ROGERS (BOTTOM).

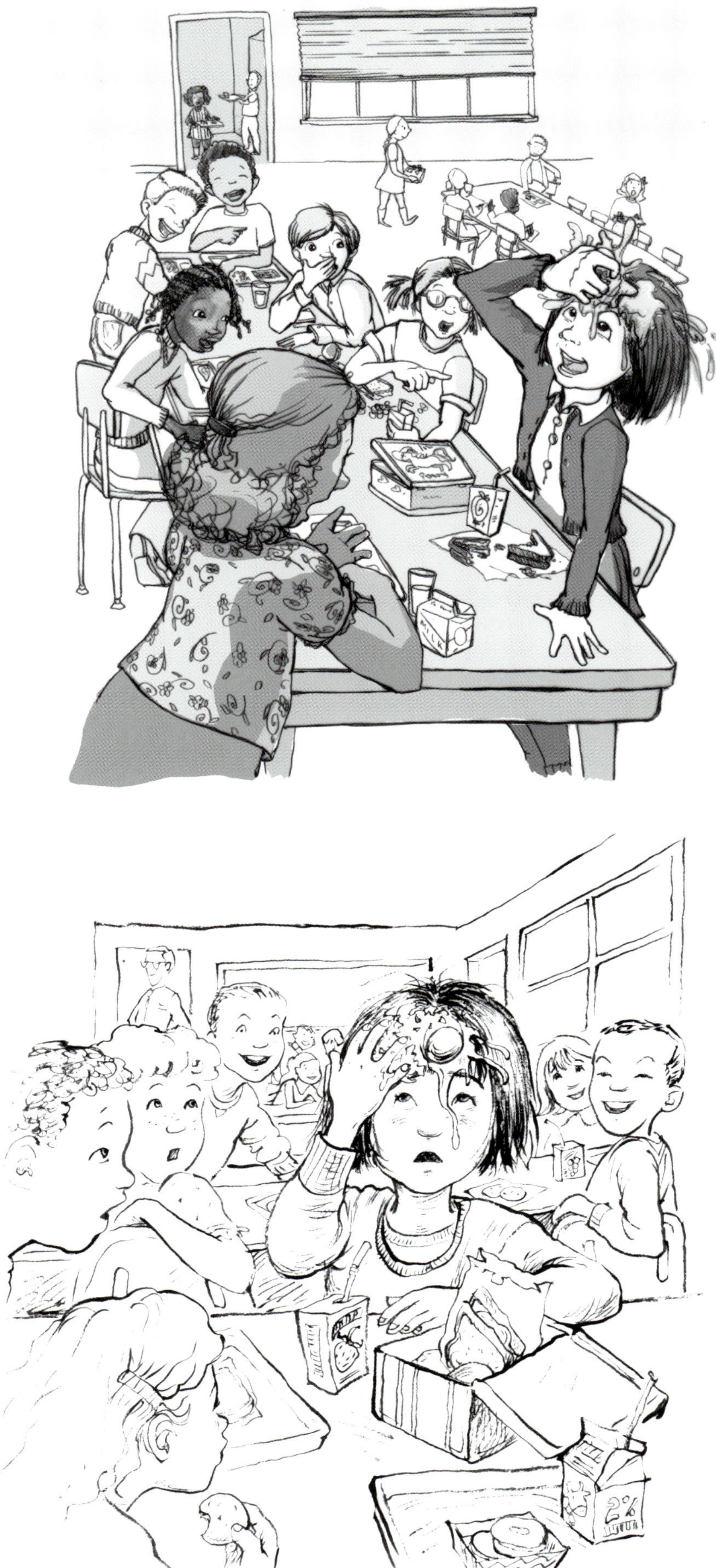

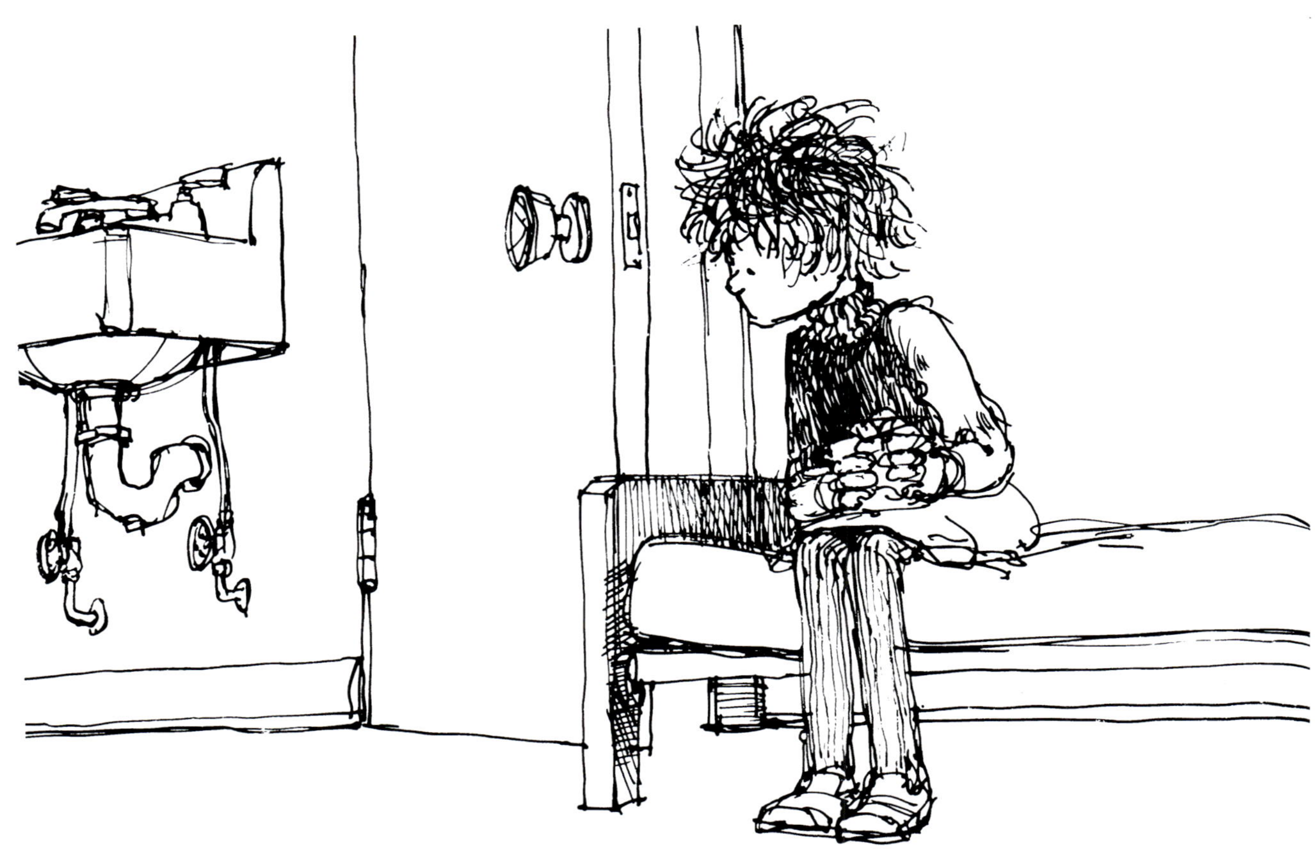

"I hear my little show-off came in with egg in her hair." She laughed and added, "What a nuisance."

Ramona was so stunned she did not try to hear Mrs. Larson's answer. Show-off! Nuisance! Did Mrs. Whaley think she had broken a raw egg into her hair on purpose to show off? And to be called a nuisance by her teacher when she was not a nuisance. Or was she? Ramona did not mean to break an egg in her hair. Her mother was to blame. Did this accident make her a nuisance?

Ramona did not see why Mrs. Whaley could think she was a nuisance when Mrs. Whaley was not the one to get her hands all eggy. Yet Ramona had heard her say right out loud that she was a show-off and a nuisance. That hurt, really hurt.

After Ramona overhears her third-grade teacher, Mrs. Whaley, talking to the school secretary, she's not sure if she'll ever be able to trust her teacher again. Tiegreen captures this moment of shock and alienation, the girl clasping tight to the damp paper towels in her hands, the oblivious grown-ups gossiping somewhere beyond the cracked door.

ALAN TIEGREEN (ABOVE) AND TRACY DOCKRAY (OPPOSITE).

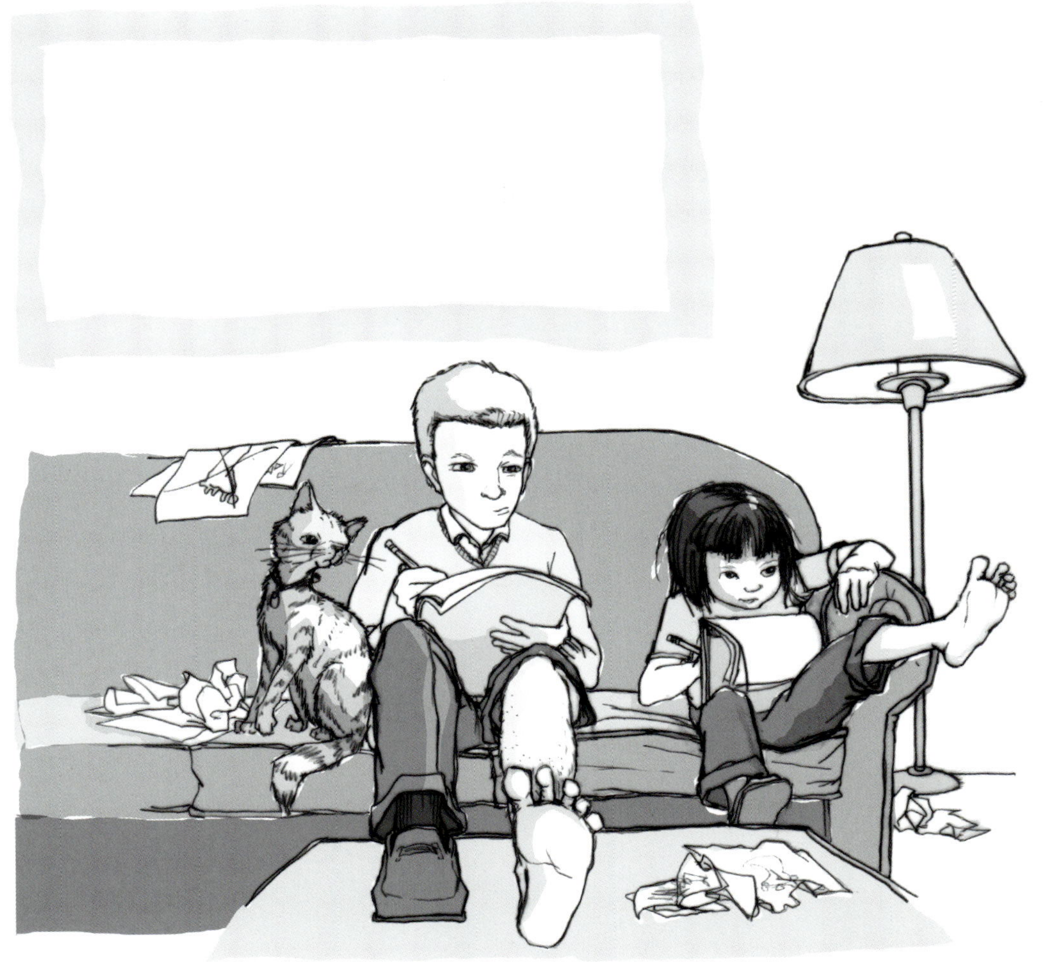

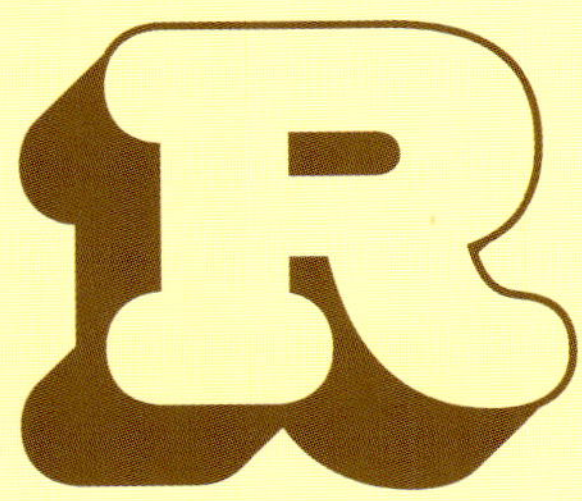

Ramona wandered around the house looking for something to do, when she discovered her father sitting on the couch, pencil in hand, drawing pad on his knee, frowning at one bare foot.

"Daddy, what are you doing that for?" Ramona wanted to know.

"That's what I keep asking myself," her father answered, as he wiggled his toes. "I have to draw a picture of my foot for my art class."

"I wish we got to do things like that in my school," said Ramona. She found pencil and paper, pulled off one shoe and sock, and climbed on the couch beside her father. Both studied their feet and began to sketch. Ramona soon found that drawing a foot was more difficult than she had expected. Like her father, she stared, frowned, drew, erased, stared, frowned, and drew. For a little while she forgot she was cross.

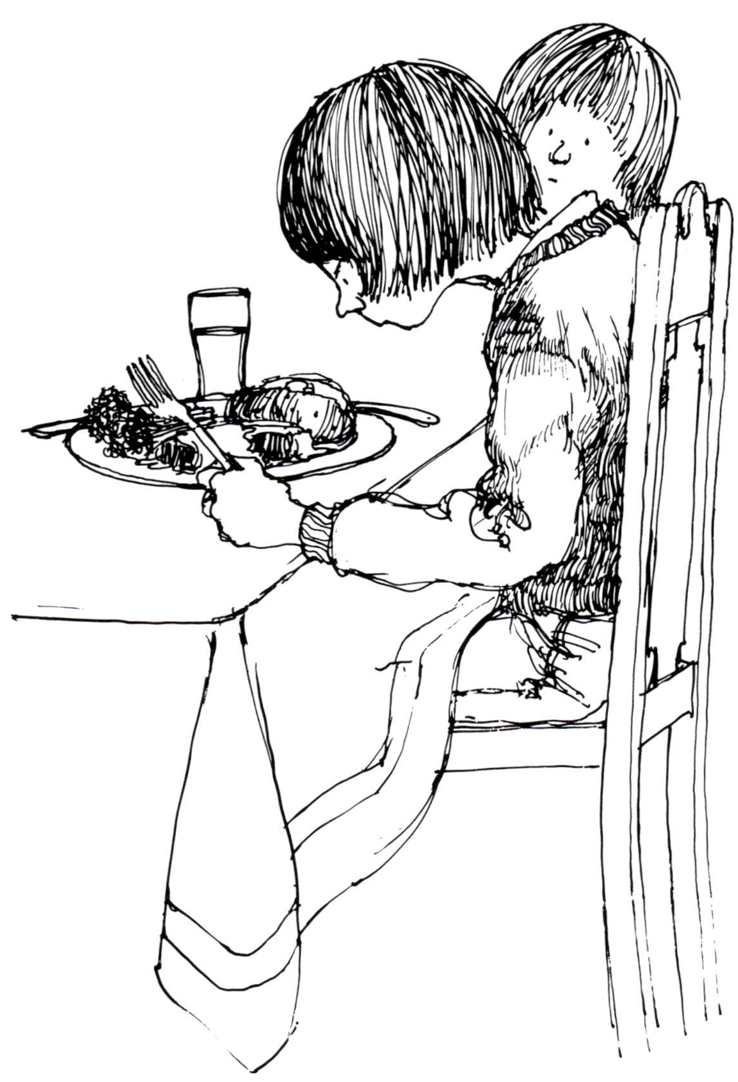

Ramona, still angry at her mother for sending her to school with a raw egg, protests having to eat tongue for dinner. Tiegreen's illustration focuses on the moment of discovery, when Ramona pushes the gravy aside and realizes that her meat is covered in tiny bumps. Rogers zooms out to show Ramona's overt expression of disgust and Beezus's subtler one, with Mr. and Mrs. Quimby doing their best to make their case—tongue is cheaper than "plain meat"—and to not lose their patience. Notice Picky-picky in the bottom center of the frame—he doesn't seem to share the girls' opinion about tongue.

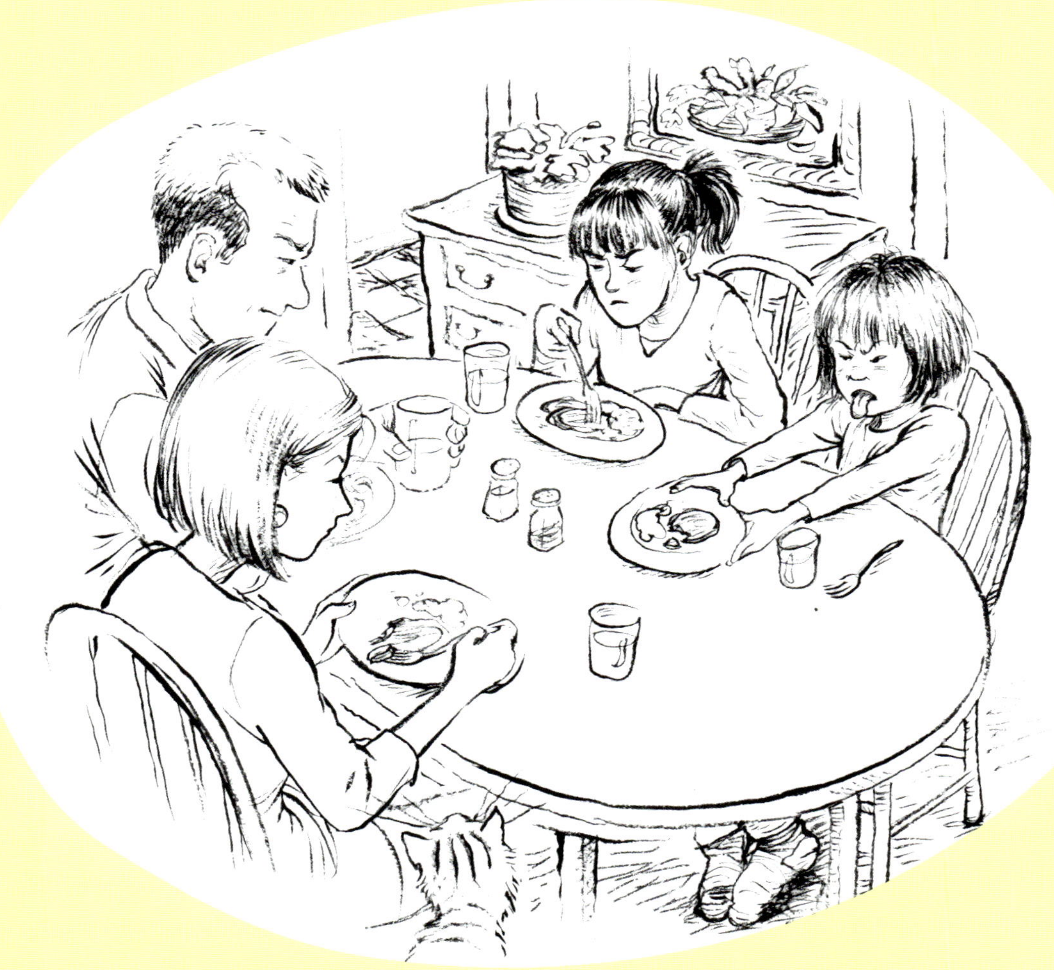

ALAN TIEGREEN (OPPOSITE) AND JACQUELINE ROGERS (ABOVE).

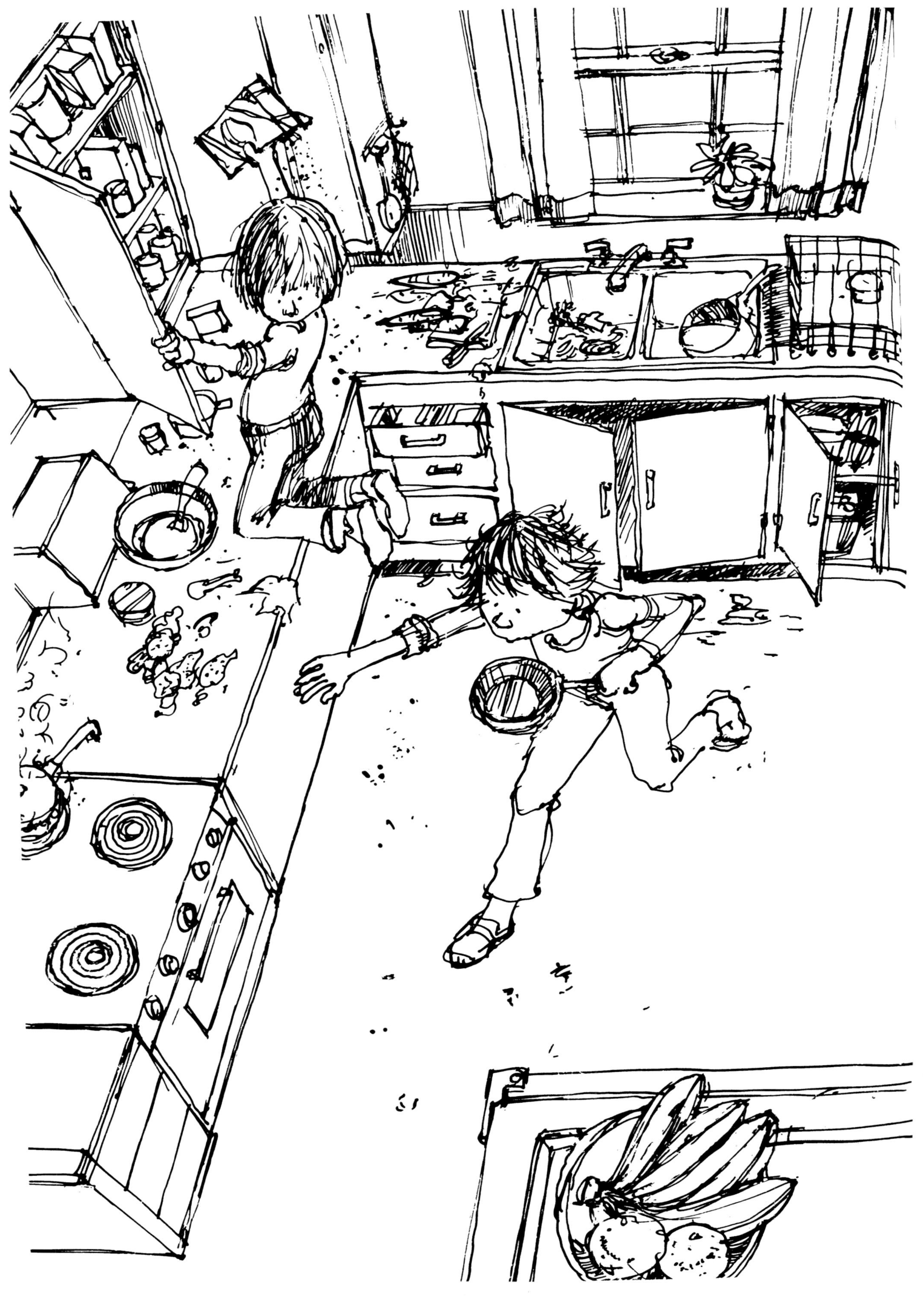

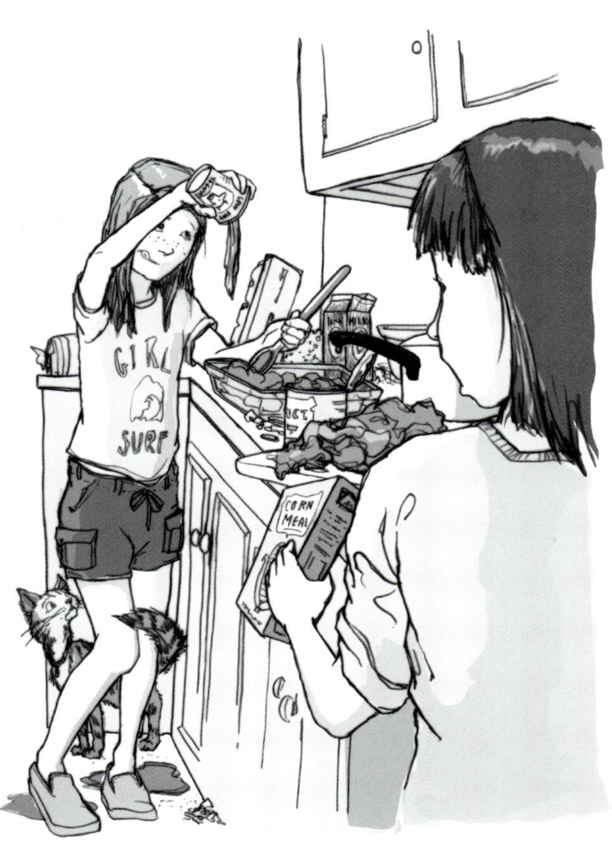

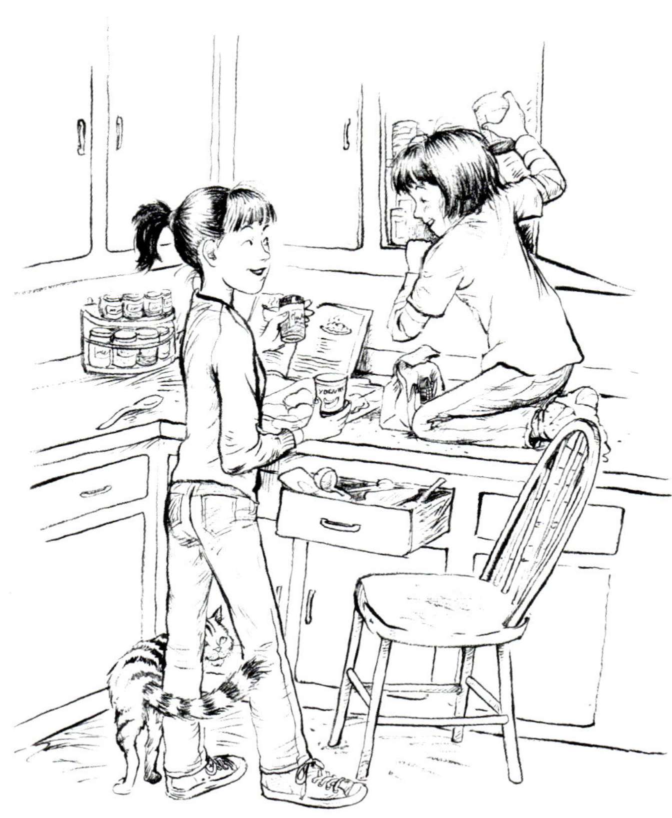

Ramona and Beezus unite.

Ramona and Beezus raid the cabinets to make dinner, their punishment for complaining about having to eat tongue the night before. Tiegreen's bird's-eye view shows the scrambling girls and chaotic kitchen in all its glory. Dockray's illustration draws the eye from the box of cornmeal in Ramona's hand up the cluttered countertop to Beezus, wearing a more modern T-shirt with the words "Girl Surf" on it and concentrating on pouring plain yogurt mixed with chili powder over raw, skinless chicken thighs. Rogers's scene takes place during the beginning stage of this improvised cook-off and focuses on a smile shared between the girls. A rare moment of sisterly comradery.

OPPOSITE: ALAN TIEGREEN. ABOVE: TRACY DOCKRAY (LEFT) AND JACQUELINE ROGERS (RIGHT).

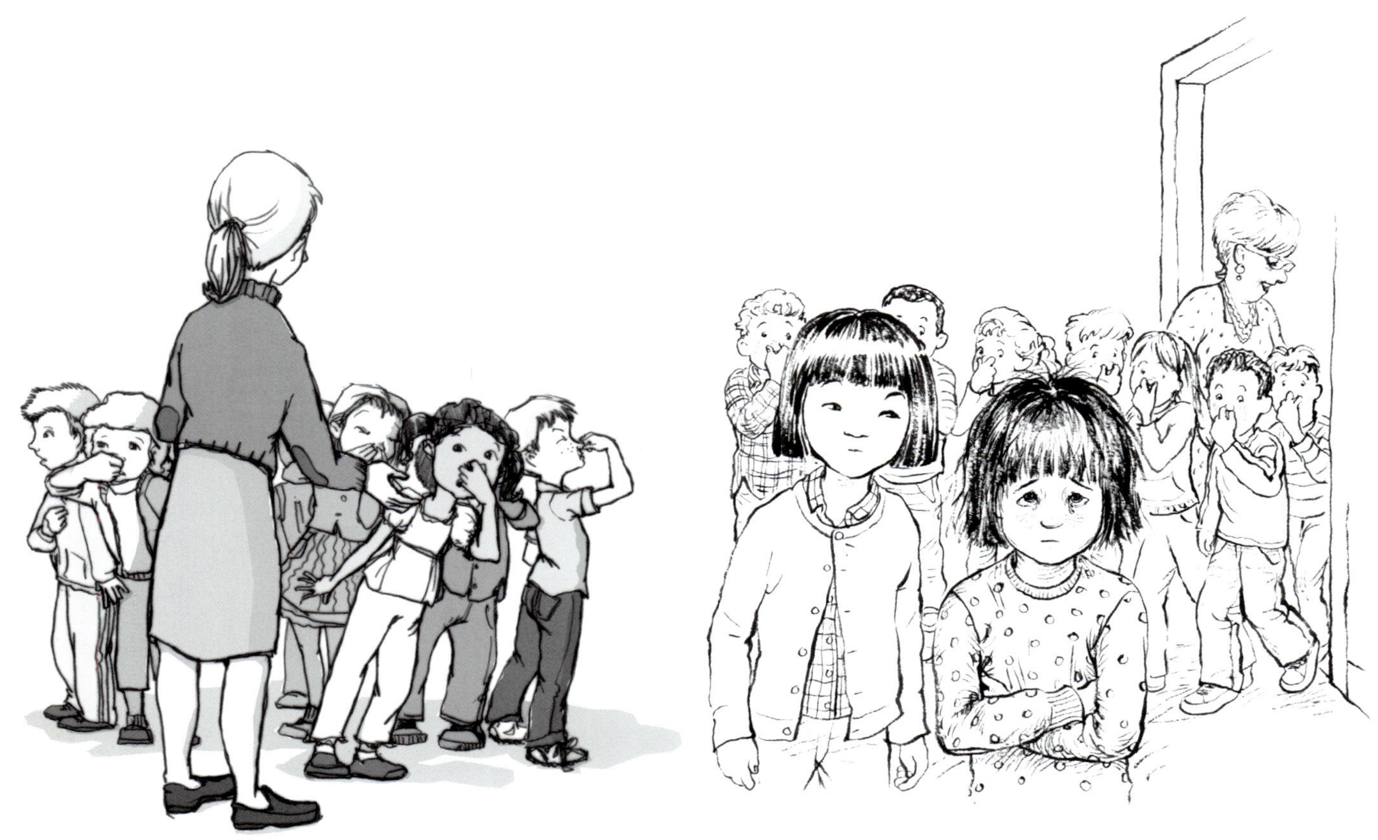

Ramona becomes a supernuisance.

After overhearing Mrs. Whaley's comments to the school secretary, Ramona has become very anxious about being a nuisance. So when she starts to feel strange, she does not call out to her teacher to ask to be excused. Then her worst nightmare comes to pass: She vomits on the classroom floor. Dockray has narrowed the perspective to show just the back of the teacher and the students pinching their noses. Rogers, on the other hand, has placed a sick and humiliated Ramona front and center, with the motherly Marsha and the disgusted third-grade class behind her.

ABOVE: TRACY DOCKRAY (LEFT) AND JACQUELINE ROGERS (RIGHT). OPPOSITE: ALAN TIEGREEN.

Carefully Ramona laid her head in her mother's lap and with every click of the meter thought, I will not throw up in a taxi.

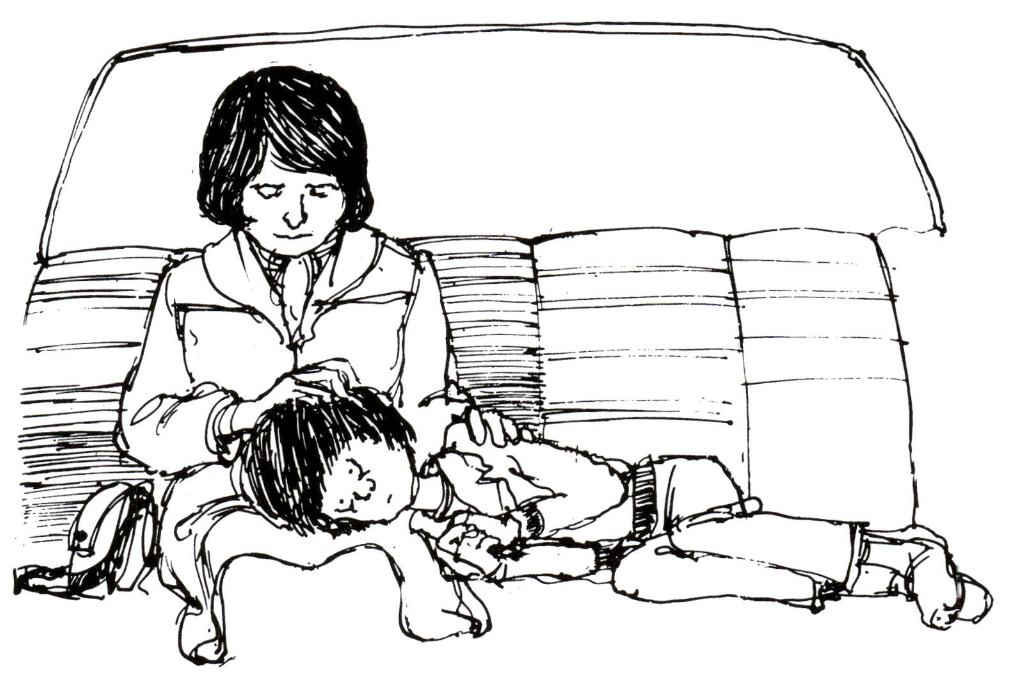

Even as her mother cares for and attempts to comfort her, Ramona, eyes wide, continues to worry.

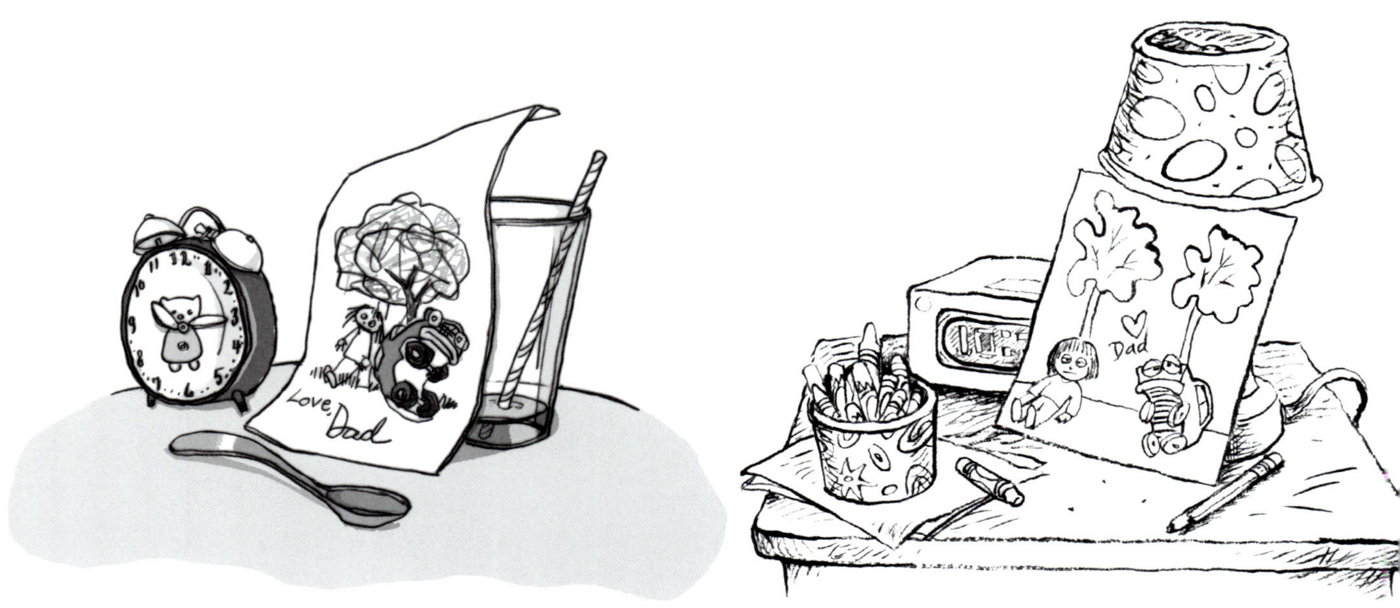

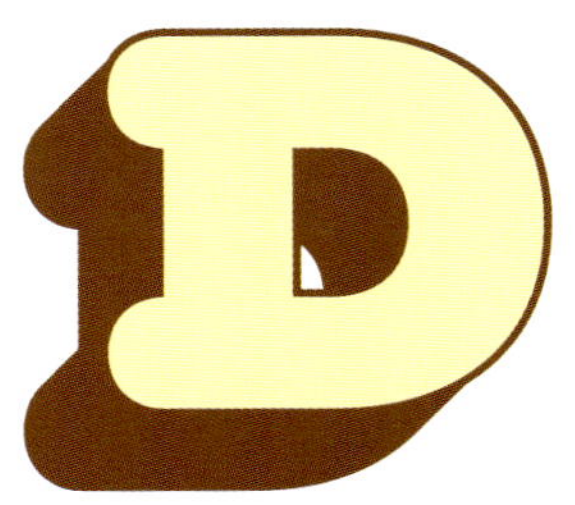

During the night Ramona was half awakened when her mother wiped her face with a cool washcloth and lifted her head from the pillow to help her sip something cold. Later, as the shadows of the room were fading, Ramona had to hold a thermometer under her tongue for what seemed like a long time. She felt safe, knowing her mother was watching over her. Safe but sick. No sooner did she find a cool place on her pillow than it became too hot for comfort, and Ramona turned again.

As her room grew light, Ramona dozed off, faintly aware that her family was moving quietly so they would not disturb her. One tiny corner of her mind was pleased by this consideration. She heard breakfast sounds, and then she must have fallen completely asleep, because the next thing she knew she was awake and the house was silent. Had they all gone off and left her? No, someone was moving quietly in the kitchen. Howie's grandmother must have come to stay with her.

Ramona's eyes blurred. Her family had all gone off and left her when she was sick. She blinked away the tears and discovered on her bedside table a cartoon her father had drawn for her. It showed Ramona leaning against one tree and the family car leaning against another. He had drawn her with crossed eyes and a turned-down mouth. The car's headlights were crossed and its front bumper turned down like Ramona's mouth. They both looked sick. Ramona discovered she remembered how to smile.

ABOVE: TRACY DOCKRAY (LEFT) AND JACQUELINE ROGERS (RIGHT). OPPOSITE: ALAN TIEGREEN.

Ramona and Picky-picky rest.

Mrs. Quimby stayed home from work to take care of Ramona, and Picky-picky, who as a rule avoids the youngest and noisiest Quimby, seems to be doing the same. (It could also be simply that she's providing extra warmth due to her illness; it's impossible to know the motivations of cats.) Ramona watches TV, and a commercial for a product that alleviates indigestion—"I can't believe I ate the *whole* thing," says a funny man after eating a pizza—makes her smile, a passing moment that will prove pivotal to the plot. Her classmates send get-well cards. Maybe they, the teacher, and Ramona's mother don't think she's such a nuisance after all. Tiegreen expertly uses perspective to capture this restful scene.

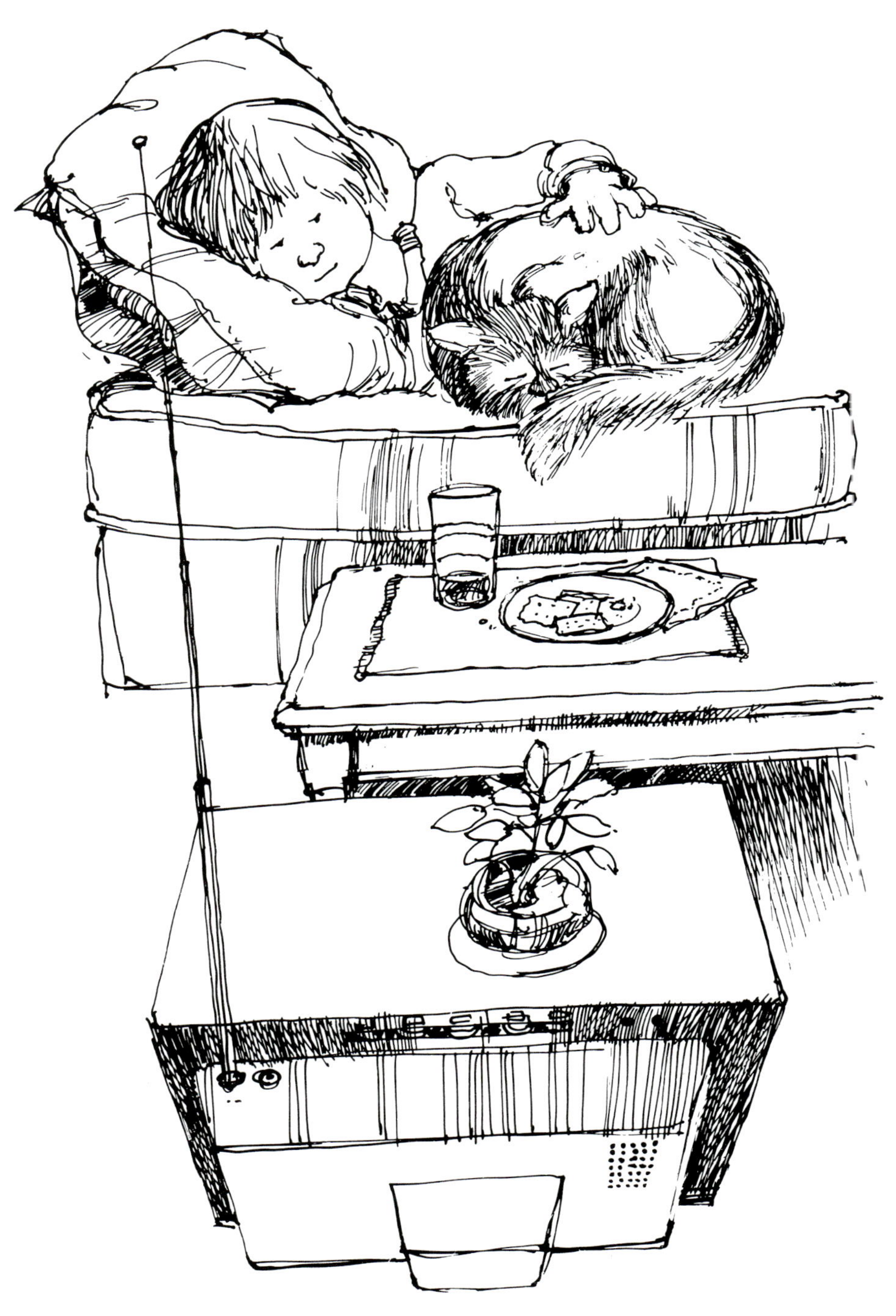

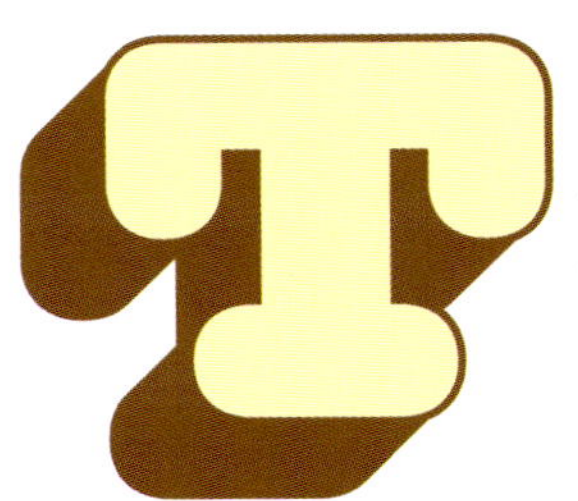

he Quimby family was full of worries. The parents were worried about managing without a car while a new transmission was installed and even more worried about paying for it. Beezus was worried about a party she had been invited to, because boys had also been invited. She was afraid it would turn out to be a dancing party, and she felt silly trying to dance. Besides, eighth-grade boys acted like a bunch of little kids at parties. Ramona, still feeling weak, moped around the house for another day worrying about her book report. If she made it interesting, Mrs. Whaley would think she was showing off. If she did not make it interesting, her teacher would not like it.

On top of everything, Beezus happened to look at her father's head as he bent over his books at the dining-room table that evening. "Daddy, you're getting thin on top!" she cried out, shocked.

Ramona rushed to look. "Just a little thin," she said, because she did not want her father's feelings hurt. "You aren't bald yet."

Mrs. Quimby also examined the top of her husband's head. "It is a little thin," she agreed, and kissed the spot. "Never mind. I found a gray hair last week."

"What is this? A conference about my hair?" asked Mr. Quimby, and he grabbed his wife around the waist. "Don't worry," he told her. "I'll still love you when you're old and gray."

"Thanks a lot," said Mrs. Quimby, not wanting to think of herself as old and gray. They both laughed. Mr. Quimby released his wife and gave her a playful slap on the bottom, an act that amused and shocked his daughters.

This scene is a perfect example of why the Ramona series has had such staying power. Young readers can relate to Beezus and Ramona's trials and tribulations, while parents and older readers can relate to those of Mr. and Mrs. Quimby.

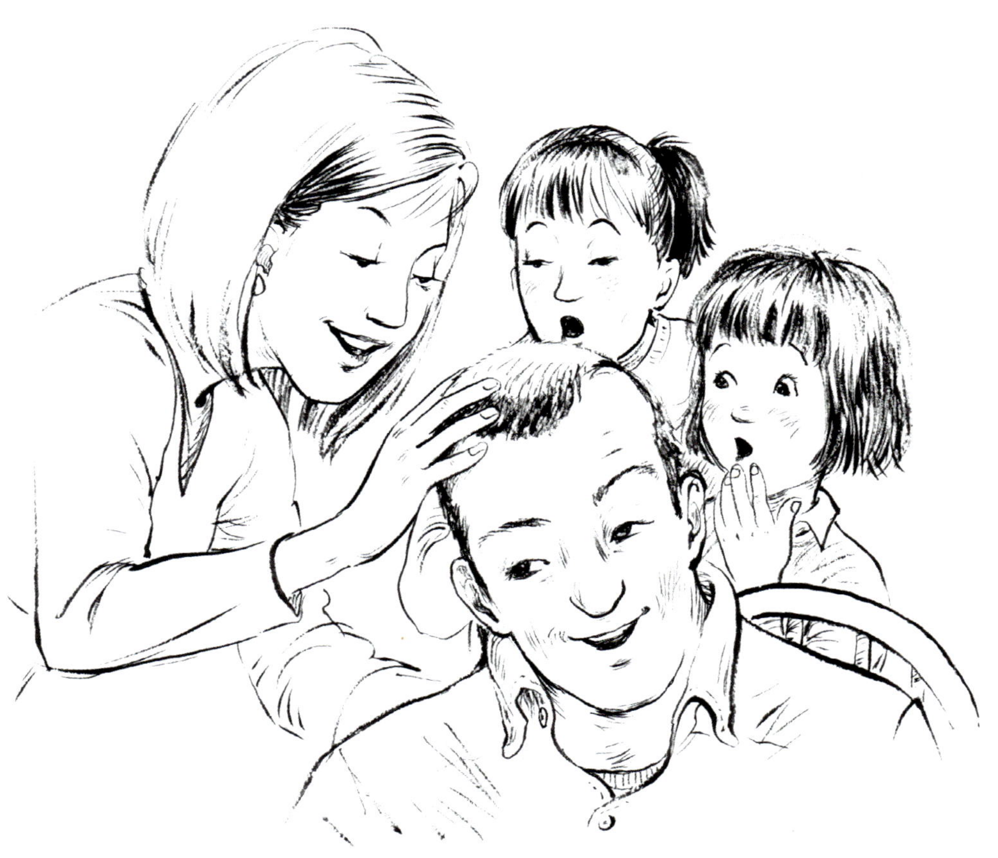

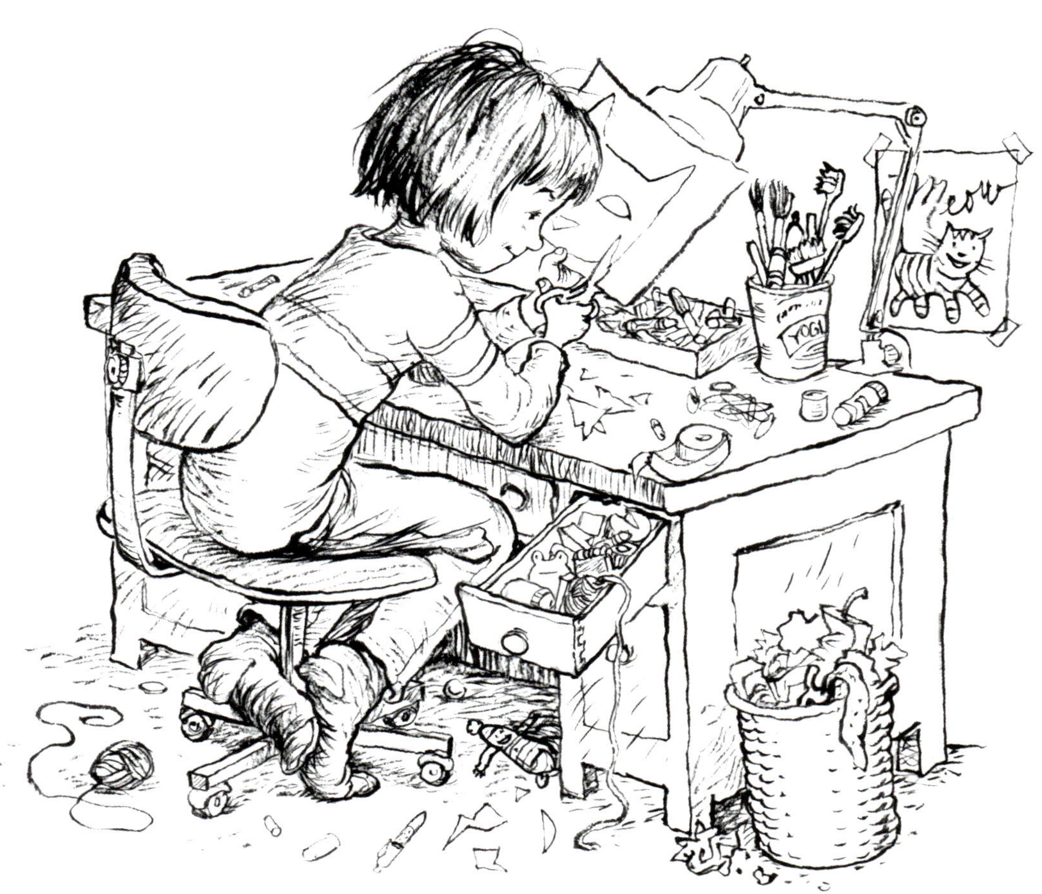

Nothing in the whole world felt as good as being able to make something from a sudden idea.

After receiving reassurance that she is not a nuisance from both her mother and her father, Ramona stops worrying (at least for the moment). Now, instead of making the classic boring book report, she can let the creative juices flow in what her family calls "Ramona's studio."

JACQUELINE ROGERS (OPPOSITE AND ABOVE).

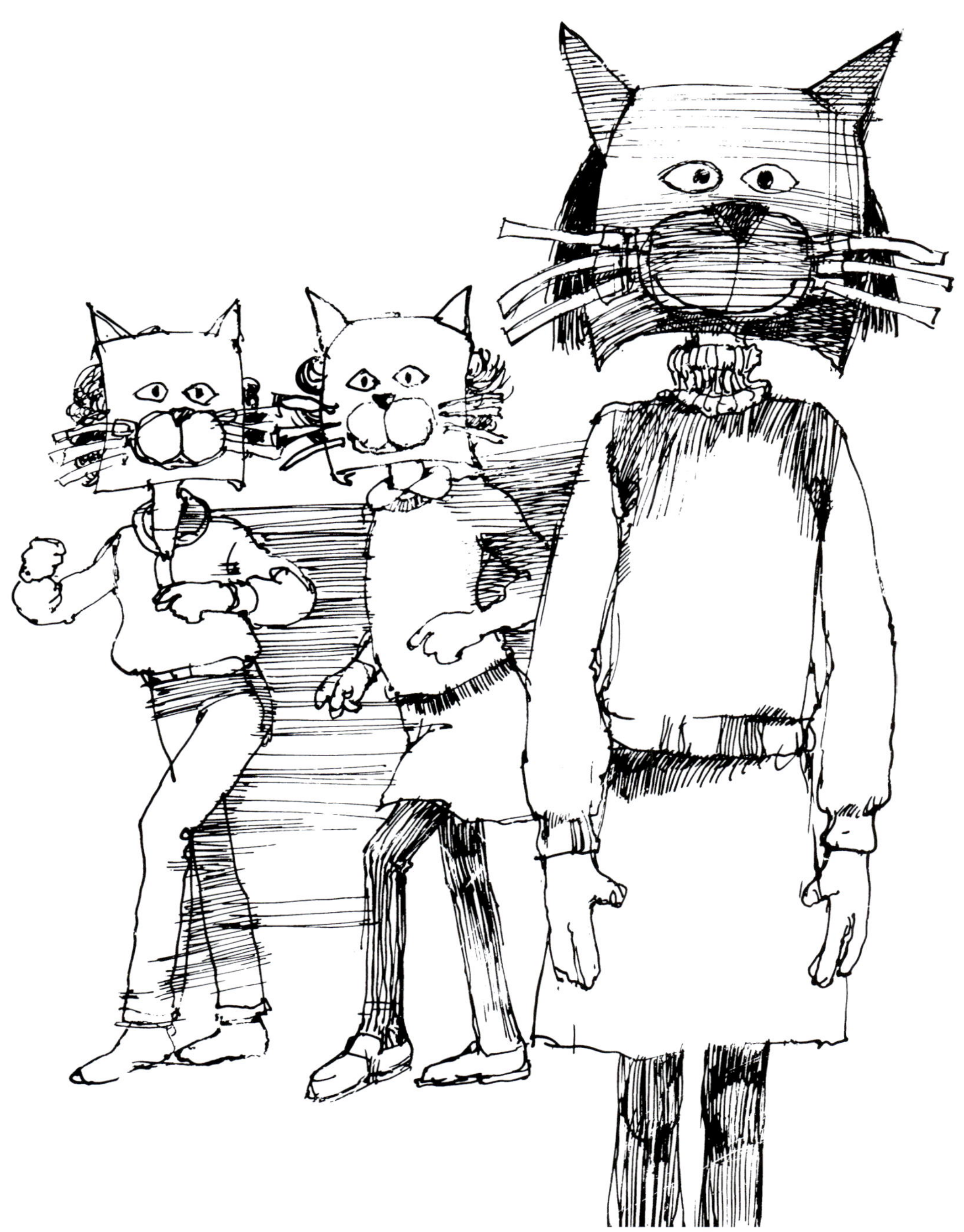

Inspired by the funny guy who ate a whole pizza in the ad on TV, Ramona decides to present her book report on *Left-Behind Cat* like a commercial. Her friends Janet and Sara provide backup, dancing like cats and chanting "Meow, meow, meow, meow." The sight of Yard Ape grinning distracts Ramona, causing her to forget the report's conclusion and forcing her to improvise. "I can't believe I read the *whole* thing!" she eventually blurts out. Tiegreen, the only illustrator who chose to draw this scene, uses motion lines extending behind the backup dancers to show their movement.

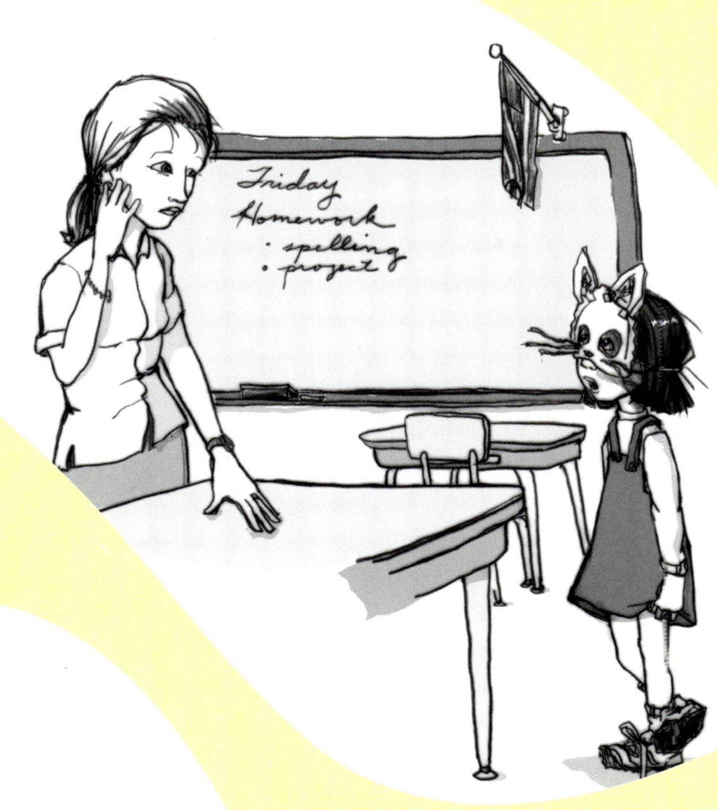

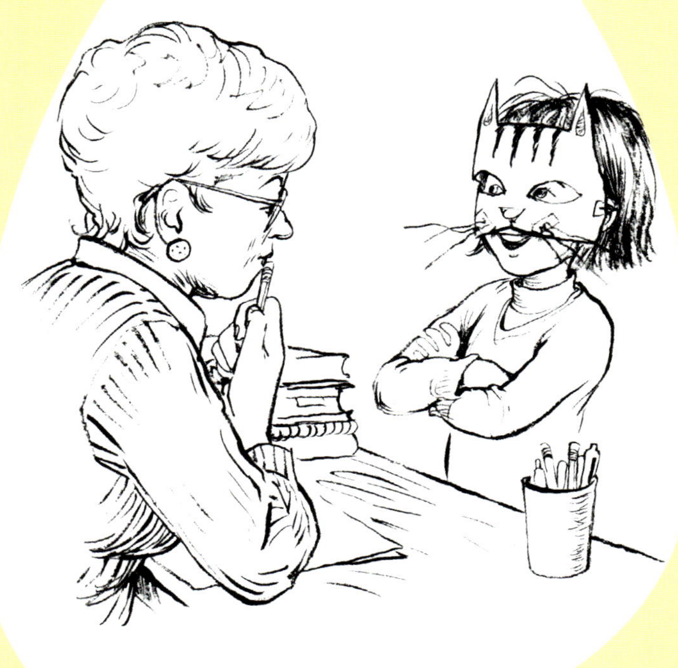

Ramona works up the nerve to confront her teacher.

After the roaring success of her book report, Ramona finally tells Mrs. Whaley that she overheard her in the nurse's office. In Dockray's illustration, Ramona stands with ankles crossed in a gesture of nervousness while Mrs. Whaley's hand on her face reveals her dismay. Rogers chose to show Ramona with arms confidently crossed in front of her and her teacher looking more confused and curious than upset.

OPPOSITE: ALAN TIEGREEN. ABOVE: TRACY DOCKRAY (TOP) AND JACQUELINE ROGERS (BOTTOM).

Mrs. Whaley's smile was mischievous. "Tell me, Ramona," she said, "don't you ever try to show off?"

Ramona was embarrassed. "Well . . . maybe . . . sometimes, a little," she admitted. Then she added positively, "But I wasn't showing off that day. How could I be showing off when I was doing what everyone else was doing?"

"You've convinced me," said Mrs. Whaley with a big smile. "Now run along and eat your lunch."

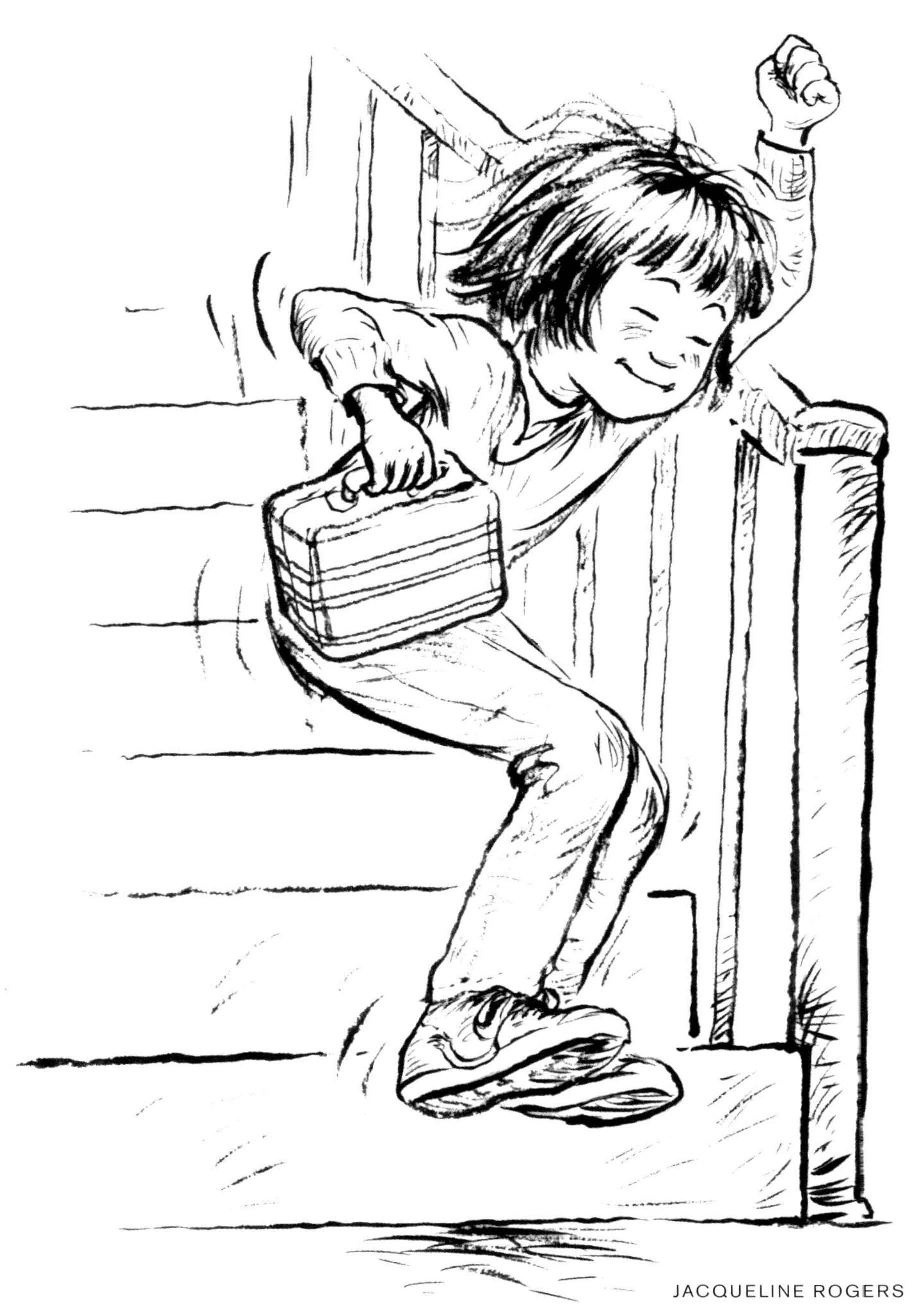

JACQUELINE ROGERS

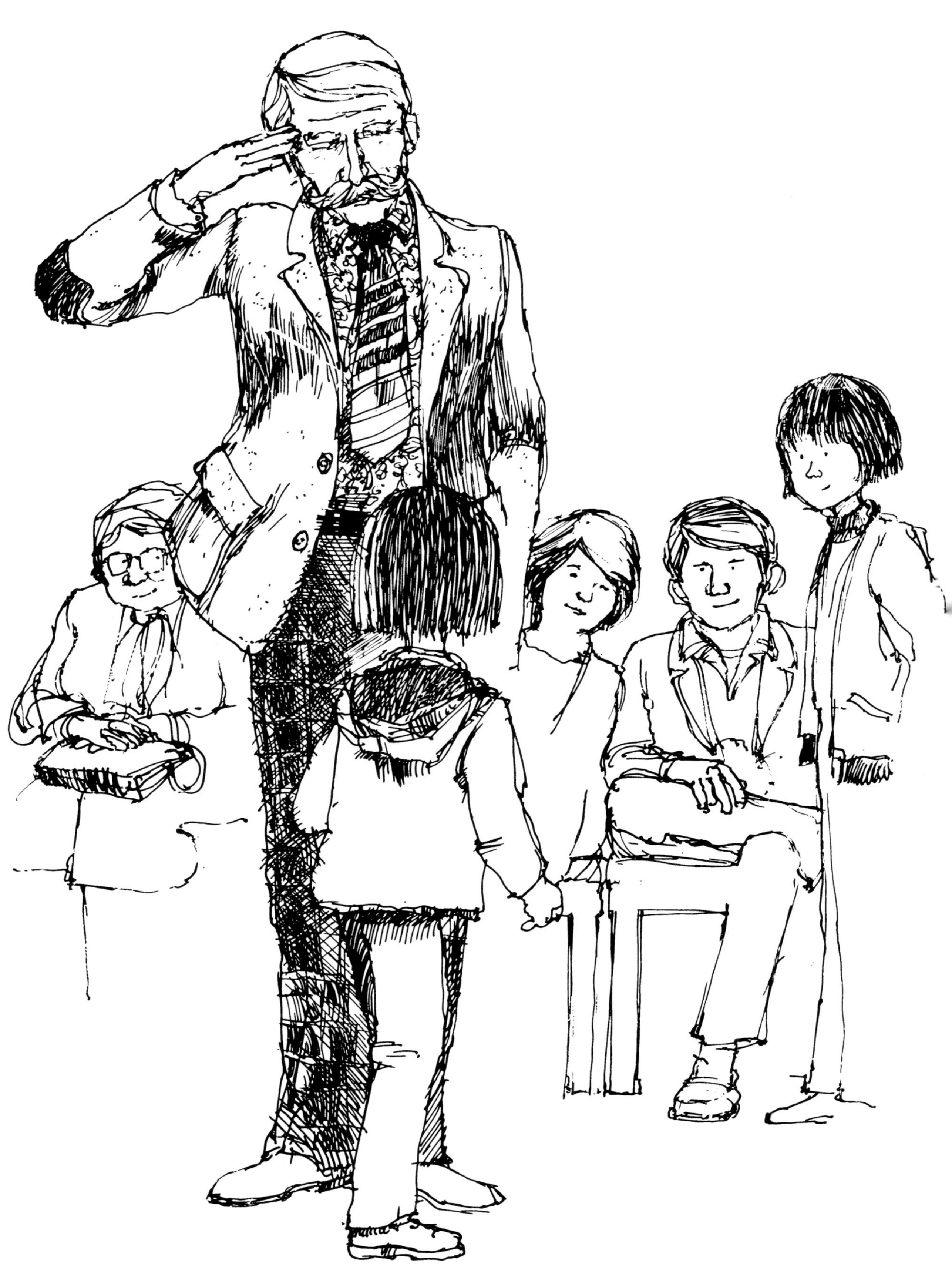

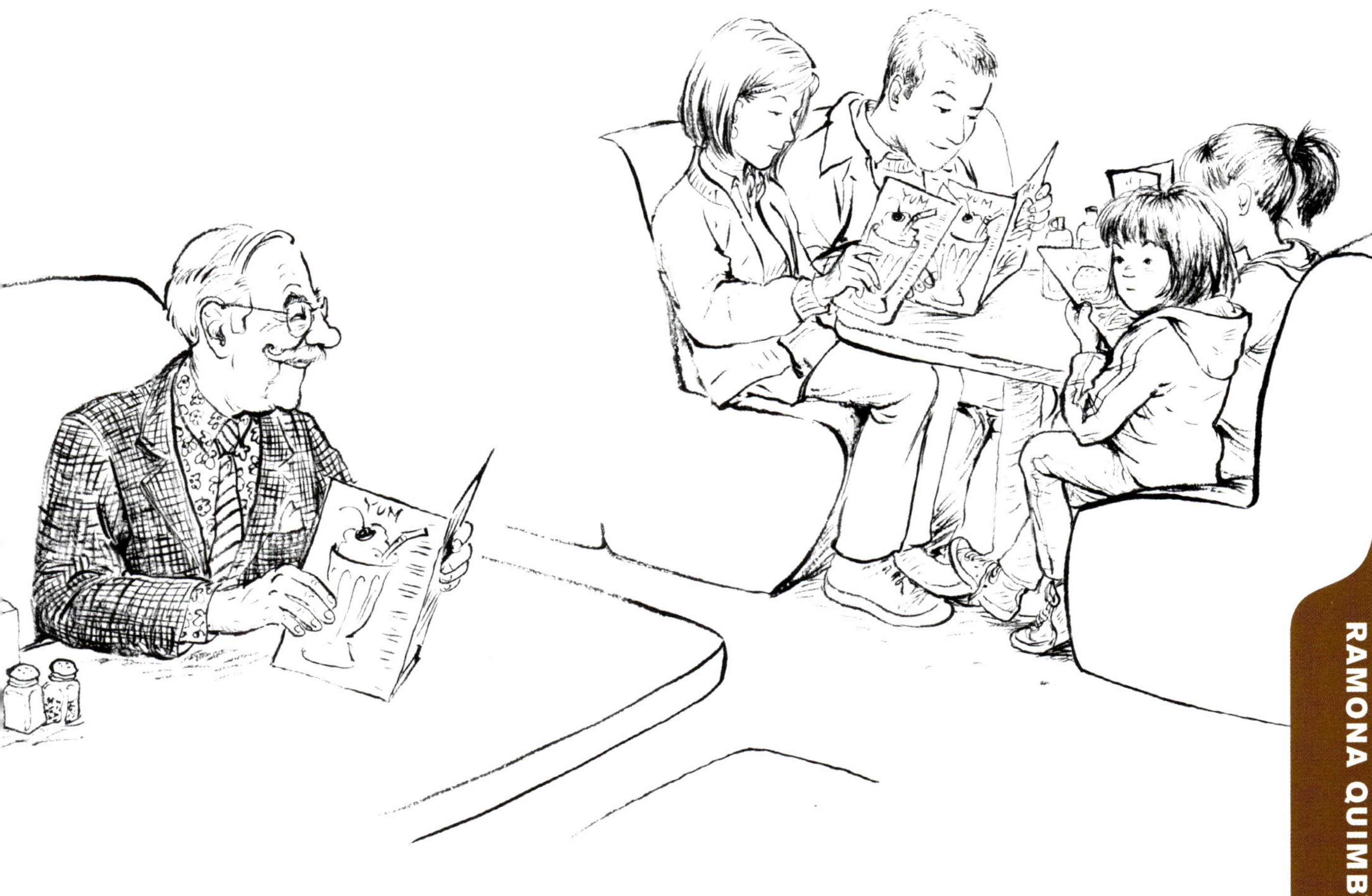

To lighten the mood on a rainy, grouchy Sunday, Mr. Quimby suggests dinner out at Whopperburger. While waiting for a table, they meet an old man with neatly trimmed gray hair and a mustache. He asks Ramona if she's been good to her mother, and Ramona, who is adamant about accuracy, doesn't quite know what to say. ("Not always" is the first response that comes to mind). Tiegreen styled the stranger in loud late-seventies fashion, with checkered pants, a patterned shirt, and a striped tie. Rogers, clearly recognizing perfection when she saw it, similarly dressed the old man, though the rest of the family wears more modern clothing. In her illustration, the family is seated; note the look of apprehension on Ramona's face. Soon the waitress will surprise them by telling them that the lonely gentleman paid for their meal.

ALAN TIEGREEN (OPPOSITE) AND JACQUELINE ROGERS (ABOVE).

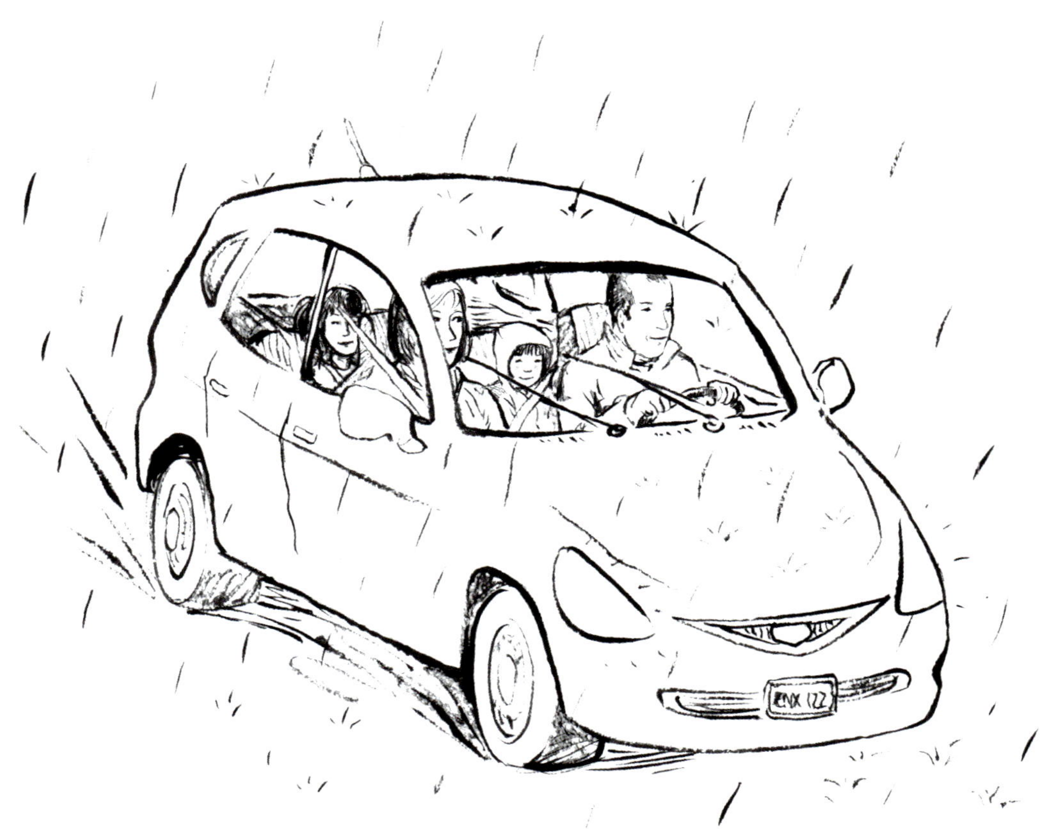

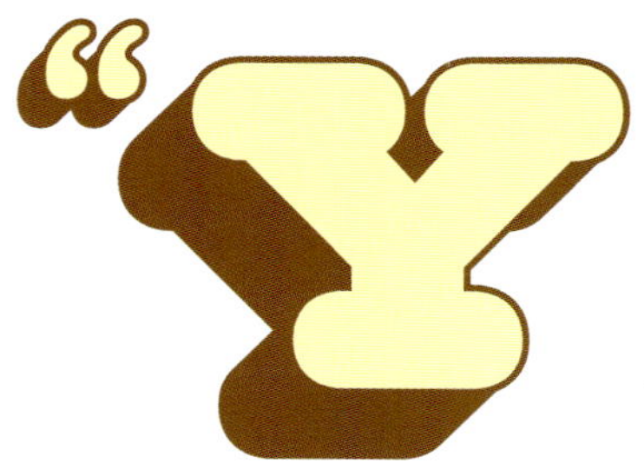

"You know," said Mrs. Quimby thoughtfully, as the car left the parking lot and headed down the street, "I think he was right. We are a nice family."

"Not all the time," said Ramona, as usual demanding accuracy.

"Nobody is nice all the time," answered her father. "Or if they are, they are boring."

"Not even your parents are nice all the time," added Mrs. Quimby.

Ramona secretly agreed, but she had not expected her parents to admit it. Deep down inside, she felt she herself was nice all the time, but sometimes on the outside her niceness sort of—well, curdled. Then people did not understand how nice she really was. Maybe other people curdled too.

"We have our ups and downs," said Mrs. Quimby, "but we manage to get along, and we stick together."

JACQUELINE ROGERS (ABOVE) AND TRACY DOCKRAY (OPPOSITE).

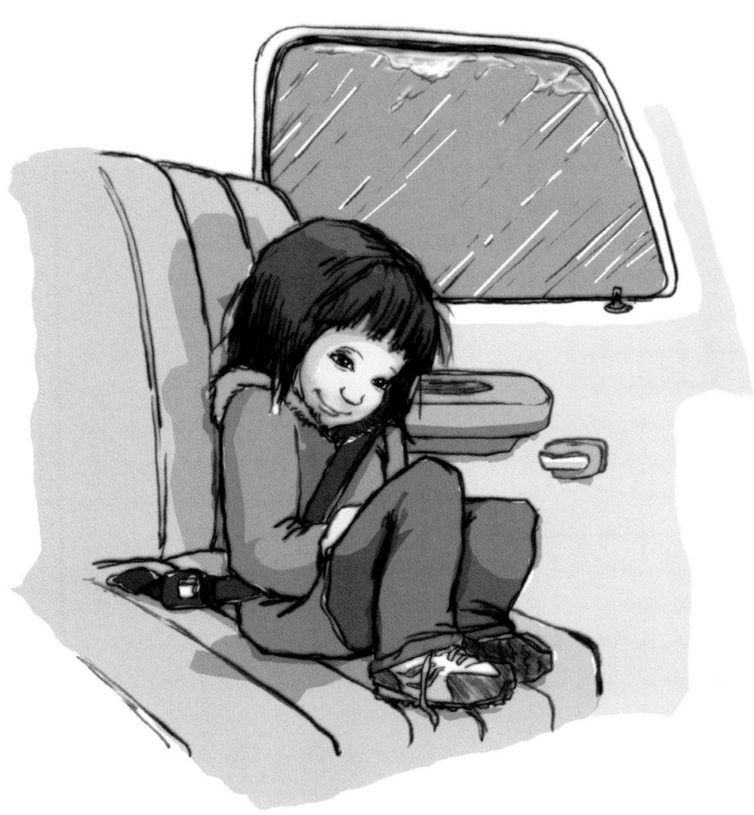

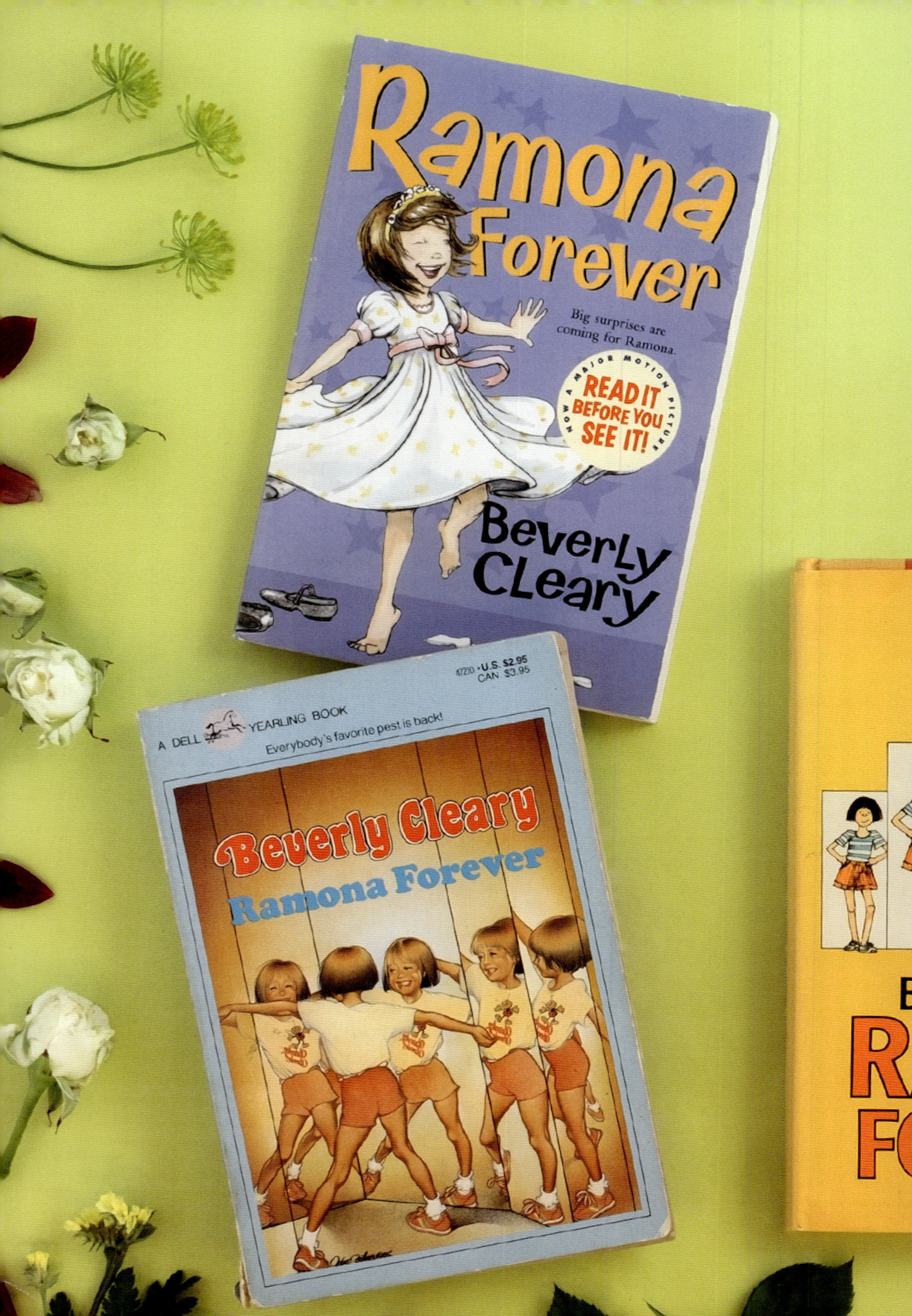
Ramona Forever
Big surprises are coming for Ramona.
NOW A MAJOR MOTION PICTURE
READ IT BEFORE YOU SEE IT!
Beverly Cleary
47210 • U.S. $2.95 CAN. $3.95
A DELL YEARLING BOOK
Everybody's favorite pest is back!
Beverly Cleary
Ramona Forever

Ramona Forever

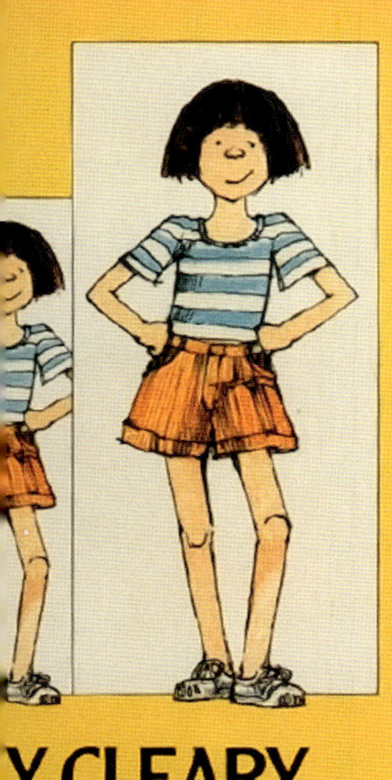

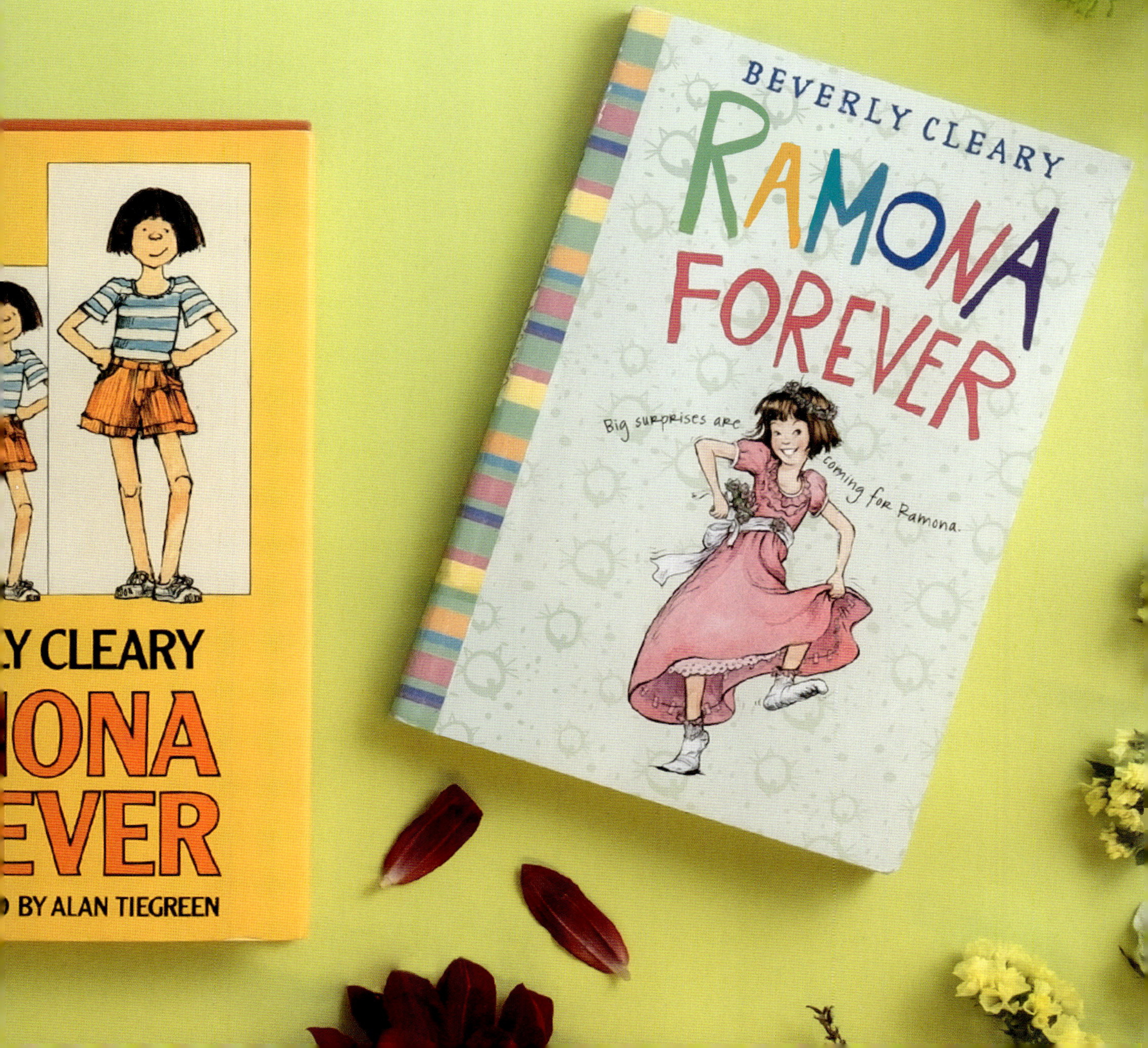

Ramona Forever

Chapter Seven

It isn't fair, Ramona told herself, even though grown-ups were always telling her life was not fair. It wasn't fair that life wasn't fair.

Five years have passed since the publication of the previous book in the series and now, in *Ramona Forever*, it's sweeps week in Ramonaland: a wedding, a death, and a pregnancy, all in one epic romp through third grade. If you want to avoid spoilers, skip this introduction. If not, here are the specifics: Howie Kemp's uncle Hobart comes into town and steals the heart of Ramona and Beezus's aunt, Picky-picky goes to the big kitty condo in the sky, Mrs. Quimby and Mr. Quimby make the shocking announcement of her pregnancy.

These are a lot of maturity-inducing events, one right after the next. The arrival of the jokey Hobart (with whom Ramona is less than impressed) prompts a certain awakening in Ramona, a new awareness of reciprocity in relationships: As much as Ramona doesn't like Mrs. Kemp, the girl realizes, Mrs. Kemp doesn't like her! (Willa Jean plays the pivotal role of pest in this scene, later described as "the accordion incident.") With this, the divide between the world of adults and the world of children blurs—the world they are living in is, in fact, one and the same. This insight will launch Ramona's fight for her independence from Mrs. Kemp's afterschool oversight. Beezus surprises her by backing her up, and her parents surprise her by agreeing to her demands.

Unfortunately, soon after the two girls start coming home after school, the ancient and much-loved Picky-picky gives up the ghost. His exit from the world of the living spurs another maturity moment—one could even call it a moment of existential angst—around death and the ephemeral nature of all things. To alleviate the girls' grief, the Quimby parents make a surprising announcement: Soon their family will go from four (humans) to five. Chaos ensues as a wedding is thrown together and, after forever (a total of nine months or so), the newest member of the Quimby clan arrives.

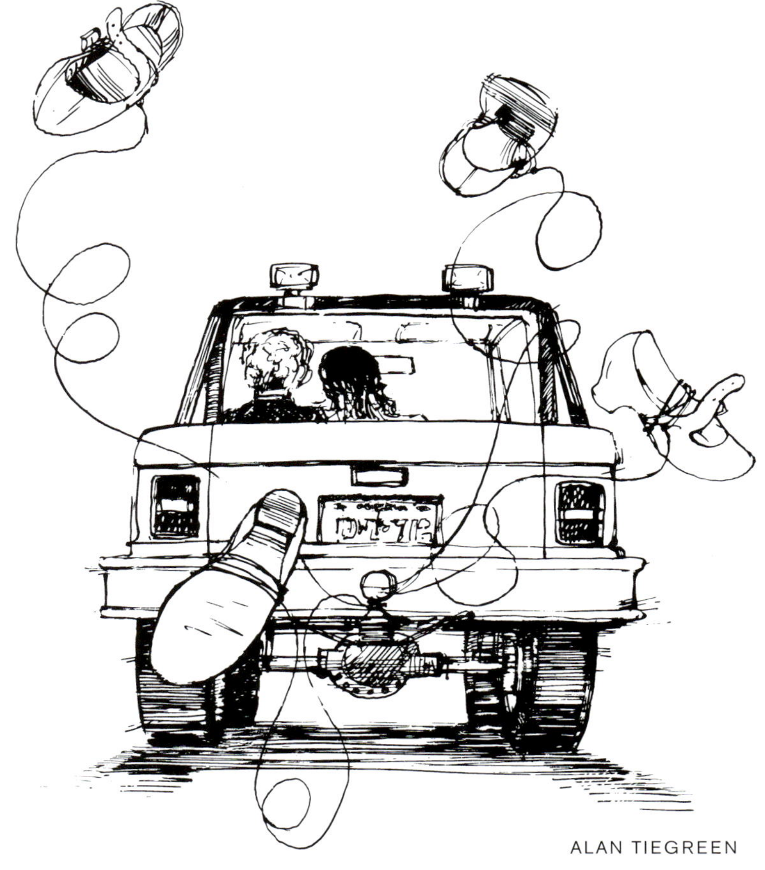

ALAN TIEGREEN

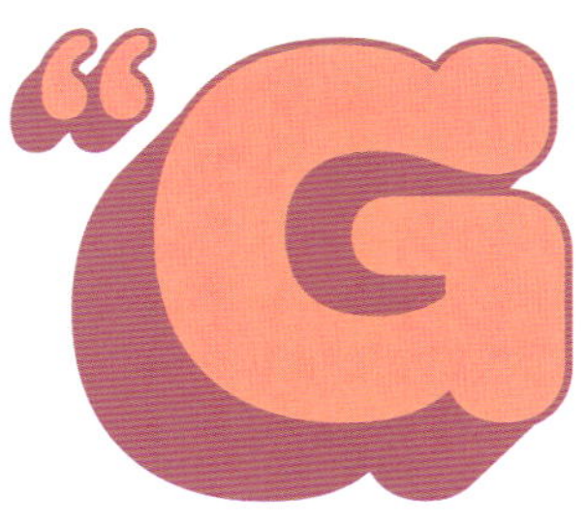

uess what?” Ramona Quimby asked one Friday evening when her Aunt Beatrice dropped by to show off her new ski clothes and to stay for supper. Ramona's mother, father, and big sister Beezus, whose real name was Beatrice, paid no attention and went on eating. Picky-picky, the cat, meowed through the basement door, asking to share the meal.

Aunt Beatrice, who taught third grade, knew how to behave toward her third grade niece. “What?” she asked, laying down her fork as if she expected to be astounded by Ramona's news.

Ramona took a deep breath and announced, “Howie Kemp's rich uncle is coming to visit.” Except for Aunt Bea, her family was not as curious as Ramona had hoped. She plunged on anyway because she was happy for her friend. “Howie's grandmother is really excited, and so are Howie and Willa Jean.” And so, to be truthful, was Ramona, who disliked having to go to the Kemps' house after school, where Howie's grandmother looked after her grandchildren and Ramona while the two mothers were at work. A rich uncle, even someone else's rich uncle, should make those long after-school hours more interesting.

“I didn't know Howie had a rich uncle,” said Mrs. Quimby.

“He's Howie's father's little brother, only now he's big,” explained Ramona.

“Why, that must be Hobart Kemp,” said Aunt Beatrice. “He was in my class in high school.”

“Oh, yes. I remember. That boy with the blond curly hair who played baseball.” Mrs. Quimby motioned to her daughters to clear away the plates. “All the girls said he was cute.”

“That's the one,” said Aunt Bea. “He used to chew licorice and spit on the grass to make the principal think he was chewing tobacco like a professional baseball player, which was what he wanted to be.”

“Where's this cute licorice-chewing uncle coming from, and how did he get so rich?” asked Ramona's father, beginning to be interested.

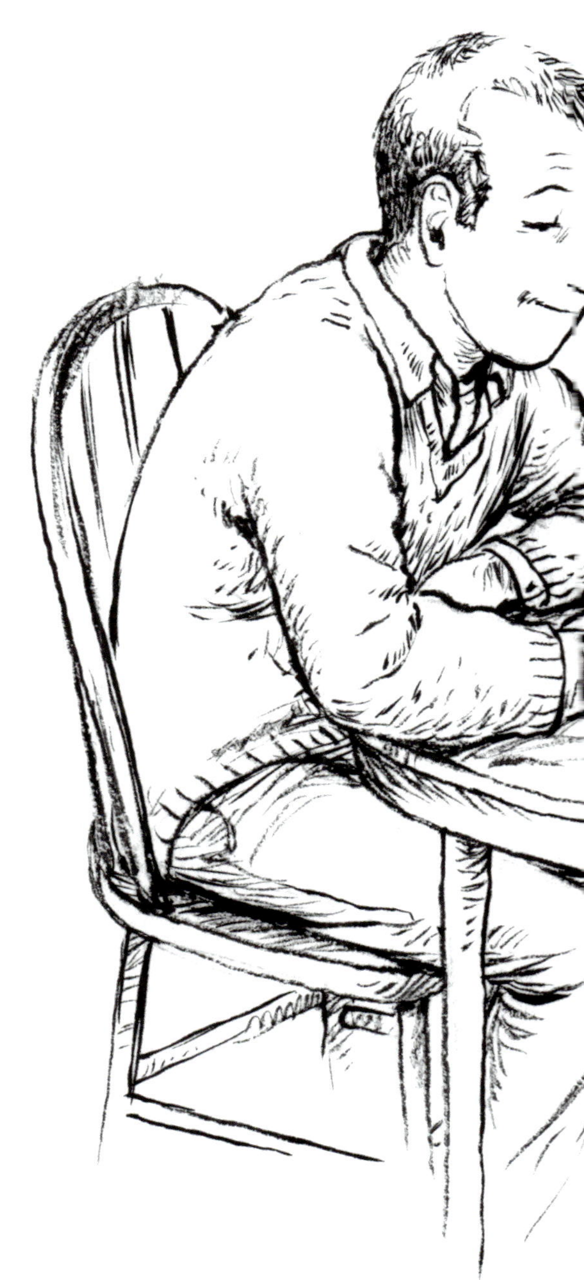

JACQUELINE ROGERS

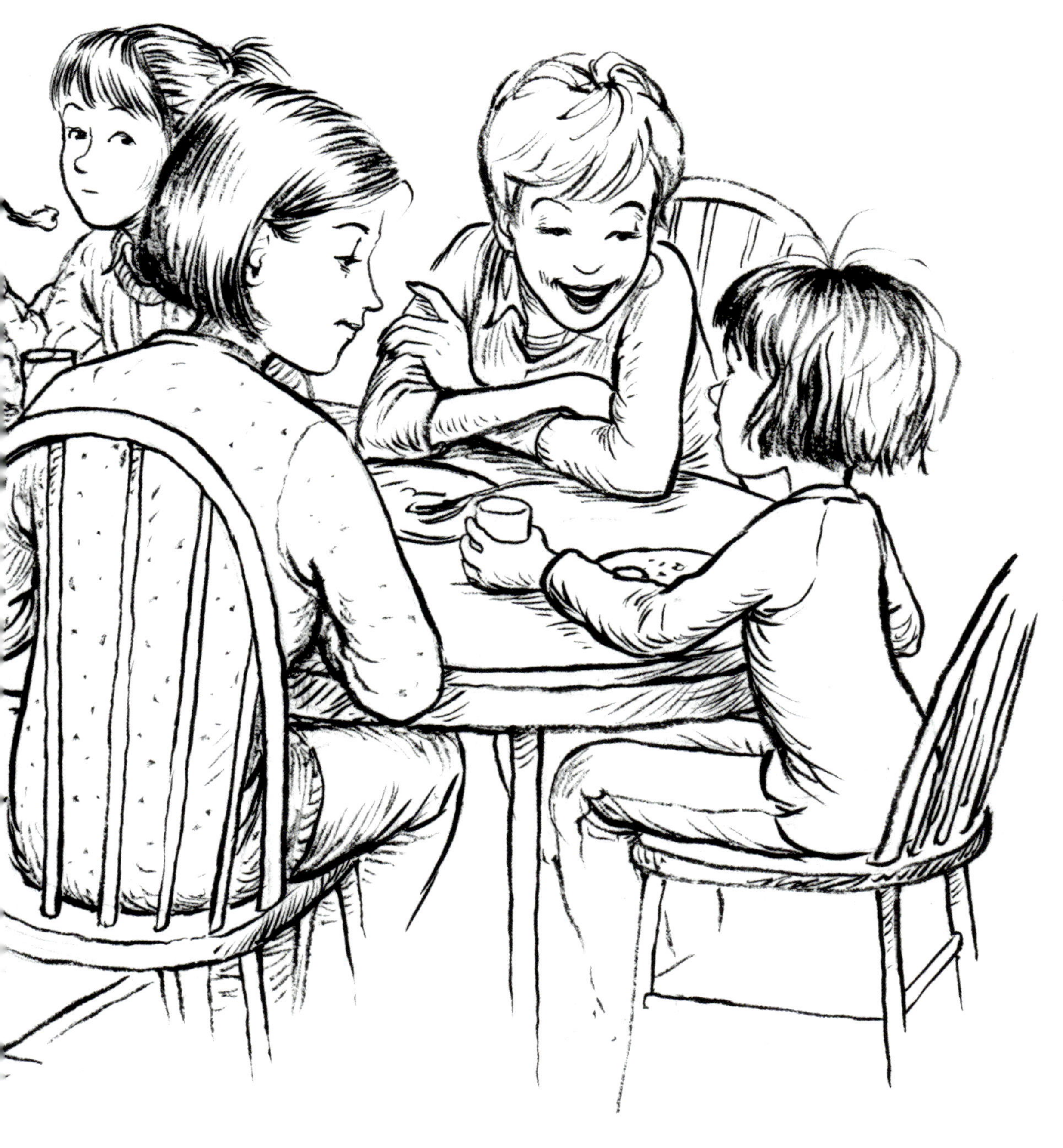

Ramona was suddenly struck by a new and disquieting thought. Mrs. Kemp did not like her.

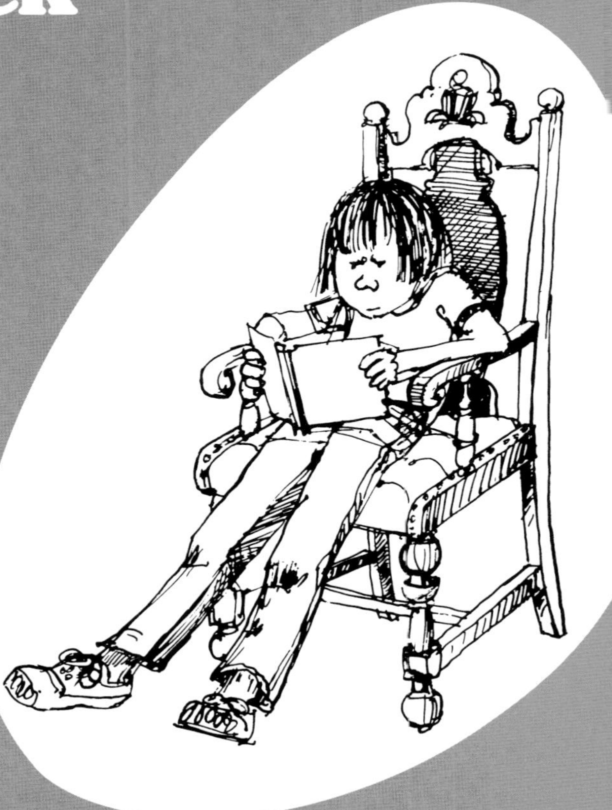

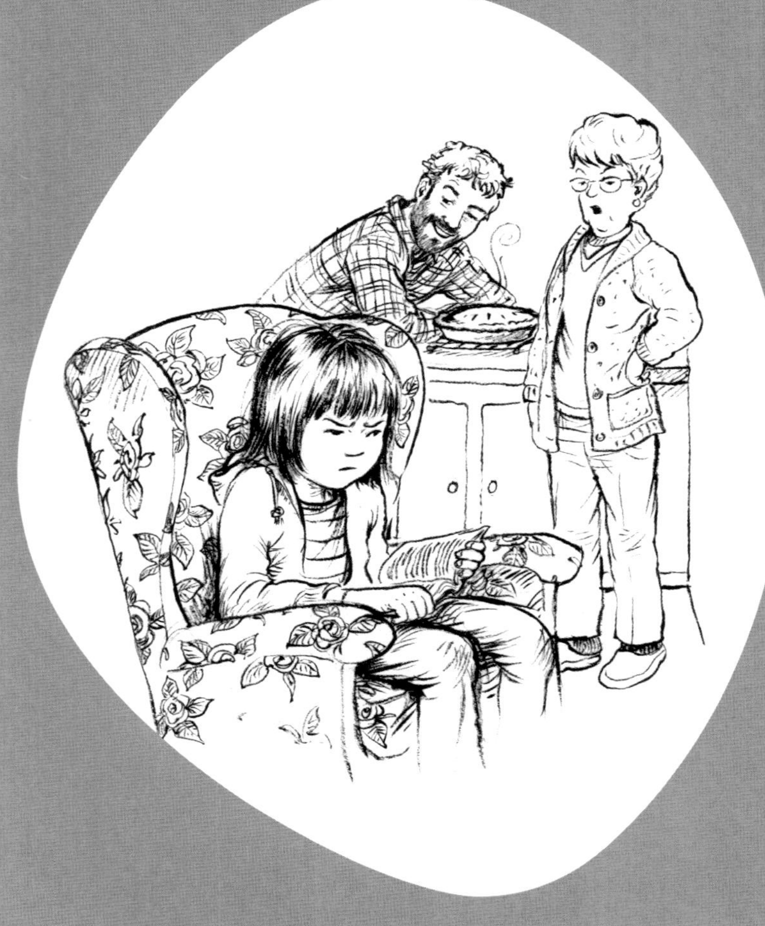

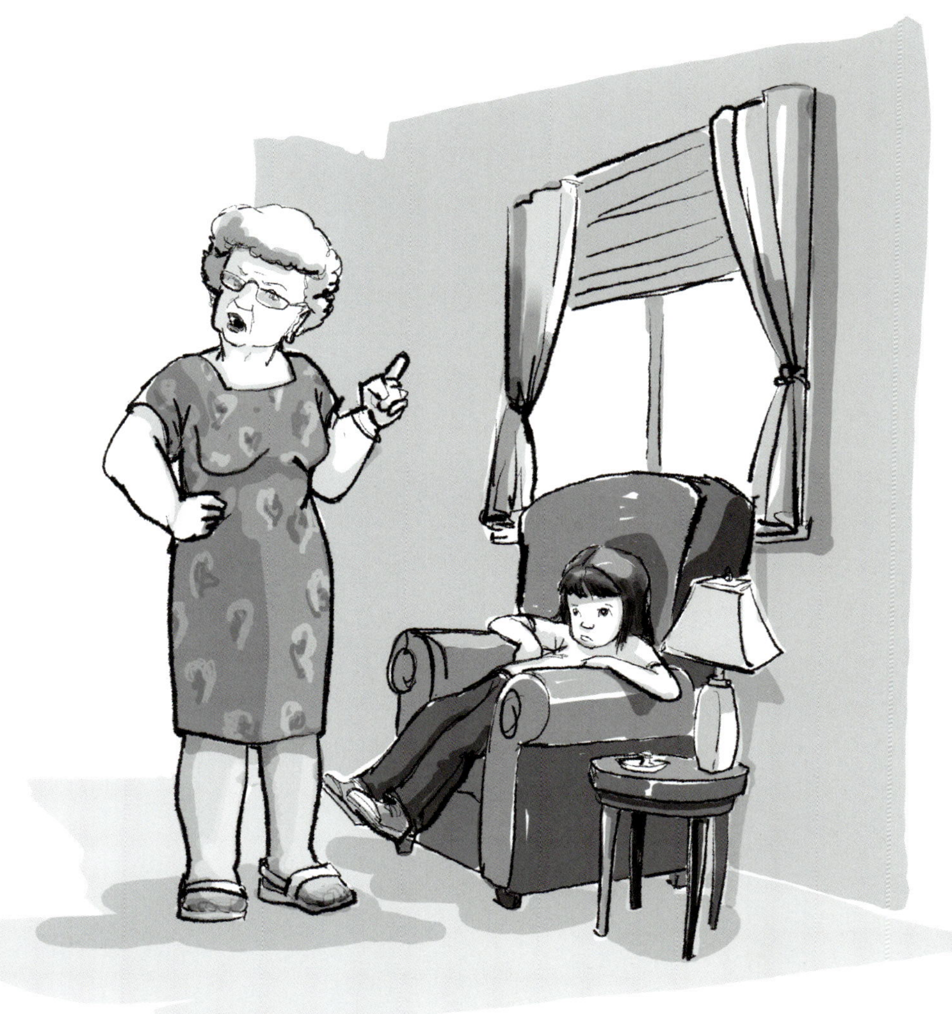

The infamous Uncle Hobart has finally arrived, bearing the kind of gifts that only a bachelor uncle would think to bring. After Willa Jean sits on her brand-new accordion—eliciting a dreadful yet satisfying piercing noise that signals its irrevocable brokenness—Mrs. Kemp scolds Ramona for the zillionth time for not watching the little pest well enough. Oh, the unfairness of it all!

Put together, these three illustrations create a zooming-out effect, from Ramona slumped angrily in her chair, to Mrs. Kemp standing over her, to Uncle Hobart trying to make peace between the older woman and the girl. Ramona does not appreciate the ally—already, she has decided that Hobart is one of those annoying grown-ups who think it's funny to tease children.

This moment could also be understood as a mental zooming out, an expansion of understanding. Ramona suddenly realizes that adults have their own feelings about children, feelings that aren't always very nice.

OPPOSITE: JACQUELINE ROGERS (LEFT) AND ALAN TIEGREEN (RIGHT). ABOVE: TRACY DOCKRAY.

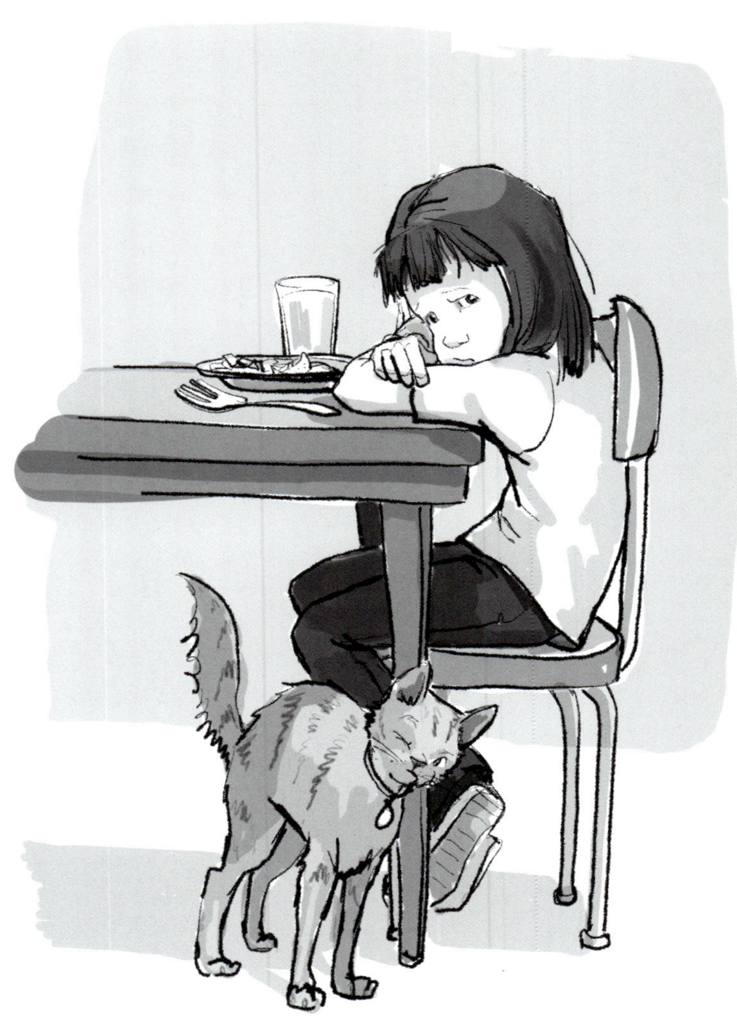

Ramona announces that she won't be going back to the Kemps.

Instead of getting excited or dismissive, Mr. Quimby asks for more information in a calm manner, an annoying habit he's developed since going back to college to study teaching and child development. In Tiegreen's illustration, Ramona is in full crying mode, while in Dockray's version, Ramona looks tragically forlorn. In both, a hungry Picky-picky awaits table scraps.

ABOVE: ALAN TIEGREEN (LEFT) AND TRACY DOCKRAY (RIGHT). OPPOSITE: JACQUELINE ROGERS.

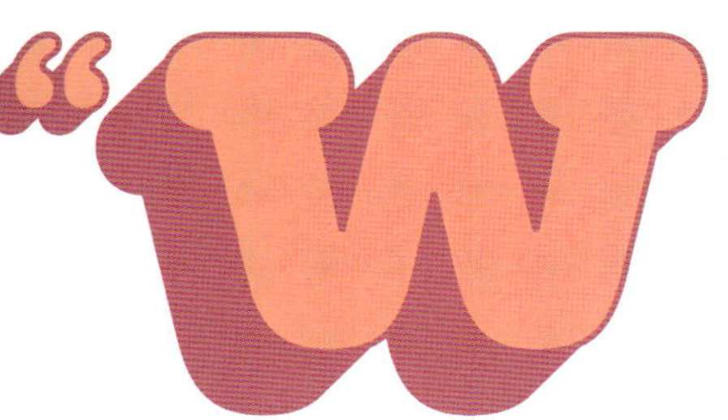

hy don't we go ask Mother?" "When she wants us to know, she will tell us. And of course, I might be wrong. . . ." Doubt crept into Beezus's voice before she said, "Oh, I hope I'm right. I love babies. I'd love to help take care of one of our own. I just know it would be darling."

Ramona sat on the bed thinking while Beezus opened her books. A little brother or sister? She did not like the idea, not one bit. If she had a little brother or sister, grown-ups would say in their knowing way, as if children could not understand, Somebody's nose is out of joint. Ramona had heard them say it many times about children who had new babies in the family. This was their way of talking about children behind their backs in front of them.

"But if it's true, I sure hope Daddy finds a teaching job fast," said Beezus. "Now go away. I have to study."

Ramona wandered into the living room, where her mother was lying on the couch watching the evening news on TV with the sound turned low so it would not disturb her husband, who was studying at the dining room table. Ramona knew she was not supposed to interrupt when he was studying, but this time she decided he wasn't really working, just doodling on a piece of scratch paper with a worried look on his face. She slipped her head up between his ribs and arm.

"Hi," said her father, as if Ramona had brought his thoughts back to the dining room.

"Hi," answered Ramona as her father quickly turned over his page of doodles, but not before she had a glimpse of dollar signs and babies, doodles that must mean he was thinking about a baby.

"You have me to be your little girl," Ramona reminded her father.

Her father rubbed his chin against the top of Ramona's head. "That's right, and I'm mighty glad I do."

"Then you wouldn't want another little girl, would you?" Ramona had to find out.

"Oh, I don't know," said Mr. Quimby. "I like little girls."

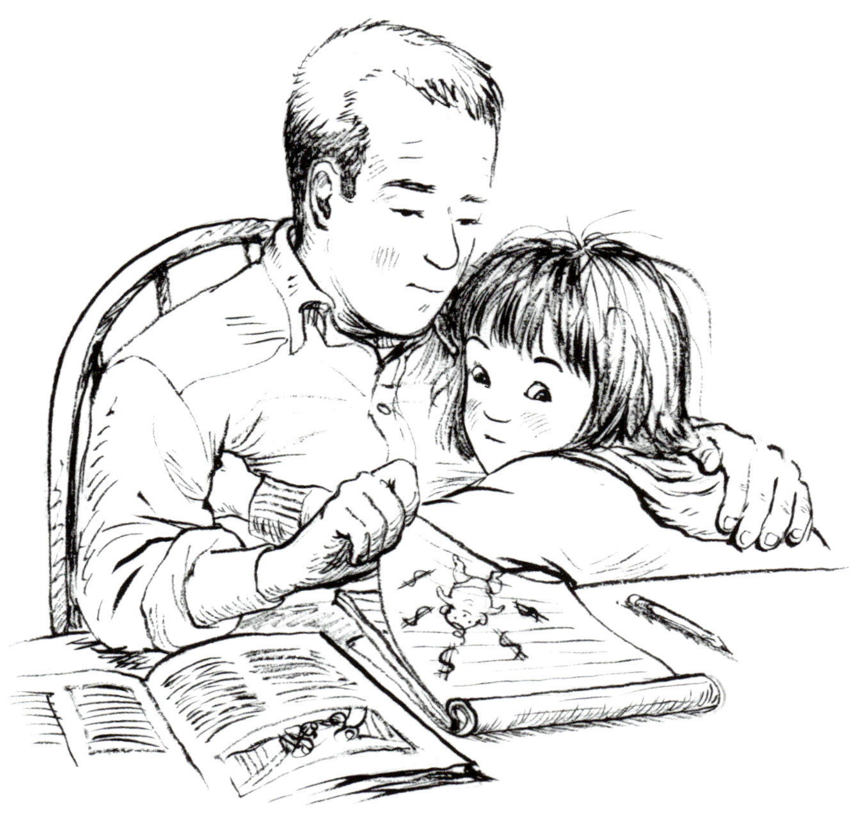

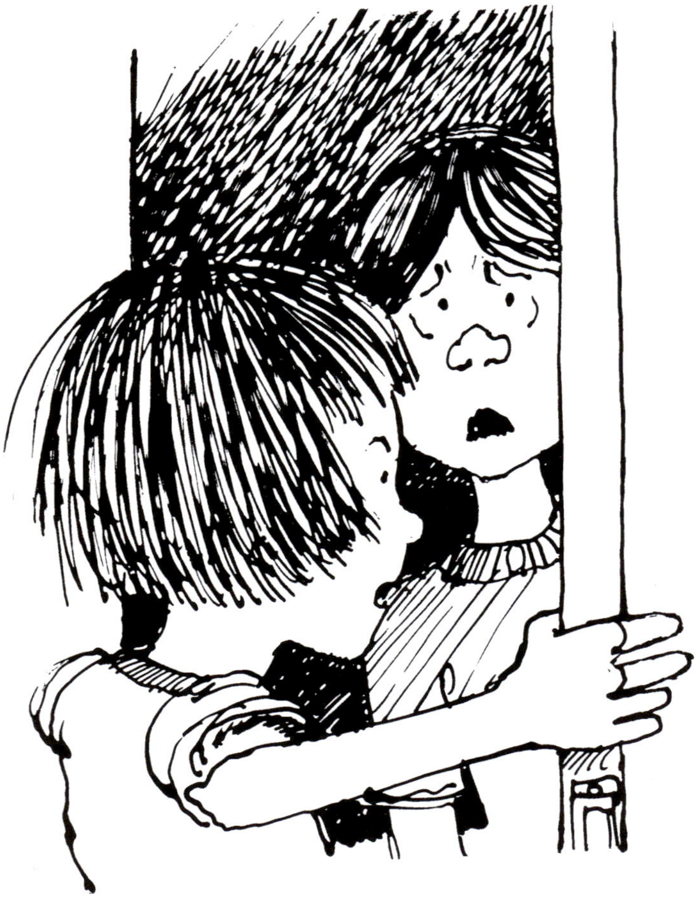

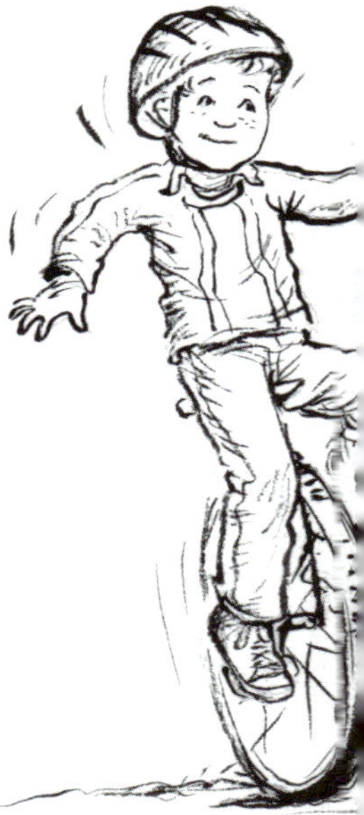

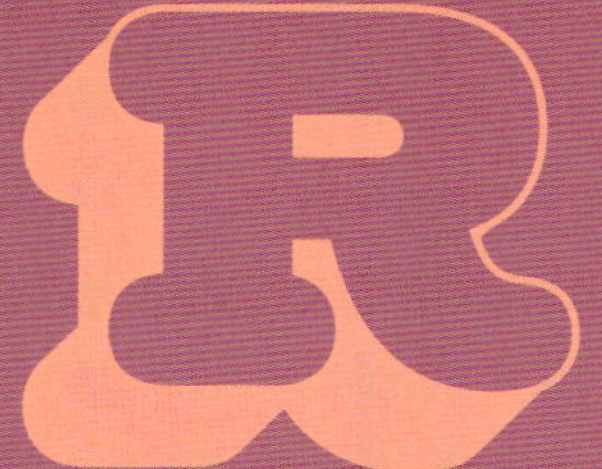amona grew more determined and contrary. "Mom always lets me go out and play with Howie."

"Just the same, if you get hurt, I'm responsible," said Beezus.

"You're just being mean," said Ramona. "So long, Pizzaface." Just before she slammed the door, she was horrified to see Beezus's face crumple, as if she were about to burst into tears.

The sisters have been working so hard to get along, a condition of their being allowed to come home after school instead of going to the Kemps'. Then Howie comes over with a bicycle for Ramona to ride, bossy old Beezus balks at giving permission, and, just like that, their peace treaty ends. Ramona will soon learn that "Pieface," a benign insult she uses often, has an entirely different meaning than "Pizzaface," especially to a junior high schooler who worries about her skin. Dockray and Rogers didn't illustrate this critical moment; only Tiegreen chose to capture poor Beezus's teenage anguish.

Ramona is less than enthusiastic after getting some more big news.

A death, a pregnancy, and now this. Ramona will have to get used to the idea of Hobart being around more, because he and Aunt Bea are getting married—in two weeks. And her parents knew all along. Traitors!

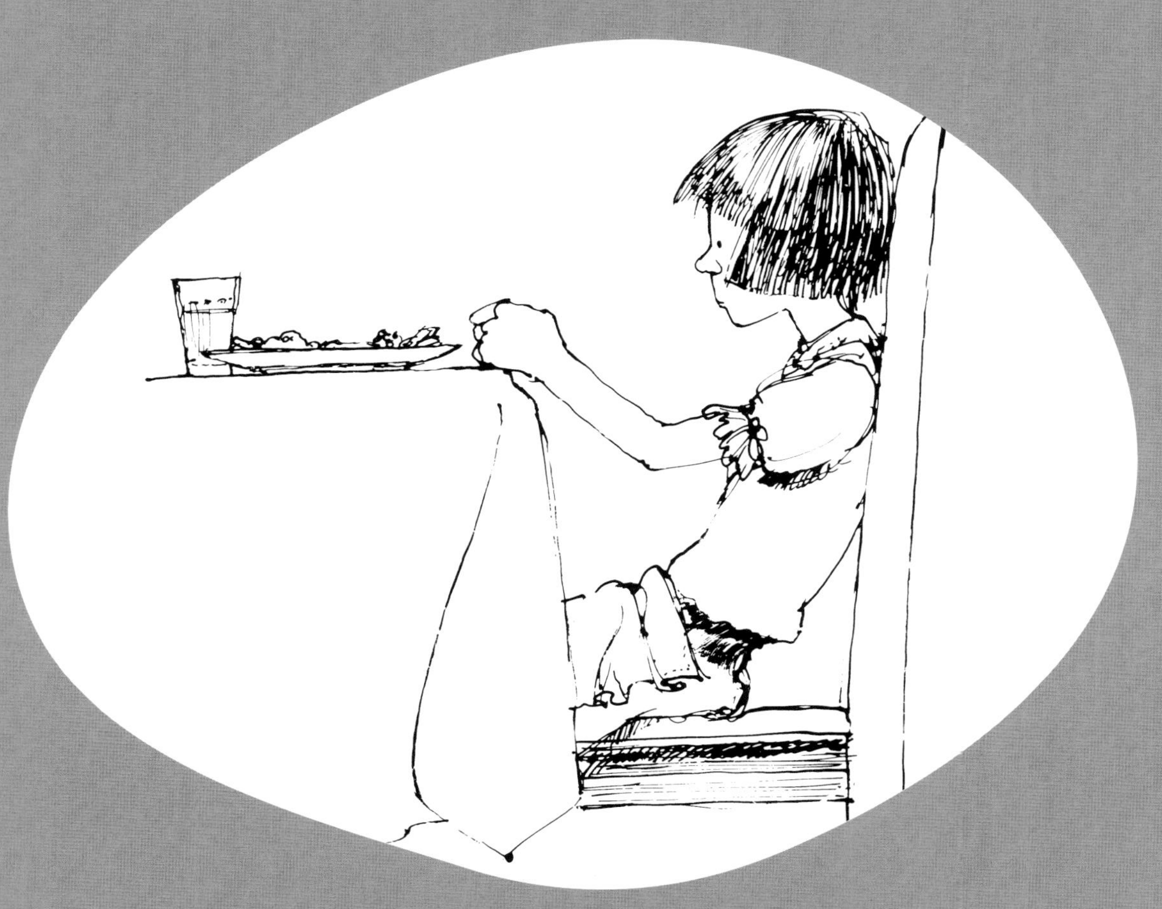

Ramona slipped over for a glimpse of herself in the three-way mirror, which reflected her back and forth from every angle. She began to dance, to watch all the Ramonas. Obediently, they imitated her, dancing on and on into the distance, tinier and tinier until they could no longer be seen. Forever me, thought Ramona. I go on forever.

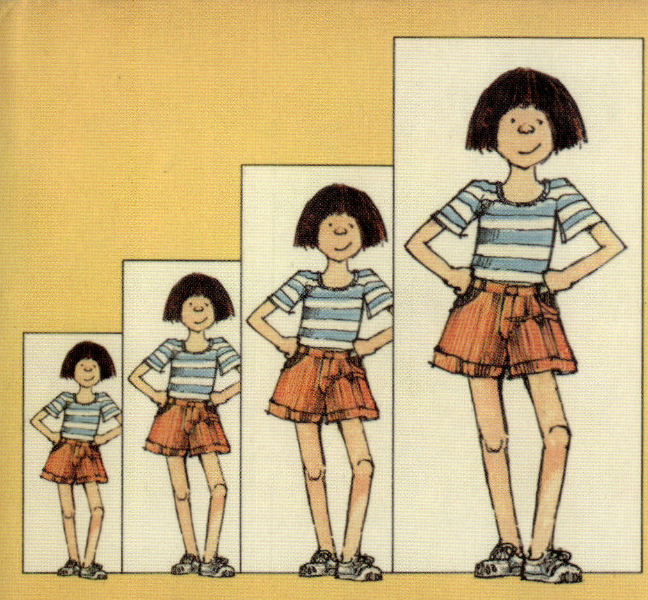

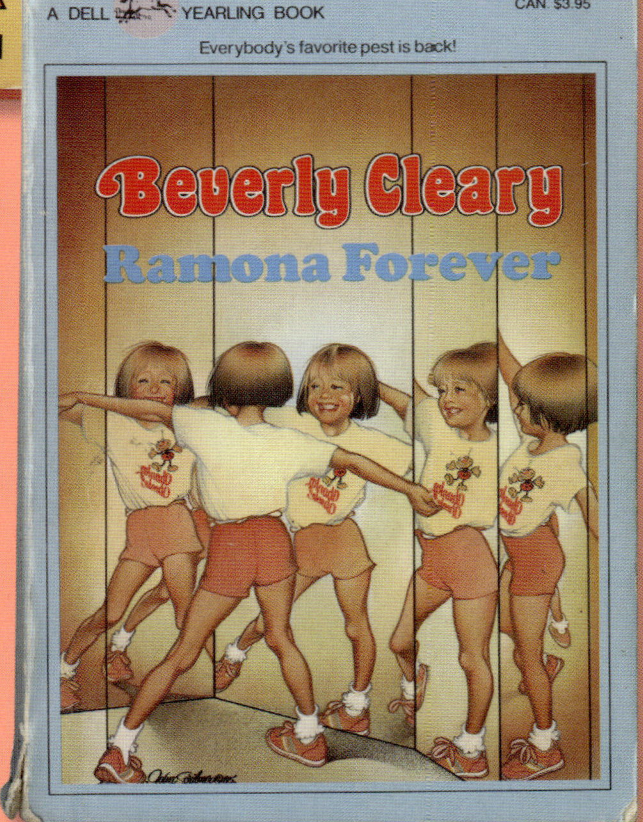

These two renowned book covers depict a pivotal moment in the dressing room of the bridal shop. Tiegreen's Ramona strikes a pose of quiet self-confidence, while Scribner's Ramona practically bursts with joy.

ALAN TIEGREEN (LEFT) AND JOANNE SCRIBNER (RIGHT).

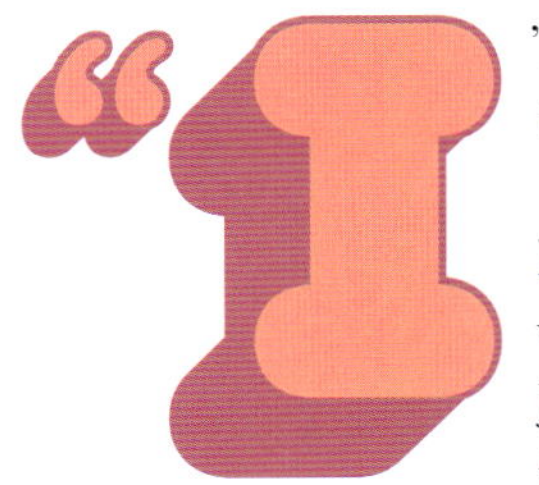

'll call the florist the first thing in the morning."

"Are you crazy?" cried Aunt Bea. "The day of the wedding, when florists are swamped with June weddings? Where would they find more flowers, especially so soon after the Rose Festival?" Worn out from progress reports, moving, and excitement, she turned to her fiancé and said, "I thought you said there was nothing to planning a wedding. Well, that just shows how wrong you can be."

"If I can be so wrong, why are you marrying me?" demanded Uncle Hobart. He looked tense, which was unusual for him. Both families tried to act as if they were not listening—except, of course, the older children, who were fascinated. Willa Jean looked as if she might cry.

"That's a good question," said Aunt Bea.

"That's a good question! That's a good question! All the years I was in school, teachers were always telling me I had asked a good question. Half the time they didn't even answer. They just asked me what I thought the answer should be, or asked some other kid to answer. Now you're telling me I asked a good question. You sound just like a teacher."

"I am a teacher." Aunt Bea's voice was cold.

Beezus and Ramona exchanged a "there-goes-the-wedding" look. Now the bridesmaid dresses no longer mattered. Howie looked hopeful, as if he thought he might escape carrying that ring on the pillow after all.

Uncle Hobart raised his voice. "Just once I would like to hear a teacher answer a question. Why are you marrying me—if you still plan to marry me?"

Aunt Bea began by sounding like a teacher. "Hobart has asked a good question," she said with a pleasant smile before she turned and shouted, "Because I love you, you cootie!" She then burst into tears.

Dockray's Ramona, her hand to her mouth, is shocked by a vocabulary word more fitting on the playground than coming from her grown-up aunt. In this version, Mrs. Quimby doesn't look too worried—perhaps she's chalking up the argument between bride and groom to pre-wedding jitters—while Willa Jean appears to be on the verge of tears. Tiegreen focused on the tense exchange between the soon-to-be newlyweds. Note the gloriously feathered hair of Aunt Bea.

ALAN TIEGREEN (TOP) AND TRACY DOCKRAY (BOTTOM).

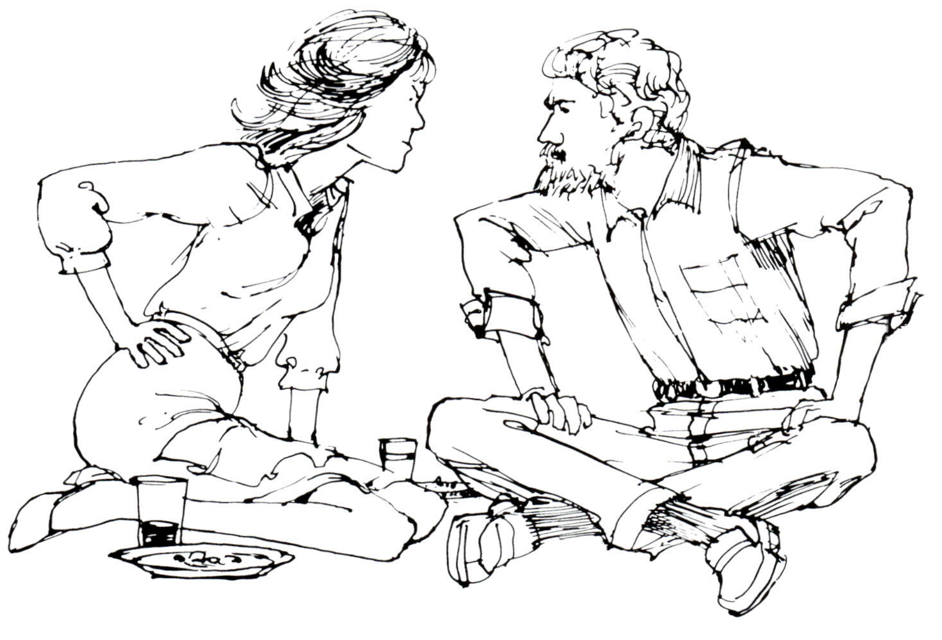

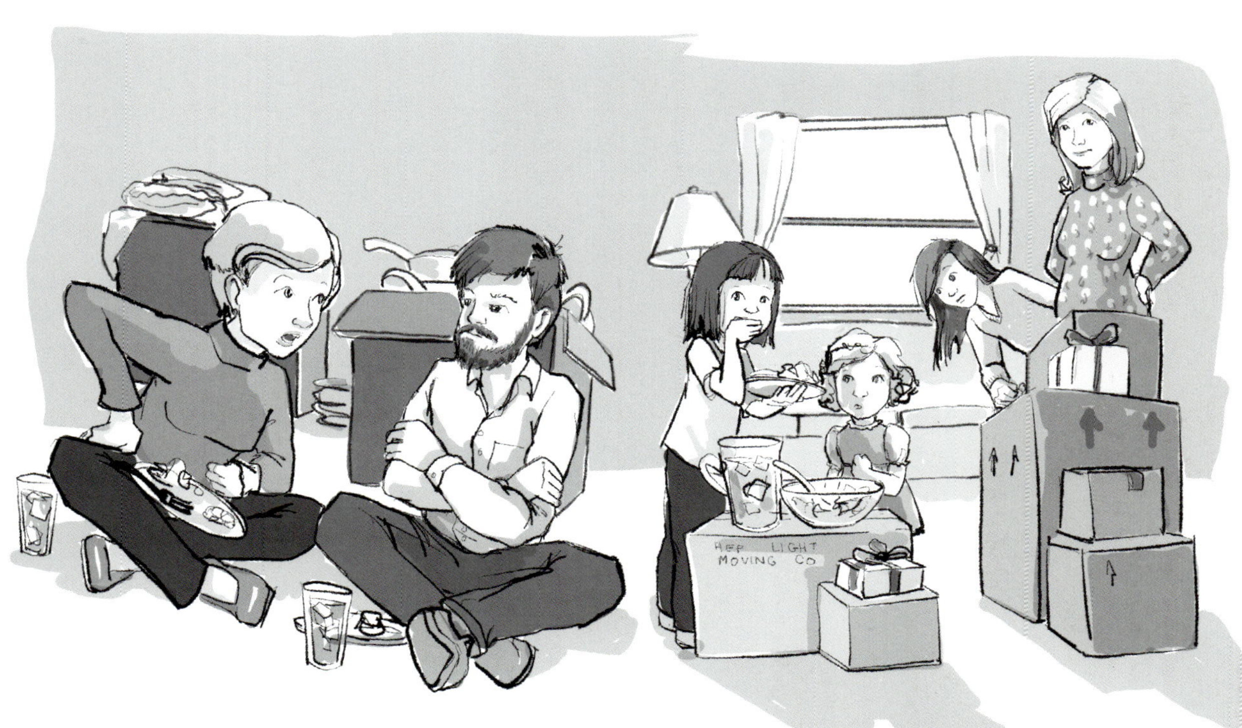
HEF LIGHT
MOVING CO

Ramona realizes that her shoes are too small.

The day of the wedding quickly arrives. Here Ramona discovers that she has outgrown her nice flats, as has Beezus. She will attend the wedding wearing her lovely bridesmaid dress, a crown of tiny pink roses, and . . . white socks.

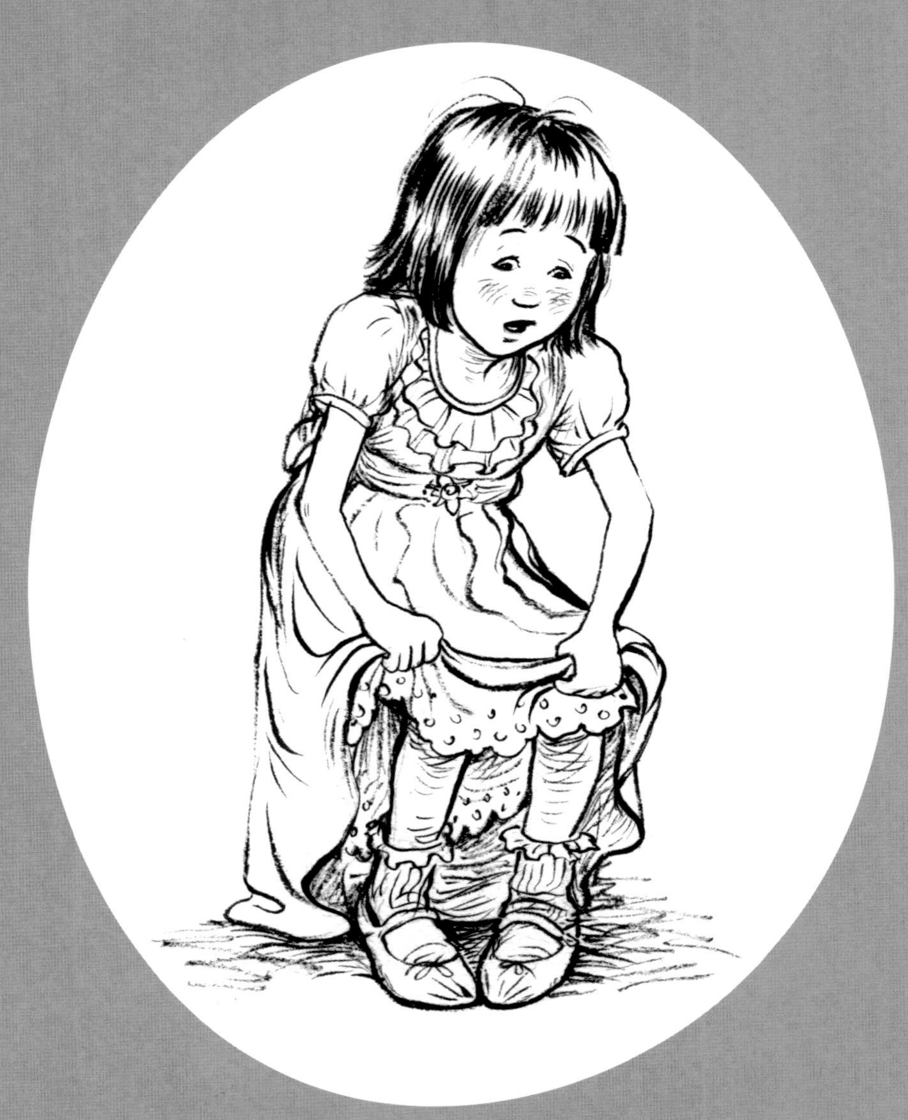

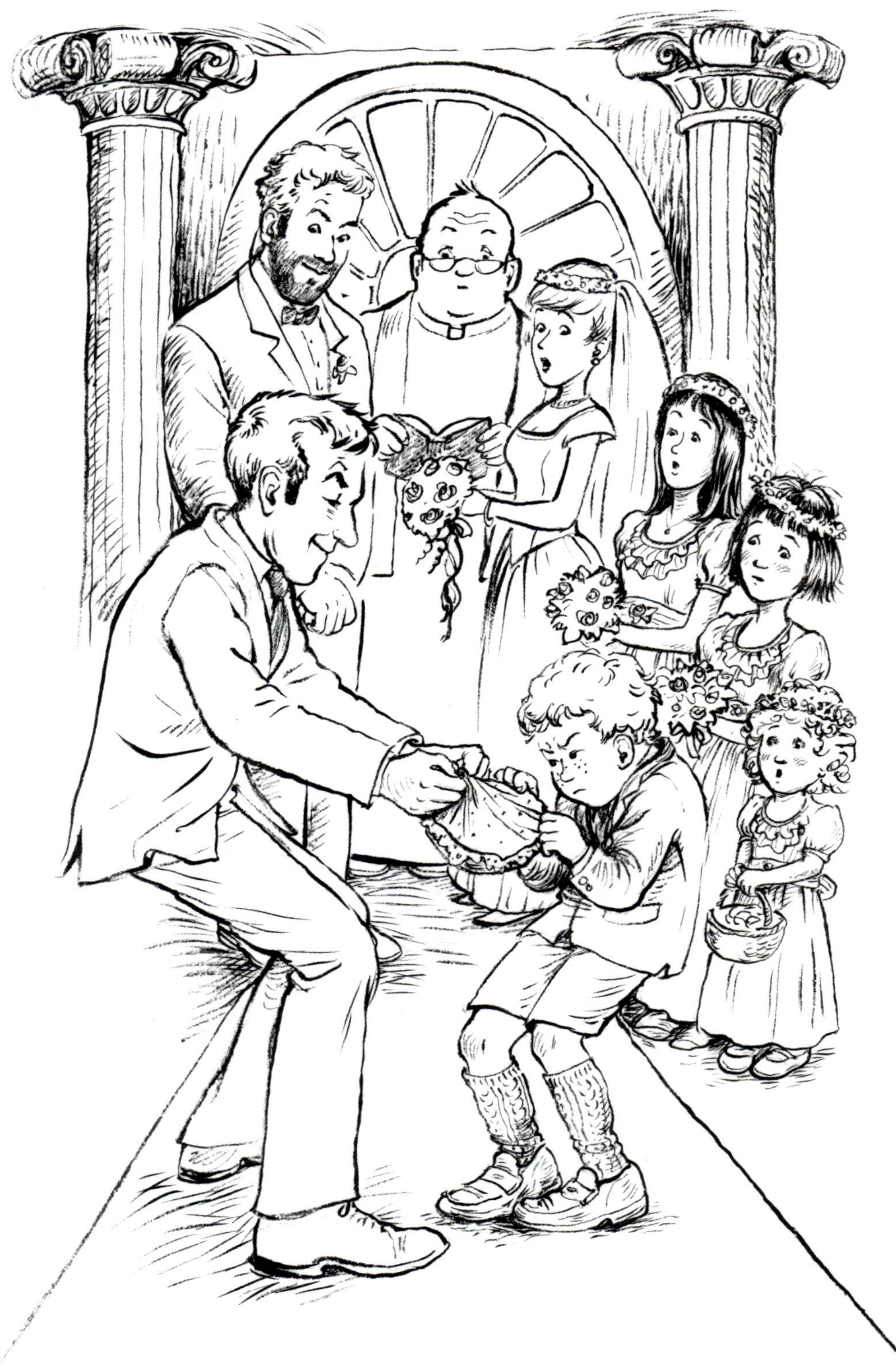

Worried that her grandson would lose the ring, Mrs. Kemp fastened it to the pillow a little too well. Howie struggles to pull it off so that he can hand it to the groom. In the next moment, the ring will be freed from the stitches and go flying through the air.

JACQUELINE ROGERS (OPPOSITE AND ABOVE).

What should Ramona do? She was under strict orders not to move, but she was the only one who knew where the ring had landed. . . . In a minute someone would snicker and set off the whole congregation. Ramona could not bear to have her aunt's wedding laughed at. She decided to act, even if it meant showing her white socks.

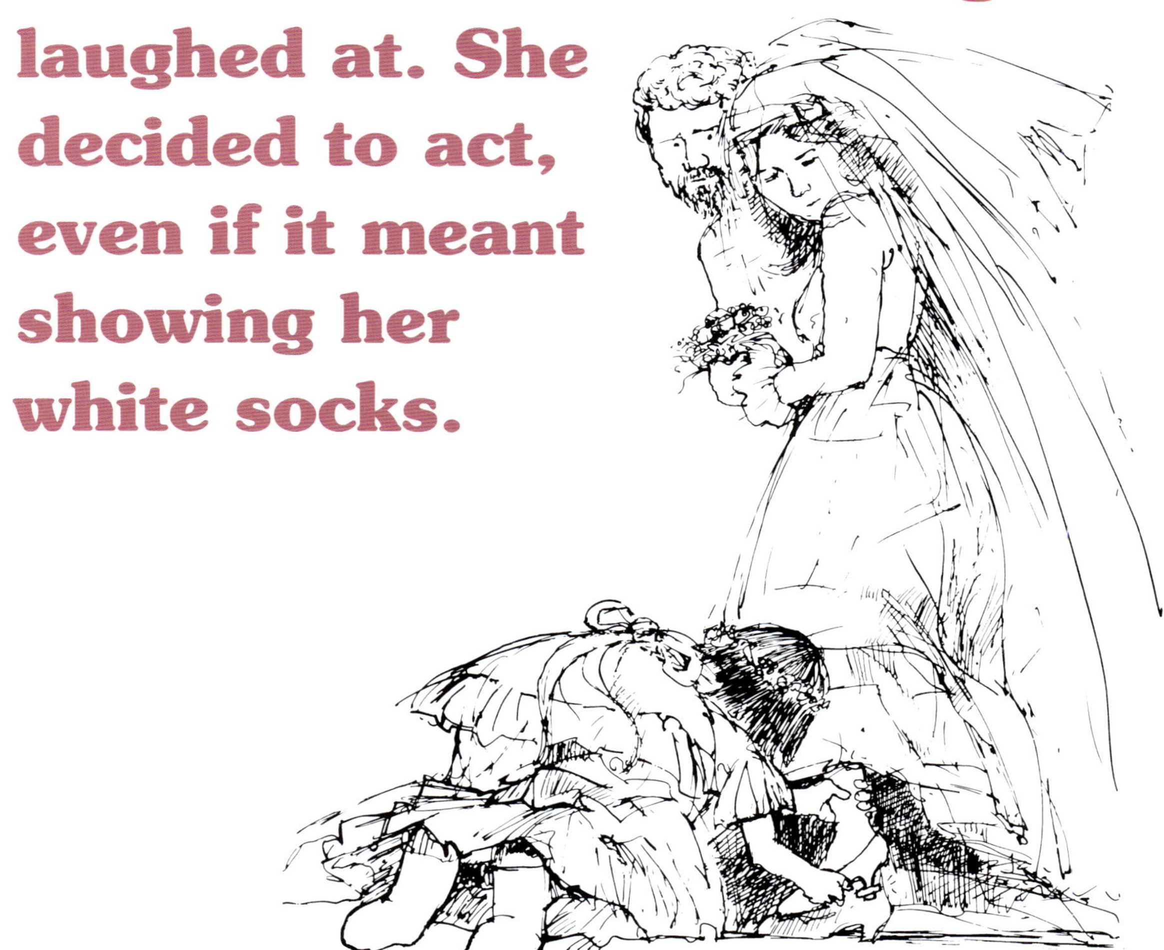

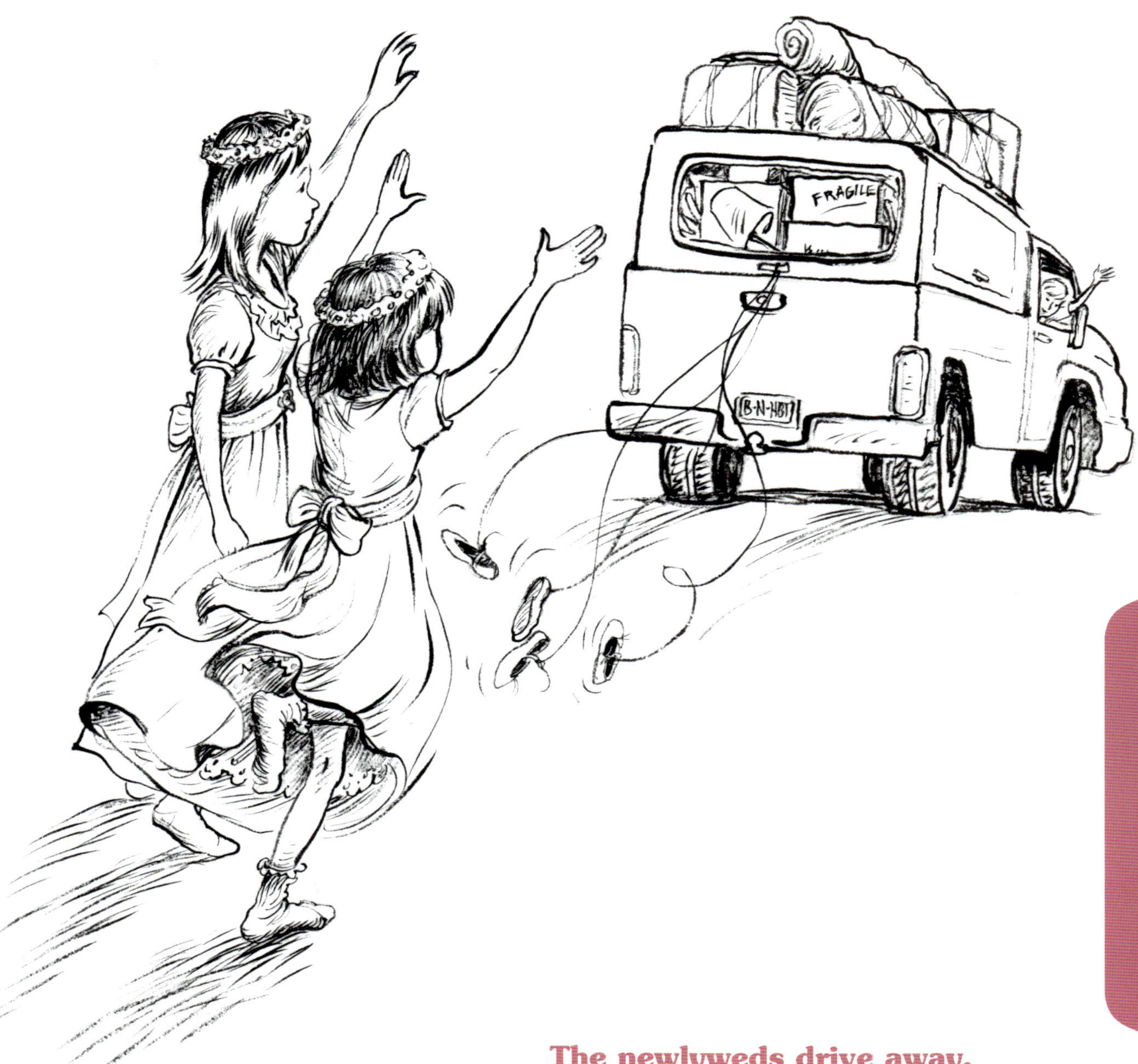

The newlyweds drive away.
Aunt Bea and Uncle Hobart's truck drags Ramona's and Beezus's too-small slippers in this classic "Just Married" ritual.

ALAN TIEGREEN (OPPOSITE) AND JACQUELINE ROGERS (ABOVE).

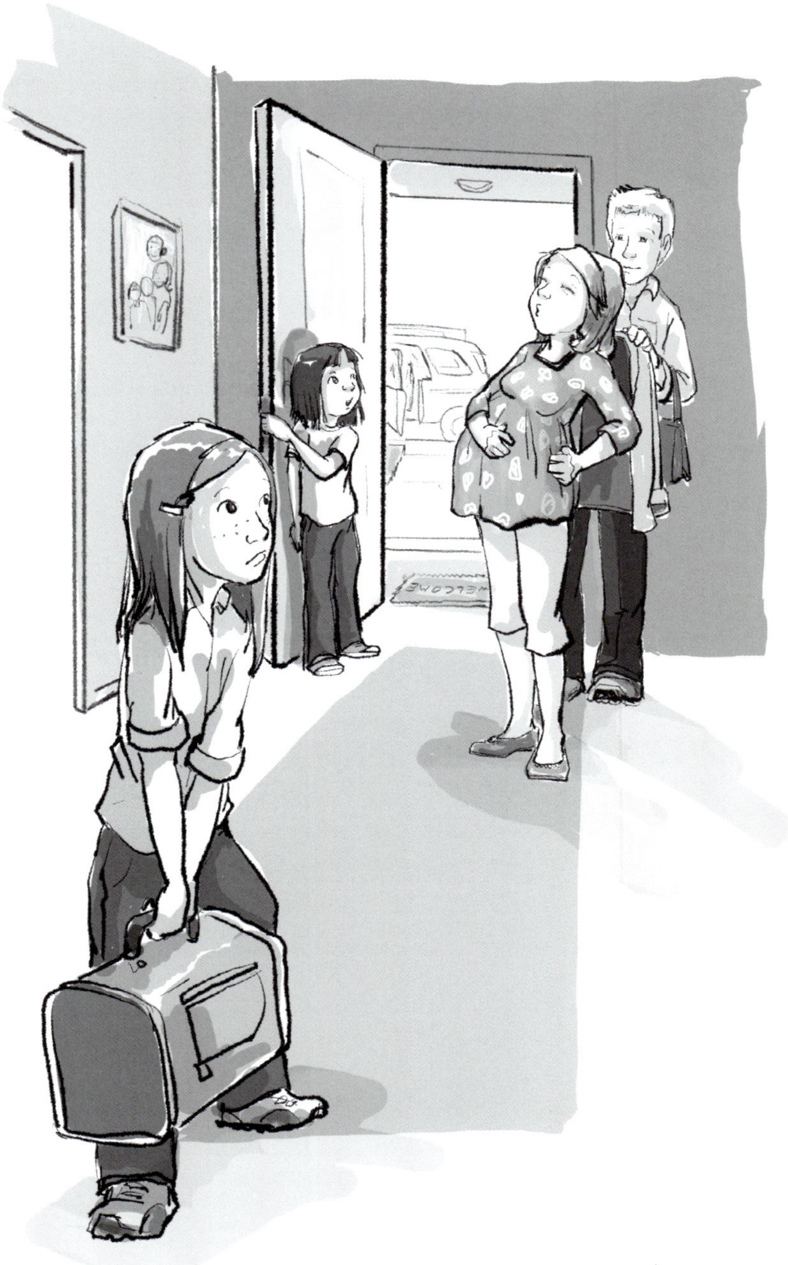

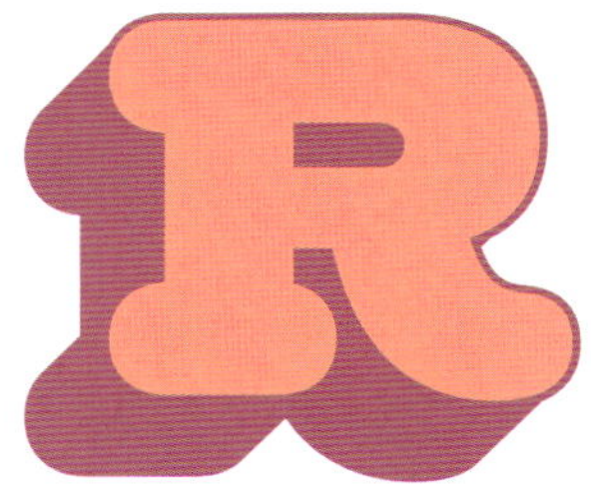

amona and Beezus, excited and frightened, looked at one another. At last! The fifth Quimby would soon be here. Nothing would be the same again, ever. Mr. Quimby reported that the doctor would meet them at the hospital. Without being asked, Beezus ran for the bag her mother had packed several weeks ago.

Mrs. Quimby kissed her daughters. "Don't look so frightened," she said. "Everything is going to be all right. Be good girls, and Daddy will be home as soon as he can."

TRACY DOCKRAY (ABOVE) AND ALAN TIEGREEN (OPPOSITE).

"She looks exactly like you when you were born," Mrs. Quimby told Ramona.

Because of the germy nature of children under the age of twelve, for four days Ramona was banished to the waiting room while her father and sister went to visit Mrs. Quimby and the baby. Finally, finally, finally, Ramona gets to meet her new sister. It's hard for Ramona to imagine that she used to be as little and funny-looking and cross-eyed as the newest member of the family. Now, with the continued work of growing up ahead of her, Ramona is no longer the baby.

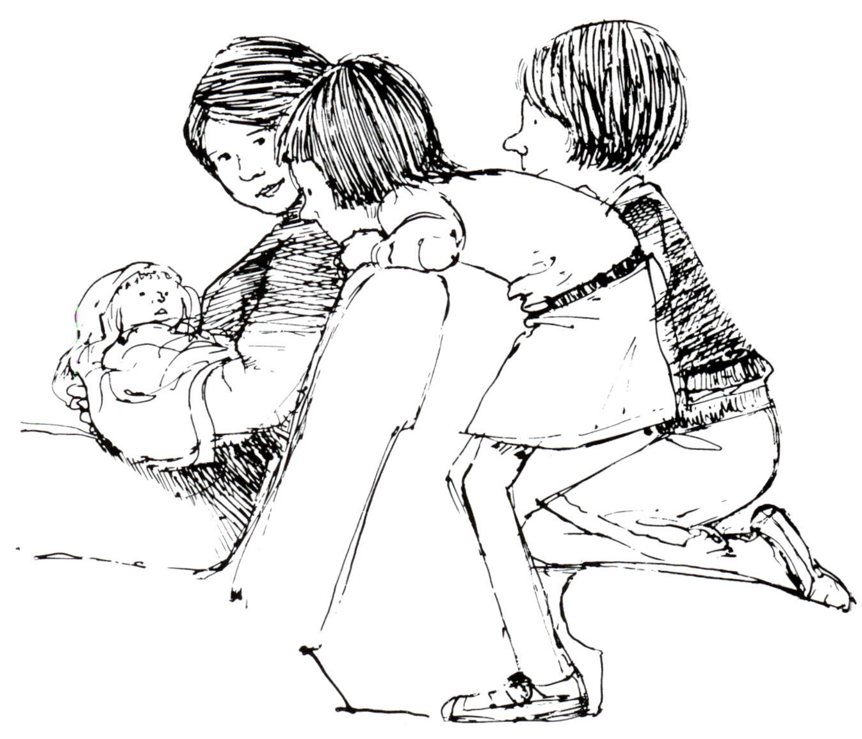

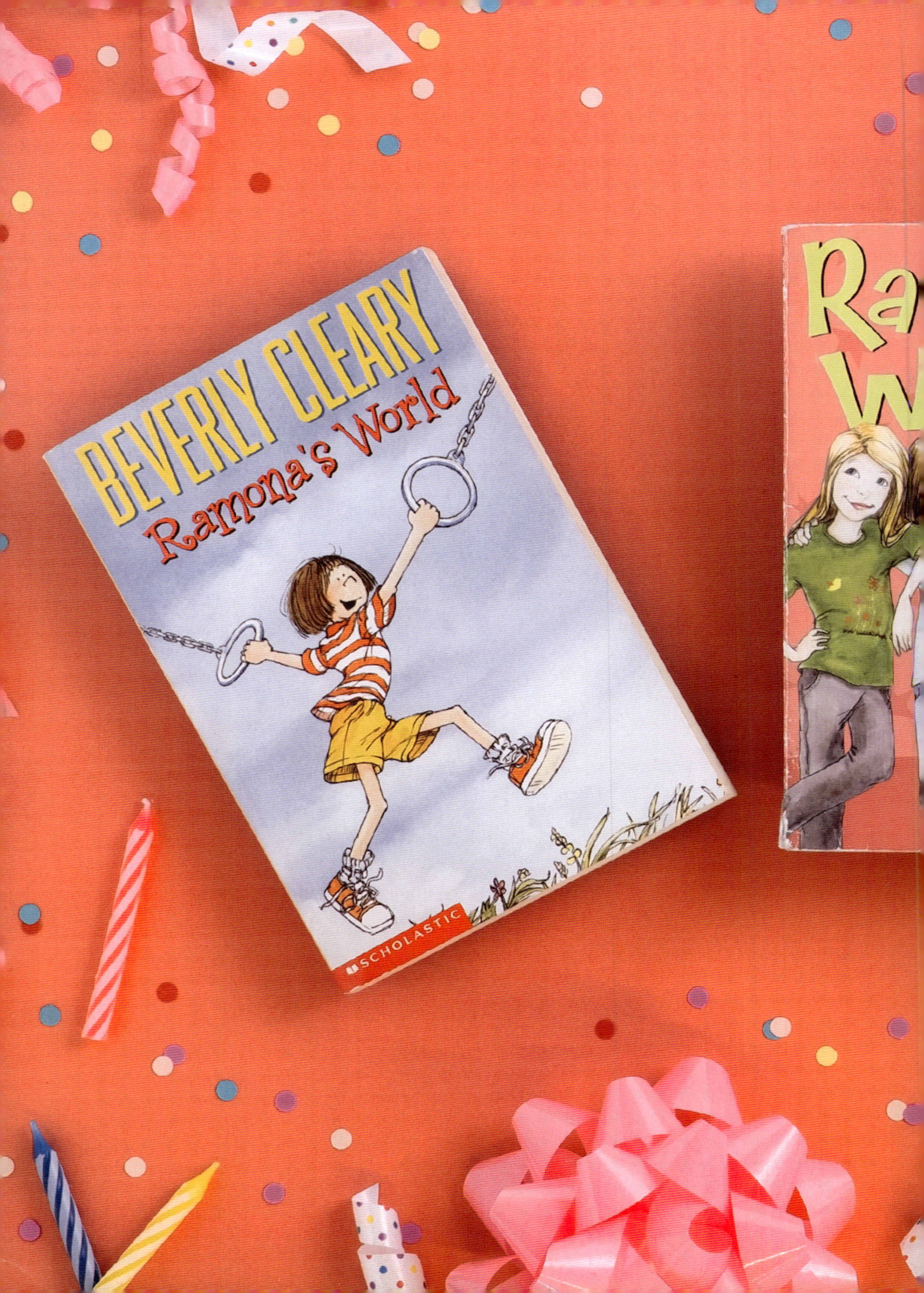
BEVERLY CLEARY
Ramona's World
SCHOLASTIC

Ramona's World

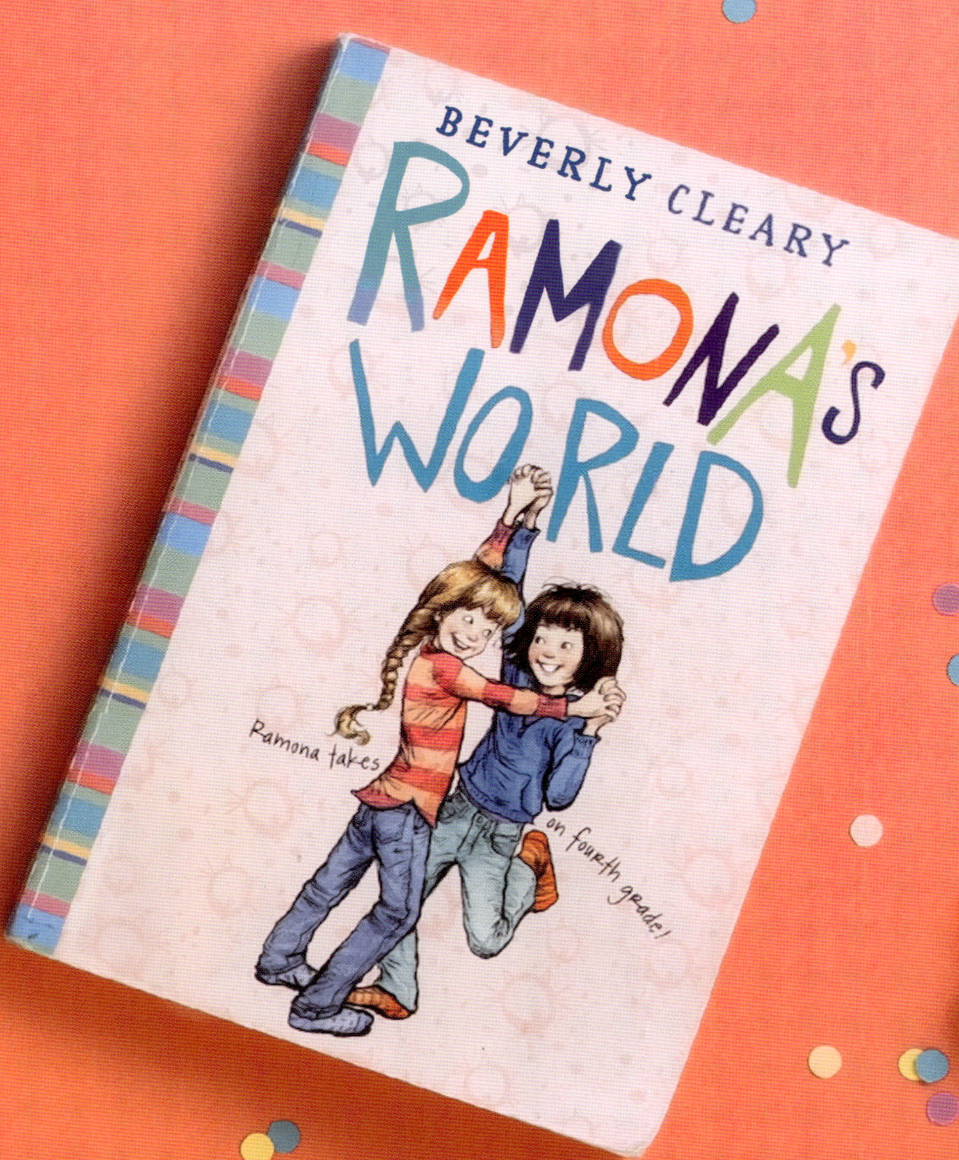

Chapter Eight

Ramona's World

She loved her baby sister, but sometimes she wished her father did not have quite so many daughters.

Ramona is a fourth-grader, a newly minted big sister, and nine going on "zeroteen" (otherwise known as ten). She has a new best friend, Daisy Kidd, and a long-held crush on Yard Ape that only grows stronger with time.

There are no big crises or excessively happy developments in *Ramona's World*, like her father losing his job or a trusted adult calling her a nuisance or a family wedding—making it the least stormy book in the series. Perhaps this is, in part, because Ramona inhabits that sweet spot between the unrestrained emotionality of childhood and the angst of teenagedom. Her burgeoning temperateness could also be attributed to Ramona's new position as Roberta's big sister—the older girl is no longer the baby of the family and has decided to act like the role model that she's supposed to be. (Another theory is that Beverly Cleary was eighty-three at the time of the book's publication, so maybe she was in a more temperate space herself.)

Not that Ramona's life is without its problems. Her fourth-grade teacher, Mrs. Meacham, is obsessed with spelling, which just so happens to be Ramona's Achilles' heel. (Why does spelling even matter if people know what you mean?) She puts a hole in her new best friend's dining room ceiling. The first time she is left alone with Roberta, the baby gets her head stuck in Daisy's cat's kitty condo. But, somehow, Ramona manages to see her way through.

For avid fans of the series and of Beverly Cleary, this last book reads like a swan song, and it's hard not to feel nostalgic as the pages turn. In fact, it was Cleary's last full-length original book. With it, we say good-bye to Ramona, Beezus, Mrs. and Mr. Quimby, and the friends and neighbors of Klickitat Street.

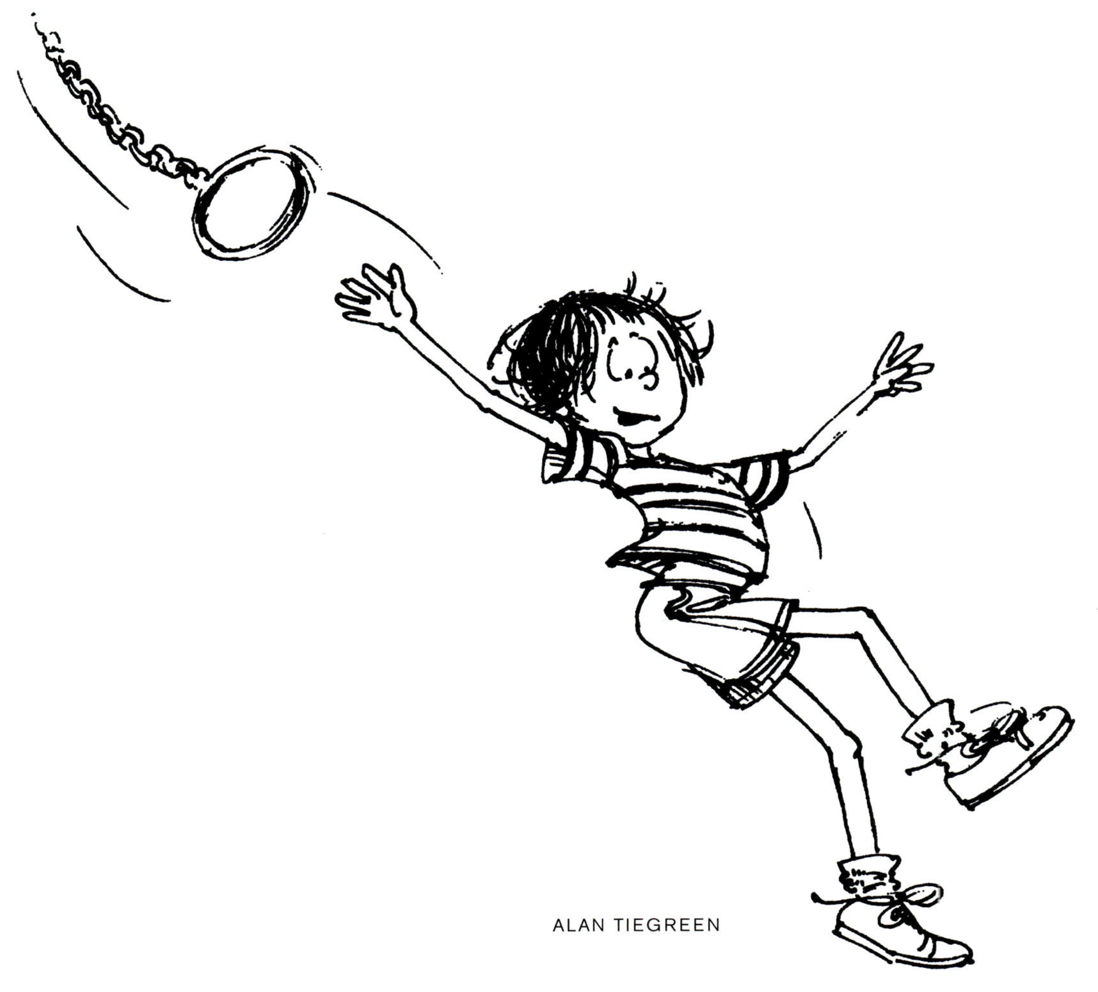

ALAN TIEGREEN

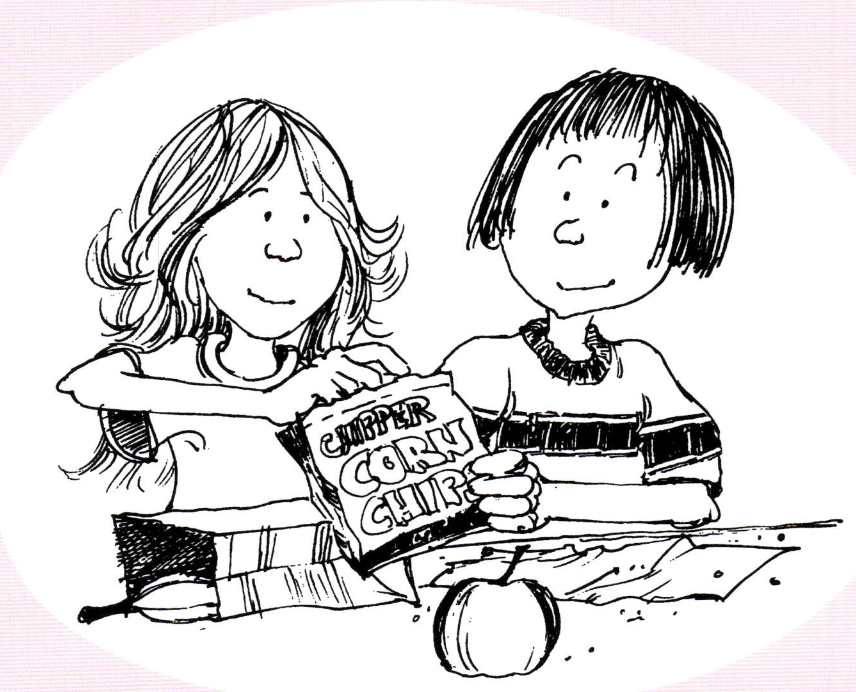

Ramona makes a new friend.

In the first seven books of the series, Ramona is content to play with Howie and, when they're not fighting, her older sister, Beezus. But these days Howie seems to prefer riding his bike with the neighborhood boys. So with the arrival of new girl Daisy Kidd at Cedarhurst Primary School, Ramona will have the opportunity to branch out. Note a prim Susan in the background of Rogers's illustration. Now that they are mature fourth-graders, she needn't worry about Ramona boinging her curls.

ALAN TIEGREEN (ABOVE) AND JACQUELINE ROGERS (OPPOSITE).

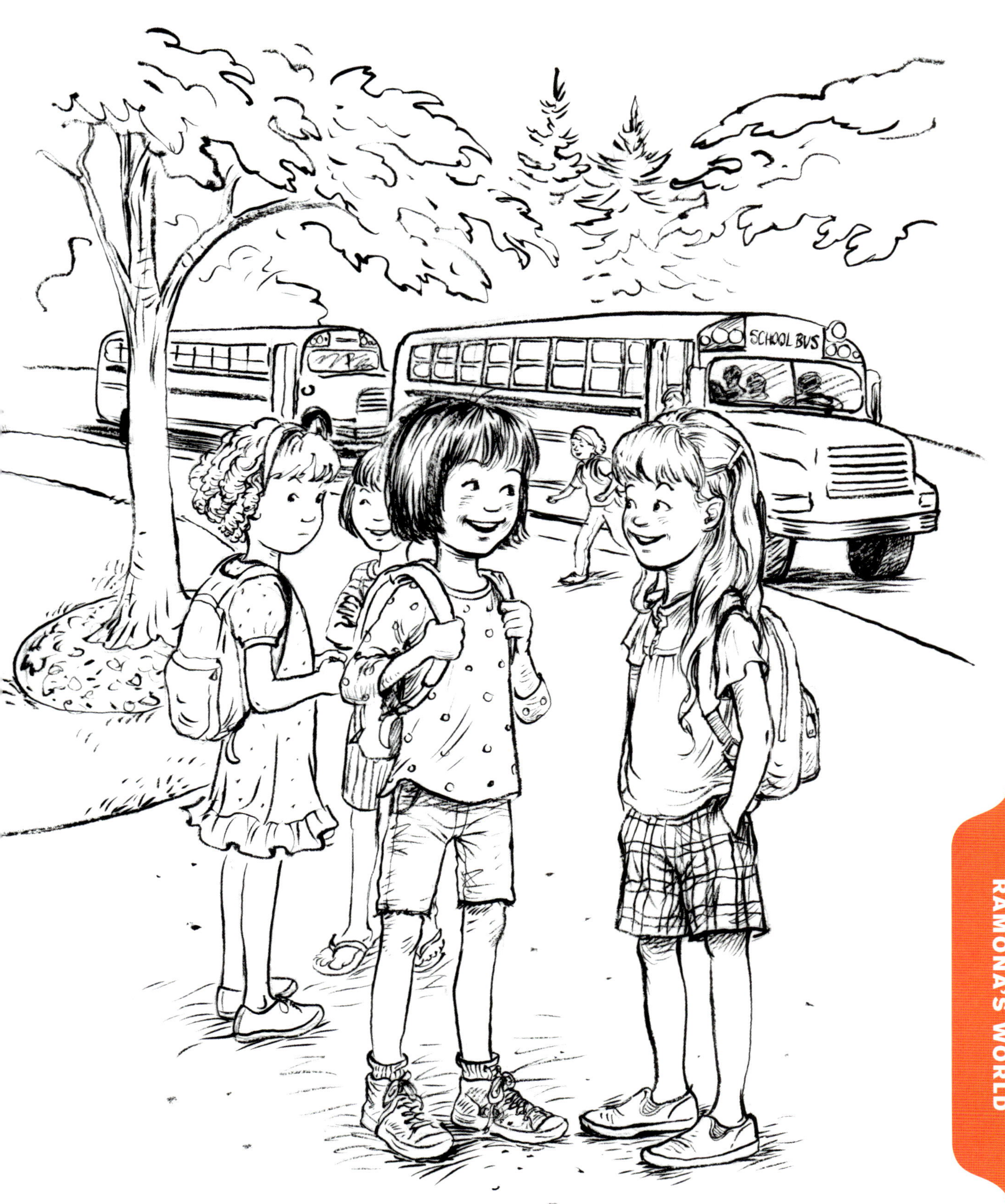
SCHOOL BUS

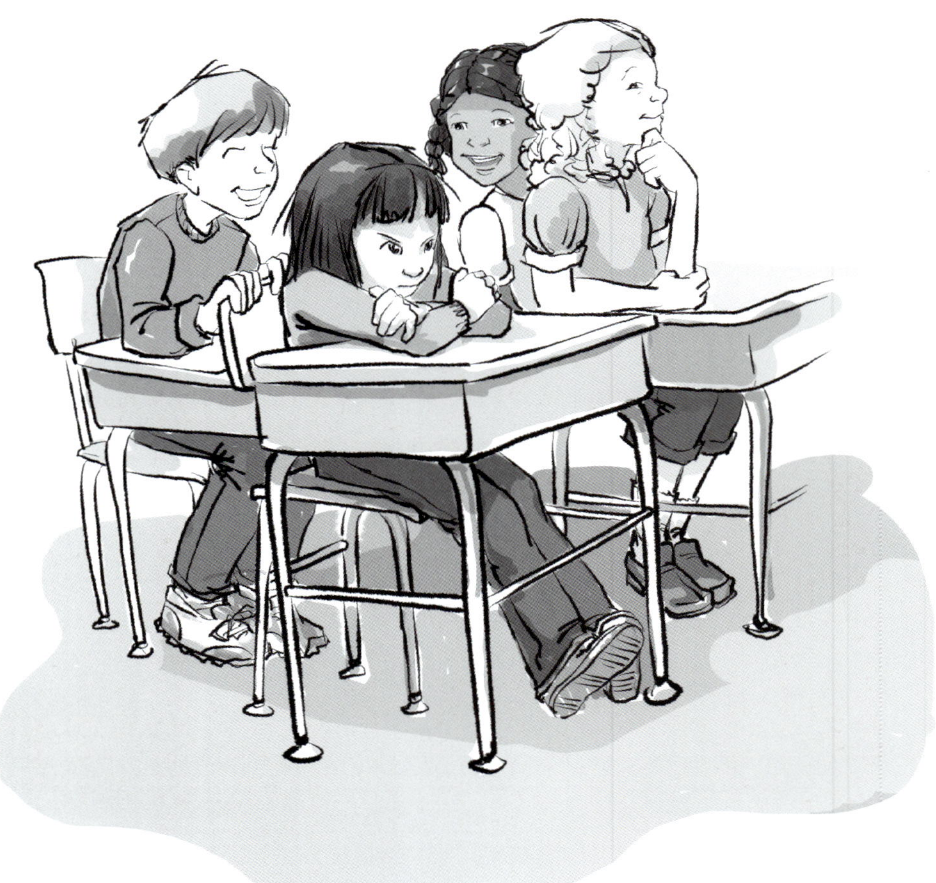

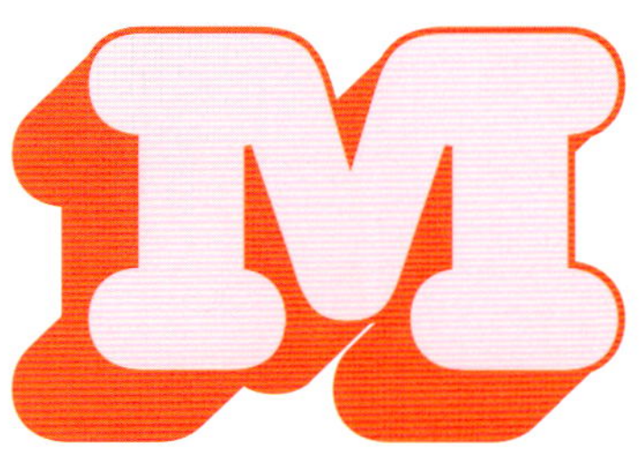

Mrs. Meacham explained. "Today we are going to study words we use. When we wrote about ourselves, we discovered words we need to learn how to spell."

Ramona looked more closely at the words on the chalkboard. Among them she saw scream, hungry, couch, finger, role, model. They looked familiar. They were familiar. They were her words. She scowled.

"Is something the matter, Ramona?" asked Mrs. Meacham, who had been quick to learn names.

Ramona decided to speak up. "What difference does spelling make if people know what you mean?" she asked.

"You wouldn't want people to think you sat on a coach instead of a couch, would you?" Mrs. Meacham asked.

The class found this funny, but Ramona did not, not when the class laughed. She felt her face grow hot. She slid down in her seat and shook her head. Mrs. Meacham knew the answer. Why did she bother to ask?

Mrs. Meacham continued, "And before lunch are you hungry or hunrgy?"

The class laughed, harder this time. The warm day suddenly seemed warmer. Ramona decided right then that she did not like Mrs. Meacham, and this was only the second day of school. Mrs. Meacham did not tell the truth. She said learning was fun, and it wasn't. At least not all the time. Not when it came to spelling.

The fourth grade suddenly began to stretch ahead, long and dreary and full of spelling.

In Dockray's illustration, three students chuckle over the teacher's lame jokes, while Tiegreen's version takes on a nightmarish tone as Ramona's classmates seem to surround her. Only in Rogers's illustration does the girl have an ally—just Daisy Kidd, in the right corner of the background, doesn't laugh.

ABOVE: TRACY DOCKRAY. OPPOSITE: ALAN TIEGREEN (TOP) AND JACQUELINE ROGERS (BOTTOM).

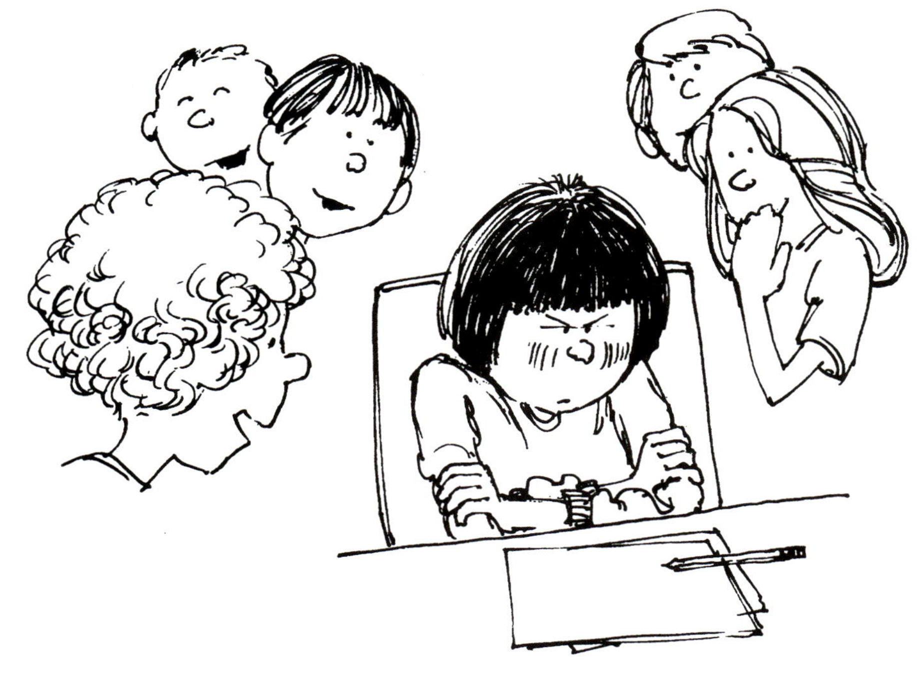

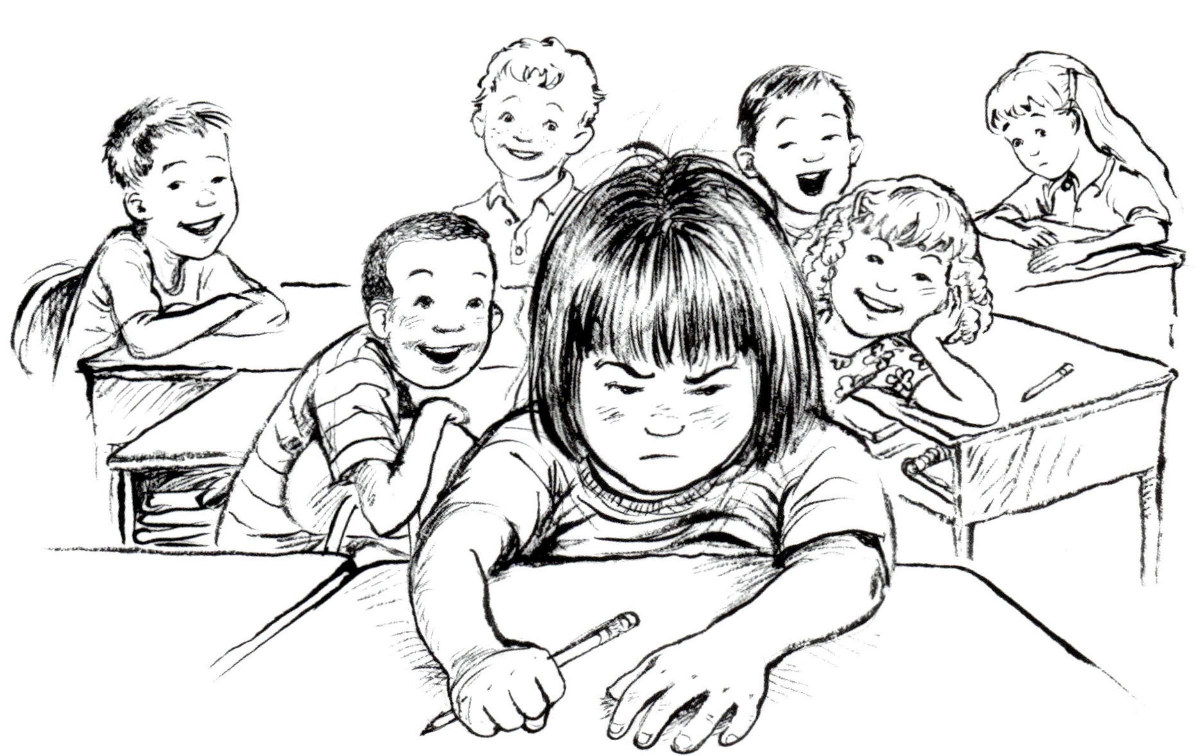

RAMONA'S WORLD

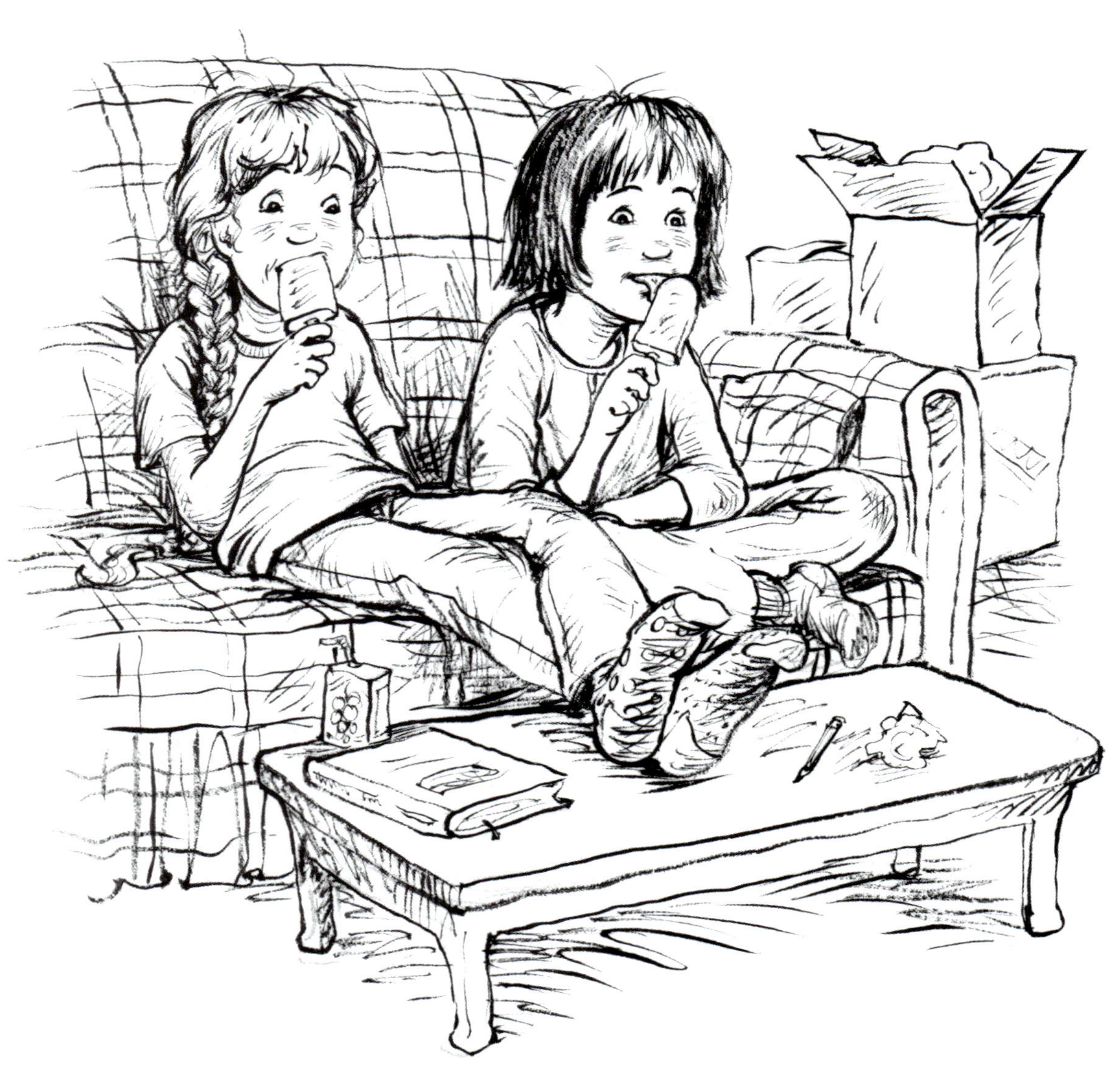

An afternoon at the Kidd home crystallizes Ramona and Daisy's friendship.

Fourth grade starts to look up (again) when Daisy invites Ramona over for a playdate and dinner after school. Petting the dog, Mutley, eating juice bars in front of the TV, vacuuming the cat—these are the kinds of things new best friends do together.

ABOVE: JACQUELINE ROGERS. OPPOSITE: ALAN TIEGREEN (TOP) AND TRACY DOCKRAY (BOTTOM).

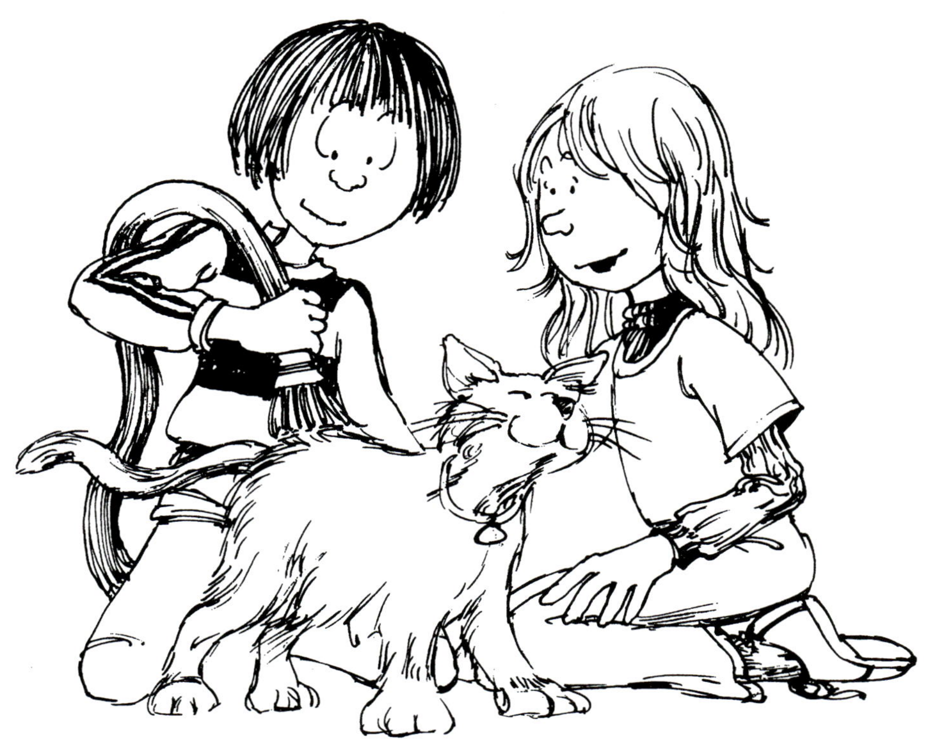

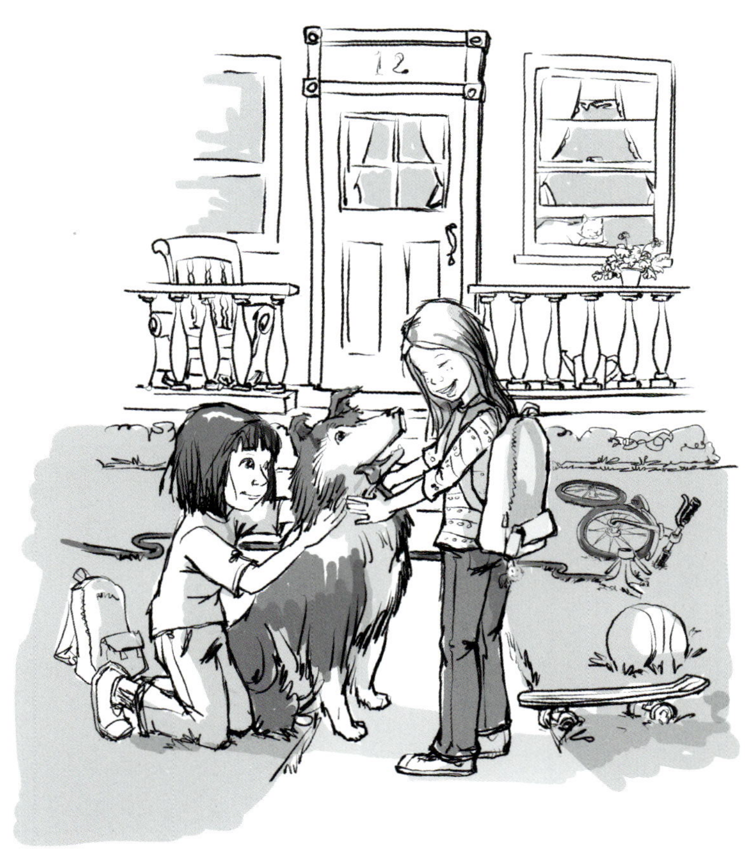
12

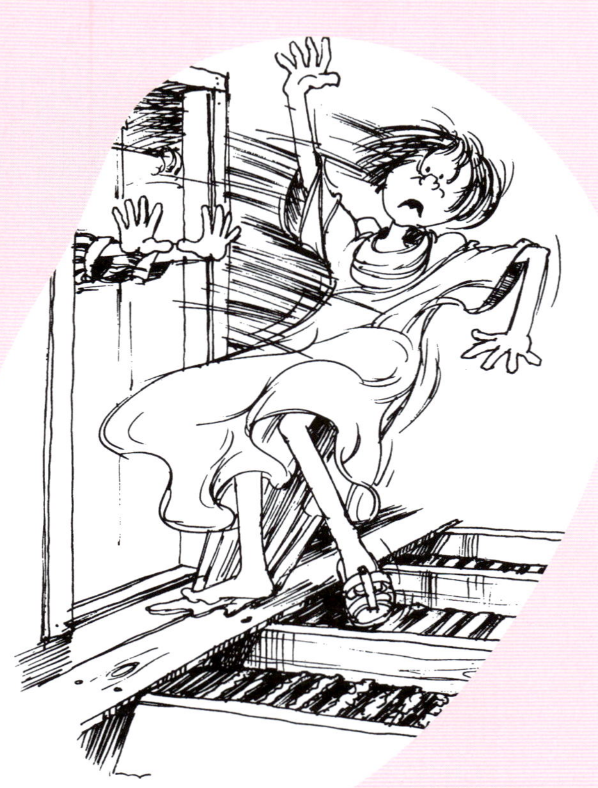

Ramona puts a hole in the ceiling.

While playing dress-up, wicked witch Daisy pushes beautiful princess Ramona. She trips on her fancy costume dress and goes flying, putting a hole in the lath and plaster of the floor of the bedroom closet, which is also the dining room ceiling. After Daisy's brother, Jeremy, comes to the rescue, scratched-and-bruised Ramona immediately worries that she'll never be allowed to see Daisy again, then panics over the cost of the repair. In Tiegreen's illustration, Ramona seems tiny compared to the giant gaping hole in the ceiling. Rogers captures the surprising reaction of Mrs. Kidd—unlike Mrs. Kemp or even Ramona's own parents, Daisy's mom reassures instead of scolding her. The only thing left to worry about? Whether Jeremy saw her underpants.

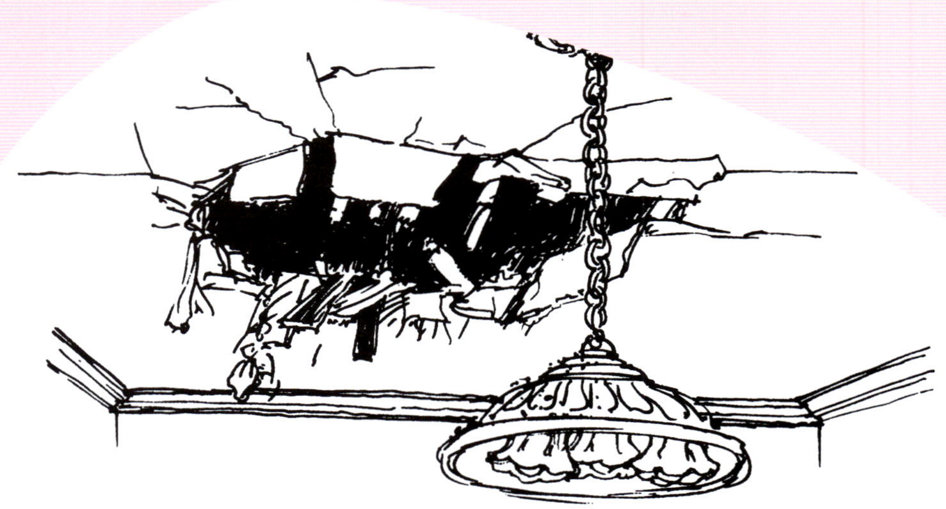

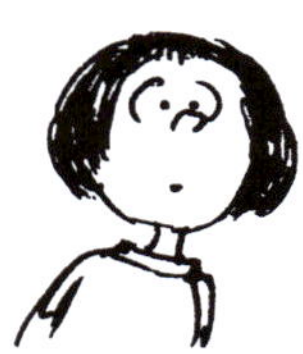

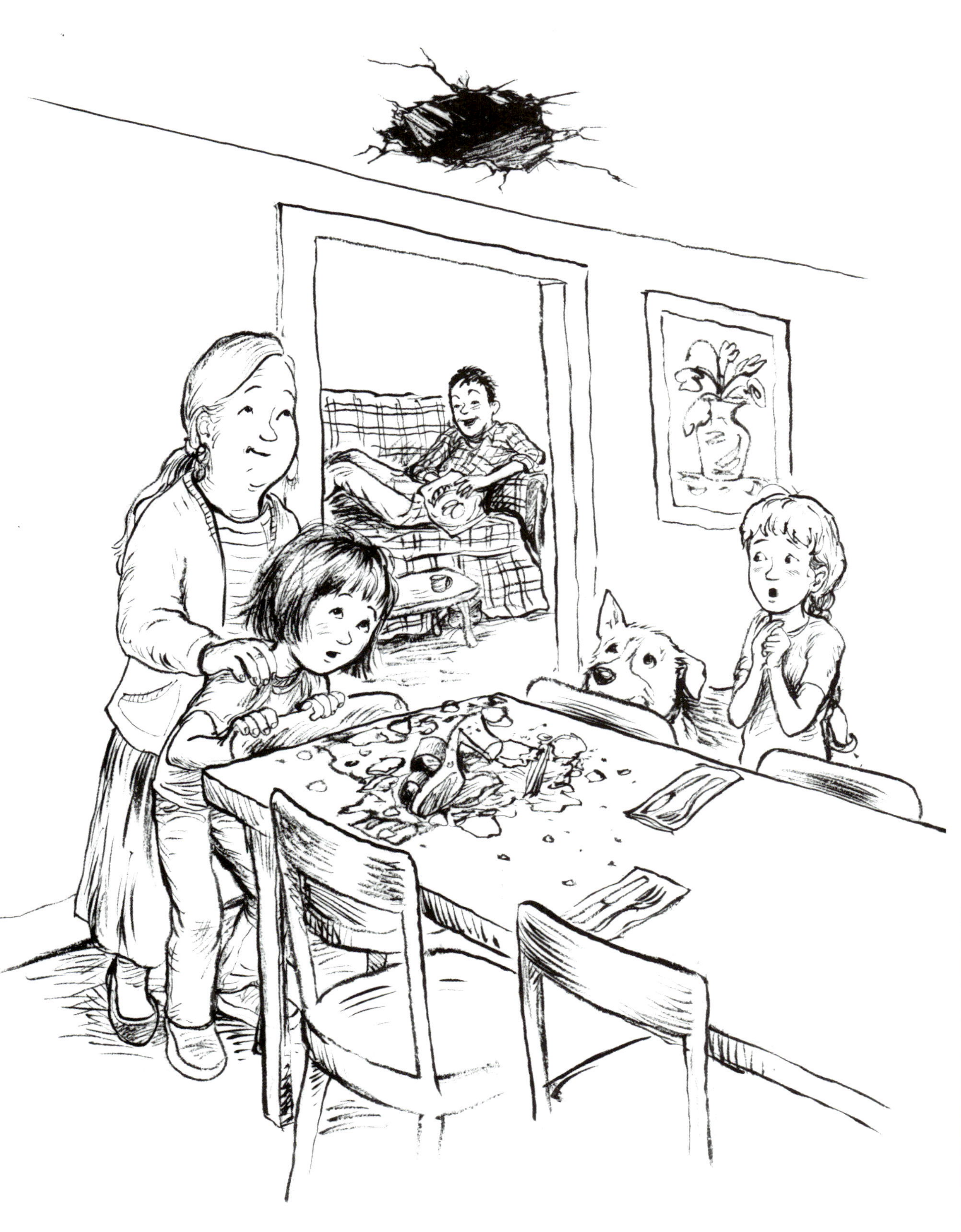

RAMONA'S WORLD

ALAN TIEGREEN (OPPOSITE) AND JACQUELINE ROGERS (ABOVE).

"I'm tired of being plain old responsible Beezus. I'm tired of people saying how sensible I am. I want to be glamorous for a change. . . . I want to wear earrings and lipstick and be somebody different. I want to look nice for the party. I want to have fun!"

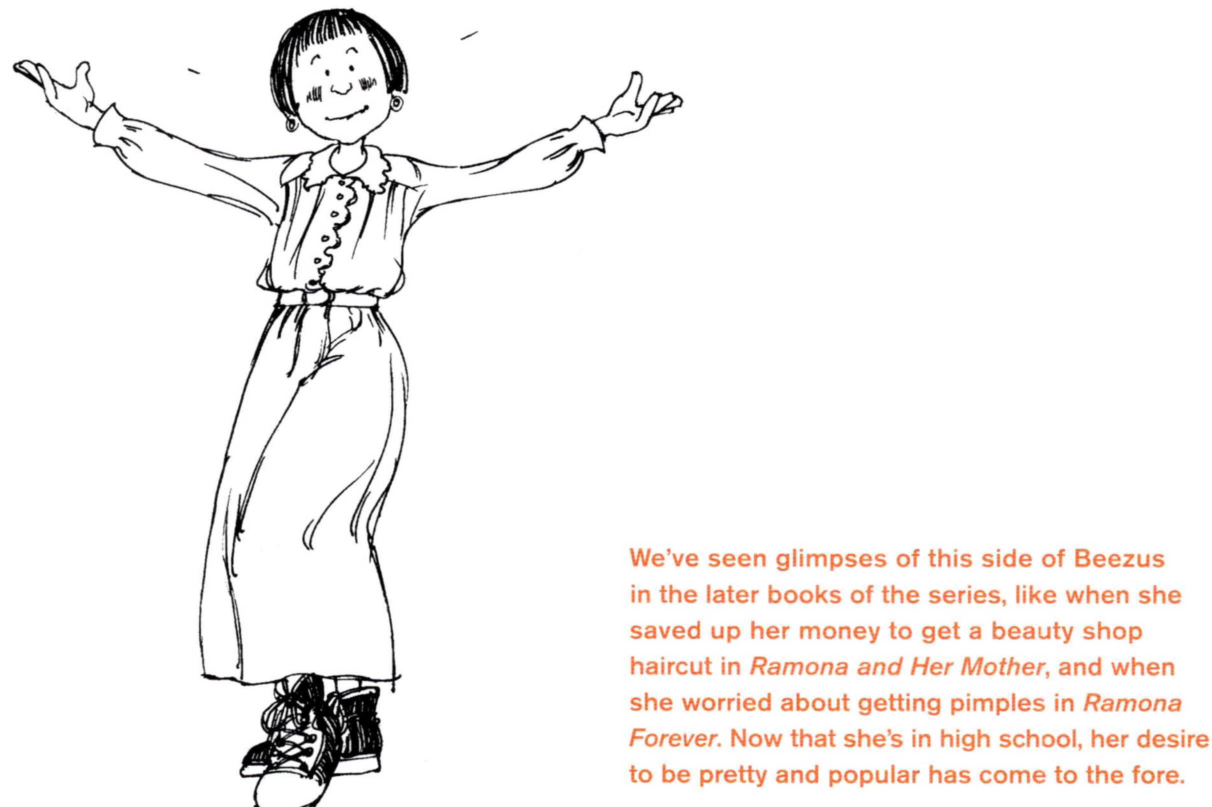

We've seen glimpses of this side of Beezus in the later books of the series, like when she saved up her money to get a beauty shop haircut in *Ramona and Her Mother*, and when she worried about getting pimples in *Ramona Forever*. Now that she's in high school, her desire to be pretty and popular has come to the fore.

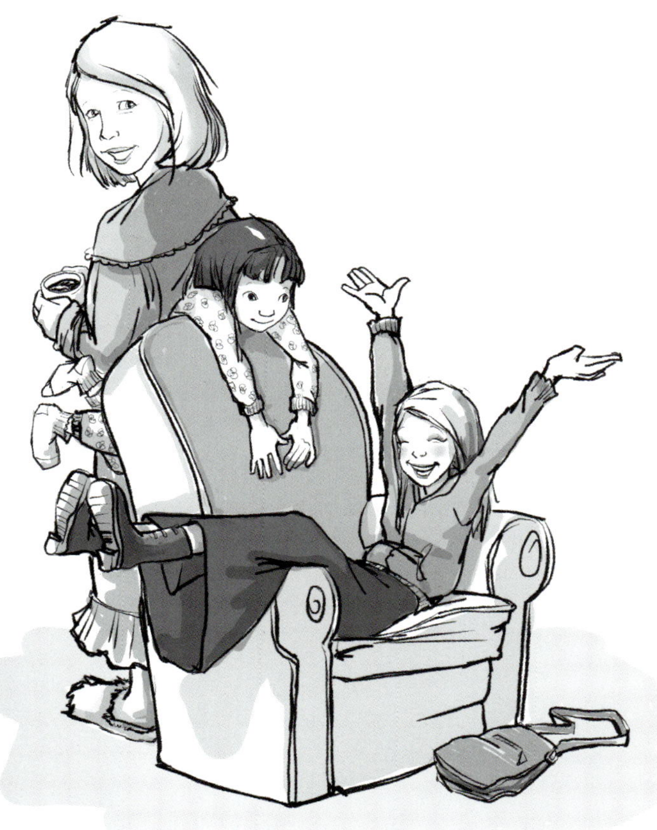

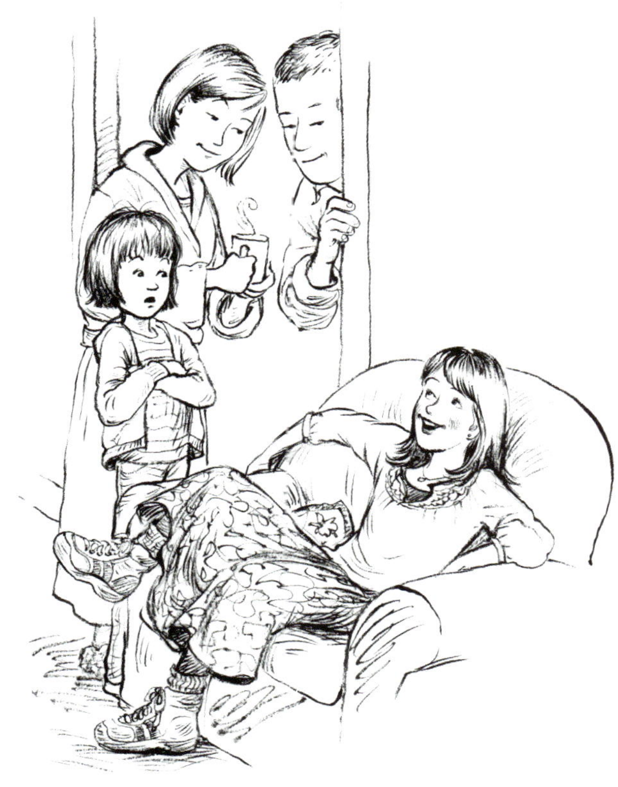

Beezus, just returned from her exciting night out, is recounting the events of the party. She wears hiking shoes (because dress-up shoes are so uncool) and dark red lipstick and green eyeshadow sampled from the host's mother's makeup. According to Beezus, even though the boys were too scared to come inside, let alone dance, the party was a great success. After her sister's description of the evening's events, Ramona promises herself that she'll never be a wallflower—if she ever wants "to do such a silly thing as dance" she won't hesitate to approach someone and ask.

OPPOSITE: ALAN TIEGREEN. ABOVE: TRACY DOCKRAY (LEFT) AND JACQUELINE ROGERS (RIGHT).

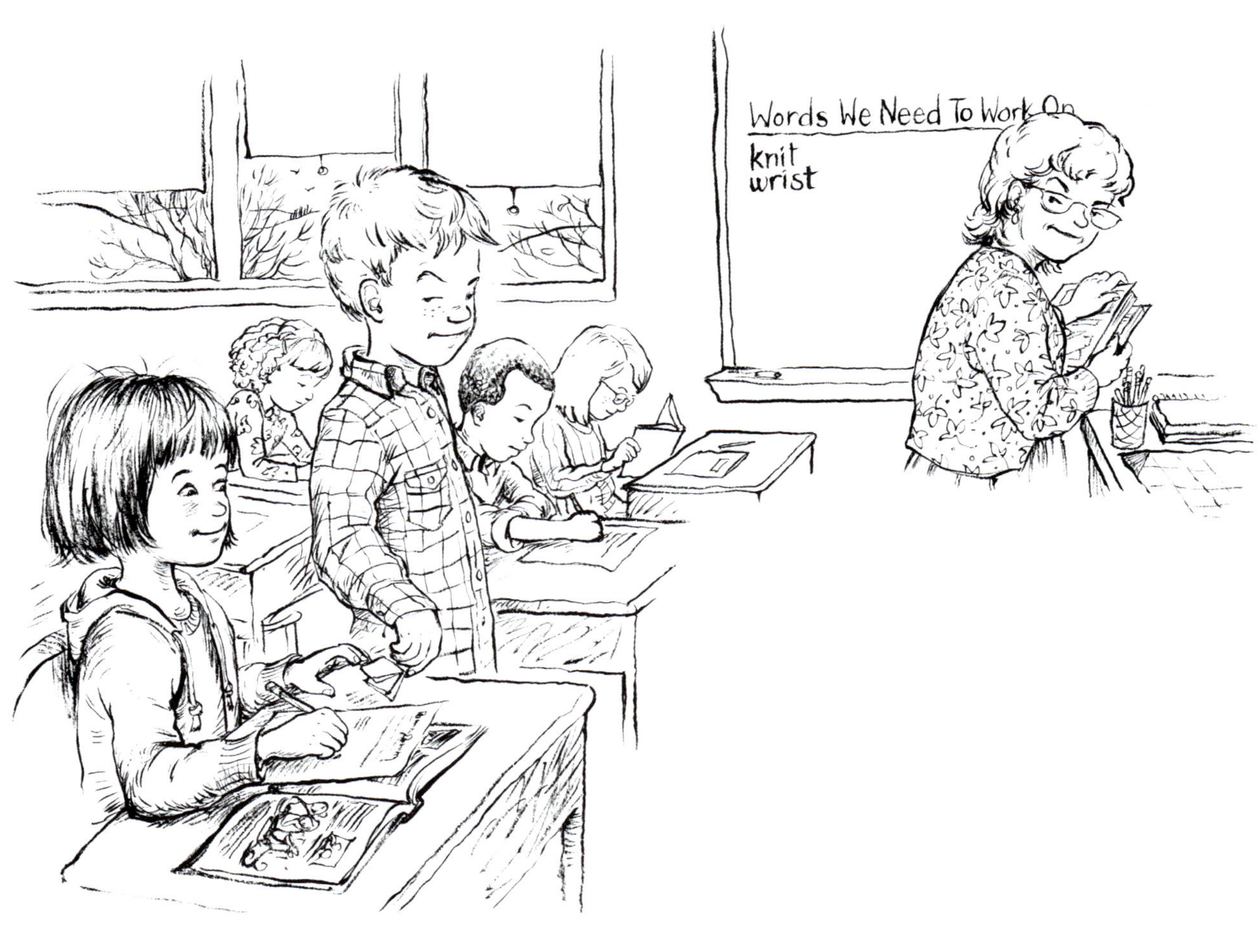

Mrs. Meacham is a stickler for spelling—even the spelling in secret notes.

Yard Ape—aka Daniel—drops a note on Ramona's desk. Unfortunately, before she can read it, the spelling-obsessed teacher confiscates it and adds insult to injury by using it to teach a lesson (and then tearing it up). Mrs. Meacham adds the word "Ramona" to the list of Words We Need to Work On on the chalkboard after reminding the students not to confuse *n* and *m*.

JACQUELINE ROGERS (ABOVE) AND ALAN TIEGREEN (OPPOSITE).

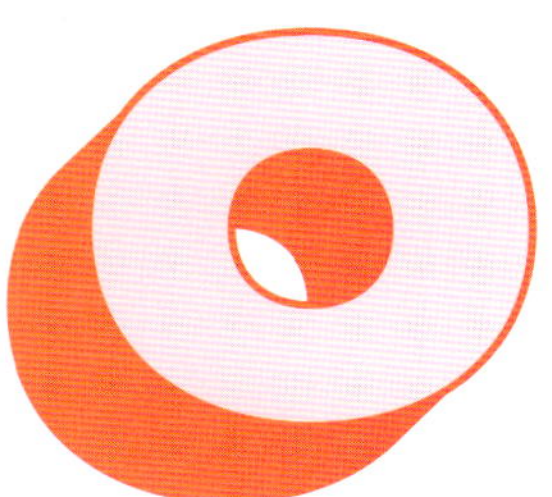

ne afternoon when she had come to Ramona's house, the girls were looking for something to do. Daisy picked up the sports section of the newspaper, which was lying on the coffee table, and began to read aloud as if she were an excited television announcer, "'Crash! Splash! $25 Cash Back! No down payments for six months!'"

Ramona picked up another part of the paper and read in a stern voice, "'Stop sneezing! Get rid of dust, mold, and fungus with our duct clean-up system'"—here, a dramatic pause—"'and keep it clean!'"

Both girls found this funny.

"Sounds like what Jeremy's room needs," remarked Daisy before she read in a dreamy voice, "'Planning a romantic wedding?'"

"Not right away," said Ramona, scanning the newspaper. "Here's a funny letter somebody wrote to some people who do income tax stuff. They put it in their ad."

"Boring," said Daisy.

Ramona ignored her and read, "'You J. K. Barker people really know your stuff. I shoulda come here last year, and I'm gonna come here next year.'" She frowned her disapproval.

Daisy was indignant. "They shouldn't put words like gonna and shoulda in the newspaper. Mrs. Meacham wouldn't like it."

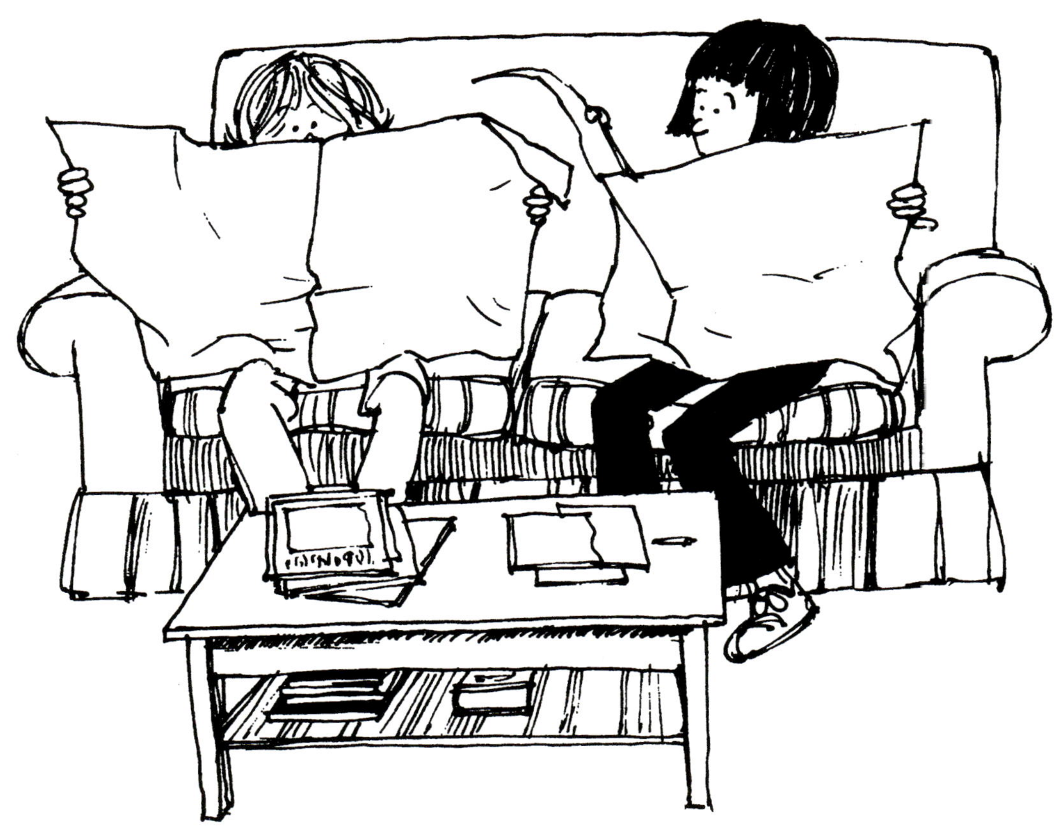

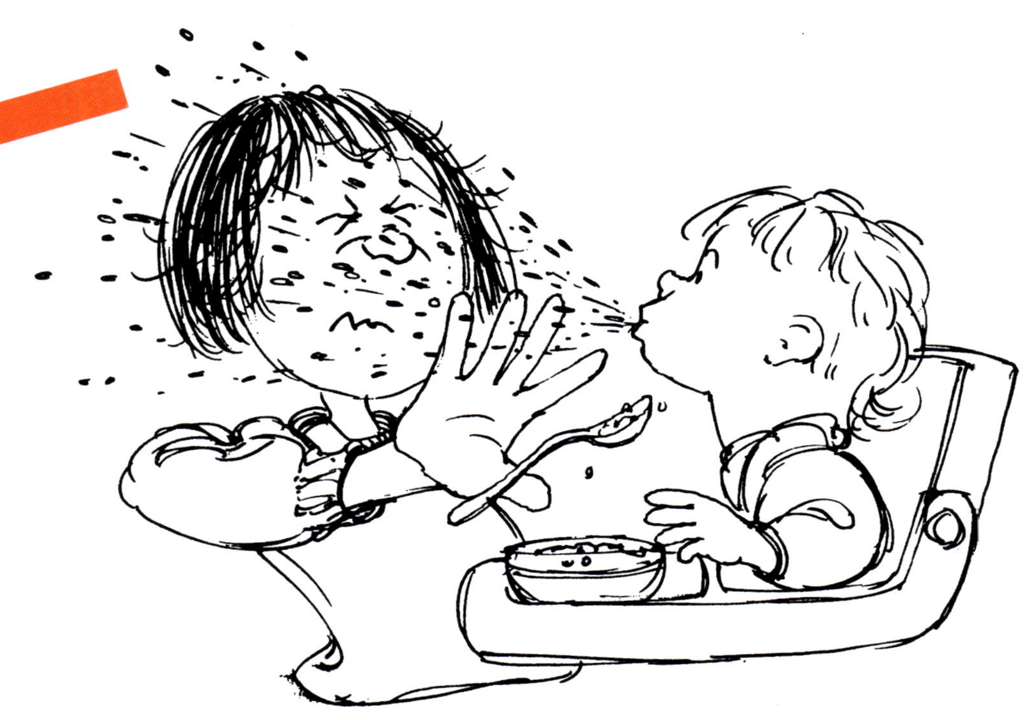

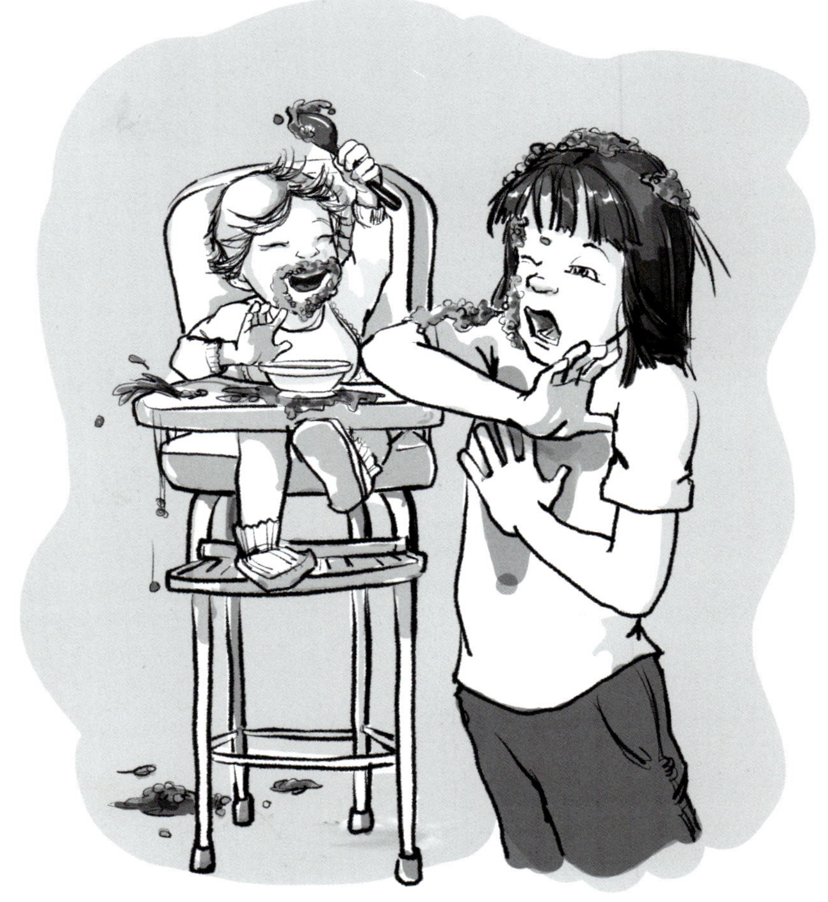

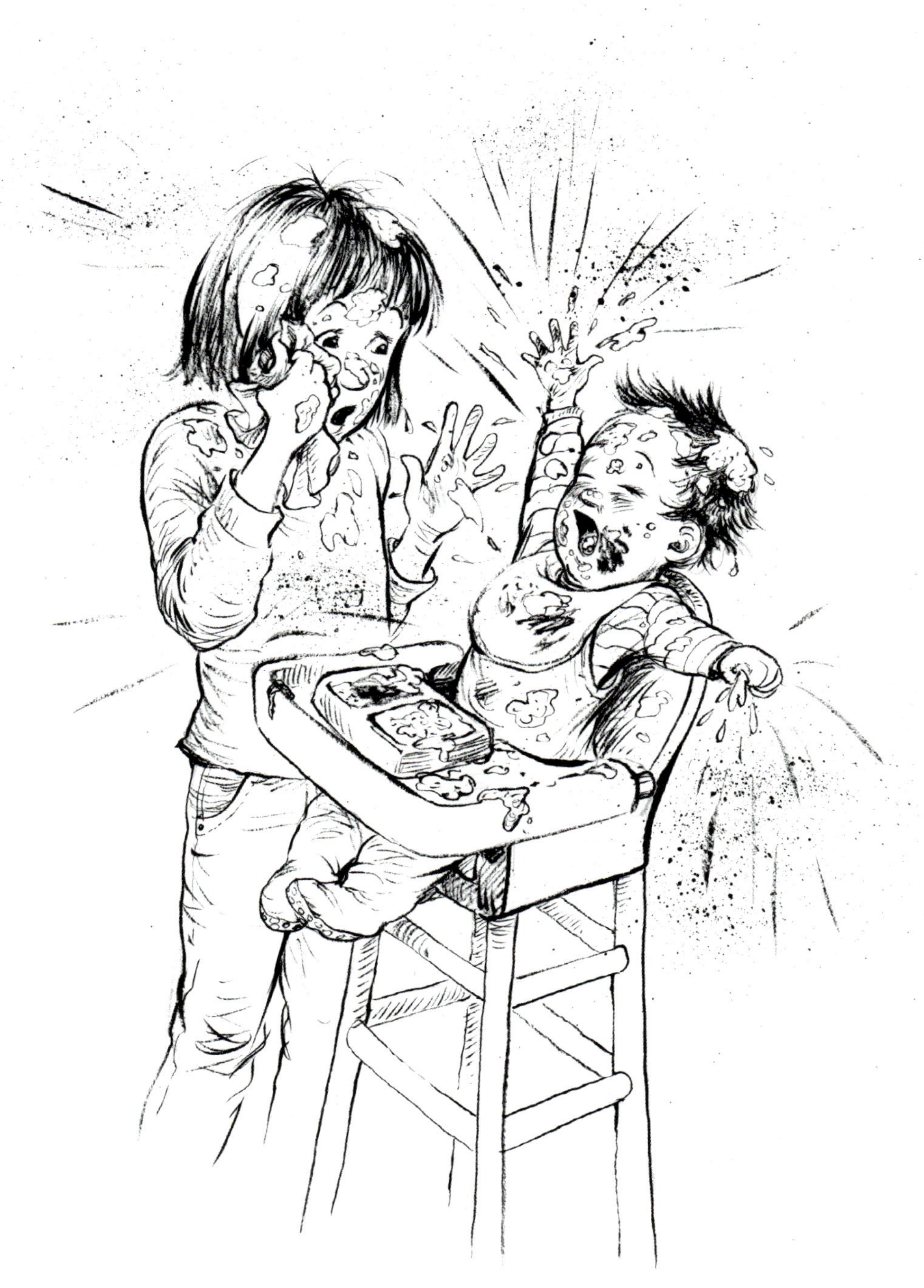

Little Roberta has developed a mind of her own.

Ramona attempts to help her mother by feeding her baby sister, who has decided that she doesn't like strained peas. Tiegreen captures Ramona and Roberta mid-spray, while Dockray's scene depicts a happy baby post-flinging of a spoonful. In Rogers's illustration, the damage has already been done.

OPPOSITE: ALAN TIEGREEN (TOP) AND TRACY DOCKRAY (BOTTOM). ABOVE: JACQUELINE ROGERS.

Susan said cheese. The camera clicked.

"Next!" said Bill as Susan stepped aside. A boy took her place. "Say cheese," ordered Bill. This went on over and over until it was Yard Ape's turn. He stood up straight, grinned, and after saying cheese did not step aside. "How come you always tell us to say cheese?" he asked. "Don't you get tired of it?"

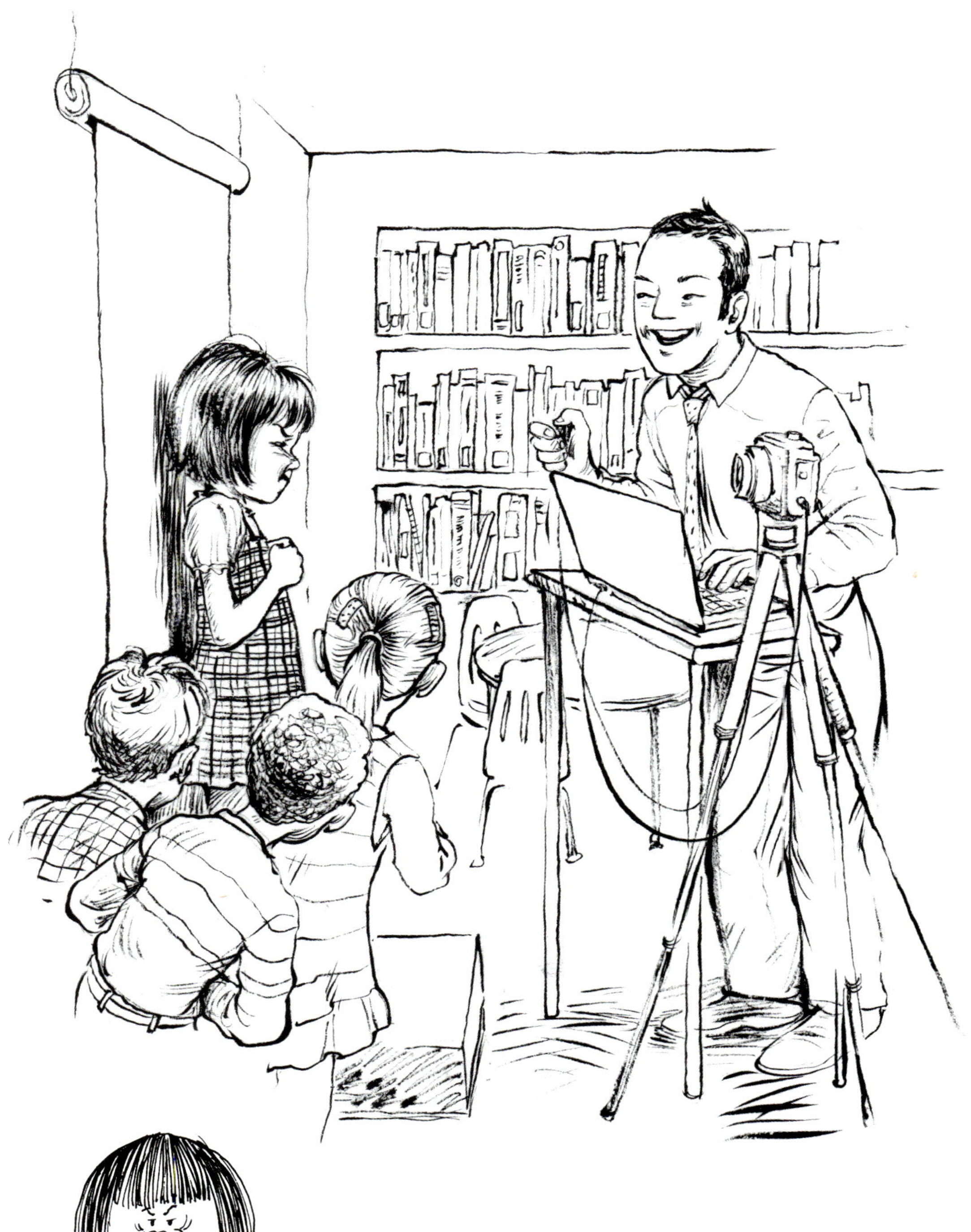

As a matter of fact, photographer Bill does get tired of saying "cheese." So when Ramona's turn comes, he shirks routine and says "peas." This sparks Ramona's memory of last night's feeding and being covered in gooshy peas and baby spit, and she instinctively makes a face. Tiegreen focuses on the scowl, while Rogers shows the photographer making the quip anc the class, laughing, in the foreground.

JACQUELINE ROGERS (TOP) AND ALAN TIEGREEN (BOTTOM).

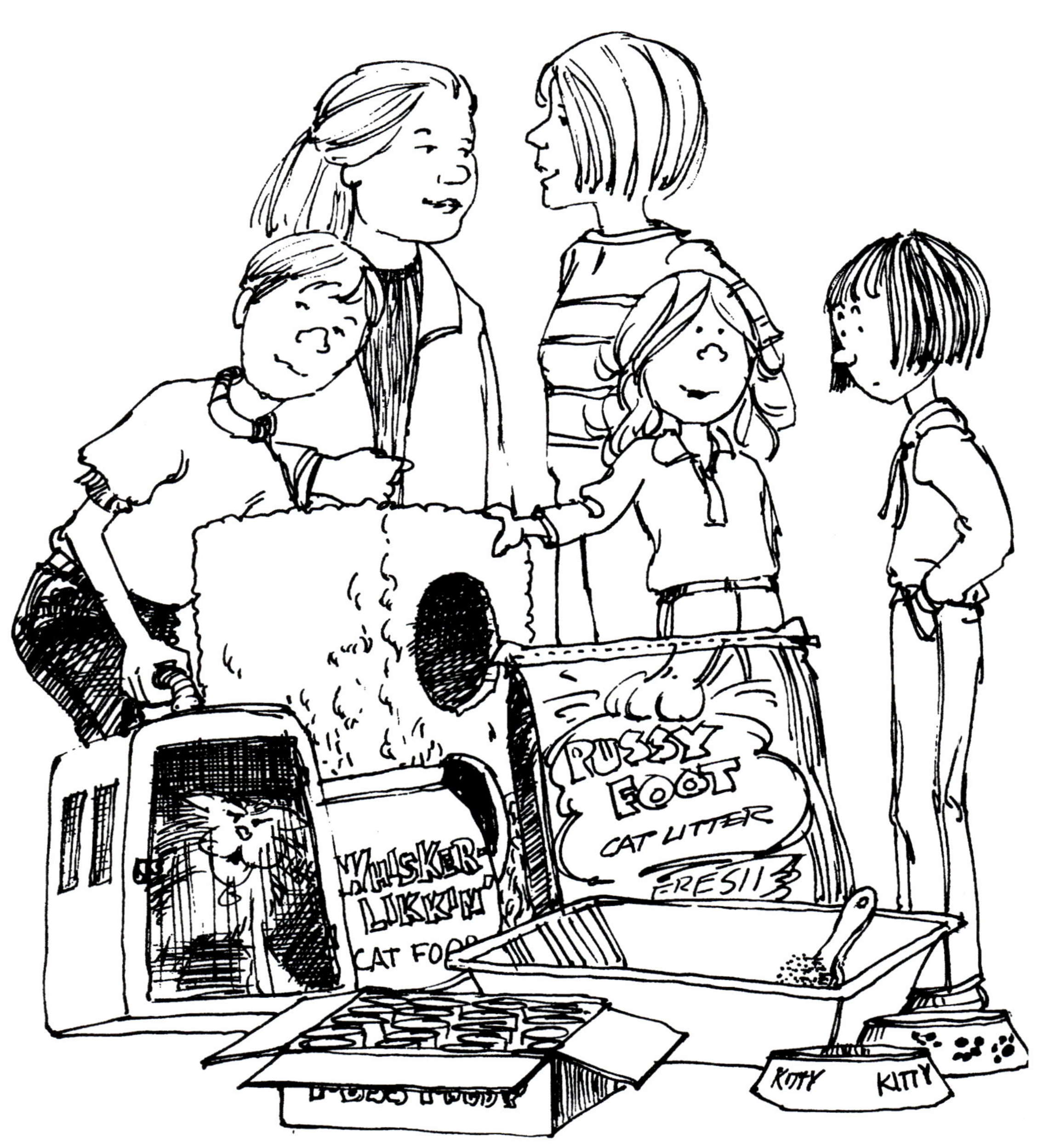

Ramona's first adventures in cat-sitting.

At nine years old, Ramona is ready for some responsibility. So when Daisy tells her that the Kidd family will be going on vacation for a week, Ramona offers to watch Clawed. Perhaps another motive is that Ramona misses her old cat, Picky-picky, who died the previous year.

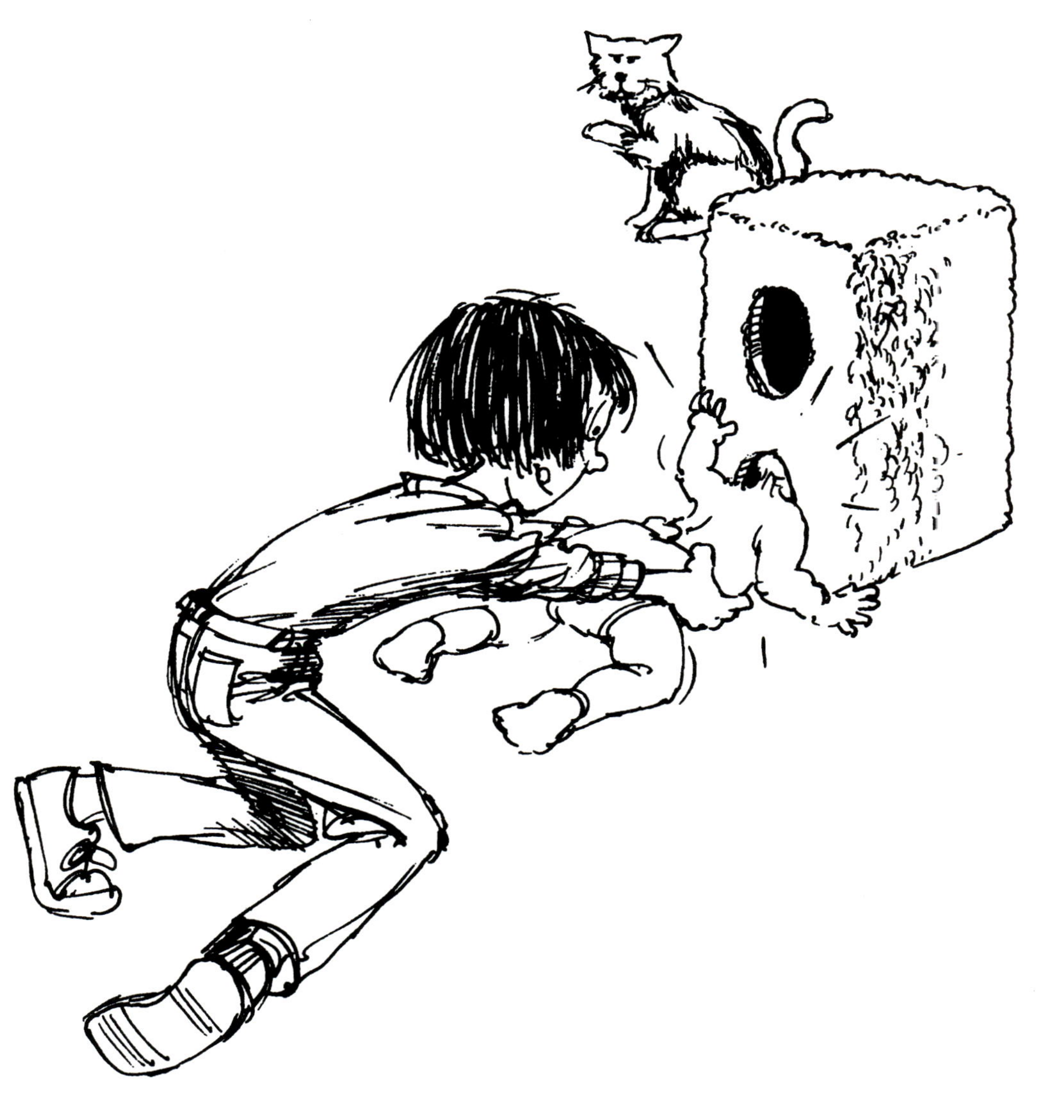

Ramona's first adventure in babysitting.

Ramona convinces her mother that she can be trusted to watch the baby during the fifteen minutes Mrs. Quimby will be gone picking up Beezus from a friend's house. Of course, that's plenty of time for Roberta to get her head stuck in Clawed's kitty condo.

ALAN TIEGREEN (OPPOSITE AND ABOVE).

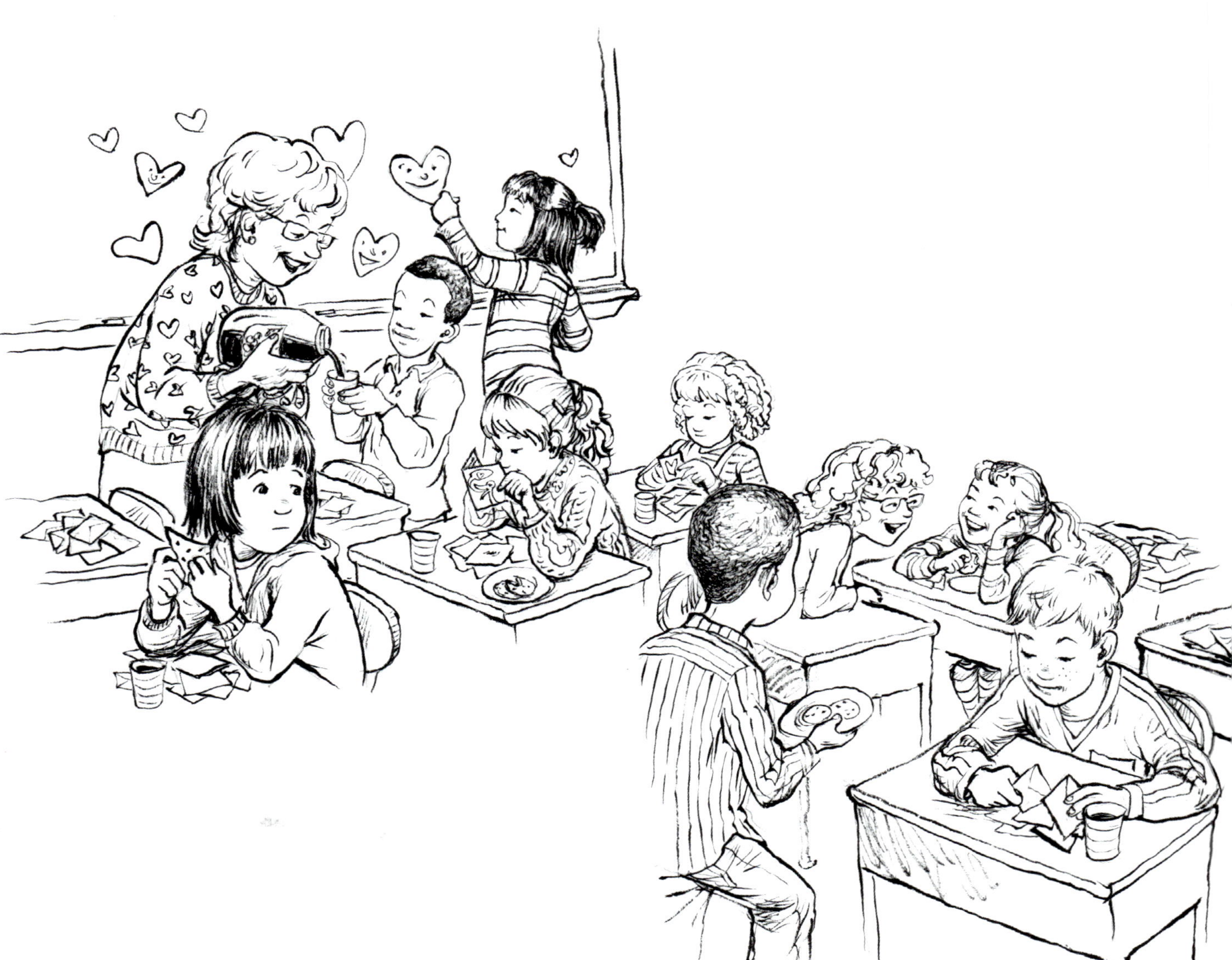

Valentine's Day in Mrs. Meacham's class.

It is mandatory that each student give a valentine to everyone else. Ramona bought valentines for most of the class and handmade some for Daisy, Janet, and Howie. But what about for Yard Ape? Fortunately, Beezus had the wonderful suggestion of giving him the school photo in which she is scowling about peas. Here they eat peanut butter cookies and exchange valentines.

JACQUELINE ROGERS (ABOVE) AND ALAN TIEGREEN (OPPOSITE).

An original poem! A poem Mrs. Meacham didn't have a chance to read. Ramona looked at Yard Ape and smiled. He smiled back. Then she carefully folded his valentine smaller and smaller until it was small enough to fit into the little box in which she kept her baby teeth at home. She would keep it forever.

IF YOU ARE EATING PEAS
THINK OF ME BEFORE YOU SNEEZE.
Signed,
Yard Ape
PRESIDENT

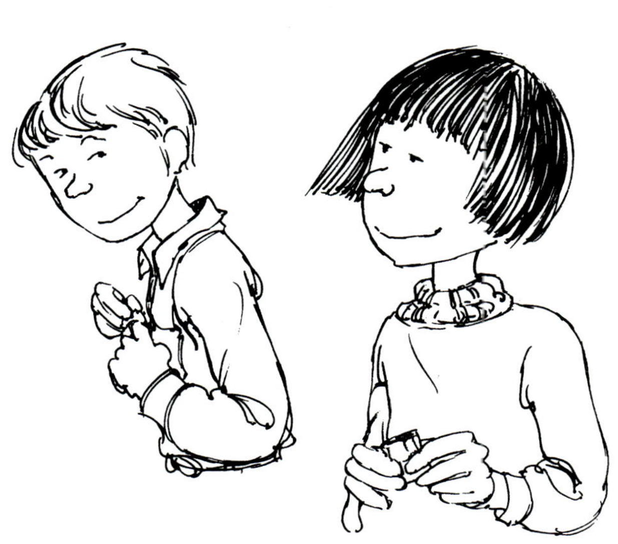

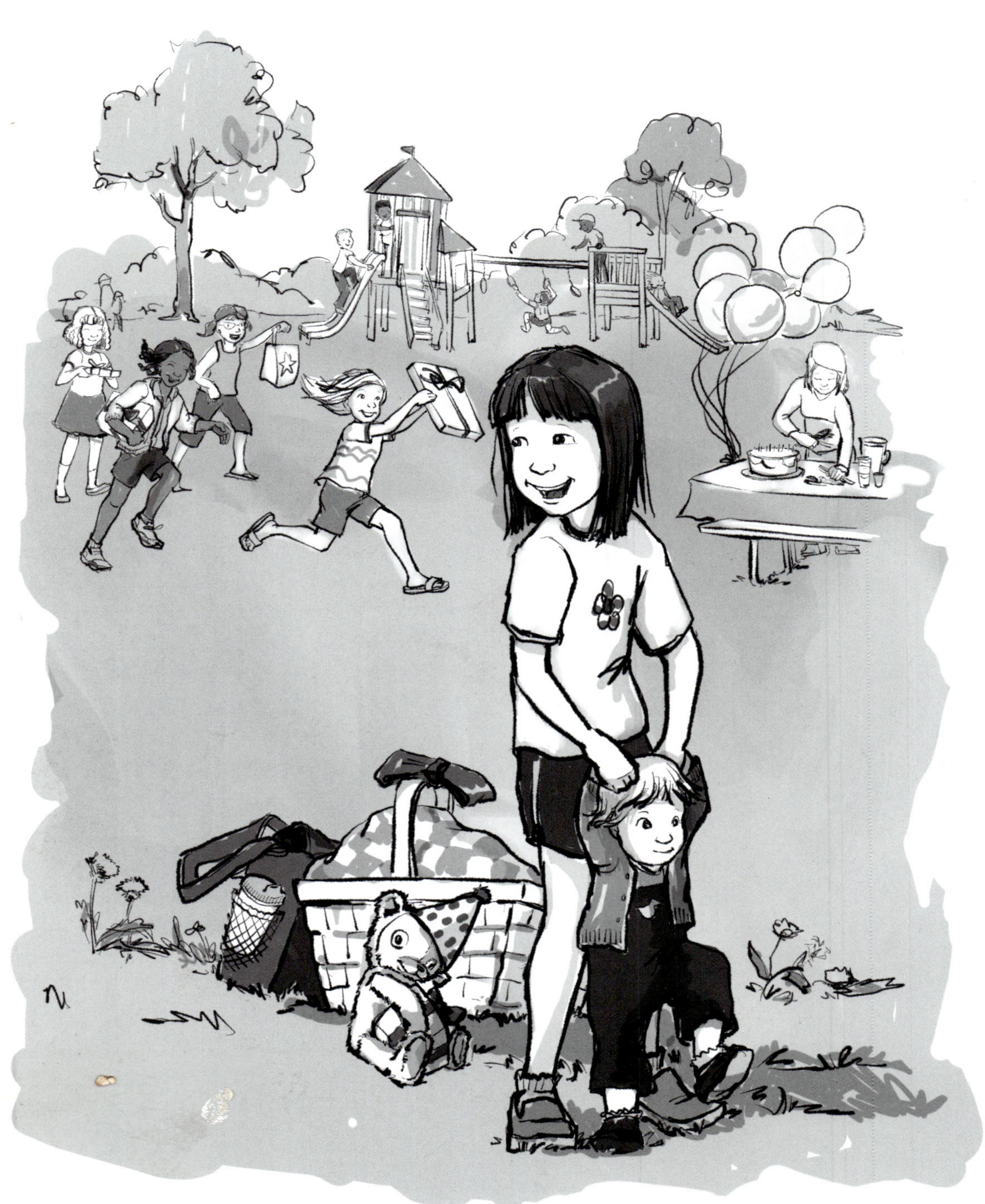

Ramona turns zeroteen.

Mrs. Quimby makes chocolate cake with lots of whipped cream, and Ramona's friends bring presents for her zeroteenth—aka tenth—birthday party. She's now officially a teenager. Well, almost.

ABOVE: TRACY DOCKRAY. OPPOSITE: JACQUELINE ROGERS (TOP) AND ALAN TIEGREEN (BOTTOM).

"I'm supposed to be perfect every single minute," said Susan, her chin quivering.

How awful, thought Ramona, beginning to feel sorry for Susan.

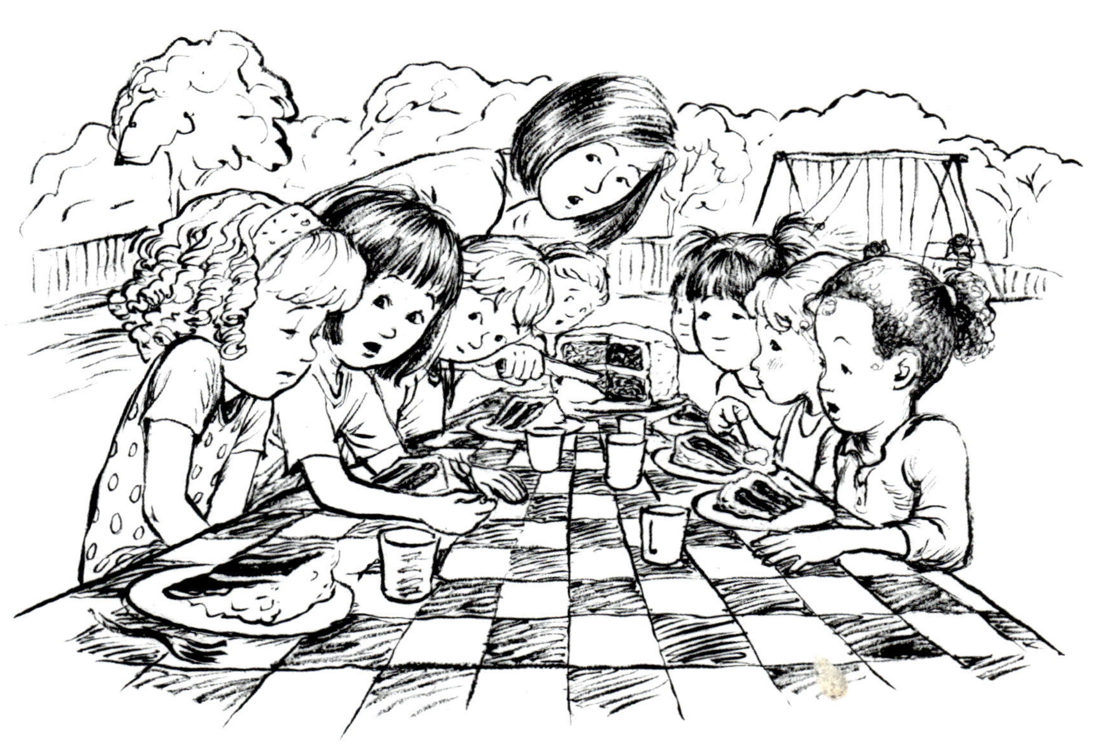

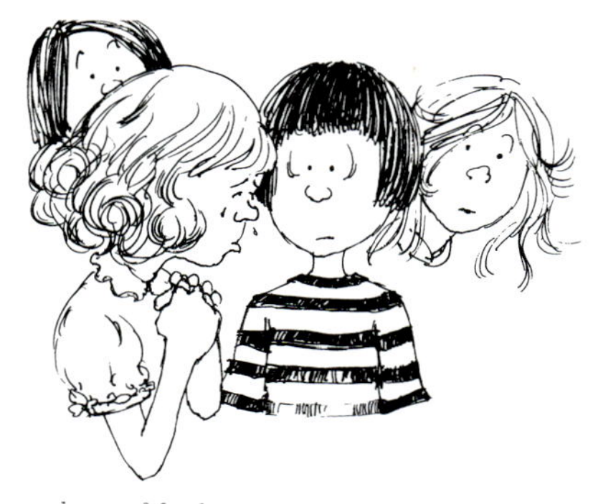

For perhaps the first time, Ramona has sympathy for her nemesis Susan, whose mother made her bring an apple to the birthday party because she read a book on staying healthy. Always having to be perfect all the time must be terrible, Ramona realizes, appreciating her own messiness and her own mess-tolerant parents. It's a moment of understanding, and an important moment of growing up.

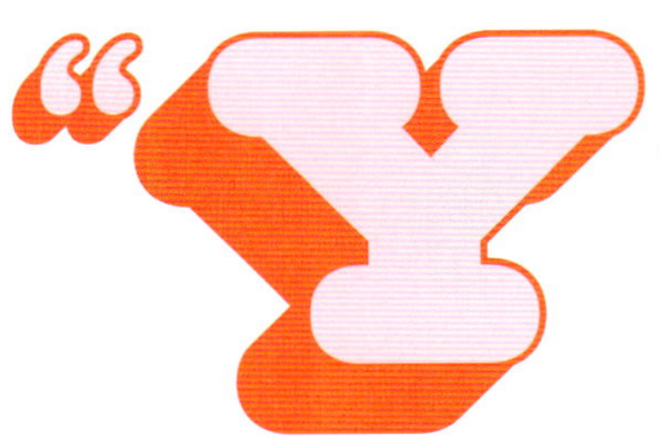

ou know, Ramona," said Mrs. Quimby, "Susan's mother isn't the only one who has read a book. The book I read said ten is the nicest age of growing up. It said ten-year-olds are pleasant and agreeable."

"That's me," said Ramona, suddenly at her pleasant and agreeable best.

Mrs. Quimby dropped a kiss on Ramona's hair before she changed the subject. "I wonder what we should do with the rest of this cake," she said. "Whipped cream doesn't keep very long."

Ramona saw Yard Ape and his merry band of two running across the grass. "Feed it to the boys," she said to her mother, and called out, "Hey, Yard Ape! Want some birthday cake?"

"Sure." Danny picked up a tennis ball a beginning player had batted over the fence and threw it back. Then he and his friends came running.

Ramona seized the knife and clumsily divided the leftover cake into three pieces. The boys picked up their cake with their fingers and sang, led by Yard Ape, "Happy birthday to you . . . happy birthday, dear Ramona. You belong in a zoo."

Ramona could ignore the part about the zoo because she was secretly pleased that Yard Ape had called her dear Ramona even if the words were part of a song everyone knew.

The boys finished their cake, licked their germy fingers, and wiped them on the seats of their germy pants. "Thank you for the birthday cake," said Yard Ape, who must have been taught manners, even if they did not show in school. "Happy tenth birthday."

"Zeroteenth," corrected Ramona. "I'm a teenager now."

Yard Ape stopped. "I never thought of it that way." He started off across the grass.

"And I'm a potential grown-up!" Ramona called after him.

"Me too!" Yard Ape shouted back.

"Come on, Ramona," one of the girls called out. "It's your birthday."

"Run along," said Mrs. Quimby as she returned Roberta to her car seat.

"I'm coming," Ramona answered. Her sticky fingers would help keep her hands from sliding off the rings. The sky was blue, little children still laughed and splashed in the wading pool, the rings clanged. She felt better about Susan. Yard Ape liked her. The day was perfect—well, not really, but close enough.

OPPOSITE: JACQUELINE ROGERS

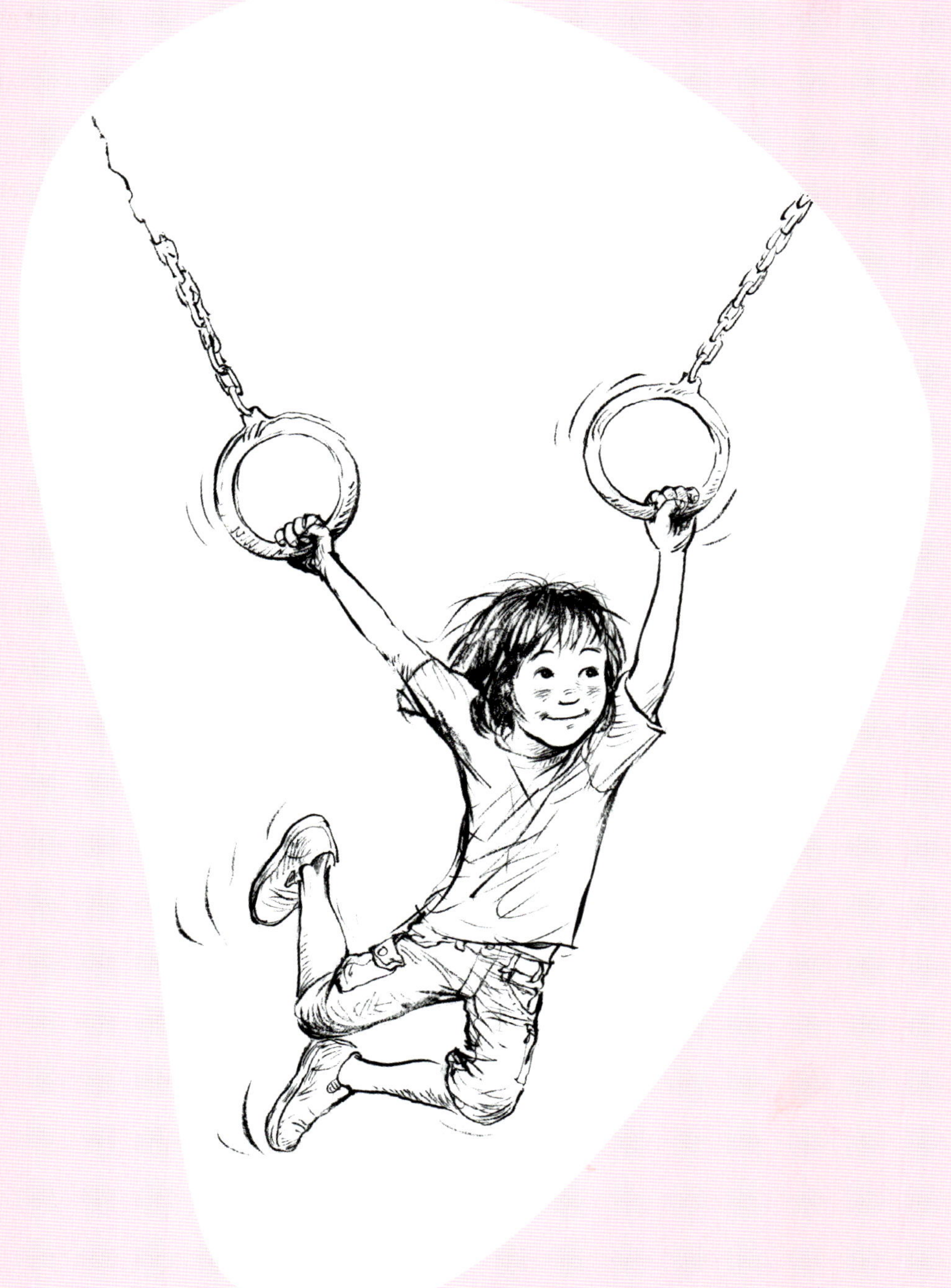

AFTERWORD

Jaqueline Rogers

On Drawing Ramona

In the spring of 2012, I received an email from Cara Petrus, an art director at Harper Collins. They were repackaging Beverly Cleary's beloved Ramona series and thought I'd be a good fit to illustrate the new edition. Cara asked if I'd be interested in trying out for the job. I'll never delete that email. I tried to keep my composure, tried not to get too excited. What a great honor! What were the chances I could get chosen? I knew there would be other illustrators trying out for the series; this was not going to be easy.

I rushed to the library and took out all eight Ramona books, hurried home, climbed into bed, and inhaled the series. I had never read the books as a child, but I knew my daughters had. I had seen a Ramona or two go in and out of their backpacks years ago. I was well aware of Joanne Scribner's classic cover art for the series. As a budding illustrator, fresh out of art school, Scribner's Ramona was a style I admired and tried to emulate. Now, in my fifties and illustrating for thirty years, I had the opportunity to bring my own version of Ramona to paper.

What a shocking realization I had while I read that first book, *Beezus and Ramona*. The sisters were remarkably like my own daughters, Martha and Emma. Though my daughters were only three years apart, their personalities were similar. Martha, my Beezus, was quiet, introspective, and so tidy, we took the bib off her at six months old—there was just no need. On the other hand, Emma, my Ramona, was like a small hurricane through the house, irrepressibly energetic, quirkily creative, and a bit mischievous. Even though they were now in their twenties, I was catapulted back to their single digits. All I needed to do was draw my daughters. They fell out of my pencil like rain, as natural as I could have ever hoped.

The competition for the series took about three weeks of back and forth, drawing Ramona from four years old to ten. I practiced over and over in a sketch book, in pencil, ink, watercolor, always with that attitude of a curious and spicy girl. I got the job! YAHOOO!

One of the most important qualities of Ramona's personality that I wanted to preserve was her indomitable spirit. How do I draw that? Facial expressions and body language for sure, but how else? I wanted my ink style to somehow follow Ramona's personality: sometimes scratchy, using a vibrant line with a variety of thick and thin, loose and full of energy. I used a brush with India ink—a messy choice, but a perfect match.

Before the digital age, I would slow down my ink line, for fear that I would make a mistake resulting in layers of white-out or even throwing out the drawing and starting over. Thanks to digital correction, I could keep my fast brush line, sloppy fingers, crooked eyes, blobs of ink, all scanned in and then corrected on the computer. The majority of my two hundred plus interior illustrations were corrected in some way or another. If you dug into my piles of art you could see my sloppy first drafts.

The full-color covers had the same style ink line with added watercolor and gouache washes. The graphic designer was in charge of coming up with the new packaging style to help freshen the series. I was to make the characters only, with no backgrounds.

It is so interesting to me to see how a classic series like this morphs through time. The colors, typefaces, and design elements show the trends of the day, and the art style as well. My style does not have a trendy, modern look; it is more of a classic style. So the new look with the bright band of colors down the spine and the fun wavy type line across the art helped my figures pop on the covers.

For me, one of the hardest parts of illustrating characters in books is to keep each character consistent in all ways: height, weight, age, skin tone, hair. Not only in how they look, but in the orientation of their bedroom, the living room, kitchen. How many pairs of shoes do they have? Is the day over and do I need to change the clothing for the next illustration? I devised a detailed chart to keep track of the time within each book so I knew when to change the outfits. For added accuracy, I drew a map of the house and yard so that I had a visual to refer to when needed.

Just as writers write what they know, so too, do illustrators draw from their own experiences. I was so absorbed in drawing my daughters that I didn't realize until long after the project was done how much these characters were mirrors of my own life as a child and the people I knew. I was a grown-up-pleasing Beezus, as well as a feisty Ramona, observing life from the youngest viewpoint in a large family. I idolized my brother, Martin. There was a scary dog we walked by on the way to school. And Mrs. Fry was at the crosswalk every day to help us safely cross that busy road. There were teachers I loved and some I did not, along with classmates, all of whom informed my school scenes. My life experiences fill my personal library with an abundance of reference material for drawings.

Emotionally connecting to my characters is the most important asset I can bring to my illustrations. The Ramona series gave me a fabulous adventure in 2012, and the honor to be part of the history of talented artists who have brought her to life over the past sixty years.

Thank you, Beverly Cleary, for your timeless and irrepressible girl, Ramona Geraldine Quimby.

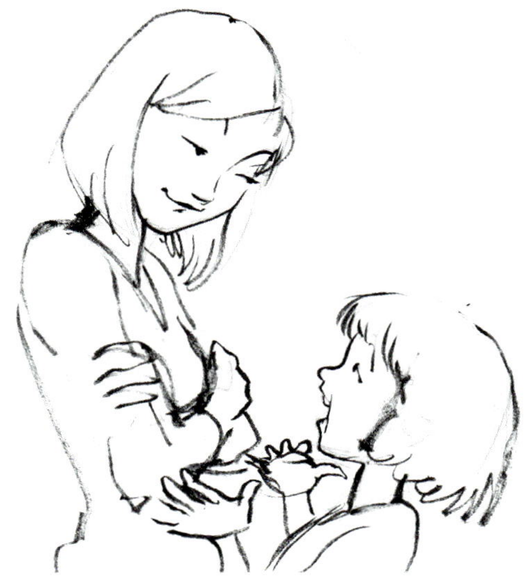

JACQUELINE ROGERS

Appendices

Louis Darling's Correspondence with Beverly Cleary

Darling illustrated twelve of Cleary's books, starting with her debut novel, *Henry Huggins*. The author and illustrator met in person only once during their twenty-year collaboration. *Runaway Ralph* was his final book with Cleary, published the year he died, in 1970.

1456 Campus Drive
Berkeley 8, California
June 17, 1950

Mr. Louis Darling
William Morrow & Company
425 Fourth Avenue
New York 16, N. Y.

Dear Mr. Darling:

I want to tell you how delighted I am with your illustrations for "Henry Huggins." You seem to know exactly what I had in mind. I laughed when I saw the pictures in the galleys, and now that the book has arrived I am even more pleased. I really can't decide which picture I like best--Henry asleep among the fruit jars, the PTA mothers altering the bunny costumes, or Ribsy at the dog show.

And thank you for the very nice quotation that appears on the jacket.

Sincerely yours,

17 JULY '50
SAXON LANE
SAUGATUCK CONN.

Dear Mrs. Cleary —

Thank you very much for your letter. It must be a bit of a strain to an author to have some unknown artist messing about on the pages of her book.

It is hard to express our enthusiasm over "Henry Huggins" the quote on the jacket was an extreme under statement. He and Ribs, Beezus, Ramona and all the others have taken their place in a very special circle of esteemed friends which can be added to, unfortunately, only once in a great while. Thank you for writing about them.

Sincerely
Louis Darling

APPENDICES

15 Dec 1954

Dear Beverly,

BEEZUS AND RAMONA has gotten started and, as usual, is illustrating itself. As I read the script the pictures just pop up and all I have to do is to make a few marks and there they are. I have illustrated a lot of other books since HENRY HUGGINS came along. It has taken a lot of pure effort to do them both in conception and execution. But HENRY and all the others from your pen have allways been complete delight. Lois and I both look forward to the period of the year, usually just before Christmas, when the annual "Cleary" book comes along. But this one, for me, is the best. As you may have gathered I am very fond of Ramona. Elisabeth says that I have an affinity for her. Perhaps it is more in the nature of admiration, when remembering my own somewhat restrained childhood, I see the courage and imagination with which she deals with her many problems especially that of Mrs. Wisser. Whatever, there is a wonderful orgy of "Ramona drawing" going on in this establishment right now.

Beezus seems to be coming out a little bit more feminine than is usual, more dresses and less jeans and shirts. She seems to do better this way in contrast to Ramona. I have noticed also that the local kids are not wearing this outfit so much now. I don't mean to imply that her character has changed basically but that she seems just a little more interested in things feminine these days or, perhaps, the subject matter of this story has brought out the rose smelling part of her nature a little bit stronger. Please let me know if you approve.

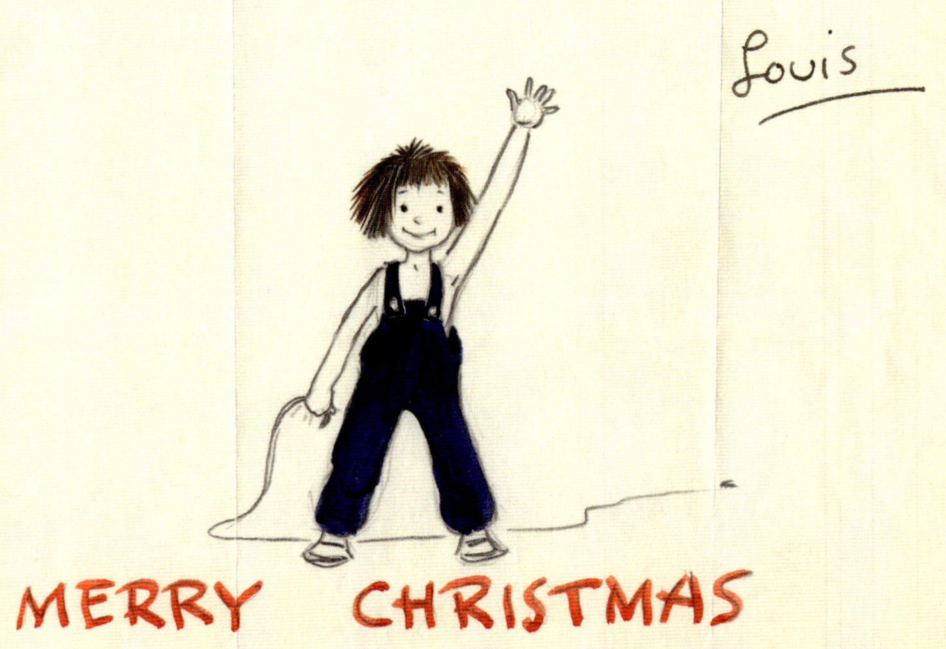

R. F. D.#2
Old Lyme, Connecticut 06371
11 September 1967

Dear Beverly,

I have the galleys for RAMONA THE PEST and am planning to commence the pictures soon. I see that Ramona is still Ramona with her own sort of illogical logic--or logical illogic--but in a environment both strange to her and to me, for her. Will you write some words of wisdom about all this to help with the pictures? clothes etc,etc.?

and a pleasure

The mouse book was very fine/to do and all that. But I did not really feel at home in that old hotel with Kieth et al. I am very glad to be back with old, good friends.

Sincerely,

Louis

1091 Creston Road
Berkeley, California 74708
September 15, 1967

Dear Louis,

It is so good to know that RAMONA THE PEST is in tried and true hands! I have been mulling over possible words of wisdom and find I do not have a great deal to say. Ramona's kindergarten is in what my generation called a "portable." It is a wooden building just large enough for one class and it supposed to be temporary but I notice that they usually stay around for years. It has it's own playground surrounded by a chain link fence and containing a jungle gym, traveling bars (I guess that is what you call a metal ladder parallel to the ground that children swing on by their hands) and traveling rings. A big circle is marked on the asphalt for games. Also hopscotch squares. Inside there is a cloakroom and bathroom at one end, a row of little cupboords along one wall and each cupboard door has a different decal for identification--frog, duck, kitten, etc. A blackboard at one end of the room. One corner filled with toy stove, refregerator, doll house, etc. A long counter under the window with a sink. A low piano in the corner behind the teacher's desk . The children sit at small tables which can be pushed around and are usually arranged in pairs toward one end of the room. For stories and show and tell the children usually sit in semi-circular rows on the floor near the teacher's desk.

About clothes--sashes are Out in kindergarten. Mean old boys yank them. Belts are all right on dresses and many girls wear simple print or corduroy shifts (consult Lois) with blouses. Girls always wear dresses with bobby socks or sometimes knee socks. They wear girls' sneakers, saddle shoes (all white) or leather sandals (child's, not thong.) Boys wear jeans or Levis, usually turned up at the bottom. Plaid or striped shirts are more In than T shirts although T shirts are still worn. On cool days wraps are a wierd assortment of sweaters, jackets, blazers and car coats. Oh yes, boys wear sneakers, leather oxfords and sometimes cowboy boots. All boys in rain gear look exactly alike. They wear brown boots, yellow rain coats that are usually too long and the kind of rain hat that has a visor and comes down over the neck and has a sort of hlf-moon space from which they peer out like little animals looking out of burrows. On clear days traffic boys wear heavy red sweaters and yellow felt caps made a soldier's folding cap. On rainy days they wear the usual yellow rain gear.

I hope all this helps. Now I find myself thinking about Ralph and that motorcycle again. That book has meant so much to a certain type of small boy, the "reluctant reader." I have seen them look at that motorcycle on the jacket and pounce on the book with a look of lust on their faces. I have a theory that if more small boys really learned to read there would not be so many big boys roaring around the countryside on motorcycles and so I am tempted to continue with Ralph. Also, all one winter a mouse and a hamster lived in cages on my kitchen t able and I found myself inventing dialogue for them. I don't know that anyone has written about the problems of animals in cages and perhaps someone should.

My daughter gave a book report on GULL'S WAY and got an A on it. That reminds me--last winter I read a novel that I enjoyed and wondered if you had read it. I believe the title was FORBUSH AND THE PENGUINS. It was about a young ornithologist spending a winter in the Antarctic observing a colony of penguins. It was most entertaining.

Sincerely,

APPENDICES

Tracy Dockray's Early Sketches

Dockray created these journal pages as part of her pitch to illustrate the Ramona book.

"Beverly Cleary created a character that we can all relate to. Ramona has the desire to do the right thing and win approval, but age and immaturity play a part in making that impossible—sometimes with hilarious result.

"I related to Ramona's imagination. She loved her crayons and was *always* creating—making those unforgettable rabbit ears, or constructing the best paper bag owl, even though Susan copied her good idea and got credit (curse that Susan and her curls!) or just hanging out with her dad and sketching their bare feet together. I will confess here that I am a secret Crayola sniffer. It reminds me of being young and creative."
—Tracy Dockray

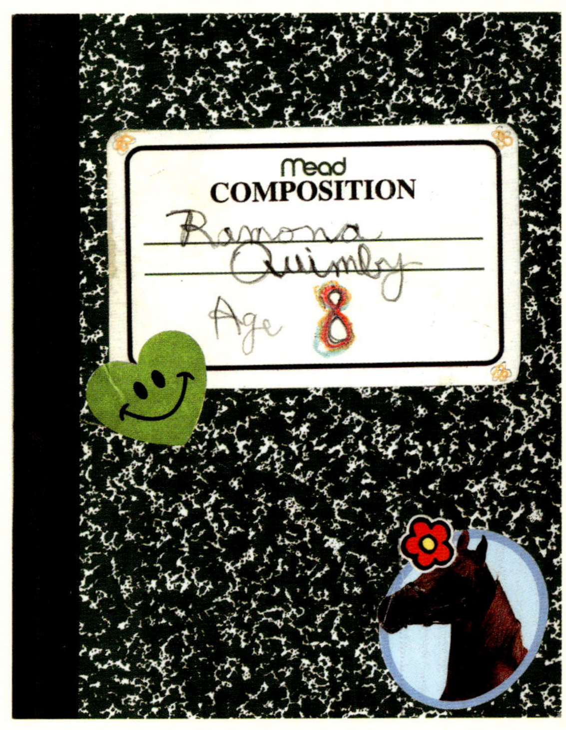

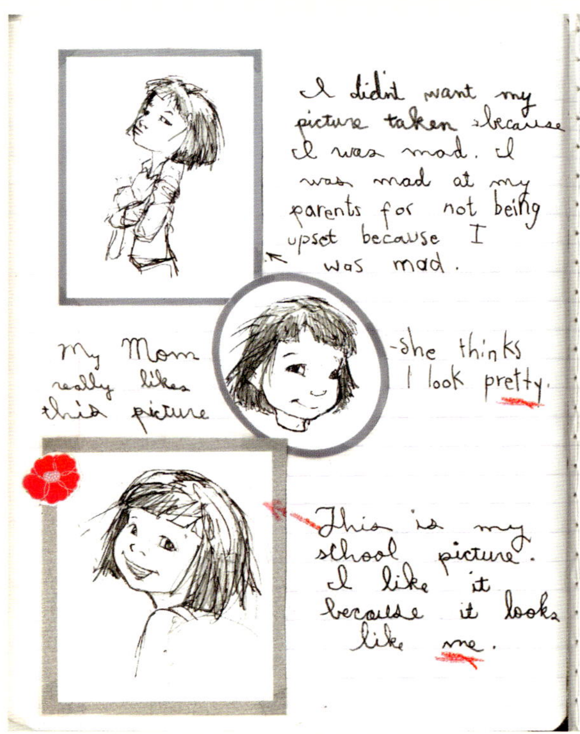

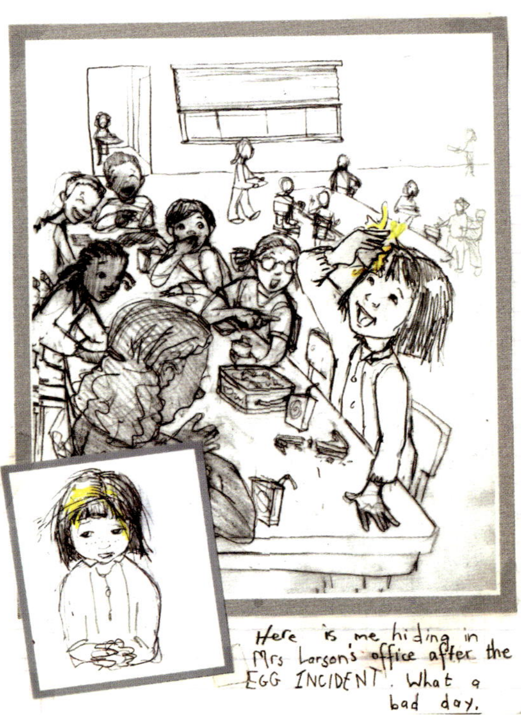

This is Howie's little sister Willa-Jean.

She thinks she's beautiful all the time. I think she's a pest. My job after school is to be nice to her while Willa-Jean's grandmother looks after us.

It's a long, hard job and I can't wait until my Mom comes to pick me up.

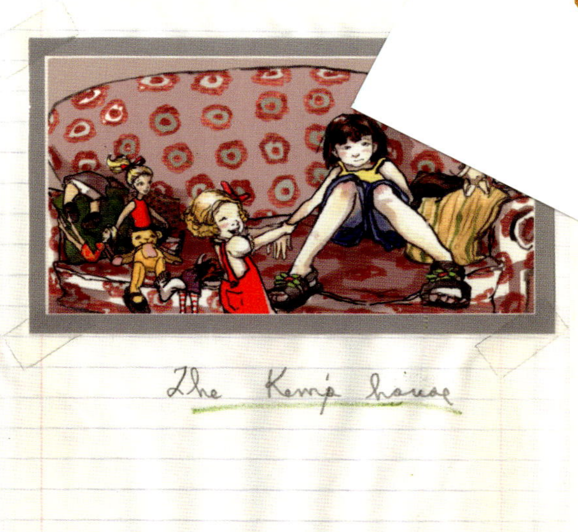

The Kemp's house

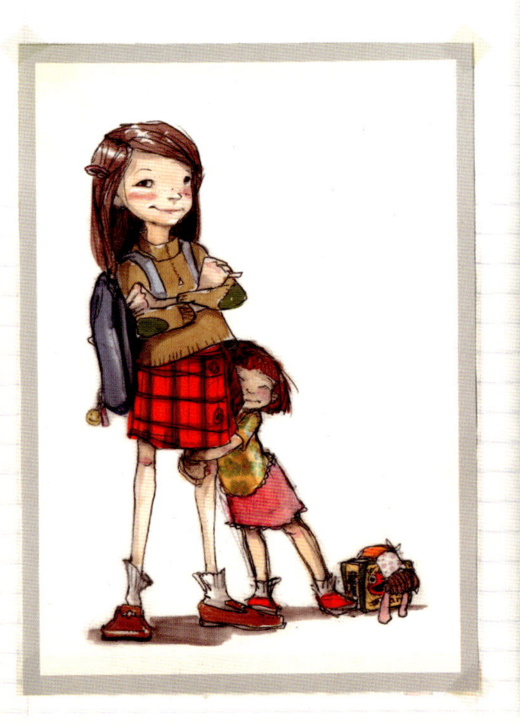

In this picture I'm giving my big sister a hug. Sometimes she calls me a pest. I don't think I'm a pest. People who call me a pest are always bigger so they can be unfair sometimes,

Ramona Quimby

Acknowledgments

First and foremost, a heartfelt thanks to Beverly Cleary. Where would we be without the Quimby family, Henry Huggins and Ribsy, Leigh Botts and Mr. Crenshaw, Socks and Ralph and all the rest of the girl from Yamhill's extraordinary characters? Where would we be without D.E.A.R.?

A big thank you to Emily Freidenrich for your friendship and professional support, and for your beautiful books *The Art of Beatrix Potter* and *Almost Lost Arts*.

For giving me both essential direction and freedom to roam the Ramona universe, thank you to editor Mirabelle Korn. Thank you to Chronicle Books and editor Bridget Watson Payne for bringing me in on this project. Thanks to designer Alison Weiner, Janine Sato and Steve Kim of the production team, managing editor Michele Posner, copyeditor Kathie Gordon, and proofreader Margo Winton Parodi for making sure everything is beautiful and polished.

Thank you to Jean McClellan at HarperCollins, and thank you to Caitlin Marineau at the University of Minnesota Libraries for the art and access to the creators' world.

An enormous thank you to Jacqueline Rogers, Joanne Scribner, and Tracy Dockray for taking the time to tell me about your experiences and creative processes. A double thank you to Tracy Dockray for contributing additional artwork, and to Jacqueline Rogers for contributing her thoughts in the form of an essay. Big thanks to Annie Barrows for her insight into the life (and ego) of a children's books writer and, of course, for the wonderful Ivy + Bean series.

As always, a very special thank you to Troy Lucero for your unwavering support and phenomenal pizza.

Image Credits